Norman N. Holland

PSYCHOANALYTIC HORIZONS

Psychoanalysis is unique in being at once a theory and a therapy, a method of critical thinking and a form of clinical practice. Now in its second century, this fusion of science and humanism derived from Freud has outlived all predictions of its demise. Psychoanalytic Horizons evokes the idea of a convergence between realms and the outer limits of a vision. Books in the series test disciplinary boundaries and will appeal to scholars and therapists who are passionate not only about the theory of literature, culture, media, and philosophy but also, above all, about the real life of ideas in the world.

Series Editors
Esther Rashkin, Mari Ruti, and Peter L. Rudnytsky

Advisory Board
Salman Akhtar, Doris Brothers, Aleksandar Dimitrijevic, Lewis Kirshner, Humphrey Morris, Hilary Neroni, Dany Nobus, Lois Oppenheim, Donna Orange, Peter Redman, Laura Salisbury, Alenka Zupančič

Volumes in the Series:
Mourning Freud by Madelon Sprengnether
Does the Internet Have an Unconscious?: Slavoj Žižek and Digital Culture by Clint Burnham
In the Event of Laughter: Psychoanalysis, Literature and Comedy by Alfie Bown
On Dangerous Ground: Freud's Visual Cultures of the Unconscious by Diane O'Donoghue
For Want of Ambiguity: Order and Chaos in Art, Psychoanalysis, and Neuroscience edited by Ludovica Lumer and Lois Oppenheim
Life Itself Is an Art: The Life and Work of Erich Fromm by Rainer Funk
Born After: Reckoning with the German Past by Angelika Bammer
Critical Theory Between Klein and Lacan: A Dialogue by Amy Allen and Mari Ruti
Transferences: The Aesthetics and Poetics of the Therapeutic Relationship by Maren Scheurer
At the Risk of Thinking: An Intellectual Biography of Julia Kristeva by Alice Jardine and edited by Mari Ruti
The Writing Cure by Emma Lieber
The Analyst's Desire: Ethics in Theory and Clinical Practice by Mitchell Wilson
Our Two-Track Minds: Rehabilitating Freud on Culture by Robert A. Paul
Norman N. Holland: The Dean of American Psychoanalytic Literary Critics by Jeffrey Berman

Norman N. Holland

The Dean of American Psychoanalytic Literary Critics

Jeffrey Berman
Foreword by Murray M. Schwartz

BLOOMSBURY ACADEMIC
NEW YORK • LONDON • OXFORD • NEW DELHI • SYDNEY

BLOOMSBURY ACADEMIC
Bloomsbury Publishing Inc
1385 Broadway, New York, NY 10018, USA
50 Bedford Square, London, WC1B 3DP, UK
29 Earlsfort Terrace, Dublin 2, Ireland

BLOOMSBURY, BLOOMSBURY ACADEMIC and the Diana logo are trademarks of
Bloomsbury Publishing Plc

First published in the United States of America 2021
This paperback edition published 2022

Copyright © Jeffrey Berman, 2021

For legal purposes the Acknowledgments on p. x–xi
constitute an extension of this copyright page.

Cover design by Namkwan Cho
Photograph © Steve Eichner

All rights reserved. No part of this publication may be reproduced or transmitted
in any form or by any means, electronic or mechanical, including photocopying,
recording, or any information storage or retrieval system, without
prior permission in writing from the publishers.

Bloomsbury Publishing Inc does not have any control over, or responsibility
for, any third-party websites referred to or in this book. All internet addresses
given in this book were correct at the time of going to press. The author and
publisher regret any inconvenience caused if addresses have changed or sites
have ceased to exist, but can accept no responsibility for any such changes.

Whilst every effort has been made to locate copyright holders the publishers would be
grateful to hear from any person(s) not here acknowledged.

Library of Congress Cataloging-in-Publication Data

Names: Berman, Jeffrey, 1945-author.
Title: Norman Holland and Identity Theory / Jeffrey Berman.
Description: New York: Bloomsbury Academic, 2021. |
Series: Psychoanalytic Horizons | Includes bibliographical references and index. |
Summary: "A study of the leading 20th-century American psychoanalytic
literarycritic"– Provided by publisher.
Identifiers: LCCN 2020039603 | ISBN 9781501372964 (hardback) |
ISBN 9781501372971 (epub) | ISBN 9781501372988 (pdf)
Subjects: LCSH: Psychoanalysis and literature. | Identity (Philosophical concept)
in literature. | Holland, Norman N. (Norman Norwood), 1927-2017–
Knowledge and training. | Literature–History and criticism–Theory, etc.
Classification: LCC PN98.P75 B47 2021 | DDC 801/.95092–dc23
LC record available at https://lccn.loc.gov/2020039603

ISBN: HB: 978-1-5013-7296-4
PB: 978-1-5013-7300-8
ePDF: 978-1-5013-7298-8
eBook: 978-1-5013-7297-1

Typeset by Deanta Global Publishing Services, Chennai, India

To find out more about our authors and books visit www.bloomsbury.com
and sign up for our newsletters.

Also by Jeffrey Berman

Joseph Conrad: Writing as Rescue (1977)

The Talking Cure: Literary Representations of Psychoanalysis (1985)

Narcissism and the Novel (1990)

Diaries to an English Professor: Pain and Growth in the Classroom (1994)

Surviving Literary Suicide (1999)

Risky Writing: Self-Disclosure and Self-Transformation in the Classroom (2001)

Empathic Teaching: Education for Life (2004)

Dying to Teach: A Memoir of Love, Loss, and Learning (2007)

Cutting and the Pedagogy of Self-Disclosure (with Patricia Hatch Wallace) (2007)

Death in the Classroom: Writing about Love and Loss (2009)

Companionship in Grief: Love and Loss in the Memoirs of C.S. Lewis, John Bayley, Donald Hall, Joan Didion, and Calvin Trillin (2010)

Death Education in the Writing Classroom (2012)

Dying in Character: Memoirs on the End of Life (2012)

Confidentiality and Its Discontents: Dilemmas of Privacy in Psychotherapy (with Paul W. Mosher) (2015)

Writing Widowhood: The Landscapes of Bereavement (2015)

Writing the Talking Cure: Irvin D. Yalom and the Literature of Psychotherapy (2019)

Off the Tracks: Cautionary Tales about the Derailing of Mental Health Care (with Paul W. Mosher). Vol. 1: *Sexual and Nonsexual Boundary Violations*; Vol. 2: *Scientology, Psychoanalyst Meets Aliens, False Memories, The Scopes Trial of Psychoanalysis, Bizarre Surgery, Lobotomy, and the Siren Call of Psychopharmacology* (2019)

Mad Muse: The Mental Illness Memoir in a Writer's Life and Work (2019)

The Art of Caregiving in Fiction, Film, and Memoir (2021)

For Julie, once again

Contents

Acknowledgments x
Foreword xii

Introduction 1
1 Writing Non-Psychoanalytically: *The First Modern Comedies and The Shakespearean Imagination* 13
2 Becoming a Freudian: *Psychoanalysis and Shakespeare* 27
3 Theorizing Psychoanalytic Literary Criticism: *The Dynamics of Literary Response* 47
4 Developing a New Model of Reader-Response Criticism: *Poems in Persons* and *5 Readers Reading* 71
5 Extending Identity Theory in the 1980s: "Re-Covering 'The Purloined Letter,'" *Laughing*, *The I and Being Human*, and *The Brain of Robert Frost* 113
6 Speaking in a Lone Voice among the New Cryptics: *Holland's Guide* and *The Critical I* 145
7 Penning Fiction: "A Cyberreader Defends" and *Death in a Delphi Seminar* 163
8 Exposing the Film Critic's Free Associations: *Meeting Movies* 195
9 Venturing into a New Field: *Literature and the Brain* 211
10 Contemplating Endings 229
Conclusion: Norman Holland's Legacy 237

Works Cited 259
Index 272

Acknowledgments

"Norman Holland's Importance to Me" was first delivered as a talk at the twenty-fifth International Conference on Psychology and the Arts in Lisbon, Portugal, in 2007. My discussion of Holland's *Death in a Delphi Seminar* appeared in a shorter and slightly different form in *Psychoanalytic Books* 7 (1996): 385–91.

I am deeply grateful to Murray M. Schwartz, Norman Holland's closest colleague and lifelong friend, and currently the editor of *American Imago*, the journal founded by Sigmund Freud and Hanns Sachs in 1939, for reading the entire manuscript, sharing his impressions with me, and writing the foreword. I've known Murray for over forty years and greatly respect him as a teacher-scholar. Special thanks to David Willbern, Holland's Buffalo colleague, who sent me a remarkable first-person account of sitting in on the Delphi seminar in the 1970s. David also sent me an eye-opening document Holland gave to his students in 1975, "About Me," his most self-disclosing statement—one that he never imagined would appear in print. "About Me" casts much light on the contrast between Holland's public confidence in his training analysis and his private doubts about its impact on his life and work. "About Me" also deepens the mystery of his childhood.

Laura Keyes Perry, one of Holland's doctoral students with an interest in genealogical research, sent me fascinating information about his parents. I'm also grateful to Holland's former colleagues, students, associates, and friends for contributing to the "Legacy" chapter: Kathy Bahr, Wendy Creed, Emily Fox-Kales, Dianne Hunter, Claire Kahane, Nelly G. Kupper, Cecilia Beecher Martins, Burton Melnick, Laura Keyes Perry, Robert Sprich, Ives Thoret, Richard P. Wheeler, David Willbern, and Meg Harris Williams. John Holland and Kelley Holland read the entire manuscript and shared with me their impressions of reading about their father's work.

I'm deeply indebted to Peter L. Rudnytsky not only for including this book in Bloomsbury's Psychoanalytic Horizons series, which he coedits with Mari Ruti and Esther Rashkin, but also for his meticulous reading of the manuscript. Holland's colleague for more than twenty years at the University of Florida, Peter challenged me with his more critical perspective on the man and his work and pushed me to show how Holland's psychoanalytic insights deepen our understanding of literature. I am also grateful to Peter for suggesting that I invite Holland's children to read and respond to my portrait of their father and for not letting me rest until I found Elizabeth

Zetzel's disguised case history of this "outstanding professional" in her Spanish-language paper.

I'm grateful to the "anonymous" reader of the manuscript who turned out to be Sander L. Gilman, distinguished professor of the Liberal Arts and Sciences as well as professor of psychiatry at Emory University. Like Norman Holland, Sander is the leading American figure in his own domain, psychoanalytic cultural criticism. Bernard J. Paris, Holland's trusted University of Florida colleague, died before he could read my manuscript. Bernie's insights into literature, particularly literary character, have indelibly shaped my own thinking.

As with my other books, I would not have been able to conduct my research without the invaluable help of the entire Interlibrary Loan staff at the University at Albany. Thanks to Timothy Jackson, Angela Persico, and Glen Benedict for fulfilling scores of interlibrary Loan requests. Special thanks to Paul Mosher for helping me locate Zetzel's case study of Holland.

I'm grateful to the entire Bloomsbury Academic staff, especially Ben Doyle, Head of Literary Studies. It has been a pleasure to work with Ben on three books. Special thanks to Haaris Naqvi, Editorial Director, and Lucy Brown, Assistant Editor for Literary Studies.

Finally, I owe the most to Julie, to whom this book is dedicated. She has helped me in every imaginable way on this and my preceding books. She alone knows the full extent of my gratitude to her.

"The Sparrow" is reprinted by permission of *The Hudson Review*, vol. 3, No. 3 (Autumn 1955). © 1955 by *The Hudson Review*.

Foreword

Murray M. Schwartz

Norman N. Holland's writings are known throughout the world and in many languages, but until now we have not had a comprehensive account of his multifaceted career as a psychoanalytic literary critic, a theorist of human identity, and a driving force in psychoanalytic education. Jeffrey Berman's *Norman N. Holland: The Dean of American Psychoanalytic Literary Critics* gives us this account, and more. With clarity, judicious summary, and careful evaluations, we are led from Holland's personal and professional beginnings through the evolution of his major works in all their interdisciplinary richness. Berman pays tribute to Holland's collegiality (many testimonies are included) but does not avoid examining Holland's personal limitations or the critical controversies in which he engaged in defense of his central preoccupations.

Although his theoretical formulations changed with developments in psychoanalysis and critical theory over half a century, Holland remained a humanist devoted to scientific and holistic methods of representing the unifying aspects of literary texts and personal experience. He was fascinated by "the way in which one person is like no other person" (p. 316), as he put it in *The I*, his magnum opus and his most comprehensive yet most neglected book. His earliest, prepsychoanalytic writings utilized the objectivizing methods of the New Criticism. *The Shakespearean Imagination* remains a model of reading for the central configuration that makes each play uniquely cohere. By the mid-1960s, he had turned to the practice of "applied psychoanalysis," summarizing the entire history of psychoanalytic writing about Shakespeare in *Psychoanalysis and Shakespeare* and, in *The Dynamics of Literary Response*, developing a model for revealing core unconscious fantasies that give rise to literary expression.

In the 1970s, there came a crucial turn in his thinking, as "reader-response" became his central preoccupation. What remained constant was his desire to articulate the thematic center of individual expression, the theme-and-variations by which he could explain how each individual enacts her or his style of being as we read or write and live through our personal idiolects within the dialects of shared cultures. He found his theoretical anchor in the speculation about infantile development proposed by the psychoanalyst Heinz Lichtenstein in *The Dilemma of Human Identity*. One of Holland's finest examples of this turn is his close reading of the poet H.D.'s personality and writing in *Poems in Persons*, a prime example of Holland's own style, accessible for a general audience and specialists alike.

Articulating "identity themes" is not a neutral activity, as Holland recognized. As a paradoxical intersubjective process, "theming," or one person's interpretation of another, is subject to the limitations of language and may be experienced as a form of recognition or of misrecognition. Berman's sensitive account of Holland's novel, *Death in a Delphi Seminar*, explores both the great acuity of Holland's intellectual style and his aversion to empathic relating.

Holland was himself paradoxical in several ways: generous yet parsimonious, self-revealing yet emotionally guarded, inclusive yet oppositional, as in his arguments with "The New Cryptics," his name for more philosophical psychoanalytic and critical styles in *The Critical I*. His generosity supported many academic colleagues and generations of students in America and abroad. His deep learning in several fields enlarged the spaces of intellectual discourse, all the way to his last book, *Literature and the Brain*, which seeks the biological structures underlying literary experience. He left us scores of interpretations of his early and continuing interest in classic films, *Meeting Movies* and *A Sharper Focus*. Within the constraints of his own identity, his curiosity transcended the confines of many academic fields.

Unlike many in the pantheon of major critics, Holland promoted egalitarian communities of scholarship and teaching. The Center for the Psychological Study of the Arts that he founded at the State University of New York at Buffalo in 1970 encouraged an authentic sharing of ideas among students and faculty from numerous disciplines, and sponsored critical teaching of psychoanalysis and its uses. In 1983, when he moved to the University of Florida, Holland together with Bernard Paris founded the Institute for the Psychological Study of the Arts to serve these purposes. Even in retirement, he created a popular film study club among his peers. The most lasting legacy, however, is the PsyArt Foundation (psyart.org), which Holland established with his wife, Jane, in order to extend the teaching of psychology and the arts in perpetuity. *Norman N. Holland: The Dean of American Psychoanalytic Literary Critics* tells a full story of how this lawyer's son defied his father's wishes in order to follow his own unique path while also putting the skills of the father to lasting, generative use.

Introduction

In his last book, *Literature and the Brain*, published in 2009, Norman Holland cites the Harvard developmental psychologist Howard Gardner's distinction between importance in one's "field" and importance in one's "domain." Importance in one's field, Holland suggests, means "professional activities like speaking at conferences, getting grants, giving public readings, dealing with publishers, or finding an agent." Importance in one's domain, by contrast, means becoming a "'must,' someone whose work, be it poetry or physics, a neophyte entering the field must study" (298).

Norman Holland (1927–2017) was unquestionably the leading American figure in his domain, psychological approaches to literature, "lit-and-psych," as he called it. Anyone interested in literature and psychoanalysis *must* study his work. Long known as the dean of American psychoanalytic literary critics, Holland produced an enormous body of scholarship that appeals to both neophytes entering the domain and advanced researchers, many of whom have been influenced by his writings. For half a century Holland raised crucial psycholiterary questions about how we read. Of all the major literary theorists, he most closely allied himself to both psychoanalysis and science—a complex alliance insofar as psychoanalysis has its tangled roots in science and art.

Toward the end of his career Holland embraced neuroscience, a field understood by few literary critics. "When we raise psycholiterary questions," he asserts in *Literature and the Brain*—"why do we enjoy, how do we empathize—then we humanists put ourselves in much the same position as the neuroscientists. For them, even more than for the humanists, the ultimate goal is the discovery of mind. What is it? How does it work? How did we get it?" (11).

Holland was a controversial, often polarizing figure, awakening strong and at times intensely ambivalent feelings in his readers. For this reason, it remains a challenge to write a book about him.

I have never written about Norman Holland, apart from reviewing one of his books. Full disclosure requires me to admit that I cannot write about him objectively—not merely because objectivity does not exist but because of my complicated history with him. Our relationship began disastrously. I was a senior at SUNY-Buffalo in 1967 when I requested a meeting with him. He had arrived a year earlier as the chair of UB's expanding English department. My mentor, Len Port, with whom I had taken several courses and developed a close friendship, had been hired as a lecturer in 1963 with the understanding that he would be appointed an assistant professor once he completed his doctoral dissertation, a study of the American literary critic Edmund Wilson. Len awakened my early passion for psychoanalysis, and it was in his freshman English class that I met the woman I later married, Barbara. When Len's three-year contract was not renewed because he didn't complete his degree, I asked Holland to extend his contract for another year. "Asked" is probably the wrong verb: "implored" or "demanded" would be more accurate. Regardless of the verb, I'm now struck by my hubris at the time. So was Holland, for I recall that he corrected my diction: in our conversation, I had used the word "relegate" when the proper word, he lectured me, was "subordinate"—or vice versa. The two words still confuse me!

Because of or, more likely, despite my request, Len's contract was renewed for a year, but he never did finish his dissertation, and he lost his job. His life began to spiral out of control. Barbara and I were married on August 11, 1968, when I was a second-year graduate student at Cornell. Two weeks later, on Labor Day, I received a telephone call from Len, from his parents' apartment in Brooklyn, telling me that he was in the process of killing himself. His suicide was devastating to Barbara and me. I needed a scapegoat, and Holland was an easy target.

Len's death compelled me to study psychoanalysis because it offered, both then and now, the best explanatory system to understand suicide. I wrote my doctoral dissertation on the theme of suicide in Joseph Conrad's life and fiction; it was published, heavily revised, in 1977 as *Joseph Conrad: Writing as Rescue*. After receiving my PhD in 1971, I taught for the next two years at Cornell as a lecturer until I received an offer from SUNY-Albany (now called the University at Albany), where I have remained my entire teaching career.

Holland reentered my life in the late 1970s, during my bruising tenure experience. In recommending against tenure and promotion, the personnel committee concluded that my scholarship revealed a "fundamental deficiency" in my ability "to handle literary texts." The verdict was shattering because it confirmed my worst fears about myself: that I was indeed intellectually inferior, unqualified to be a college teacher. I ultimately prevailed in receiving tenure and promotion, thanks in large part to strong outside letters of support, including one from Holland, who mailed me a photocopy of the evaluation he had sent to the university personnel committee. Bad father had become good father!

Holland's support turned out to be crucial. It is no exaggeration to say that without his endorsement I might never have received tenure, which meant, in effect, abandoning hope for an academic career. During my sabbatical in 1980, I began studying psychoanalysis in New York City at the National Psychological Association of Psychoanalysis (NPAP), the first nonmedical institute in the country, founded by Freud's student, Theodor Reik. (Freud wrote *The Question of Lay Analysis* in 1926 in support of Reik, who was not allowed to practice psychoanalysis in Vienna because he lacked a medical degree.) I studied at NPAP for three years, not to become an analyst but to deepen my understanding of psychoanalysis for my teaching and scholarship.

"Norman Holland's Importance to Me"

On the occasion of Holland's eightieth birthday, in 2007, I was one of two people (the other was Murray Schwartz) who honored him at the twenty-fifth International Conference on Psychology and the Arts in Lisbon, Portugal. Here are excerpts from my talk:

> For the past forty years Norman Holland has been the Dean of American psychoanalytic literary critics. He was one of the first proponents of reader-response criticism, the theorist of readers' identity themes, and the author of a baker's dozen of books that have become classics in the field. In addition, he is the creator and moderator of PsyArt, the online Literature and Psychology listserv that has over one thousand subscribers, and the guiding force behind the annual International Conference on Literature and Psychology, in which we are all happily participating. More than anyone in the country, indeed, the world, he has insisted that if psychoanalysis and psychoanalytic literary criticism are to survive, they must be based on good science rather than on speculation.
>
> I never had the pleasure of taking a course with Norm when I was an undergraduate at SUNY-Buffalo in the early 1960s, but I found myself drawn irresistibly to his writings when I was in graduate school and began experimenting with psychoanalytic criticism. His groundbreaking work on reader-response criticism and identity theory awakened my own interest. His commitment to psychoanalytic pedagogy inspired me thirty years ago to ask my students to write a weekly Freudian diary. He has been a role model for me both professionally and personally.
>
> I have learned so much from Norm's books. To begin with, I learned that studying psychoanalysis is a lifelong passion, one that requires not simply an understanding of Freud's writings but also an awareness of the historical evolution of psychoanalytic theory. Norm has insisted that as important as a reading knowledge of psychoanalysis is, it is not enough.

One must explore one's own unconscious processes and, if one has the time and money, to undergo a personal analysis. He has also encouraged us to be aware of developments in related fields, such as clinical psychology, biology, and now neuropsychology, all of which he has eagerly and systematically studied. Though trained as a New Critic, he was one of the first truly interdisciplinary literary critics. As he writes in *Holland's Guide*, "in my experience, the more you study psychoanalysis per se, especially clinical psychoanalysis, the better psychoanalytic criticism you will write. It is a mistake to read only psychoanalytic literary criticism and then try to practice it." (3)

Reading Norm's books, I have learned to value clarity. His conversational prose style makes him accessible to scholars and nonscholars alike. He writes with wit, verve, and urbane intelligence. He often writes about polymaths, but he is one himself: his interdisciplinary knowledge is extraordinary, but he is never showy. Long opposed to "lit-crit" jargon, he writes with a transparency that is never condescending or reductive. He uses his knowledge not to demolish opponents but to show them how conflicting theories can be synthesized. His own theories are controversial, and he has long been a lightning rod for the opponents of psychoanalysis, yet he remains a model of scholarly grace in his argumentation. He always speaks respectfully of his opponents, and he goes out of his way to credit those from whom he has learned. I have never encountered a more generous scholar.

"Immature poets imitate," T. S. Eliot quipped; "mature poets steal." I have stolen many of the statements Norm makes in his books, such as "when psychoanalysis is good, it is very good; when it is bad, it is horrid." I regularly tell my students, echoing Norm, that "all knowledge is personal knowledge." At psychoanalytic conferences I politely but firmly avoid talks on Lacan, finding from experience that a diet on what Norm calls "French Fried Freud" gives me heartburn. I have always appreciated Norm's heartfelt dedication of each book to his beloved Jane; I dedicate my books to my beloved Barbara, who was my muse in life and now in death.

I want to end on a note of respectful disagreement with Norm. "One repays a teacher badly if one remains only a pupil," Nietzsche observed wryly, and I think that Norm has never sufficiently appreciated the role of the teacher in general or his own teaching in particular. And here I want to draw a parallel between the therapist-patient and the teacher-student relationships. The existential psychiatrist Irvin Yalom states in his masterful 2005 novel *The Schopenhauer Cure* that "*It's not ideas, nor vision, nor tools that truly matter in therapy. If you debrief patients* at the end of therapy about the process, what do they remember? *Never* the ideas—it's *always* the relationship. They rarely remember an important insight their therapist offered but generally fondly recall their personal relationship with the therapist" (62–3). Yalom makes a similar observation in *Love's Executioner*: "It's the relationship that heals, the relationship that heals, the relationship that heals—my professional rosary." (98)

The same is true about education. Students remember best those teachers who have made a difference in their lives, who have encouraged and supported students rather than simply imparted knowledge to them. Were it not for Norm's professional endorsement of my work, I might not have received tenure in the late 1970s. What I will always remember about Norm is not his publications, as important as they are, but his confidence in me, a confidence that I desperately needed at the time, and that I have tried to instill in my own students.

I realize, in retrospect, that the tone of my remarks is not only celebratory but also perhaps panegyrical, as if Holland had already passed into the darkness of history. Eulogies, someone once said waggishly, are best delivered when the subject is still alive and can appreciate effusive praise. Holland was, of course, very much alive: he and Jane were beaming during the two talks honoring his birthday. Every word I expressed was heartfelt. I tried to convey my deep admiration for Holland's work without sounding like a disciple, which I never was. And yet a psychoanalytically oriented writer who asserts that every word is "heartfelt" must be suspect—another example of my complex history with Holland. Was my tribute an opportunity to praise Holland or bury him? As he himself admits in his penultimate book, *Meeting Movies*, published in 2006, a "hard truth from psychoanalysis" is that even "our most profound love includes its opposite, something quite unlovable, hatred, fear, malice, spite, envy, competitiveness." We need to accept the ambivalence of love, he reminds us: "we carry it on to our last sigh" (94).

There was a special irony about my tribute to Holland on his eightieth birthday, for when Freud was honored on his *seventieth* birthday, he made a comment that nearly every psychoanalytic scholar, including Holland, has quoted without being able to cite the precise source of the quotation, as I point out in a footnote in my 1985 book, *The Talking Cure*:

> In his famous essay "Freud and Literature," in *The Liberal Imagination*, Lionel Trilling writes: "When, on the occasion of the celebration of his seventieth birthday, Freud was greeted as the 'discoverer of the

unconscious,' he corrected the speaker and disclaimed the title. 'The poets and philosophers before me discovered the unconscious,' he said. 'What I discovered was the scientific method by which the unconscious can be studied.'" (32)

Virtually every psychoanalytic literary critic, including myself, has dutifully cited Trilling's words but, since he does not footnote the quotation, it has been hitherto impossible to track down the source. Even after I systematically read all of Freud's writings and correspondence, I still could not locate the quotation. Nor were the other psychoanalytic critics with whom I spoke able to solve the mystery. Did Trilling fabricate the saying? Just when I began to think so, I located the source of the quotation. A physician named Philip R. Lehrman, Professor of Neurology and Psychiatry at Columbia University, wrote an essay called "Freud's Contributions to Science" appearing in the Hebrew journal *Harofe Haivri*, vol. 1 (1940), 161–176. Trilling apparently took the quotation from this article.... According to Lehrman, Freud made the remark in Berlin in 1928 to a Professor Becker, the Prussian Minister of Art, Science and Education. (*The Talking Cure*, 304, n.40)

A Paradoxical Figure

One encounters in Holland's work many paradoxes. He was a scholar committed to reader-response criticism who nevertheless remained fiercely private about disclosing anything personal about his life—his upbringing, his relationship to his parents, his religion, his earlier academic degrees in electrical engineering from MIT in 1947 and law degree from Harvard in 1950, and his medical crisis when he was in his sixties. There's no reason a literary critic must be self-disclosing, but reader-response criticism is by its nature highly personal, and Holland's willingness to disclose his identity theme as a reader stands in stark contrast to his refusal to reveal anything about his private life. Only in *Meeting Movies*, published when he was seventy-nine, did he publicly let down his guard. Another paradox was his lifelong struggle between critical monism, the belief in the possibility of an objective reading of a text, and critical relativism, the recognition of the subjectivity of reading. Another paradox was that Holland's early books showed little interest in psychoanalysis, but when he emerged as a psychoanalytic literary critic in his third book, he was among the most faithful upholders of Freudianism, an orthodoxy that changed slowly, often imperceptibly, over the years. Another paradox was Holland's belief that a teacher could use psychoanalysis in the classroom as an explanatory system, a way to discover a reader's identity theme, without mobilizing the power of the talking cure as a therapeutic (or, occasionally, a countertherapeutic) force—a paradox that is most evident in *Death in a Delphi Seminar*. Still another paradox was that beneath his warm geniality and charm was an intellectual aggressivity that could be fiercely combative, something I did *not* comment on in my talk. Nor did I comment on Holland's wariness of empathy, which, like Freud, he did not have in abundance.

In writing a book about Norman Holland's psychoanalytic literary criticism, I am reading him with my characteristic identity theme, that of a mid-septuagenarian who, driven by Freud's repetition-compulsion principle, returns repeatedly to a fraught time in my early professional life, a half-century ago, that proved impossible for me to understand. Freud's repetition-compulsion principle, as Holland often suggested, does not reveal a "death instinct" but rather the attempt to master a traumatic experience, to relive it again and again to achieve control over it. Holland is thus associated with two of the three harrowing events of my life: my mentor's suicide and the near-loss of my job (the third was Barbara's death from pancreatic cancer in 2004 at age fifty-seven). Writing about him reawakens these troubling memories.

One of the driving forces behind my teaching and scholarship, I noted in "'The Grief That Does Not Speak': Suicide, Mourning, and Psychoanalytic Teaching," published in the same edited volume, *Self-Analysis in Literary Study* (1994), in which Holland also has an essay, is a "reparative fantasy in which, by attempting to 'rescue' fictional characters, I replay my discussions with Len and strive for a more positive outcome" (43). The suicide has irrevocably changed my life, recalling Feste's words in Shakespeare's *Twelfth Night*: "Any thing that's mended is but patched." Writing the first book about the significance of Holland's psychoanalytic literary criticism, I hope to introduce his scholarship to readers who may not yet be familiar with his work. He is a "must-read," as I attempt to show in the following pages. A book on Holland is also a study of twentieth-century American psychoanalytic literary criticism, a subject of vital importance to the psychoanalytic community he did much to create.

Throughout this book, I can hear two distinctly different voices coming from me, the personal voice, when I talk about "Norman Holland's" importance to me, and the scholarly voice, when I discuss the significance of "Holland's" achievement. Both voices, the personal and the scholarly, reflect my complicated feelings toward the man and his work. These two voices conjure up my many different feelings toward him, fear, and anger when I was an undergraduate, affection, admiration, and trust years later.

The Plan of This Book

Throughout this study I take a chronological approach to Holland's work, showing the continuities and discontinuities of his thinking. I comment on all 15 of his books (which have been translated into 13 languages) and many of his nearly 250 scholarly articles published in popular and professional journals. (A bibliography of his work is available at http://users.clas.ufl.edu/nholland/bibliog.htm.) Holland sometimes reverses positions, not always telling us about these reversals. He usually writes in character, emphasizing rationality, agency, and self-control, no surprise for a person who believes in the consistency of identity themes, but sometimes he startles us by writing out of character. He has his share of blindnesses, as we all do.

Chapter 1 focuses on Holland's early non-psychoanalytic books, *The First Modern Comedies* and *The Shakespearean Imagination*. Both works reveal that he was steeped in the assumptions of New Criticism, explication de texte, the dominant theory of literary criticism at the time. His comments on psychoanalysis in these two books are largely negative and dismissive, making his "conversion" to psychoanalysis a few years later improbable. His lifelong interest in science, however, can be seen in these early writings. He raises a question in *The Shakespearean Imagination* that appears in many of his books: can a fictional character be treated like a real person? His initial answer is a thunderous no, yet he changed his mind about this question, and his final answer, nuanced and persuasive, appears in his last book.

Chapter 2 shows how Holland transformed himself into a psychoanalytic critic with the publication of *Psychoanalysis and Shakespeare*, which represents a sea change in his thinking. *Psychoanalysis and Shakespeare* is not exactly a recantation of *The Shakespearean Imagination*, published only two years earlier, but it shows striking differences in methodology and theoretical assumptions. The book inaugurated Holland's career as the leading American psychoanalytic critic of his age, but his vision of Shakespeare could not be more different from that of Harold Bloom, who used psychoanalytic theory to formulate the century's most influential theory of poetic creativity, the anxiety of influence. Holland and Bloom were neither academic friends nor rivals; instead, they lived in parallel universes, each imbued with different understandings of Freud's legacy.

Chapter 3 highlights *The Dynamics of Literary Response*, the beginning of Holland's career as a psychoanalytic literary theorist. The book for which he is probably best known, *The Dynamics of Literary Response* was the outgrowth of his long personal analysis with Elizabeth Zetzel, an event that became a turning point in his life. He applied the insights he had gleaned about himself, particularly the role of fantasies, desires, fears, and defenses, to construct a new model of reading. Holland's personal analysis was the source of his new self-knowledge, but his analysis was based on the psychoanalytic assumptions of the 1950s and 1960s, assumptions that would soon be called into question and in some cases repudiated by later psychoanalytic theorists, including Holland himself. He confesses to a bias in *The Dynamics of Literary Response*, an intense desire for intellectual understanding, a hint of his reliance upon "intellectualization" that is a crucial element of his identity theme.

Chapter 4 explores *Poems in Persons* and *5 Readers Reading*, where Holland develops a reader-active rather than a text-active or bi-active model of reading. He drew inspiration from the 1961 article "Identity and Sexuality" by the Prussian-born psychoanalyst Heinz Lichtenstein, who had moved to Buffalo where he became the only practicing analyst at the time. Holland's painstaking research for the two books was based on prolonged interviews with several undergraduates who offered their free associations to selected stories. The result of this unprecedented empirical research convinced Holland that reading was a far more subjective act than anyone had imagined. Both the first edition of *Poems in Persons*, published in 1973, and the revised edition, published in 2000, discuss the poet H.D., who was analyzed by Freud and later wrote about her experience. Holland's discussion of H.D.'s identity theme was not well received by feminist scholars, however, in part because of his reliance upon Freud's discredited idea of "penis envy." In *5 Readers Reading* Holland offers his own identity theme, but he fails to comment on the obsessional nature of his hyperrationality, an obsession that recalls Freud's discussion of the obsessional personality that characterizes, I believe, Holland himself.

Chapter 5 looks at Holland's playful essay "Re-Covering 'The Purloined Letter'" as well as the three books he wrote in the 1980s: *Laughing, The I* (retitled in 2011 as *The I and Being Human*), and *The Brain of Robert Frost*. By this time he was no longer an orthodox Freudian, having distanced himself from some of psychoanalysis's problematic views. Criticizing Lacanian and deconstructive critics' reliance on outdated Saussurean linguistics, Holland became a lightning rod for poststructural theorists; he returned fire with fire, never fleeing from heated debate. He was still wary of self-disclosure in the 1980s, but he made one revelation, about his temperamental need for parsimony, that casts additional light on his own identity. *The I* demonstrates Holland's keen insights into F. Scott Fitzgerald's identity theme, that of a "promising writer" who is always disappointed. *The Brain of Robert Frost* shows how psychoanalysis and cognitive science bear upon literary criticism—and how the insights of brain research, still in its infancy, help us understand the act of reading.

Chapter 6 examines Holland's writings in the early 1990s. *Holland's Guide* presents readers with an intellectual roadmap of the growing field of literature and psychology. Unlike other bibliographical tools, it contains succinct and lively outlines of all types of psychoanalytic approaches. The breadth of the book is impressive, covering Freudian and Jungian psychoanalytic criticism, feminist psychoanalysis, and psychoanalytic film criticism. The authoritative tone of *Holland's Guide* contrasts the embattled tone of *The Critical I* in which Holland, regarding himself almost as a solitary voice in the wilderness, criticizes Lacanians and Derrideans for their assault on the humanistic self.

Chapter 7 discusses Holland's unlikely transformation into a fiction writer. His science fiction story "A Cyberreader Defends" betrays the fear that Lacanians have severed his "lifeline," leading to a professional and perhaps personal crisis, fear over the validity of identity theory. Set in the near future, the story contains two characters who engage in a spirited debate over academic politics, a young female professor, "Norma," who is worried about not receiving tenure, and her colleague "Norbert," a grumpy elderly scholar who has been marginalized by French Fried Freud. "A Cyberreader Defends" was the warm-up for the postmodern murder mystery *Death in a Delphi Seminar*, where Holland ingeniously shows how reader-response theory helps to solve a crime—two crimes, as it turns out. The inspiration behind Holland's only novel was the "Delphi seminar" that he co-taught with Murray Schwartz at SUNY-Buffalo. There are, however, striking differences between the real and fictional Hollands, as we discover from a document curiously titled "About Me."

Chapter 8 turns to Holland's most autobiographical work, *Meeting Movies*, where he boldly reveals for the first time his free associations, thus allowing us new insight into his identity. He traveled far out of his comfort zone in offering these free associations. And yet, in contrast to other literary scholars who have written about psychoanalytic self-disclosure, including David Bleich, Bernard J. Paris, Daniel Rancour-Laferriere, and myself, he admits almost nothing about his adult life. Nevertheless, *Meeting Movies* remains a notable achievement, an example of how a film critic's identity theme shapes his interpretations and evaluations of cinema.

Chapter 9 considers Holland's last book, *Literature and the Brain*, where he charts new territory for literary scholars. Less interested in how we read literature than in why we read, he turns to the burgeoning field of neuroscience for explanations. He returns to the old question of whether to treat fictional characters as if they are real people, and gives us a new answer based on neuroscientific research. Most of the questions Holland raises in *Literature and the Brain* have only partial and provisional answers, but his pleasure in reading literature and his intellectual curiosity remain beyond question.

Literature and the Brain is an eloquent swan song, a tribute to a man whose intense rationality never prevented him from feeling or expressing joy.

The final chapter, the most personal, includes my correspondence with Holland in the late 1990s, when he contemplated "rational suicide" following a diagnosis of lung cancer in 1991. I don't know how seriously he considered suicide, but fortunately his cancer never spread, and he lived another twenty years, dying at the age of ninety, fulfilled deeply in love and work. I include my correspondence with Holland after his wife died in 2015 as well as Murray Schwartz's announcement of Holland's death in 2017.

In the conclusion I consider Holland's vast legacy, particularly his efforts to create a digital psychoanalytic community that would welcome everyone interested in the relationship between psychology and the arts. I include the comments of Holland's former colleagues, students, and friends who reveal his significance to them. John Holland and Kelley Holland had strikingly different relationships with their father, highlighting different aspects of his personality.

Throughout my study I discuss Holland's closest colleagues, including Murray Schwartz, Bernard J. Paris, and Leslie Fiedler, as well as his fiercest critics, Frederick Crews, David Bleich, and Jonathan Culler. A book about Norman Holland is also a study of American psychoanalytic literary criticism; accordingly, I have tried to mention his contemporaries and students who made their own distinctive contributions, including Christopher Bollas. Whenever possible, I relate Holland's evolution as a psychoanalytic literary theorist to new developments in psychoanalysis. Although my study is not biographical, I try to interweave the story of Holland's life and his work. Bennett Simon's statement about another interdisciplinary academic, Jonathan Lear, is no less true of Holland: "Good interdisciplinary work is not for the faint of heart. To be good it takes discipline and work" (155).

Surprises

Reading Holland's fifteen books systematically for the first time, from the beginning of his long career to the end, I've been repeatedly surprised both by the continuities and discontinuities of his work. It's fascinating to see his sudden emergence as a psychoanalytic scholar, sprung, fully grown, like the goddess Athena from Zeus's forehead—only in Holland's case, he erupted from Freud's head, or brain, armed for academic battle, citing chapter and verse from the *Standard Edition*. Holland *never* seriously criticized Freud, though over the years he subtly distanced himself from the more objectionable aspects of psychoanalytic theory. It's instructive to see how he writes about other scholars, friends and foes alike. And it's startling to learn from "About Me" that he had doubts about the value of his personal analysis.

    Holland could be an intellectual provocateur, and sometimes he was taken aback by the reception of his work—and on more than one occasion he struck back. He identified closely with Freud, and I suspect that he regarded himself as one of the disturbers of the world's sleep. In light of his radically new theory of reading, I believe that he identified secretly with Freud's observation to Wilhelm Fliess in 1900: "I am by temperament nothing but a conquistador—an adventurer, if you want it translated—with all the curiosity, daring, and tenacity characteristic of a man of this sort" (*Letters to Fliess*, 398). In studying Holland's writings, I sometimes found myself muttering to myself, "Yes . . . but," transported back into time, half a century earlier, when I was an inarticulate college senior, encountering an intimidating department chair who left me tongue-tied.

1

Writing Non-Psychoanalytically

The First Modern Comedies and *The Shakespearean Imagination*

Holland never wrote a memoir, but in 1999 his fourteen-page essay "The Story of a Psychoanalytic Critic" appeared in *American Imago*. The essay is not elegiac, as one might expect, but it represents a summing up of his life. He remarks in the opening paragraph that two discoveries shaped his intellectual life and career: New Criticism and psychoanalysis. The second discovery, he admits ruefully, proved the first one wrong, though it would take him decades to realize this.

New Criticism, a form of literary criticism that became popular in the 1930s and flourished until the 1960s, emphasized the organic "unity" of the text. "Always something of a rebel, I came to believe passionately in this way of reading" (246). Holland thought that New Criticism "democratized literature" by freeing it from the grasp of academic authorities who maintained they knew everything about the questionable facts of literary history. "New Criticism seemed to me a high point in Western writing about literature. It still seems so to me, even after several decades of reaction and discrediting. Yes, even though later critics have proved the assumptions of New Criticism wrong, in my eyes, too. We were mistaken, but we did good work, given our premises" (246).

"*Jude the Obscure*: Hardy's Symbolic Indictment of Christianity"

That good work can be seen in Holland's first published article, a study of suicide in Thomas Hardy's 1895 novel *Jude the Obscure*. I find it odd, though, that his first publication was on suicide—odd in that there is often a personal reason why a scholar writes about this subject, as in my own case but apparently not in his. The article appeared in *Nineteenth-Century*

Fiction in 1954, when Holland was only twenty-seven and still a doctoral student at Harvard. The essay is admirable in every way, reflecting the critical sophistication of a much more experienced scholar. I cited the article in my 1990 book, *Narcissism and the Novel*, though I was writing on different issues in *Jude* and arrived at different conclusions. In rereading the article for this book, I was startled to discover that he referred to himself as "Norman Holland, Jr.," a name he did not use in later publications.

Holland began his literary career as a New Critic, as the article demonstrates. "The imagery in *Jude* reveals a unifying meaning that seems to have gone unnoticed" (50), he remarks in the opening paragraph. Arguing for the artistic unity of the novel, Holland disagrees with the critical consensus, as Irving Howe stated it more than a decade later, that the suicide of Jude's son, Little Father Time, is aesthetically flawed: "botched not in conception but in execution: it was a genuine insight to present the little boy as one of those who were losing the will to live, but a failure in tact to burden him with so much philosophical weight" (145–6). Holland cites several scholars, including Magdalene Meusel's 1937 dissertation *Thomas Hardy und die Bibel*, from which he quotes a long paragraph in German, part of which he translates into English. Holland analyzes in depth the characters' names (including the name *Jude*, which means "Jew" in German), the symbolism of Arabella's slaughter of a pig, the characters' attitudes toward sexuality, the allegorical nature of Father Time, and the parallels between the boy's suicide and the crucifixion of Christ. Particularly impressive is Holland's discussion of the recurrent pagan, Jewish, and Christian religious imagery. I have taught the novel dozens of times, but I missed a subtle detail that Holland points out. Phillotson, the novel's Philistine, "calls his wife 'Soo,' the traditional call for pigs, which symbolizes his sexual attitude" (56).

Holland makes at least one statement that can be challenged, the assertion that self-sacrifice is not part of Jude's character. On the contrary: after the young Jude finds out that his mother drowned herself, he attempts suicide in the identical way by walking on a partly frozen pond, a striking example of suicide contagion. As I observed in *Narcissism and the Novel*, the "cracking ice manages to sustain his weight, temporarily thwarting his self-annihilation" (188). Holland also ignores Sue's complicity in Father Time's suicide. When the severely depressed boy asserts, despairingly, that "It would be better to be out o' the world than in it, wouldn't it?", Sue morbidly agrees, instead of reassuring the scared boy that she and Jude love him. And when Father Time expresses the Job-like wish never to have been born, she responds, "You couldn't help it, my dear," heightening his worst fears about himself. Sue's empathic failure triggers his inner violence, culminating in hanging his two young siblings and then himself.

In writing about the theme of self-sacrifice in *Jude the Obscure*, Holland had no particular interest in the theoretical or clinical research on suicide. Nor was he yet interested in how different readers respond to the novel's crucifixion imagery. The closest he comes to offering his own perspective on the novel is in the following instructive sentence. "Hardy is saying through Jude and the others that the only part of Christianity worth saving is not an ideal of sacrifice, but rather the notion that somehow we can make this life under Fate's rule more bearable by love for our fellow men" (57), a statement that reveals Holland's own view of Christianity at the time.

The First Modern Comedies

Holland was only thirty-two when *The First Modern Comedies: The Significance of Etherege, Wycherley, and Congreve* appeared in 1959, an accomplishment that becomes more remarkable in that he had a law degree before beginning graduate study in English. He wasted no time in launching his academic career. He was always a fast, prolific writer. He may have suffered from writer's block in his short-lived career as a poet, as he discloses in *Meeting Movies*, but not as an academic writer.

One could not predict from *The First Modern Comedies* that Holland would emerge as the country's leading psychoanalytic literary critic. Restoration comedy, also called comedy of manners, is English comedy from the restoration of Charles II in 1660 to 1710. It is not a literary period that lends itself to psychoanalytic theorizing, mainly because the plays are filled with stock or "humor" characters. Even the non-humor characters are two dimensional, lacking in psychological complexity. Holland presumably chose to study this literary age because of his lifelong interest in humor. His primary concern in discussing three Restoration comic writers, George Etherege, William Wycherley, and William Congreve, is to study the "intricate art" of their plays, not to make "moral, sociological, or aesthetic judgments about them" (*The First Modern Comedies* 208). Examining eleven comedies, Holland argues that they deal primarily with the contrast between appearance and nature. This may appear to be an overly general theme, but he explains why it is useful. "Both language and action represent human conduct split under the pressure of conformity into a visible, social appearance and a personal, private nature. Folly is the confusion of the two; wisdom is their separation and balance" (37).

Holland opens the book with a chapter called "Ground Rules" in which he rejects the prevailing view that Restoration comedy is immoral. "The purpose of literature is to me simply pleasure, the pleasure of understanding, first, the coherence and structure of the work itself and, second, the relation of the work to the reality it represents" (3). He could have stopped there, but he adds a personal remark that some readers might find provocative if not provoking. "If anyone these days is so thin-skinned that the comedies' indecency does block the pleasure they can give, then we best part company here" (4). After acknowledging what he calls the book's "modest plan and arrangement," he then offers the "shamelessly grandiose hope" that it will produce a "total revaluation of" Restoration comedy (8).

Holland's attitude toward earlier scholars is respectful but not deferential. The bibliography in the field is "mountainous," he opines, "but the mountain has brought forth a mouse" (209). Holland doesn't define himself in the book as a New Critic, but his literary assumptions and methodology point in this direction, as does his bibliography. He proceeds from the hypothesis that everything in each play—plots, characters, events, and language—all fit together into a unified whole. In seeing this unity, he admits, he has tried to be "over-ingenious rather than conservative, because I think the reader would rather have something he disagrees with than complete silence on a particular topic" (7).

Holland indeed succeeded in provoking critical disagreement, though he could not have been pleased about John Harrington Smith's harsh review in *Modern Philology*. Smith faults Holland for overstating the claim that everything in the eleven plays begins and ends with language. He also criticizes Holland for the tendency to "set down the meanings that the plays evoke in him, as if he were a poet rather than a scholar or critic" (275)—a prescient remark that, in retrospect, may be seen as a strength rather than a weakness of the book. Smith, it turns out, is one of the mice to which Holland refers, naming him not in the text but only in a footnote (259, n. 32).

Early Comments on Freud

Holland refers to Freud four times in *The First Modern Comedies*; the only significant reference occurs in his discussion of Pinchwife in Wycherley's *The Country Wife*, when the aging rake threatens to use his sword against his wife, Margery, in the letter-writing scene. "Write as I bid you, or I will write Whore with this Penknife in your Face," Pinchwife snarls, which elicits Holland's comment:

> Wycherley, of course, had not read Freud; we cannot expect that he was aware of the overtones of swords and knives. Nevertheless, the

insight here is brilliant. Pinchwife—his name is significant—fears and distrusts women; these fears create a hostility that tends to make him an inadequate lover: unconsciously, he satisfies his aggressive instincts by frustrating and disappointing women he makes love to. Disappointing women, in turn, creates further situations that increase his fears. Thus he falls into the typical self-defeating spiral of neurosis. As Pinchwife himself puts it, free of the cumbersome jargon of psychotherapy, "The Jades wou'd jilt me, I cou'd never keep a Whore to my self." (74–5)

What's significant here is not Holland's reference to Freudian sexual symbolism, a subject that never awakened much interest in him, even after he became a psychoanalytic literary critic, but his attention to the second stage of psychoanalytic development, ego psychology. Thus, Holland implies that Pinchwife *projects* his sexual fears onto women, which only increases his hostility and mistrust of them. Holland also seems to be invoking *projective identification*, Melanie Klein's term to describe how a person, after projecting hostile feelings onto others, then sees them as persecutory objects. As Glen O. Gabbard notes in *Long-Term Psychodynamic Psychotherapy*, "the projector exerts interpersonal pressure that nudges the other person to experience or unconsciously identify with that which has been projected" (159–60). After making this literary interpretation, Holland then draws an implicit contrast between Freud, the originator of this insight, and those clinicians, popular writers, and perhaps even psychoanalytic literary critics whom he judges guilty of using "cumbersome jargon."

Holland's most astute psychological insight in *The First Modern Comedies* appears in his discussion of Manly, the nominal sea-captain hero of Wycherley's last play *The Plain-Dealer*. Like Pinchwife, Manly is a case study of guilt and aggression projected onto others, with disastrous consequences:

The one thing that makes us think of Manly as heroic is his raging, furious honesty. Because his own exterior is a true reflection of his inner self, he expects the same of others and is enraged when he does not find it. That rage is the only large, heroic thing about him, and even though it expends itself on absurdities, it is in some sense praiseworthy. A psychologist, I think, would say that Manly felt too guilty about own failings. His guilt makes him aggressive and hostile and makes him punish himself by attacking insincerity or "adjustment" in others. By these attacks he not only punishes himself by tempting others to dislike him, but at the same time he persuades himself that he is better than they are because he judges them. His concept of plain dealing is simply raw hostility. (99)

A subtle difference between the two interpretations, both based on ego psychology, is that whereas in the first passage Holland refers condescendingly to psychologists who are guilty of psychobabble (a word not yet coined), in the second passage his attitude toward psychologists is unambiguously positive.

Holland never addresses the question in *The First Modern Comedies* whether a fictional character can be treated like a real one, though he does raise this question in many of his later books. Interestingly, his ego psychology interpretations of characters like Pinchwife and Manly assume that they function like real characters, with the same or similar complexity of motivation, projective tendencies, and conflicted desires.

Holland's interest in science is already evident in his first book. Seventeenth-century scientific discoveries demonstrated that "truths which not so long before had seemed blatantly obvious were in fact purely and simply not so. Men's senses were not to be trusted, and it was science that had shown their falsity" (55). Holland's faith in science never wavered, particularly in the emerging fields of cognitive psychology and neuropsychology. He points out that disguise, however frivolous, became in the seventeenth century a matter of "cosmic significance," largely as a result of the new physics (45). Surprisingly, in "The Story of a Psychoanalytic Critic" he states that literary criticism is one of the social sciences (246) rather than part of the humanities.

Holland's fervor for literature appears throughout *The First Modern Comedies*. He understands the conventions of art but questions why literature should falsify reality. "The underlying assumption that the dramatist ought to administer poetic justice is a childish oversimplification," he writes: "it leads to the most magnificently absurd kind of ending, as any reader of eighteenth- or nineteenth-century drama can testify, or indeed anyone who sees many Hollywood films in which 'good guys' win and 'bad guys' lose. The drama ought to take some account of the fact that in life good guys sometimes finish last" (203). Not many scholars of Restoration comedy, or of any other academic period, are forthright enough to make this observation in their first book. *The First Modern Comedies* doesn't give much indication of the trajectory of Holland's future scholarship, but we can already see that his character and method of writing were uniquely his own.

Apart from his insights into literary character, Holland's analysis of language is incisive and original, as can be seen in his commentary on Congreve's *The Double-Dealer*. "Both in language and action everything goes in and out. The images of penetration or nonpenetration parallel on a linguistic level the actions of the wives who refuse their husbands intercourse so they can sleep with other men" (154). Perhaps his most noteworthy linguistic observation is that the fundamental differences between Elizabethan and Restoration plays are in the latter's greater use of similes than metaphors. "The 'like' and 'as' are essential because the implicit metaphorical correspondences of the Elizabethan world-picture are no longer so strongly felt in the Restoration" (231). Observations like this, calling attention to linguistic as well as psychological details, abound in *The First Modern Comedies*, supporting George Falle's recognition in his enthusiastic review published in the *University of Toronto Quarterly* that the "flexibility and range of Professor Holland's critical method allow for evaluations which are remarkable for their perception and sensibility" (100).

The Shakespearean Imagination

Holland's second book, *The Shakespearean Imagination*, published in 1964 and reprinted in 1968, was based on a television course he taught through Harvard's Commission on Extension Courses. He doesn't use the word "grandiose" in the preface to describe the nature of his scholarly task in writing the book, but he comes close. "So ambitious a book should have been written at the end of a lifetime of teaching Shakespeare, and I can claim a scant eight years" (vii). He acknowledges that he doesn't credit individual critics for the insights into Shakespeare that appear throughout the book: "I can only plead that I have treated myself as stingily, making no effort to single out my own originations" (viii). Many insights, though, seem uniquely his own. He raises the following daring questions about Feste, the fool whose spirit presides over *Twelfth Night*. Referring to Feste as a "wheedler of gifts and a kind of miraculous child," Holland asks:

> Is it not possible to think of the Christ Child as some sort of ultimate entertainer, an ambiguous person, half human, half divine, a god-man on whom we project our wishes, to whom we pay rich gifts and love, whose kingdom is one of universal love in which there are no masters, no servants? And is he not the ultimate *festus* sacrificed to pay for our folly? (192)

Holland's delight in puns and wordplay is evident throughout *The Shakespearean Imagination*, as when he analyzes a hidden pun in *King Lear*:

> We can start with a number, the number that starts all the rest of the numbers, one. "One," the single, sole, and solitary self, a number that seems to hover between numbers in general and qualities, one or nothing. But "one" comes up in this play not so much as "one" but as

"I," the individual. "I" leads us into a favorite Shakespearean pun on the letter "I" and the organ "eye." Gloucester loses his eyes, but Lear loses his "I" in the other sense, his self, his mind, the thing that makes him what he is. Then, there is still another sense of the sound "I": "aye," the affirmative, and both Lear and Gloucester get into trouble because they do not affirm by their actions what they seem to believe, namely, that medieval view of nature as an ordered and harmonious hierarchy. "One," "I," "eye," "aye"—this audio-visual pun, in a sense, underlies the whole of *King Lear*. (255)

Shakespeare was a great punster, and Holland is, too, a master of using and decoding wordplay. Significantly, the passage bespeaks not only Holland's rhetorical flourish but also his use of alliteration: "single, sole, and solitary self"; "still another sense of the sound"; "harmonious hierarchy." The literary critic's language does justice to the playwright's. Two of Holland's books, *The Critical I* and *The I*, exhibit this wordplay: the interplay of the I of identity, the eye of vision, and the aye of reading.

The Shakespearean Imagination abounds not only in insights but also in Holland's characteristic humor, as when he observes that the Elizabethan idea of the great chain of being, like any hierarchical system, combines fact and value. "An assistant professor is a bigger and better thing than a mere instructor but a far less grand thing than an associate professor" (38). Lest there be any doubt about Holland's own academic rank, we learn from the back cover of the 1968 edition that the author is professor and chair of the Department of English at SUNY-Buffalo. Nor is he averse to acknowledging his own limitations. After offering several criticisms of the staging of Shakespeare's plays, he admits, "I suppose it's just as well I'm a critic and not a director" (112).

Written for a television audience consisting of a wide variety of people, *The Shakespearean Imagination* has a conversational tone that is never dull or pedantic. Holland always wears his vast knowledge lightly, whether he speaks about the Elizabethan world view, so different from our own, the history of Shakespeare's productions, or the critical receptions of his plays. Witness this observation about those who have tried to deny that Shakespeare was the author of the plays that bear his name. "The facts are that Shakespeare came from a solid, middle-class, even upper-middle-class, background, exactly the same background as most of the other Elizabethan popular playwrights, and that he was about as well educated as a modern college graduate, or, at least, as well educated as the people who say Shakespeare was an unlettered peasant" (2). I learned much while reading *The Shakespearean Imagination*, and I found Holland to be a captivating author, one to whom I felt close. *The Shakespearean Imagination* was published around the time of my ill-fated encounter with him, and I suspect that if I had read the book before speaking with him, the meeting might have gone better.

Historical Critics and New Critics

In commenting on the long tradition of Shakespeare scholarship, Holland singles out both historical critics, who study biography, history, intention, evaluation, and background, and the New Critics, who emphasize textual unity. He praises both methods, which have in common a concern for language, but implicitly he identifies himself as a New Critic. Throughout the book he analyzes meticulously the structure, parallelisms, and recurrent images and themes of thirteen (out of thirty-seven) Shakespeare plays. He locates in *The Shakespearean Imagination* four qualities that give value to a literary work: "the balance of stock response and complexity," "unity of tone," "density," and "unity in general" (89). His need for organic unity never wavered, even when deconstruction came along and postulated radical disunity. "Good reading or good seeing, the 'new' critic says, proceeds first and foremost by paying close attention to the work itself, putting aside value judgments and matters of biography or historical background until we have really understood the words themselves" (43).

Every interpretation of Shakespeare, Holland reminds us, is a reflection of the age when it was written. Every interpretation also uncovers something about the interpreter. It's fascinating to read *The Shakespearean Imagination* in light of what it reveals—and conceals—about Holland's life at the time. "If I can put it in crude, naturalistic terms, the same crude terms in which Lady Macbeth becomes simply an ambitious corporation wife, the whole question in *Macbeth* is whether the son will inherit his father's business, or some interloper from outside will come in" (63). The reader will need to wait forty-two years, until the publication of *Meeting Movies*, for Holland to tell us that the greatest personal crisis in his life was the decision to reject his parents' wish for him to inherit his father's patent-law business. Some of Holland's statements were not likely to raise many eyebrows at the time, such as the following comment about the late play *The Winter's Tale*, where Shakespeare "pays a beautiful tribute to women. Man creates art, invents philosophies and musics, makes money, sets up courts and ranks and ceremonies, writes plays, publishes criticism; man does all these things, but woman does the really important thing—she has babies" (303). Now, of course, few women would regard this as a beautiful tribute.

A Warning

The Shakespearean Imagination is the first though by no means the only book in which Holland warns against the danger of treating fictional characters as if they were real ones, as many distinguished literary figures have asserted. Holland feels strongly enough about this dangerous tendency to post a warning to his readers. "It seems to me very suspect to treat literary characters as though they were the equivalent of real people. It is true, a literary character is in part the illusion of a human being, but that does not mean that he will necessarily behave with the same consistency as a human being" (117). Apart from the questionable assertion that human beings are consistent, Holland maintains an absolute distinction between fictional and real people. "Beware of treating Shakespeare's characters as though they were real people. What a striking action it is for Falstaff to carry Hotspur off on his back, but it tells us nothing about his personality; it tells us only that he is a creation out of a quite traditional form of drama" (129).

The Wrong Question about *Hamlet*

Of all Shakespeare's plays, *Hamlet* is the longest and has generated the most commentary from psychoanalytic and non-psychoanalytic critics alike. It's not surprising, then, that Holland spends so much time analyzing Hamlet's character; the chapter on *Hamlet* is the longest and most incisive. What *is* surprising, however, is Holland's approach to the play. He raises what has long been the most intriguing question about Hamlet's character: why does he delay so long in fulfilling the ghost's injunction to revenge his most foul and unnatural murder? "As we shall see," Holland responds, not entirely giving away his hand, "this is an odd and perhaps down-right wrong way of trying to grasp the tragedy. It is, though, the one most people take, and far be it from me to spurn anything so useful as a jumping-off place" (150).

Holland examines three answers to this question, revealing a thorough mastery of the psychohistorical scholarship. He rejects the first answer to the question, which denies that Hamlet does indeed delay. There is simply too much textual evidence to ignore, he rightly points out. He also rules out the second answer: Hamlet delays because otherwise there would be no play, an answer that trivializes the play. He devotes most of his attention to the third answer: there is something in Hamlet's character that causes the delay. Some of the greatest nineteenth-century poet-critics, including Goethe and Coleridge, formulated interpretations based on this answer. Goethe saw

Hamlet as too sensitive to fulfill the ghost's command, while Coleridge saw Hamlet as too intellectual and averse to action. Holland effectively refutes both theories of Hamlet's delay. He also informs us, almost as an aside, that hardly any actor playing Hamlet looks like the character Shakespeare describes concretely in the play: in Holland's words, "thirty years old, bearded, fat, and still going to the University" (a reference to the stage actor Richard Burbage, the first person to play the role of Hamlet), to which Holland adds, "If you want to lift him out of the play, you can see him as a recognizable type that you might find around, say, New Haven or Harvard Square: the perpetual graduate student" (157-8).

Those familiar with Holland's psychoanalytic writings would expect him to embrace the Freudian explanation of Hamlet's delay. Holland does, up to a point, but he is not overly impressed with it. He gives an accurate history of Freud's theorizing on the play, commenting as a historical footnote, expressed epigrammatically, that "it was not Freud who brought the Oedipus complex to Hamlet, but Hamlet who brought the Oedipus complex to Freud" (158–9), a remark that he repeats in his next book, *Psychoanalysis and Shakespeare* (59). To show how literature influenced Freud's thinking, Holland quotes Freud's October 15, 1897, letter to Wilhelm Fliess in which he expresses the central epiphany of his life as a result of reading *Oedipus Rex*: "I have found love of the mother and jealousy of the father in my own case too, and now believe it to be a general phenomenon of early childhood" (*The Shakespearean Imagination* 159; *Letters to Fliess* 272). Immediately following this, Holland tells us that in later life Freud said, "Not I, but the poets discovered the unconscious" (159), neglecting to add that Freud thanked the philosophers, too.

Psychoanalysts Not Welcome

Holland also cites Dr. Benjamin Spock's support of the existence of Oedipus complexes in children but then argues that the pediatrician's description is too tame. "The child's imagination is somewhat more lurid than Dr. Spock— and I—are willing to say, but that is the essence of it, and there is plenty of scientific evidence for this fact, and also evidence in your own experience, and mine" (158). Some readers might be startled by the apostrophe. To eliminate any doubt about the validity of the Oedipal explanation of Hamlet's delay, Holland then offers his own opinion: "it seems to me that the logic of this scientific reading is unimpeachable." But there's a problem. "The reading is correct, and settles the question—except that the question was wrongly asked in the first place" (159).

Holland, it turns out, has a major problem with the answer because Hamlet is not a living person but part of a play. "He delays because that is part of the play" (159). If that sounds tautological, he is quick to point out that the best interpretation will focus on the entire play: how all the characters, plots, and themes fit into a unified whole. One does not need to invoke psychoanalysis, he avers, to see that the whole play, with its unified structure, dramatizes the tragedy whereby thought and action are antithetical to each other. Citing the gravedigger's words—"An act hath three branches, it is to act, to do, and to perform"—Holland argues that "everywhere we turn in this tragedy, we find this sense of fragmentation, splitting, decomposition" (167). That is *Holland's* answer to the question of delay, a New Critical answer, not a psychoanalytic one.

Holland's response to the detailed psychoanalytic approach to *Hamlet* is not exactly, "so what?", but he is not moved by it in any way, neither intellectually, emotionally, nor aesthetically. Some of his references to psychoanalysis are dismissive, as when he writes about the closeness of love to hate in *Romeo and Juliet*. "At this point, I suppose, we stretch out our Freudian antennae, but the Elizabethans needed no psychoanalyst come from the couch to tell them how close love is to fighting" (72). One can't accuse Holland of ignoring or misreading Freud. He declares without much enthusiasm that some producers of *Macbeth* refer to the three witches as embodying the "dark forces in man's mind dredged up from some proto-Freudian nightmare" (52). He agrees with Freud's explanation of Falstaff's appeal: in Holland's words, "We enjoy Sir John because we need not condemn him," but then he adds, in a subtle put-down, "I think, though, we can find a no less psychological, but more literary answer" (118). After noting the disease imagery in *Macbeth* and commenting that the Macbeths are "sick," he reminds us, coining a neologism, that "Disease, in this metapsychosomatic sense, is not just something you take to your neighborhood psychiatrist. This kind of disease goes deeper than medicine" (55). Similarly, "*Twelfth Night* shows us a world rather like the psychiatrist's ink blots, except that the ink isn't blotted—it's still sloshing around" (185).

Sometimes Holland invokes a Freudian idea to illuminate a character's complexity, but his motive appears mainly to convince us that he understands the psychoanalytic approach to literature rather than finds the approach useful in his own literary practice. Speaking about the purity of Othello's mind, which Iago, his dark double, is easily able to destroy, Holland remarks that a "psychologist would speak of the 'return of the repressed'" (207). The problem play *Measure for Measure* dramatizes contradictions and opposites. "You could put the contrast in psychological terms: we see in others the restraining government of ego or superego; inside is the drive of the primitive id" (231).

Holland regards Shakespeare as the world's greatest playwright, and yet he believes, unexpectedly, that the bard's plays betray a "quite limited conception of human psychology" (327). We read Shakespeare's plays, Holland suggests throughout the book, not for their insights into psychology but for the power of his literary imagination. Tellingly, Holland makes an implicit distinction in *The Shakespearean Imagination* between psychoanalysis, of which he remains wary, and psychology, which he equates with "poetic truth," as when he says about *Othello* that Shakespeare is "trafficking in psychological or poetic time, not real time" (199). Similarly, Lady Macbeth's childless motherhood answers to a "kind of poetic or psychological necessity" (71). We should not look in Shakespeare for a "story truth, a truth of character and motivation and plot," but rather for a "poetic or psychological truth, a truth that resonates in our minds perhaps because it is not literal, factual realism" (197).

A Sentimentalist?

Nor does Holland have much interest in viewing literature as disguised autobiography. With one possible exception, he argues that none of Shakespeare's plays was autobiographical. The one exception, he concedes, is Shakespeare's last play, *The Tempest*, where generations of readers have interpreted Prospero's breaking of his magical staff, and closing words, "Our revels are now ended," as the playwright's adieu to his audience. "There is no real evidence that it is Shakespeare's farewell, but if it makes you feel good as it makes me feel good, if it gives you a warm sentimental feeling in your abdomen as it gives me a warm sentimental feeling in my abdomen, then let us by all means think of it as Shakespeare's long farewell." To drive the point home, Holland confesses that he is "basically a sentimentalist," which gives him the "cue to exit" the book (322). Once again, the reader must wait more than four decades before Holland expounds on his own sentimentalism.

2

Becoming a Freudian

Psychoanalysis and Shakespeare

The year 1966 was pivotal for Holland. After teaching in the Department of Humanities at MIT for eleven years, first as an assistant and then as an associate professor of English, eventually becoming head of the literature section, Holland departed for his new position as department chair at SUNY-Buffalo, where he became the James H. McNulty Professor of English. Within a few years Holland, along with Robert Rogers, Murray Schwartz, Joseph Masling, Claire Kahane, David Willbern, and Jim Swan, established one of the country's first PhD programs in literature-and-psychology. In the same year, Holland completed his formal psychoanalytic training and personal analysis, which he began in 1959, as a nonmedical candidate at the Boston Psychoanalytic Society and Institute, of which he became an affiliate member in 1965. The year 1966 was also the year Holland's essay "Freud and the Poet's Eye" appeared in *Hidden Patterns: Studies in Psychoanalytic Literary Criticism*, edited by Leonard and Eleanor Manheim. Holland's essay is one of sixteen, including reprinted essays by Freud and Jung. The Manheims point out in the introduction that despite the pioneering efforts of such literary giants as Thomas Mann, the "academic fraternity of scholar-critics has been slow to accept studies like ours as valid contributions; young and less influential scholars were understandably timid in venturing into a field that was generally considered suspect" (2).

There's nothing timid about "Freud and the Poet's Eye." Holland offers shrewd insights into Freud's deep ambivalence toward artists. "That is, he admires writers and artists greatly, but at the same time he compares them invidiously to scientists, calls them children, likens their creations to daydreams, and assigns them venal motives" (153). By creating psychoanalysis, Holland continues, "Freud became both the scientist who changes reality through knowledge *and* the artist who fantasies a changed reality into being" (164). Though Holland has not yet offered his own identity theme—that will come years later—his observation about the most basic motive in Freud's character, his curiosity and need to understand and master the riddle of human existence, is no less true of himself.

The year 1966 also saw the publication of *Psychoanalysis and Shakespeare*, a tour de force, a comprehensive study of nearly everything written on the subject, beginning with Freud. Holland surveyed over 400 interpretations of Shakespeare's plays and poems, ranging from brief comments to prodigious tomes. In addition, he compared psychoanalytic interpretations of the playwright to pre-psychoanalytic ones, a herculean task in light of the 350-year commentary on Shakespeare. Holland's scholarship is encyclopedic in scope, his critical judgments engaging, insightful, and often playful. Had he written nothing else, one would marvel at his accomplishment.

Astonishingly, *Psychoanalysis and Shakespeare* appeared only two years after *The Shakespearean Imagination*, yet it represents a sea change in his thinking. It is rare in the history of scholarship for a literary critic to write back-to-back books on the same author, penned only a couple of years apart, which illustrate fundamentally different approaches, visions, and conclusions. Holland observes in his note to the reader that he totally rewrote *Psychoanalysis and Shakespeare* after completing his psychoanalytic training. The initial draft of the book, he remarks ruefully, was based on only a "reading knowledge" of Freud. Reading knowledge, he argues, is insufficient for a full understanding of psychoanalysis. He singles out the help of Dr. Elizabeth Zetzel, to whom he remains "uniquely thankful" (viii). He thanks her in several of his books, disclosing for the first time in *The I* that she was his personal analyst while he was in psychoanalytic training.

Psychoanalysis and Shakespeare succeeds in speaking to three interrelated groups of people: those interested in psychoanalysis, those interested in Shakespeare, and those interested in humanistic thought. Part I offers a psychoanalytic view of literature that contains everything Freud wrote about art; Part II summarizes psychoanalytic interpretations of nearly everything Shakespeare wrote, both poems and plays; and Part III consists of "Conclusions Logical" and "Conclusions Not So Logical." He goes out of his way to help readers, regarding himself as their guide (anticipating *Holland's Guide*). "Rather than read this *Guide Michelin* continuously," he observes, "you may prefer to consult it for particular plays, poems, or topics that interest you" (vii). Like a guide or encyclopedia, the major part of the book, the detailed psychoanalytic discussion of Shakespeare's poems and plays, is arranged alphabetically, from *All's Well That Ends Well* to *The Winter's Tale*. Over 400 pages long, the book contains a comprehensive subject and author index. The notes are themselves highly readable, often entertaining, as when he laments the unreliability of Shakespeare bibliographies and the difficulty of getting long out-of-print articles. "I am mentioning these miseries not so much to gain your sympathy as your forbearance if you do not find in the chapters hereafter all you seek. Perfection in matters bibliographical, I fear, is to be hoped for rather than achieved" (365). He also refers to a large number of supplementary notes on books and articles that contain fleeting psychoanalytic comments on Shakespeare. "I list them here in the hope of saving time for anyone wishing to do further work on psychoanalysis and Shakespeare."

With characteristic thoroughness, Holland appears to have read every word of Freud in the eighteen-volume German edition, *Gesammelte Werke* (volumes 1 through 17 appeared between 1940 and 1952; volume 18, the index, appeared in 1968) and the twenty-four-volume English translation, *Standard Edition* (1953–74). He refers to the *Minutes of the Vienna Psychoanalytic Society*, observing that only the first volume was available at the time of writing. (The first volume was published in English in 1962, the fourth and final volume published in 1975.) In addition, he read all of Freud's extensive correspondence published up to 1964. *Psychoanalysis and Shakespeare* appeared before the *Concordance to the Standard Edition* was published in 1984, yet Holland has an uncanny ability to recall, as a result of a near-encyclopedic memory, every time Freud quoted (and sometimes misquoted) from a literary author. For example, he notes that Freud's favorite expression, Hamlet's statement, "There are more things in heaven and earth, Horatio, / Than are dreamt of in your philosophy," appears five times in his writings (62). Throughout *Psychoanalysis and Shakespeare*, Holland makes allusions to Freud's writings that he assumes, correctly or not, his readers will identify, as when he says in the opening chapter that he wrote the book "in hopes that where conflict was, there shall insight be—and perhaps even acceptance" (4), an echo of Freud's statement in *New Introductory Lectures on Psycho-Analysis* (1933), "Where id was, ego shall be" (*Standard Edition*, vol. 22, 80).

Vulgärfreudismus

Holland's major challenge in writing *Psychoanalysis and Shakespeare* is not to convince those who lack knowledge of Freud that psychoanalytic insights can illuminate the poetry and plays. Rather, he intends to correct those who distort real psychoanalysis into a caricature, *Vulgärfreudismus*: namely, literary critics who, bandying about what they crudely think is depth psychology, (mis)apply psychoanalytic theory to literature. "Instead of data generating theory," Holland complains, "theory generates data. The intellectual Freudian typically begins with a 'reading knowledge' of Freud (neglecting other analysts, despite the great importance of ego psychology, largely developed after Freud's death)" (5–6).

Making this criticism is tricky, however, partly because the history of psychoanalysis betrays the ease with which Freud and his disciples banished "dissidents" like Jung, Adler, and Rank from the psychoanalytic community, and partly because Holland is, in effect, repudiating or at least radically revising his own approach to Shakespeare in a book published only two years earlier. Holland's odd neologism, *Vulgärfreudismus*, which he uses twice early in the book (5, 51), suggests his efforts to distance himself through Latin from his academic colleagues who mistakenly, in his view, call themselves psychoanalytic literary critics.

Holland makes few references to *The Shakespearean Imagination*, largely ignoring his earlier dismissive attitude toward psychoanalysis. Neither a recantation nor an apologia, *Psychoanalysis and Shakespeare* represents Holland's life-transforming epiphany—and his devout wish to accompany new converts to the promised land. He reveals nothing about his training as a New Critic, apart from statements like "the text in literature becomes an end in itself, removed from 'nature' and author alike" (8). He still values textual unity, however, and he praises interpretations that seek to understand the inner consistency of a text.

Freudolatry

In *The Shakespearean Imagination* Holland explores the long history of bardolatry, reminding us that Ben Jonson loved his friendly rival "on this side of Idolatry." One can say without much exaggeration that in *Psychoanalysis and Shakespeare* Holland presents us with his own vision of Freudolatry, a promethean thinker who changed the course of history. Freud's discovery of the unconscious at the end of the nineteenth century was likely to be, in Holland's view, the "defining event in the intellectual life of the twentieth" (3).

Holland's idealizing identification with Freud corresponds to that of Ernest Jones, whose influential three-volume biography *The Life and Work of Sigmund Freud* (1953–7) is a hagiography. Volume two opens with the sentence: "By 1901 Freud, at the age of forty-five, had attained complete maturity, a consummation of development that few people really achieve" (3). None of the other major Freud biographies, no matter how sympathetic, endorses this glorified view. Jones sees Freud's self-analysis as the greatest feat in his life, one of the greatest intellectual feats in history. "His determination, courage and honesty made him the first human being not merely to get glimpses of his own unconscious mind—earlier pioneers had often got as far as that—but actually to penetrate into and explore its deepest depths. This imperishable feat was to give him a unique position in history" (3-4). Holland did not particularly admire Jones's literary theorizings, but he agreed with Jones's view of the heroic Freud, the Freud whose roots lie in the age of Enlightenment. Holland never believed that Freud's obsession with fame betrayed grandiosity and messianic thinking, a view propounded by Frank J. Sulloway in *Freud, Biologist of the Mind* (1979), Richard Webster in *Why Freud Was Wrong: Sin, Science, and Psychoanalysis* (1995), and Frederick Crews in *Freud: The Making of an Illusion* (2017), all of whom, in my view, present an overly critical view of the creator of psychoanalysis.

Holland acknowledges in *Psychoanalysis and Shakespeare* Freud's "false starts and changes in direction" (5), but he never doubts the enduring scientific truth of Freud's discoveries. Sometimes, Holland admits, Freud appears to be guilty of what the modern literary critic would call the "intentional fallacy," the belief one can know an artist's intentions and motivations, but then Holland observes that Freud ultimately avoided the intentional fallacy because of his insistence that an author's conscious and unconscious mind must be determined by the work itself.

Holland characterizes Freud as a lover of Shakespeare, an "*amateur* in the finest sense." He singles out Freud's remarks on Shakespeare for two reasons. "First, he had some extraordinary insights into Shakespeare's works; second, his treatment of Shakespeare—much greater in bulk than his comments on any other writer—established the basic methods of applying depth psychology to literature" (73). Freud had, like Holland himself, a droll sense of humor, as when Holland cites the following anecdote before pushing through a "rather tangled thicket" of scholarly criticism. "One of his students was giving a seminar paper on *Hamlet*, and he began by apologizing for the number of quotations from Shakespeare he would have to use. 'Bring as many quotations as you can,' Freud dryly remarked. 'They will certainly be the best part of your paper'" (152). A professor reading a student's seminar paper on Holland, who was always an elegant and witty prose stylist, might feel the same way.

Bloom Brontosaurus Bardolater

Any discussion of psychoanalysis and Shakespeare must mention, however, briefly, Holland's near-exact contemporary Harold Bloom (1930–2019).

Called variously America's most influential, prodigious, and controversial literary critic, he wryly referred to himself in his acclaimed 1998 book *Shakespeare: The Invention of the Human* as "Bloom Brontosaurus Bardolater, an archaic survival among Shakespearean critics" (589). Bloom's 1973 book *The Anxiety of Influence*, translated into forty-five languages, offers a strikingly Oedipal theory of creativity, where "strong poets," whom he defines as "major figures with the persistence to wrestle with their strong precursors, even to the death" (5), assert their originality by deliberately misreading their precursors. "The history of fruitful poetic influence, which is to say the main tradition of Western poetry since the Renaissance, is a history of anxiety and self-saving caricature, of distortion, of perverse, wilful revisionism without which modern poetry as such could not exist" (30). The world's greatest writer, in Bloom's view, was Shakespeare, who, by "inventing what has become the most accepted mode for representing character and personality in language, thereby invented the human as we know it" (*Shakespeare* 714). A more conservative way of stating this, Bloom declares in the beginning of his 745-page tome (which lacks footnotes, a bibliography, or an index), "would seem to me a weak misreading of Shakespeare: it might contend that Shakespeare's originality was in the *representation* of cognition, personality, character" (xviii).

But the irrepressible Bloom was never conservative in his provocative literary pronouncements. He regarded Freud as one of the century's greatest creative writers, believing, as he opines in *The Western Canon* (1994), that Freud was far greater than his creation, psychoanalysis. "Freudian literary criticism of Shakespeare is a celestial joke; Shakespearean criticism of Freud will have a hard birth, but it will come, since Freud as a writer will survive the death of psychoanalysis" (350). One week before his death, Bloom was scheduled to give a talk on Freud to the American Psychoanalytic Association in New York City. No doubt it would have both pleased and dismayed his audience. He believed that Shakespeare anticipated everything valuable in Freudian theory. Freud is "essentially prosified Shakespeare," Bloom claimed. "Shakespeare's Vienna is a pre-Freudian joke against Freud, a Shakespearean revenge for Freud's ardent support for the delightful argument that the low-born 'man from Stratford' had stolen all his plays from the mighty Earl of Oxford" (*Shakespeare* 377). Bloom asserts near the end of the book that, "as ever, Shakespeare is the original psychologist, and Freud the belated rhetorician" (714). As an example, "Freudian ambivalence is simultaneous love and hatred directed toward the same person; Shakespearean ambivalence, subtler and more frightening, diverts self-hatred into hatred of the other, and associates the other with lost possibilities of the self" (190).

Bloom was always interested in literary character, despite (or perhaps because of) prevailing theoretical assumptions of the death of the self.

[M]ostly because of the peculiarities of modern criticism, the time has come around when it seems salutary to speak again of "literary and dramatic character" in order better to comprehend Shakespeare's men and women. Very little is gained by reminding us that Hamlet is made up of and by words, that he is "just" a grouping of marks upon a page.

Tellingly, although Bloom has no investment in what Holland later calls identity themes, he refers to character as a "person's habitual way of life" (*Shakespeare* 16).

Bloom was a unique literary phenomenon, sui generis, a "monster of reading" who could devour a 400-page book in an hour and then remember it word for word, thanks to a photographic memory. Though temperamentally different—Bloom was saturnine, Holland, sanguine—they had much in common apart from their lifelong devotion to Freud. Both regarded Samuel Johnson as among their favorite critics and often cited him in their writings: Holland regarded Johnson as giving literary theory a dose of common sense; Bloom stated that Johnson's "Falstaffian vitalism is always my first thought when I reread, teach again or continue brooding upon the canonical critic of Western literature" ("The Critic's Critic"). Both admired the Canadian literary critic Northrop Frye. Both were intellectual rebels who later came to be regarded by younger youngers as reactionary in their rejection of poststructural criticism. Holland would agree with Bloom's statement that the "death of the author, Foucault's post-Nietzschean invention, convinces academic partisans gathered under Parisian banners, but means nothing to the leading poets, novelists, and dramatists of our moment, who almost invariably assure us that their quest is to develop further their own selfish innovations" (*Shakespeare* 724).

Both were polarizing figures. Bloom's irritation with the "school of resentment," by which he meant the feminists, Marxists, multiculturalists, and postcolonialists who believe that the main value of reading literature is for social and political change, has its counterpart in Holland's annoyance with the "New Cryptics" who privilege language over the self. Both were known primarily as literary theorists, but each wrote a single novel: Bloom's *The Flight to Lucifer* (1980) preceded *Death in a Delphi Seminar* by fifteen years. Holland was not known for championing the "Western canon," as Bloom was, but his favorite authors were Bloom's: Chaucer, Shakespeare, and Milton. And both believed that the most compelling reason to read literature is for aesthetic pleasure.

Opening with a Joke

Psychoanalysis and Shakespeare opens with a joke, a dialogue between two cannibals. "Did you ever eat a psychoanalyst?" "Eat one!" replied the other, "Did you ever try to *clean* one!" (4). Behind the joke, which Holland ingeniously explicates in terms of oral sadism, lies another one that we might miss. "Would the joke work with 'lawyer'? Probably, but probably not with 'engineer,' except perhaps among a group of engineers. How would the joke go over with a group of psychoanalysts? (That was where I first heard it, and it went over very well—perhaps the unconscious feeling was, 'We're dirty and we like it.')" (36). Hardly any reader of *Psychoanalysis and Shakespeare* would know that Holland was himself both an engineer and a lawyer before he became an English professor. He must have chuckled to himself when later in the book he describes a literary critic who, influenced by Wilhelm Reich's character types, describes Shakespeare's Coriolanus as a "phallic-narcissistic character." Holland then adds, as an aside, "the kind of man who becomes an athlete, an aviator, soldier or engineer," a person, in short, who tends to be "haughty, aggressive, self-confident; his narcissism reveals itself in exaggerated displays of dignity" (157).

Scholars have long been fascinated by Shakespeare the man. Our scant knowledge of him has only deepened academic interest. Holland offers several useful recommendations about evaluating biographical conclusions reached by both psychoanalytic and non-psychoanalytic scholars. "A single play or a single character is, after all, only a tiny fraction of Shakespeare's whole achievement. While it is undoubtedly true that each work will reveal his personality, one feels on surer ground when the analyst approaches the author through patterns of action that run throughout several plays or, even better, through Shakespeare's whole output" (103). The same advice is true for understanding, biographically, any author, including Holland himself.

As he did in his first two books, Holland generally treats respectfully the hundreds of scholars whose writings he summarizes and evaluates in *Psychoanalysis and Shakespeare*. But there are exceptions. He describes two scholars who studied extensively Shakespeare's imagery, Caroline Spurgeon and Edwin Armstrong, as not "burdened by any particular scientific knowledge of the human mind" (122). He praises Ella Freeman Sharpe's writing on *Hamlet* "despite occasional misreadings and a generally mad ring to it" (113), a comment that we can later understand when he describes her speculation on the "bowel movements of the infant poet-to-be" (169).

Throughout his long career, Holland showed little interest in psychobiography, believing it was too speculative to reveal anything meaningful about the biographical subject. Given the mystery surrounding

Shakespeare, including debates over authorship—Freud maintained, for example, that the Earl of Oxford was the real author, a belief that his fellow analysts tried vainly to convince him was looney, which happened to be the unfortunate name of the man, J. Thomas Looney, who proposed the idea—Holland concludes that we would like a portrait of the playwright, but "psychoanalysis can only offer an X ray" (139).

A Sketch of Shakespeare

After summarizing a large number of highly speculative studies of Shakespeare's personality, Holland agrees with the overwhelming number of psychoanalytic scholars who conclude that the central conflict in Shakespeare's plays focuses on the fraught father-son relationship, based on love-hate ambivalence. "The figures that dominate Shakespeare's stage are men, and the leading figures in the plays are almost without exception cast in the roles of fathers and sons" (133). Holland offers additional details about Shakespeare's personality, beginning with the obvious: he was a man with a remarkable verbal wit, a fondness for jokes and puns, and a delight in finding the perfect words to characterize others. But then Holland makes the paradoxical claim that despite Shakespeare's dramatization of murder, rape, incest, suicide, sadistic mutilation, and cannibalism, subjects that might imply a pathological personality, he "enjoyed remarkably good mental health":

> In our own day, as in Shakespeare's, such is the stuff as dreams are made on, and unfortunately, in our cheery age, they sometimes make up reality, too. These fantasies speak not of sickness, but of life. The man who tries to carry such foul imaginings into reality is sick, of course, as is the man who is frightened by them or unaware of them, who cannot face them squarely. A man who, like Shakespeare, can accept such imaginings and not only come to grips with them, but transmute them into moral, even bourgeois, drama, such a man has an extraordinary strength and beauty of mind. (133)

Apart from being a "remarkably normal man," "armed with a rich repertoire of defenses and a great deal of energy at the service of his well-developed ego" (136), Shakespeare was, in Holland's view,

> rather more interested in other people than the self-contained man's man usually is. He does not, however, collect people or depend on them or seek to pry into them; in fact, his feelings toward others are rather

difficult to describe, but he seems to like to confront, as it were, the essence of the people around him, to experience (as opposed to "know") what they are really like.

Holland's next comments are more general. "He seems to work on the assumption that other people are not exactly what they seem—they are more complicated than that, often made up of two quite inconsistent characteristics as he himself is" (140–1).

Extending psychoanalytic inferences about childhood into adult character, Holland conjectures that "aggressive masculinity" served Shakespeare as a "defense against passive feminine needs rather than passivity as a defense against aggression felt as threatening or overwhelming." He then elaborates on the conjecture in one of the longest footnotes in any of his books:

> I think the aggressive was, for several reasons. Had he tried to master aggression by passivity, we would have gotten the picture of a relatively inactive individual given to sporadic nastiness and obstruction, an oral rather than a phallic character. But his contemporaries record a "gentle Shakespeare" (i.e., gentlemanly), and we know he was active in his company, in lawsuits, and in business. The plays abound in images of sports and violent action, particularly the explicit acting out of parricide and fratricide. The plays, it seems to me, probably mirror the man: they are explicitly aggressive in a phallic and oedipal way but at a deeper level uneasily passive (for example, in Shakespeare's constant acceptance and violation of monarchical order). Thus, Shakespeare's application for a coat of arms and his purchase of New Place would show how in life he placed his aggressive, phallic drives toward business success at the service of oral wishes to be accepted into a larger, nurturing social order. (141–2).

And of Holland Himself?

I'm not enough of a Renaissance scholar to say whether this portrait is true of Shakespeare, but I think it is partly true of *Holland* himself. Not that he was Shakespearean in every way. Some of Holland's statements about Shakespeare are obviously not self-characterizations. He goes out of his way to say that Shakespeare "was not the kind of man who is compulsive about details and possessions in the manner of a bookkeeper, a scholar, or a miser" (139). Holland was surely compulsive about details—he was a meticulous scholar, highly systematic and attentive to the smallest details. He acknowledges his compulsiveness in "The Story of a Psychoanalytic Critic" when he talks about his temperamental need for organic unity. "Making such unities was reassuring, so much so as to become a compulsion with me. It was a useful compulsion. It led to the enthusiastic writing of articles explicating this or that text, articles that were suitably rewarded by academic notice and promotion and professorial fame" (246). Like Bloom, Holland believed Shakespeare had the greatest imagination the world has known, but Holland then made the counterintuitive assertion that Shakespeare was not a man of great intellectual curiosity: "the itch to 'find out' things was not particularly strong in him" (139). For Bloom, we should note, the opposite is true: Shakespeare's curiosity was "unappeasable" (189). Regardless of which critic was right about Shakespeare, we can say that Holland's intellectual curiosity is evident in all of his books.

Apart from these differences, most of what Holland says about Shakespeare is true of Holland himself. He comes across in all of his writings as intellectually aggressive and self-confident even when (*especially when*) he contradicts a comment he had expressed dogmatically in an earlier book. An example: unlike his unenthusiastic remarks in *The Shakespearean Imagination* about Hamlet's Oedipal complex, now he states, with no sense of contradiction or chagrin, "Certainly no one can say an oedipal reading of *Hamlet* is reductionist, although it is not, of course, the only possible reading" (178).

Like the gentlemanly Shakespeare, Holland was perceived by many of his psychoanalytic colleagues, myself included when I later became friends with him, as urbane and friendly. He worked tirelessly as a teacher, scholar, and organizer. Like Shakespeare, who succeeded in most of his efforts, Holland was always savvy in the academy, the Marston-Milbauer Eminent Scholar in English at the University of Florida. He was the "foremost psychoanalytic literary critic in America," according to the *Encyclopedia of World Literature in the 20th Century*, a comment Holland posted proudly on his website. He both accepted and challenged academic order, reminding scholars when he thought they were right or wrong in their theorizings. Like the Shakespeare he envisioned, he placed his aggressive, phallic drives at the service of oral wishes (he was a voracious reader). He always sought to be accepted into a larger, nurturing social order.

Holland's other statements about Shakespeare apply to himself, as when he describes the inner man as a "very tender, gentle person, even weak and wavering, someone who could cry easily, who dislikes violence and cruelty, who submits easily to others, particularly if they impose interest or tenderness on him" (141)—a description that strikingly foretells aspects of his own inner self, as revealed in *Meeting Movies*. Many of his students saw him as kindhearted, as I discuss in the final chapter. The father-son conflicts that take center stage in Shakespeare's plays were also central in his own life, as he admits in *Meeting Movies*, when he struggled as an adolescent and young man to free himself from his father's controlling influence. Another statement he makes about Shakespeare—"At times he becomes almost motherly, particularly toward younger men" (141)—describes Holland himself, supporting young psychoanalytic scholars like myself.

"Out of Their Depth"

Holland's aggressive masculinity can best be seen in his discussion of psychoanalytic interpretations of *Hamlet*. "Whether the critic is pro, con, or whimsical, there seems little question that the Freud-Jones view of *Hamlet* is very widely known and probably this century's most distinctive contribution to Shakespearean criticism" (165). It is easy to agree with Holland here. But a few pages later he makes an incendiary pronouncement:

> It is a little surprising that there should be any literary critiques of this kind, that is, attacking the Freud-Jones analysis of *Hamlet*, not from a literary but a psychological point of view. With all due respect to my literary colleagues, it seems to me that they are somewhat out of their depth, psychologically. Surely criticisms of a psychoanalytic diagnosis as such are the province of the expert—in psychoanalysis. For literary critics not trained in psychoanalysis there are plenty of cogent criticisms of the Freud-Jones view of *Hamlet* that can be made from the point of view of an expert in literary criticism: misreadings, misunderstandings of tone, treating a play as a puzzle, reading back to Shakespeare, treating the characters as real people, and so on. It seems to me the purely literary critic would do well to confine himself to those, if he wishes to object. (185)

Elsewhere in *Psychoanalysis and Shakespeare*, Holland comes across as authoritative without being authoritarian, but this dictum would offend all but the most orthodox psychoanalytic literary critic. He declares that psychoanalysis is a science, thus, objective, verifiable, and unassailable. He refers to his own approach to literature as a "scientific one" (36). To challenge the findings of psychoanalysis is irrational and foolhardy, Holland implies, though he softens the words with *tries*. "Psychoanalysis is that science which tries to speak objectively about subjective states, specifically, subjective states resisted but arrived at in the psychoanalytic interview" (4–5). Having completed his psychoanalytic training, Holland now sees the light; non-analyzed psychological critics remain, alas, in the stygian darkness.

To my knowledge, Holland was the first literary scholar to have graduated as a research candidate from a psychoanalytic institute, paralleling the art critic Ernst Kris, whose 1952 book *Psychoanalytic Explorations in Art* Holland greatly admired. Holland regarded Kris as one of the most brilliant psychoanalytic theorists after Freud. Several literature professors, including Peter L. Rudnytsky, have completed psychoanalytic training and become practicing clinicians, something Holland had no desire to do, but none has claimed that non-psychoanalytic colleagues are out of their depth, psychologically, in critiquing psychoanalysis. One may cite here the comments of Nancy Chodorow, who earned a PhD in sociology and taught for several years before beginning analytic training to become a full-time clinician. In a 2005 interview, she disagreed with Paul H. Elovitz's assertion that having a personal analysis is the single most important step in learning psychoanalysis. Chodorow didn't minimize the value of being in analysis, but she made a noteworthy qualification: "there are plenty of independent scholars around who do splendid research and writing in history, or sociology, or biography, based on no more than an undergraduate degree" (Elovitz and Lentz, 140).

Adam Phillips, one of the world's most celebrated psychoanalysts and literary critics, calls into question literature professors who claim special expertise as a result of being in analysis:

> It is one thing to say that people who have been in analysis have a different understanding of the literature, but quite another to say that they have a better one, or, indeed, a real one. After all, where does this betterness reside, and where do the criteria come from? Or is it simply the case that the initiates have produced the most persuasive readings, the most persuasive, that is, to anyone other than themselves? (*Promises, Promises* 368)

I don't know whether Holland rued making the statement, but it could not have done much to help him win friends and allies in academia. Holland knew that psychology, as Dostoevsky pointed out in *The Brothers Karamazov*, is a double-edged sword; in retrospect, Holland's cutting remarks were a self-inflicted injury.

Holland could not foresee in the mid-1960s that Freud was already coming under fierce attack from both inside and outside the psychoanalytic community. Nor could he foretell that the marriage between literature and psychoanalysis would need to be equal in order to survive. From its inception, the union between the two disciplines was one-sided, with the psychoanalyst holding the privileged position of authority and power. But a marriage cannot succeed, or at least flourish, if one partner dominates the other. Holland assumed early in his career that literary scholars could learn much from psychoanalysts, but he didn't realize that psychoanalysts could learn as much from literary scholars. As I wrote in the foreword to New York University Press's Literature and Psychoanalysis series (1991–7):

> The literary critic's insights into psychoanalysis are no less valuable than the psychoanalyst's insights into literature. Gone are the days when psychoanalytic critics assumed that Freud had a master key to unlock the secrets of literature. Instead of reading literature to confirm psychoanalytic theory, many critics are now reading Freud to discover how his understanding of literature shaped the evolution of his theory. In short, the master-slave relationship traditionally implicit in the marriage between the literary critic and the psychoanalyst has given way to a healthier dialogic relationship, in which each learns from and contributes to the other's discipline.

Many literary critics have offered insights into Freud's formation of psychoanalytic theory, including the blind spots in both the creator and his creation. Madelon Sprengnether examines in *The Spectral Mother* (1990) Freud's ambivalence to the figure of the mother and his resulting inability or unwillingness to theorize the pre-Oedipal period. In *Mourning Freud* (2018) Sprengnether shows how Freud could not admit the painful feelings evoked by multiples losses and disruptions in his childhood. The Oedipus complex, in her view, "serves to obscure a deeper, more private, and conflicted drama of mourning that Freud was unable to articulate" (242). Other literary critics, such as Mark Edmundson in *Towards Reading Freud* (1990), similarly see Freud's emphasis on the Oedipus complex as concealing deeper aspects of his personality that he would not or could not acknowledge.

Holland never seriously challenged the foundation of psychoanalysis, neither in *Psychoanalysis and Shakespeare* nor elsewhere. Unlike Otto Rank, who "broke with Freud" after a "period of twenty years in the bosom of orthodoxy" (89), Holland remained in the same bosom, a land of milk and honey, once he became a psychoanalytic critic in the mid-1960s, regarding Freud as the source of all that was good and nurturing. Yet to his credit, Holland is not so rigid in *Psychoanalysis and Shakespeare* that he forces his readers to choose between competing and often conflicting interpretations of the writer. Holland reminds us that with respect to aesthetic theories, "either-or must give way to both-and" (46). He urges us to be as open-minded as possible, as he is in presenting hundreds of different psychoanalytic interpretations of Shakespeare. Sometimes, however, he cannot resist taking a pot-shot at an influential critic, as when he refers to Edmund Wilson as the "*pontifex maximus*" (297), not realizing that other literary scholars would make the same criticism of him.

Erik Erikson's Influence

One doesn't think of Erik Erikson (1902–94) as a Shakespeare scholar, but he was one of the high priests of psychoanalysis, the most influential twentieth-century American analyst. Holland praises Erikson's 1962 essay "Youth: Fidelity and Diversity" (republished in *Identity: Youth and Crisis* in 1968) in which he discusses Hamlet's developmental crisis. "In particular, Erikson sees Hamlet as a delayed adolescent, facing in his thirtieth year the issues most men work out in their early twentieth" (*Psychoanalysis and Shakespeare* 174). Erikson "whimsically" sees, Holland adds, in Polonius, with his sententious "I have found the very cause of Hamlet's lunacy," a caricature of the psychiatrist. It's not surprising that Erikson, whose major work centered on identity issues, should find an ally in Holland, whose major work focused on the reader's identity theme. It's likely that Erikson, along with Heinz Lichtenstein, inspired Holland with the idea of applying identity theory to the act of reading.

Tellingly, in *The Critical I*, published in 1992, Holland reveals for the first and only time an obstacle he encountered, early in his academic year, when he began developing an interest in psychoanalysis. He recalls being a student at Harvard, around 1960, when he wanted to take a course with Erik Erikson who taught at Harvard Medical School. Advisers from the English department "energetically" discouraged Holland from taking a course with Erikson. (Murray Schwartz reports a similar experience in his intellectual memoir, "Psychoanalysis in My Life": while he was a doctoral student at UC Berkeley, a member of his exam committee abruptly quit when Schwartz refused to remove Erikson's *Young Man Luther* from his reading list.) Now, thirty years later, Holland writes in *The Critical I*, "if you are a literary theorist, you brand yourself passé if you cannot talk easily of Freud and Lacan, perhaps Winnicott or conceivably Kohut or Kernberg (but not Kris or Hartmann or Erikson or Laing—they are as grandly 'over' as the Beatles)" (84).

After praising Erikson's developmental approach to Shakespeare, Holland points out that the analyst treats Hamlet "as a real person, psychosocially interacting with a real culture" (177). Holland doesn't want to say, categorically, that this approach is wrong, as he would have said (and did indeed say) in *The Shakespearean Imagination*, though he knows it goes against the overwhelming weight of twentieth-century literary authority. "But this question, to apply or not to apply psychoanalytic experience to literary characters, constitutes a major problem that runs all through psychoanalytic criticism. It had best wait" (193).

Returning to *Hamlet*

Erikson's interpretation of *Hamlet* is only one of nearly 100 commentaries on the play discussed by Holland in *Psychoanalysis and Shakespeare*, enough material on *Hamlet* alone to constitute a book by itself. "Psychoanalysts seem to take to *Hamlet* like kittens to a ball of yarn" (163), Holland wryly says. His discussion of the play is forty-three pages long and is divided into several sections: The Freud-Jones View, Restatements of the Freud-Jones View, Stagings of the Freud-Jones View, Amplifications of the Freud-Jones View Within Orthodox Psychoanalysis, Variations of the Freud-Jones View, Literary Critiques of the Freud-Jones View, and Semi- or Anti-Psychoanalytic Views. The last section has seven subsections: Poison in the Ear, Hamlet's Madness, The Play Within the Play, Ophelia's Madness, The Graveyard Scene, Osric, and Particular Speeches. I mention this to point out the thoroughness of Holland's scholarship and the clarity of the book's organization.

No text has been of greater interest to psychoanalysts than *Hamlet*, and nearly every twentieth-century scholar, psychoanalytic and otherwise, has commented on his princely Oedipus complex. The "discovery of Hamlet's oedipus complex seems almost like a rock upon which Freud founded his theory," Holland remarks, a rock that has "withstood a good deal of wash and wear" from the myriad of critics who have proposed theories. Holland makes several acute comments about the play's matricidal imagery that speak to an earlier developmental stage, the pre-Oedipal, which few psychoanalytic studies of the play had investigated at that time. Holland sees Hamlet's hostility toward his mother, and, by extension, toward women in general, especially Ophelia, as "stemming from a pre-oedipal oral conflict that paved the way for this solution to the later oedipal issues" (183). He then adds, however, that such clinical speculations that treat a fictional character like a real person would not be well received by a "purely literary critic," meaning, Holland himself a few years earlier, or, more accurately, the Holland who still could not silence his inner New Critical voice.

Mind the Gap

Holland has his own preferred psychoanalytic approach to Shakespeare, but he finds nuggets of truth in other approaches, even those he admits that are built on a shaky foundation. After referring to two unconvincing readings of *A Midsummer Night's Dream*, by Weston A. Gui and Donald F. Jacobson, he cites Morton Kaplan, who criticizes the readings as a "ratiocinative exercise and sterile criticism," devoid of any insight. But then Holland unexpectedly defends the two readings. "While I agree with Professor Kaplan that both readings are grossly overstated, I do feel they point the way for a proper psychoanalytic study" (245). One can see Holland building bridges from one psychoanalytic approach to another. "Mind the gap," Holland would often say at European psychoanalytic conferences, referring humorously to the audible or visible warning phrase used to remind passengers on the London Underground to tread carefully while crossing the precarious space between the subway door and the station platform. Much of Holland's later commentary was to remind readers to mind the gap—respecting and bridging the distance between themselves and others.

In "Conclusions Logical," Holland rejects the "here-a-phallic-symbol-there-a-phallic-symbol" approach to psychoanalytic literary criticism. No surprise there. He was never interested in this type of criticism. Nor is it a surprise that he repudiates treating fictional characters as if they were real people, "character-mongering" (303), as he calls it. Literary character, he never tires of telling us, is shaped primarily by artistic concerns: Homo Fictus and Homo Dramaticus operate according to different laws from Homo Sapiens. There are three ways to approach the subject, he reminds us: studying the author's mind, a character's mind, or the audience's mind. He rejects the first approach, insisting that psychobiographical criticism is not literary criticism. He rejects the second approach, repeating the criticisms he expressed in his first two books: "literary personages exist only as words and what we call their 'character' is only an inference or abstraction from the text" (303). Only the third approach is justifiable, studying the audience's mind, or, as he suggests in his next book, the reader's mind, which is for him reaching bedrock.

In "Conclusions Not So Logical," Holland begins to think aloud about the future direction of psychoanalytic literary criticism, in particular, his own future research, devising a comprehensive psychoanalytic theory to understand our response to literature, something that has not yet been done. Such a theory, he suggests, will have a complex feedback system between author and text, text and audience (or reader). This feedback system resembles that between analysand and analyst. He ends *Psychoanalysis and Shakespeare* with a subtle allusion to *A Midsummer Night's Dream*, Theseus's speech to Hippolyta affirming the poet's imagination to give form to things unknown. "Psychoanalytic literary criticism can help literature do what men have always thought it could do, namely, give to airy nothing a local habitation and a name" (349).

Psychoanalysis and Shakespeare remains a remarkable scholarly achievement, the best single book on the subject up to its time. Writing in *Shakespeare Quarterly* in 1968, Maurice Charney characterizes Holland's book as a "significant contribution to the history of Shakespearean criticism, and also, as a necessary by-product, to the cultural history of our own age" (401). No Freudian, Charney criticizes Holland's "embarrassing 'scientism,'" his "acolytic warmth," but he nevertheless acknowledges Holland's efforts to "lay the basis for a more responsible psychoanalytic criticism" (403).

Always a Shakespearean

When Holland first became interested in psychoanalysis, in the late 1950s, he advertised himself as a Shakespearean scholar, not a psychological critic. "As my wife used to say," he quips in "The Story of a Psychoanalytic Critic," "Shakespeare was my fig leaf" (254). He never stopped being a Shakespearean even after he became a psychoanalytic theorist. He contributed an essay on "Hermia's Dream" to *Representing Shakespeare: New Psychoanalytic Essays* (1980), coedited by Murray Schwartz and Coppélia Kahn. Another essay, "Sons and Substitutions: Shakespeare's Phallic Fantasy," appeared in the 1989 volume *Shakespeare's Personality*, which he coedited with Sidney Homan and Bernard J. Paris, both of whom were colleagues at the University of Florida. The two Shakespeare books reveal Holland's eagerness to encourage his colleagues' own scholarship and, whenever possible, to collaborate with them in the cowriting or coediting of a scholarly book.

"Sons and Substitutions" has intriguing biographical interest for both Shakespeare and Holland scholars. He begins the essay by announcing that rebellion is his theme; in "The Story of a Psychoanalytic Critic," we recall, he describes himself as "[a]lways something of a rebel" (245), an observation that becomes clearer in *Meeting Movies*, where he writes about his painful rebellion against his father. Holland's statement about Shakespeare in "Sons and Substitutions" appears to be true of himself, a young man still in his father's shadow. "In these phallic or oedipal rivalries good sons (and often the bad ones, before they go bad), are their fathers' right hands, their swords, their hawks, their horses, their hounds—all symbols for the father's phallic power" (72). Holland ends the essay by acknowledging that he is writing about his own image of Shakespeare, which might be different from the reader's image.

"Shakespeare" becomes a way of representing his works to myself and thus of evoking a human truth rather than a quasi-metaphysical meaning. I imagine such a Shakespeare, but he is not *the* Shakespeare, who never was available to us anyway. He is *a* Shakespeare, *my* Shakespeare, Shakespeare as I realize him, a gambit, a try—finally, the opening to a conversation. (85)

3

Theorizing Psychoanalytic Literary Criticism

The Dynamics of Literary Response

Dedicated to his "mothers and fathers," *The Dynamics of Literary Response*, published in 1968, marks a turning point in Holland's life, the beginning of his career as a psychoanalytic literary theorist. In the preface, he expresses his indebtedness to his fellow members of the Group for Applied Psychoanalysis and the Boston Psychoanalytic Society. Without explaining why, he singles out Dr. Elizabeth Zetzel for her "particular help."

Elizabeth Zetzel

Elizabeth Zetzel's father, James N. Rosenberg, was a prominent jurist who served on a committee for the passage of the Genocide Convention at the United Nations after the Second World War. She, too, had a distinguished career, not in the law but in psychoanalysis. After receiving an undergraduate degree at Smith College, she studied medicine at the University of London and completed analytic training at the British Psychoanalytic Society, where she was analyzed by Ernest Jones, the first English analyst. Holland was not impressed with Jones's book on *Hamlet*, but he must have felt that by being analyzed by a woman who was herself analyzed by Freud's biographer and right-hand man, he was connected to the founding father of psychoanalysis. Zetzel (1907–90) was briefly excited by Melanie Klein, but a more formative influence was D. W. Winnicott, the pediatrician-turned-child analyst whose theory of the transitional object and potential space inspired Murray Schwartz, Holland's most trusted colleague, to write two key articles: "Where Is Literature?" (1975) and "Critic, Define Thyself" (1978). Zetzel was one of several women—Helene Deutsch was another—who largely subscribed to Freud's discredited theory of female psychology but who nevertheless had an illustrious career, thus, in effect, belying the theory.

Returning to the United States, Zetzel became an associate clinical professor of psychiatry at Harvard Medical School and a vice president of the International Psycho-Analytic Association. She began practicing psychiatry and psychoanalysis in 1938 and continued until her death in 1970 at age sixty-three, the same year her book *The Capacity for Emotional Growth* appeared.

Zetzel comes across in her book as a classically trained analyst who is a moderate in the highly charged ideological debates that roiled the psychoanalytic community. She sought to integrate psychiatry and psychoanalysis while at the same time recognizing that the techniques of one are not always helpful to the other. Typical of her measured views is the following comment about Melanie Klein's controversial theories.

> It is always essential in any science, but perhaps particularly in our own, to remember to distinguish between that which we believe to be true and which, as far as powers of validation go, we feel proved to be true, and that which offers suggestive and fruitful hypotheses which may be true but which must so far be considered unproved. (80)

Her words convey a cautionary wisdom that speaks to psychoanalytic critics in particular. How does one know the scientific truth of a theory? This remains a bedeviling question.

Many contemporary analysts, however, regard the "scientific" credibility of psychoanalysis as irrelevant. Whereas Holland regarded Freud as an Enlightenment thinker, Adam Phillips presents us with a "post-Freudian Freud," a man who was "always ahead of himself, and who we are beginning to catch up with" (*Terrors and Experts* 6). Psychoanalysis for Phillips is a theory of the "unbearable" (13), more confounding than comforting. Instead of achieving enlightenment, Phillips suggests, one learns to live with and appreciate unknowability, which is not the same as ignorance. Joel Whitebook uses the expression "dark enlightener" in his 2017 book, *Freud: An Intellectual Biography*. These views are antithetical to Zetzel's—and Holland's.

Zetzel begins the chapter called "The So-Called Good Hysteric" with what she calls a familiar nursery rhyme:

> There was a little girl
> And she had a little curl
> Right in the middle of her forehead.
> And when she was good
> She was very, very good,

But when she was bad
She was horrid. (229)

Holland had used the last two lines, which come from Henry Wadsworth Longfellow's poem "There Was a Little Girl," in *Psychoanalysis and Shakespeare*: "when psychoanalytic criticism is bad, it is horrid" (77). I, too, used the quotation in my talk honoring Holland. The challenge for every psychoanalytic critic is to emulate the good girl—and avoid making the antifeminist mistakes of the horrid one.

Analyzability

Zetzel coauthored a second book, *Basic Concepts of Psychoanalytic Psychiatry*, with W. W. Meissner, that was published in 1973, three years after her sudden death. As Meissner writes in the preface, "Her death was felt as a severe and acute loss by the psychoanalytic community in the Boston area and by many others to whom her clinical and teaching influence extended." The book, based on a series of public lectures she gave at the Massachusetts Mental Health Center, was designed to be an introduction to psychoanalytic theory for medical students and psychiatric residents. What's most interesting about the book for our purpose is its discussion of the criteria for analyzability conducted by the Boston Psychoanalytic Institute a number of years earlier. Zetzel and Meissner report the results of 100 patients who were analyzed for several years. The discussion reveals the types of patients who entered into and succeeded in analysis:

> The patients who presented themselves as potentially healthy individuals and who seemed to meet the criteria for analyzability seemed to fall into typical patterns of neurotic difficulty. By far the most common difficulty for adult analyzable women was in the area of capacities for heterosexual object relations. This usually reflected the influence of an hysterical personality organization. In contrast, the analyzable men were likely to present with symptoms of a more obsessional nature together with inhibitions in the area of their work. Patients referred to the instutute [sic] for therapeutic analysis fell into these two large categories. The women came because of their failure to make a satisfactory heterosexual object choice; the men sought help because of a work problem. This was quite frequently the problem for graduate students who were experiencing difficulties in completing their dissertations. (254–5)

American Ego Psychology

American psychoanalysis in the 1950s and 1960s was largely ego psychology, influenced by Anna Freud and Heinz Hartmann. As Nancy Chodorow points out in *The Psychoanalytic Ear and the Sociological Eye* (2020), ego psychology represented a "radical 'one-person' intrapsychic perspective centered on fantasy, drive-derivative wishes, resistances, defenses, and compromise formations" (3). Believing that we create our psyches mainly from within rather than through relationships with others, as interpersonal analysts Harry Stack Sullivan and Karen Horney maintained, ego psychologists represented, Chodorow notes, American individualism. They were originally the most critical of countertransference, Chodorow adds, advocating a neutral "objective" analytic stance, as Freud did. This objectivity implied the belief in an authoritarian model of analysis, an all-knowing analyst. Holland believed, along with Zetzel, that the analyst's purpose was to tell patients the truth about themselves rather than, as a contemporary two-person model suggests, analyst and patient cocreating the meaning of truth. Ego psychologists were, unlike European analysts, particularly the French, optimistic, pragmatic, and empirical, qualities that temperamentally appealed to Holland.

Holland didn't enter analysis to help him figure out how to complete his dissertation—he received his PhD in English from Harvard in 1956, before he began treatment with Zetzel—but in "The Story of a Psychoanalytic Critic" he describes his useful compulsions, thus making him a good candidate for analysis. The men who succeed in analysis, Zetzel and Meissner add, have "relatively well-defended personalities" (255), again true of Holland. Other personal characteristics predictive of analyzability include the "ability to achieve and maintain a positive therapeutic alliance," the "capacity to work through the terminal phase of analysis," the "development of certain defenses which prove to be prophylactic against undue regression during the analytic process," and, perhaps most important, the "capacity to tolerate anxiety and depression" (263). After commenting on the many factors that must be present for analytic success, Zetzel and Meissner conclude that psychoanalysis is not a treatment for all or perhaps even most people. "Much of the disenchantment with and devaluation of psychoanalysis in recent years has stemmed from attempts to apply psychoanalytic techniques inappropriately to patients who did not meet the criteria for analyzability. Therapeutic success with such patients is predictably foredoomed" (265). It should be noted, however, as Peter L. Rudnytsky has pointed out (personal communication, May 6, 2020), that Zetzel's pronouncements about analyzability are outdated.

"The Unity of the Human Self"

"The Story of a Psychoanalytic Critic" contains limited information about Holland's training at the Boston Psychoanalytic Institute, including his seven-year analysis with Zetzel. He learned from his psychoanalytic seminars two noteworthy insights that he applied to literary analysis, beginning with *Psychoanalysis and Shakespeare*. First, literary texts, like people, are multilayered. "A given text could have different levels of fantasy, from the earliest oral issues of self and other up to the loves, hates, and jealousies of the oedipal triangle. These different levels would be continuous. The higher levels would be transformations of the lower, more primitive ones" (249). Second, the psychoanalytic concept of defense could also be applied to literature. "Until the early 1960s, I do not believe anyone had used the idea of defense to analyze literature, except, of course, for Freud on jokes" (249). These two ideas, pre-Oedipal stages and defense, are central to *The Dynamics of Literary Response*.

But as important as these insights were from his Boston Psychoanalytic Institute seminars, Holland gained other truths about himself from his personal analysis with Zetzel:

> There I discovered a far more important unity than the unity of literary texts, the unity of the human self, the unity of me. I came to believe— by finding it true in myself—that purely intellectual activities (like my enthusiasm for the New Criticism) expressed personal needs deeply rooted in early life. Furthermore, one could trace in adult life aspects of these same themes in widely varying areas of behavior. Intellectual beliefs expressed the same needs as one's relations with friends and colleagues, superiors, one's children, or one's mate. In particular, one's sexual preferences expressed those needs most directly and explicitly, although one had to penetrate repression and denial to find that out. Thus, there was a far more important unity than the unity of texts, the unity of the human self. (249)

Holland's "most strange discovery" from his personal analysis was a hard psychoanalytic proverb: "What we wish, we also fear, and what we fear, we also wish." He includes the same psychoanalytic maxim in *The Dynamics of Literary Response* (295) without telling us that he acquired this insight from his own analysis. The specific example he gives us in "The Story of a Psychoanalytic Critic" is hardly specific: "My New Critical power over texts also defended against a fear of being passive toward the text, simply enjoying it" (250). One can imagine worse fears than being passive toward a pleasurable literary text! The key issue to Holland was the need to gain power over a poem or play rather than helplessly submitting to it.

A few pages later in "The Story of a Psychoanalytic Critic" Holland includes another example of a merged fear/wish: the increasing popularity of psychoanalysis in the 1950s and 1960s. He then cites Oscar Wilde's paradoxical statement, "When the gods wish to punish us, they answer our prayers." But the result is not what Holland expected. "The literary professoriate took to psychoanalysis like kittens to yarn. I am sorry to say I have found the resulting tangle singularly unsympathetic. It became psychoanalysis-as-philosophy, profoundly abstract and intellectualized, profoundly dehumanized" (254). Shades of *Vulgärfreudismus*!

"The Story of a Psychoanalytic Critic" offers only a tantalizing hint of Holland's personal analysis, which was paid for by his wife's psychoanalyst-uncle, G. Henry Katz (1893–1985), whose help the grateful analysand acknowledges in several books. Holland never discusses, for example, why he entered analysis, what he specifically learned about himself, what resistances he had to overcome, and how analysis changed his life. Although Holland decided to drop the "junior" after his name well before he completed analysis, it's likely that his conflicted relationship with his father was a central issue of therapy. He seems to suggest this when he explains why unity was such a powerful reassurance to him. "I discovered the roots of my craving in my childhood in a one-bedroom New York apartment" (247), the site where Holland played out the family dynamics that subtly influenced the literary dynamics of his emerging model of reading. His analysis was, in short, a life-transforming event in which he learned that he would be no one's junior or disciple, except, perhaps, Freud's.

Holland's need for privacy prevented him from giving us any of the details of his analysis, but other writers, analysts and non-analysts alike, have cast light on their own analyses. James T. McLaughlin (1918–2006), a training analyst associated with the Pittsburgh Psychoanalytic Institute for over half a century, offers us in his 2005 book *The Healer's Bent* the most poetic description I have come across of an experience that seems almost phantasmagoric:

> The insights that I have had in my own analyses, that I have encountered in my patients and in myself in the day-to-day analytic work over the past 40 years, have been fitful happenstance, nothing that I set out deliberately to achieve. They have been as fireflies: elusive on the wing and enigmatic in the grasp; illuminating in the moment seen, rather dull and diminished when closely scrutinized. Was the guiding glow really there, or imagined in my head? Once in hand, how to keep it glowing? (88)

"A Monastic Ritual"

Holland's personal analysis represented the beginning of his lifelong commitment to psychoanalysis. His analysis, however, may have given him an overly optimistic sense of human knowability. Erik Erikson has suggested in *Young Man Luther* that a training analysis, a rite of passage or induction into the profession, is a monastic ritual. "Young (and often not so young) psychoanalysts in training must undergo a training procedure which demands a total and central personal involvement, and which takes greater chances with the individual's relation to himself and to those who up to then have shared his life, than any other profession except monkhood" (151). The initiation requires and reinforces orthodoxy. Indeed, Holland twice refers to Freud, with hardly any irony, as "The Master" (22, 79). Freud embodies to Holland a "truly Germanic faith in *wissenschaft* [science]" (17); he is "ever the apostle of rationality" (43). Holland's analysis was a life-transforming event. From this moment on, he viewed everything through a psychoanalytic lens; there is no evidence that he called into question any of the conclusions he reached from his analysis or needed to return for a second analysis, as sometimes occurs.

"The Next New Criticism"

Without stating he was in analysis, Holland wrote "The Next New Criticism" that appeared in *The Nation* in 1961. Psychoanalytic criticism and New Criticism not only complement each other, he argued, but they are also strikingly similar in method and in their preoccupation with language. "Where the New Critic, working with a conventional dictionary and grammar, draws conclusions in terms of intellectual content, the psychoanalytic critic, working in much the same way, but with a darker dictionary and grammar, tells us what the work says in the language of the unconscious to the unintellectual parts of our minds" (340). Holland may have been the first and only literary critic to comment on these parallels. Most New Critics, he laments, have ignored psychoanalytic criticism; but both methodologies "rest uneasily like two momentarily divided but potentially dangerous chunks of plutonium" (340). The explosive simile was designed to alarm readers already frightened by Cold War threats of nuclear apocalypse, but Holland reassures readers that the combination of New and psychoanalytic criticism does not pose a danger to readers; "it will, however, be a revolution on a revolution." He then makes a shrewd prophecy. "Inevitably, it seems to me, criticism in the next fifty years will turn from its received form, the text-as-text, to face and reason with the hard fact of our own subjectivity" (341).

In "The Next New Criticism" Holland generously praises those scholars who, in his judgment, effectively use psychoanalytic criticism, including the distinguished Henry James scholar Leon Edel, Leslie Fiedler (soon to be his Buffalo colleague), Lionel Trilling, Gordon Smith, Simon Lesser, and Louis and Selma Fraiberg. Holland often pays tribute to his intellectual forbears. In "The Story of a Psychoanalytic Critic," for example, he similarly praises those established scholars who welcomed him into their discipline of literature and psychology: Leonard and Eleanor Manheim, who published the journal *Literature and Psychology*; Simon Lesser; and Norman Kiell, the creator of an indispensable bibliography.

Holland's darker side emerges, however, when he argues that psychoanalytic criticism of audience is another name for motivational research and then, referring to a popular hair cream in which a man "nudges the erect tube of Brylcreem which promptly ejaculates a white drop of pure sex appeal," he makes the following sarcastic comment about the country's two leading dramatists: "When Arthur Miller shows us an aging long-shoreman languishing oedipally over his daughter, when Tennessee Williams has his loverly hero castrated in the last act, we are no more taken in than by the Brylcreem ad" (340). In *The Dynamics of Literary Response* Holland objects to the "intolerable degree of smugness" (195) found in many contemporary critics; he generally avoided this problem in his books, but sometimes condescension mars his articles written for a wide audience, where he felt the need to exhibit his wit and erudition.

Intellectualization

Holland confesses to a bias in the preface to *The Dynamics of Literary Response* that readers must keep in mind throughout the book. "For me, the need to see and understand is very strong. To put the matter as exactly and with as much ambiguity as possible, I need to be sure that I am understanding all that I am seeing" (xvi). There's hardly anything sensationalistic or lurid about this confession; indeed, isn't this bias true of most authors: the desire to know? He admits to this bias in nearly all of his subsequent books, but it's a self-disclosure that is bound to make little impact on readers because of its lack of concreteness. The bias would have been more meaningful if he acknowledged the *fear* of not understanding, a fear which, paradoxically, an author would then need to elaborate on, and, in the process, perhaps overcome. Or he could have stated that the need for knowing interferes with the desire for being.

Another way the bias would have been more meaningful was if he stated that the desire for intellectual understanding clashes with the fear of emotional knowledge, but he never stated this. And so the reader doesn't know what this bias means or how it affects Holland's life as a scholar or teacher. We will soon see, however, that this bias is central to his identity as a reader.

Holland doesn't use the word "intellectualization" to describe his own bias, but he does use the word in *The Dynamics of Literary Response*, in a mildly pejorative sense, to describe people attracted to puzzling intellectual films. These films appeal to intellectual audiences by enabling adult intellectuals to use their *defenses* to master childhood fears and mysteries:

> For example, most intellectuals have a good deal of curiosity. The reason psychologists give is that their early attempts to solve the puzzles of childhood become a way of life. In technical jargon, infantile curiosity became sublimated into the intellectual and aesthetic curiosity of the adult. Now the puzzling movie comes along and enables us to do, or think we can do, just what our life style has been wanting to do all along: solve the riddle of emotions and sexuality by purely intellectual means. Would that we could!
>
> The puzzling movies play into the intellectual's life style in another way. Academics and intellectuals often present the appearance to other people of "cold fish," the reason being that it is typical of the highly intellectualized person that he puts up a barrier between sensuous emotional experience and the intellectual problems with which he concerns himself. The puzzling movie enables him to do this again— to put aside the emotional mysteries of the film and see it coldly, using intellection as a defense. (171)

The more one reads Holland's writings, the more convinced one is that he was thinking about himself in this passage. But he did not want the reading public to know this. And so he writes about "intellectuals," not himself, yet to gain credibility with the reader, he reluctantly uses "technical jargon," invoking the authority of psychoanalysis. The quest to unlock through psychoanalysis the mystery of all mysteries is so fraught, Holland implies, that it is easier said than done—hence, the expression: "Would that we could."

It's curious, however, that Holland implies that intellectualization is a defense mechanism when speaking about people drawn to puzzling intellectual films, yet he omits mentioning intellectualization elsewhere in *The Dynamics of Literary Response* when he includes a list of defenses. For example, in the chapter "A Dictionary of Fantasy" he lists the following major defenses: regression, denial, reversal, reaction-formation, undoing, projection, introjection, identification with the aggressor, turning against the self, regression, splitting, symbolization, sublimation, and rationalization. Not a word about intellectualization. Nor does the word appear in the glossary of psychoanalytic terms at the end of the book or in the index. Was this omission an oversight, a reluctance to speak about something so central to his identity, or an uncertainty whether intellectualization was a major defense mechanism?

Significantly, Anna Freud refers to intellectualization in *The Ego and the Mechanisms of Defense*. "This intellectualization of instinctual life, the attempt to lay hold on the instinctual processes by connecting them with ideas which can be dealt with in consciousness, is one of the most general, earliest, and most necessary acquirements of the human ego" (163). Intellectualization is so essential, she continues, that it is regarded not merely as an activity of the ego but as one of its essential components. Most of Anna Freud's discussion involves intellectualization at puberty and emphasizes its positive value. "The focusing of the intellect on instinctual processes is analogous to the alertness which the human ego has found to be necessary in the face of the objective dangers which surround it" (164).

What's wrong with intellectualization? It can be, as Glen O. Gabbard suggests, "using excessive and abstract ideation to avoid difficult feelings" (37)—thinking instead of feeling. In the hierarchy of defense mechanisms, intellectualization is considered high-level, along with sublimation, rather than "primitive," such as splitting and projective identification. Intellectualization can thus be a defense against a painful thought or feeling. Unlike a closely related word, rationalization, which implies misusing reason to deny a truth, intellectualization implies avoiding a disturbing truth, often unconscious, associated with fears and anxieties.

Holland never implies that his intense need for knowledge has limited his understanding of people or texts. A bias is not a prejudice. Holland never strikes me as a cold fish in his writings, and he did not seem that way in person. Throughout *The Dynamics of Literary Response* he is engaging and always passionate in his observations and conclusions. Admittedly, he takes a highly intellectual approach to affective issues, which can be unsettling to some readers. In the chapter on Affect, he offers an unusual chart of the interplay of fantasy, management of fantasy, and emotion. For example, the category of "puzzling movies" involves the fantasy of sexual looking, implies a displacement to intellectual issues, and results in affect block. In light of Holland's intense need for knowledge, it's not surprising that the solution of plot involves the fantasy of hungry expectance, leading to gratification and finally satisfaction. The failure to resolve plot, by contrast, involves the same fantasy of hungry expectance, leading to frustration and finally anger. Clearly, Holland is writing about himself here. His chart of twenty-five groupings of fantasies and affects may seem cerebral, but his discussions are never dry. As often as not, his humor shines through—and it's his humor that connects him to Freud. Interestingly, Freud regarded humor, as he wrote in *Jokes and Their Relation to the Unconscious* in 1905, as the "highest" of the defense mechanisms. "It scorns to withdraw the ideational content bearing the distressing affect from conscious attention as repression does, and thus surmounts the automatism of defence" (*SE*, vol. 8, 233). And it was Freud's analysis of humor in his great joke book that first drew Holland, a kindred spirit, to him. Freud's theory of humor was the only one that made sense to Holland, a theory that led him to close textual analysis. "I came to wonder," he writes in the preface to *The Dynamics of Literary Response*, "if psychoanalytic psychology could offer a theory for literature in general, not just jokes. Thus the book began" (xiii).

Developing and Applying a New Model of Reading

The Dynamics of Literary Response represents Holland's first systematic effort to develop a model for the interaction of literary works with the human mind—a model that explains subjectivity. Acknowledging in the preface the book's "ambitious" nature, he singles out two "excellent" books that have made similar attempts, Ernst Kris's *Psychoanalytic Explorations in Art* and Simon O. Lesser's *Fiction and the Unconscious*. Holland's book goes well beyond the others, though, in showing how literature transforms fantasies into meanings discoverable through psychoanalytic interpretation.

The Dynamics of Literary Response is divided into two parts, "The Model Developed" and "The Model Applied." Each part consists of six chapters. Part I develops the idea of literature as transformation, offers a brief dictionary of psychosexual fantasies, discusses Coleridge's iconic expression the "willing suspension of disbelief," explores the evocative idea that form is defense, shows how language transforms unconscious fantasy into language, and outlines how meaning leads to psychological mastery. After sketching the outline of his model, Holland then applies it in Part II to related literary topics: evaluation, style, myth, characterization and identification, affect, and morality.

Torn between Critical Relativism and Monism

Holland is always at his best when offering close textual readings. Part I opens with a discussion of two "texts" that could not be more different, a joke from *Playboy* and the Arthurian tale of Chaucer's Wife of Bath. Despite their differences, both illustrate a cornucopia of oral, anal, urethral, phallic, and Oedipal fantasies. A central theme of Holland's book is that meaning does not reside entirely in a text: rather, meaning is something we "construct for the text within the limits of the text" (25). This principle explains the wide range of meanings readers reach from looking at the same text, as he shows in the Chaucer tale. But this principle, Holland confesses, in what turns out to be far more self-disclosing than his intense need for understanding, fills him with ambivalence.

> If you are a critical relativist (as I am on Mondays, Wednesdays, and Fridays), you will simply accept each of these different readings as valid to the extent it brings all the elements of the story together to a single "point." If you are a critical monist (as I am on Tuesdays, Thursdays, and Saturdays), you will carry one step further the process of successive abstraction that led us to these several meanings ... all together into one abstraction that covers all these possible meanings. (25)

On Sundays, we can speculate, Holland writes about the conflict between his two approaches to reading.

Holland's struggle between interpretive relativism and monism betrays an irresolvable ambivalence that appears in his subsequent books. Without pathologizing this ambivalence, we may point out that Freud believed ambivalence is a symptom of obsessional neurosis. "In obsessional neurotics," he declares in his 1912 essay "The Dynamics of Transference," "an early separation of the 'pairs of opposites' seems to be characteristic of their instinctual life and to be one of their constitutional preconditions. Ambivalence in the emotional trends of neurotics is the best explanation of their ability to enlist their transferences in the service of resistance" (*SE*, vol. 12, 107). "The Dynamics of Transference" is noteworthy in the history of psychoanalysis because it is the first time Freud uses the word "ambivalence," which had been coined two years earlier by his Swiss colleague Eugen Bleuler. Holland puts his own ambivalence to good use in his scholarship, where his obsessive pursuit of detail is always evident, and where he will sometimes change his mind, suddenly, inexplicably, unapologetically.

"Dover Beach"

Despite Holland's opening sentence in the preface that he has not written a book of literary criticism, the most incisive and original aspects of *The Dynamics of Literary Response* lie in its readings of individual texts—his

New Critical insights. His audacious reading of Matthew Arnold's "Dover Beach" seems at first reductive yet cannot be dismissed. Reading nearly a score of widely different explications of the poem, which, according to the textbook he cites, is the most widely reprinted poem in the English language, Holland finds that none touches on what he believes to be its core fantasies and defenses:

> The poem is evoking in me, at least, and perhaps in many readers, primitive feelings about "things that go bump in the night," that they are disturbing, but exciting at the same time. As in the "tomorrow" speech [in *Macbeth*], there is a well-nigh universal sexual symbolism in this heard-but-not-seen, naked fighting by night. This is one way Arnold's poem turns our experience of disillusionment or despair into satisfaction, namely, through the covert gratification we get from this final primal scene fantasy. Arnold is talking about hearing a sexual "clash by night," just as children fantasy sex as fight. In fact (it has been suggested to me), the "darkling plain" may evoke in us thoughts of a bed, the "struggle" a man's active role in the sexual act, and the "flight" a woman's more passive situation (perhaps even that a wish that she would be in "flight" rather than lying there). (121)

What shall we make of this passage? To begin with, it is signature Holland, conveying his own unique reading identity—though he has not yet formulated this concept. He tells us what this poem evokes in *him* though he offers little of a specific nature. There is nothing self-disclosing here despite the hint of being personal. We sense that this interpretation of "Dover Beach," based on a primal scene, may have arisen from Holland's personal analysis, but he doesn't reveal his own experience with primal scene memories until *Meeting Movies*. None of the various explications of "Dover Beach" comes close to Holland's own interpretation. He gives credit where credit is due, telling us, parenthetically, that someone suggested to him the sexual nature of the "darkling plain," around which he constructs his own interpretation.

To single out only one thread of the interpretation of "Dover Beach," Holland points out that that the reference to the ancient Greek dramatist in the second stanza, "Sophocles long ago / Heard it on the gan," prepares us for the poem's final line, "Where ignorant armies clash by night," an allusion to the ancient Athenian general and historian Thucydides who wrote about the ill-fated Sicilian expedition against the Greeks during the Peloponnesian War. "As elsewhere in the poem," explains Holland, the image of the darkling plain "deflects our attention from a pair of lovers in a sexual situation and sublimates it into a distant, literary, and moral experience, a darkling plain from Thucydides" (121). He then tells us, matter-of-factly, that Matthew Arnold's father edited the writings of Thucydides.

Truth versus Ideology

Holland's interpretation of "Dover Beach" runs into problems, however, when he invokes what he thinks is the scientific truth of psychoanalytic theory. What's perhaps most controversial about Holland's thesis in *The Dynamics of Literary Response* is not simply the ubiquity of unconscious fantasies, although that is controversial enough, but the assertion that of all the meanings of a text, the "psychoanalytic meaning underlies all the others" (27). Psychoanalytic readers will probably accept this; non-psychoanalytic readers will not. Another statement is even more polarizing. "Psychoanalysis is not an ideology. Rather, it is clinical and experiential, and the fantasy it discovers in a literary work provides a base for our experience of that work just as fantasies—projections, imaginings, anticipations—provide a base for our experience of life itself" (31–2). One can only assume that when Holland made this statement, he was still in the throes of his analysis with Zetzel, one of his new mothers, who was herself a faithful disciple of Freud, Holland's lifelong idealized intellectual father.

Holland's implicit acceptance of psychoanalytic "truth" informs his discussion of "Dover Beach." His discussion of the unnamed male speaker's "active role in the sexual act" contrasts the woman's "more passive situation." This observation is consistent with the psychoanalytic view at the time, which Holland never seriously challenged, that masculine is active, feminine passive. But why did Holland accept this ideology—which he denied was ideology? How do we explain his unquestioning acceptance of Freud's belief in the psychic and moral consequences of the anatomical differences of the sexes? Here is Holland's summary, in his own words:

> The little girl's development is somewhat different because she feels, as it were, that the damage has already been done. In her case, the threat of castration is no longer meaningful. She, however, may give up the mother for a different reason, namely, that the mother is contemptible in that she too has lost the precious organ. The little girl may become as we say, a tomboy, trying to be as like her father as possible. Even so, the pressure to identify with the father is less. The little boy incorporates into himself his fears of his father, and in this surrender develops his superego or conscience, the basis for his later social behavior, in which his father's commandment lives in his brain unmixed with baser

matter. Freud was fond of saying that in women the conscience was less developed. (48)

Conscience less developed? Holland makes the statement casually, affectionately, unselfconsciously, but it's hard to imagine that he did not find it unproblematic, not to mention infuriating to feminists. He does not cite Freud's precise words, which are even harsher than Holland's summary. In his 1925 essay "Some Psychical Consequences of the Anatomical Distinctions between the Sexes," Freud makes what is surely his most misogynistic statement. The psychical consequences of "penis envy" have the most far-reaching consequences, he opines. "After a woman has become aware of the wound to her narcissism, she develops, like a scar, a sense of inferiority." She then begins to "share the contempt felt by men for a sex which is the lesser in so important a respect," and, at least in holding that opinion, insists on "being a man." The psychological truth is offensive, Freud admits, but he will not be deterred from unflinchingly expressing it:

> I cannot evade the notion (though I hesitate to give it expression) that for women the level of what is ethically normal is different from what it is in men. Their super-ego is never so inexorable, so impersonal, so independent of its emotional origins as we require it to be in men. Character-traits which critics of every epoch have brought up against women—that they show less sense of justice than men, that they are less ready to submit to the great exigencies of life, that they are more often influenced in their judgements by feelings of affection or hostility—all these would be amply accounted for by the modification in the formation of their super-ego which we have inferred above. (*SE*, vol. 19, 257–8)

Writing with evangelical fervor, Holland embraces all aspects of psychoanalytic theory. There is no critique of psychoanalytic theory in *The Dynamics of Literary Response*, no discussion of the limitations of Freudian theory, particularly with respect to female psychology. In *Psychoanalysis and Shakespeare*, Holland complains that psychoanalytic criticism has "languished in the antechambers of acceptability." He gives the following example of this unacceptability. "The man who tells us the skulls in that Danish graveyard are testicles or that Desdemona suffers from penis envy meets, not unsurprisingly, a certain amount of puzzlement if not downright scoff." He then asks rhetorically, "Is, then, a notion of penis envy or something like it so farfetched?" (323). Holland often quoted Freud but never the analyst's incredulous question to Marie Bonaparte: "The great question that has never been answered and which I have not yet been able to answer, despite my thirty years of research into the feminine soul, is 'What does a woman want?'" (Jones, vol. 2, 421).

Another Contentious Subject

Holland admits when speaking about Shakespeare's sonnets that nothing angers traditional scholars more than the belief that the poems affirm homosexual love. In arguing that, according to psychoanalytic theory, most males go through a homosexual phase in childhood, he then states that "a man needs to accept the feminine components in himself to be a good heterosexual lover" (86). Tellingly, he did not write about a good homosexual lover. Recall Elizabeth Zetzel's statement that the most common difficulty for adult analyzable women was in their *heterosexual* object relations. The implication is that homosexual women are not good candidates for analysis.

Holland did not have much to say about homosexuality, but he seemed to have accepted, at least early in his career, the psychoanalytic community's unenlightened attitude toward gays and lesbians. Freud regarded homosexuality not as an illness but as a developmental arrest, a fixation at an earlier stage of psychosexual development. "Homosexuality is assuredly no advantage, but it is nothing to be ashamed of, no vice, no degradation," he wrote in a 1935 letter: "it cannot be classified as an illness; we consider it to be a variation of the sexual function, produced by a certain arrest of sexual development." Freud believed that many of the greatest men of history were homosexual, including Plato, Michelangelo, and Leonardo da Vinci. "It is a great injustice to persecute homosexuality as a crime—and a cruelty, too" (*Letters* 423). Freud also signed a 1930 petition to decriminalize homosexuality in Austria and Germany.

Nevertheless, psychoanalysis was conservative both socially and politically. The American Psychoanalytic Association (APsaA) supported the American Psychiatric Association's (APA) decision to include homosexuality as a "sexual deviance" in the 1968 edition of the *Diagnostic and Statistical Manual of Mental Disorders* (*DSM*-III). As Aaron Levin relates in *Psychiatric News*, one of the most memorable moments in the history of the American Psychiatric Association occurred at its annual meeting in 1972 when "Dr. H. Anonymous," his face hidden behind a Halloween mask, asserted he was a homosexual psychiatrist. Virulent stigma against homosexuality within the mental health community had forced him behind the mask. "My greatest loss is my honest humanity," he was quoted as saying. "How incredible that we homosexual psychiatrists cannot be honest in a profession that calls itself compassionate and helping." The anonymous gay psychiatrist, identified twenty-two years later as John Fryer (1938–2003), was the catalyst behind the APA's decision in 1973 to eliminate the homosexuality diagnosis from the *DSM*. But APsaA refused to endorse the APA's decision, and it was not until 1991, when confronted with an anti-discrimination lawsuit, that APsaA allowed for the training of gay and lesbian analysts. Marking the fiftieth anniversary of the Stonewall uprising in New York City protesting discrimination against the LGBTQ community, APsaA issued a formal apology to the LGBTQ community on June 21, 2019. The apology occurred at the beginning of APsaA's 109th Annual Meeting:

> In 1969, homosexuality was considered a mental illness and sexual orientation was conflated with gender identity by the mental health field. This led to many being coerced, either by force or choice, into traumatic and harmful methods to "cure" homosexual desires and non-conforming gender identities. This belief also contributed to widespread discrimination and prejudice in housing, employment, healthcare, and in society at large.
>
> "Regrettably some of that era's understanding of homosexuality and gender identity can be attributed to the American psychoanalytic establishment," said Lee Jaffe, president of APsaA. "It is long past time to recognize and apologize for our role in the discrimination and trauma caused by our profession." (Tene)

As with so many other aspects of his psychoanalytic thinking, Holland later quietly changed his mind and modified his views of female psychology and homosexuality without admitting that the early theorists were wrong. Jane Holland, an ardent advocate of women's rights, doubtlessly helped modify her husband's thinking about female psychology. His female colleagues may have also played a role in his enlightenment. "A bright spot in the jargon-ridden morass of today's critical theory is feminism," Holland asserted in "The Story of a Psychoanalytic Critic":

> To be sure, some feminists are bogged down in deconstruction or Lacan. Others, however, insist on the vital, formative, and creative role of gender in reading and other experiences. They thus make the same intellectual turnaround as my work in reader-response. For the best feminist theory, "humanist" is not only not a term of opprobrium but the aim of the game. So too for more recent developments, gay and lesbian studies, "queer theory" and the various ethnic and political developments: Hispanic-American, African-American, and so on. (255)

Precarious Autobiography

By temperament if not by training, Holland was averse to all public self-disclosure. His references in *The Dynamics of Literary Response* to personal experience betray uncharacteristic hesitation, awkwardness, and self-consciousness. He offers only the briefest apologia in the preface as to why he is no longer a New Critic. He still believes that literature "means in a general, not a personal way" (5). He makes statements like "from my own experience, I would say that the single most common fantasy-structure in literature is phallic assertiveness balanced against oral engulfment" (43), but he remains silent about the autobiographical determinants of his own experience. He precedes a discussion of a Shakespeare sonnet with the words, "At the risk of being personal" (50), though he never says anything personal. He repeatedly invokes personal experience but just as repeatedly fails to be specific: "the key to the most successful literary works (in my experience, anyway) is that their very defenses give me pleasure" (131–2). Does he believe, as Freud did, that speaking about himself in public would compromise his authority? Freud was reluctantly willing to do this, as he admitted in *The Interpretation of Dreams*, but at the cost of his cherished privacy. "There is some natural hesitation about revealing so many intimate facts about one's mental life; nor can there be any guarantee against misinterpretation by strangers. But it must be possible to overcome such hesitations." Freud then quotes the French psychologist Joseph Delboeuf: "Every psychologist is under an obligation to confess his own weaknesses, if he thinks that it may throw light upon some obscure problem" (*SE*, vol. 4, 105).

After declaring that the most "exquisite moments" in Fellini's film *8½* are the most intensely autobiographical, Holland admits that autobiography can be "fun" but also "somewhat precarious" for the writer. He provides a general explanation for why he thinks this is true. If the autobiography is mainly factual, he argues, as it is for those penned by John Stuart Mill and Edward Gibbon, readers respond in the same way they do to all historical writing. If, on the other hand, writers disclose their fantasy life, they are likely to arouse the reader's defenses: "we will feel this as disgust, anxiety, boredom, or any one of a number of negative reactions" (221).

Holland could not foresee in the 1960s the explosive growth of the memoir and other forms of autobiographical writing that would occur only a few years later. Interest in personal writing shows no sign of abatement in the first two decades of the twenty-first century. Readers devour memoirs—to use an appropriate oral metaphor—because of their identification with writers in distress, whether it is from physical or mental illness, sexual abuse, disability, or family dysfunction. Yes, some readers may feel disgust, anxiety, boredom, or other negative emotions, but they also experience satisfaction and pleasure when writers overcome a problem. They also take delight in a writer's resiliency. Holland didn't anticipate this in his early books.

"Something of a Puritan"

The most Holland is willing to disclose about himself in *The Dynamics of Literary Response* is that he alternates between being a critical relativist and a critical monist and that he is, as one of his critics charged, "something of a Puritan" (222). Fortunately, Holland remains a Puritan with a sense of humor, a scholar who tries his best to avoid egotism. One can only agree with his hope that critical evaluation "can cease to be the smug assertion of one's own superiority in taste or vision or morality and become an exploration and acceptance of our common, fallible humanity" (224). He goes out of his way to praise earlier and contemporary psychologically oriented literary scholars, though he points out that not all claims to be a Freudian are valid. He cites Gaston Bachelard's *The Psychoanalysis of Fire* and then adds, parenthetically, "quite unpsychoanalytic, despite its title" (331). No one can answer the chicken-or-egg question whether Holland's wry sense of humor was the cause or effect of his scholarly interest in comedy. Near the end of *The Dynamics of Literary Response*, he questions whether reading literature makes people more humane, citing Northrop Frye's belief that this is true. "Yet, if this were true," Holland cannot help remarking ruefully, "English departments would be filled with saintly men, whereas, in fact, English departments are widely thought to be the most cantankerous of all" (333), a statement that foreshadows the novel he would write twenty-seven years later.

Returning to an Old Question

In both *The Shakespearean Imagination* and *Psychoanalysis and Shakespeare*, Holland takes a dim view of treating fictional characters as if they were real people. He admits that this idea is logically unsupportable in *The Dynamics of Literary Response*, but he then makes a stunning reversal.

> I have seen by the dozens psychoanalytic studies which diagnose Shakespeare's characters as though they were real people on couch or in clinic; and these critics give ample, more than ample, evidence from the plays themselves. Psychoanalytic critics regularly apply psychological

concepts from the world of everyday reality to characters who exist in a wholly different kind of world—it should not work but it does. (267)

After showing how psychoanalytic critics can talk perceptively about Mercutio's character and motivation in *Romeo and Juliet*, Holland cites a fascinating 1944 experiment conducted by two psychologists, Fritz Heider and Marianne Simmel, at Smith College. In Holland's words,

> To a group of undergraduates, they showed an animated cartoon detailing the adventures of a large black triangle, a small black triangle, and a circle, the three of them moving in various ways in and out of a rectangle. After the short came the main feature: the psychologists asked for comments, and the Smith girls "with great uniformity" described the big triangle as "aggressive," "pugnacious," "mean," "temperamental," "irritable," "power-loving," "possessive," "quick to take offense," and "taking advantage of his size" (it was, after all, the larger triangle). Eight per cent of the girls even went so far as to conclude that this triangle had a lower I.Q. than the other. Now if Smith girls can see that much in a triangle, how much more they—or we—are likely to see in Mercutio. (272)

Holland remained preoccupied with this vexing question for the rest of his life, seeking answers in the latest brain research as to why readers continue to treat fictional characters as real people. For now, however, we may simply note his willingness to change his mind about something he had once felt strongly about—without bothering to inform the reader that he had changed his mind.

The line between having strong opinions and being opinionated is often ambiguous. As often as not, Holland knows that his readers may not accept his own views, and he respects these differences. "Sometimes, I am sure, my experience will coincide with yours," he writes in the preface to *The Dynamics of Literary Response*. "At other times, you may feel that my response is idiosyncratic—so be it. The important thing is that we be as candid as we can, I in my assertions, you in your disagreements" (xiv–xv). The I-thou relationship he creates here and elsewhere is one of the book's successes.

Reviews: Frederick Crews

The reviews of *The Dynamics of Literary Response* were largely negative, often reflecting the reviewers' mistrust of psychoanalysis. The review that must have wounded Holland the most came from Frederick Crews, his former friend whose help he acknowledges in the preface. Unlike Holland, who became the leading American psychoanalytic literary critic of his generation, Crews went on to become the country's leading Freud castigator, a scholar who recanted his early books in a way that continues to mystify and bedevil his former students and colleagues. Crews's trajectory from Freud idolater to Freud basher is long and fascinating and betrays the dangers of idealization turning into virulent devaluation—and then demonization. In lurching from one extreme view of psychoanalysis to the opposite extreme, Crews misses the nuanced insights of the murky middle, where most of the truth lies.

Crews began his career as a brilliant psychoanalytic scholar, authoring *The Sins of the Fathers: Hawthorne's Psychological Themes*, published in 1966. Ironically, the back cover of *The Dynamics of Literary Response* contains an ad for Crews's book, both published by Oxford University Press around the same time. Crews's early writings reveal his belief that Freud was a heroic figure who, single-handedly, created an explanatory system that was a master key to unlock all human knowledge. The image of Freud as a Faustian figure may be seen in *The Sins of the Fathers*, in which Crews uses psychoanalysis to cast light on the mysteries of Hawthorne. Only Freud, in Crews's view, could expose the meaning of Hawthorne's ambivalence toward his ancestors, ambivalence that appears in his most powerful stories.

Significantly, Crews never doubts the scientific basis of psychoanalysis, a question that would obsess him after writing *The Sins of the Fathers*. Like Holland, Crews believes unquestioningly that psychoanalysis is the preeminent study of human subjectivity, a method to understand our waking and sleeping lives. Sometimes he seems so embarrassed by the obvious truth of his psychoanalytic statements that he feels obliged to add "of course," as when he declares, "For a Freudian, of course, there is nothing startling in the idea that fictional plots may gratify fantasies and strike subtle compromises with obsession" (154). That which is "offensive to moral logic," such as Dimmesdale's psychology of self-punishment, "perfectly observes the logic of psychoanalysis" (261).

Given Crews's nuanced use of psychoanalysis in *The Sins of the Fathers*, it's astonishing to come across a statement implying an all-or-nothing approach to Freud's work. "Revolutionary as his influence has been, Freud did not alter human nature: either we are entitled to use Freudianism retroactively or we must say that it is false" (258-9). One cannot imagine *any* contemporary analyst endorsing this statement. Freudian theory has undergone continuous revision, first by Freud himself, then by his disciples, including those who remained loyal to Freud and those who broke away to form their own movements.

In the following years, as doubts began undermining his faith in psychoanalysis, Crews rejected other psychoanalytic scholars who in his view lacked Freud's capacious imagination. Crews was still a Freudian, though barely, when he edited the 1970 volume *Psychoanalysis & Literary Process*. His comments about Holland are glaringly contradictory. In the preface Crews praises *The Dynamics of Literary Response* (1968) for its "unmatched clarity and rigor" (vi), but a few pages later admiration turns to condemnation.

> A criticism that cheerfully catalogs the unconscious tricks we play on ourselves and equates literary power with a judicious recipe of wishes and tactics, introjection and intellection, cannot avoid becoming a new version of anaesthesia—a version using Freud's terminology but lacking Freud's sympathy for the way great artists court unconscious engulfment in order to recreate the conditions of a human order. (19)

One can disagree with Holland's literary criticism for many reasons, but it is always impassioned, never anaesthetic. *Psychoanalysis & Literary Process* grew out of a graduate seminar in psychoanalytic criticism that Crews led at UC Berkeley in 1967. The five young scholars—all men—who attended the seminar included Albert D. Hutter (1941–2004), David Leverenz (1942–2017), Sheldon R. Brivic (1943), Richard L. Stein (1943), and Murray Schwartz (1942). All went on to have notable careers as college English professors and literary scholars, three of them (Hutter, Brivic, and Schwartz) in the area of psychoanalytic literary criticism. None of them repudiated psychoanalysis, as did Crews.

Other Reviews

Some of the other reviews began promisingly only to end with a deadly sting. Calling *The Dynamics of Literary Response* a "complex and interesting book" filled with many lively analyses, A. D. Nuttall then goes on to observe that "In general it may be said that to the believer in psychoanalysis they will appear—I will not say convincing (for the conceptual latitude of that science affords great scope for dissension)—but at least plausible. The present reviewer found in them little which he did not enjoy reading and almost nothing in which he could begin to believe" (244). Robert M. Adams panned *The Dynamics of Literary Response* in *The New York Review of Books*, dismissing it as a "vigorously reductive Freudian argument," and when Holland unwisely wrote a letter ("Shrinking Literature") in protest, he gave Adams another opportunity to savage the book: "There was no hint in my review that his sin was original; what I registered was a sense of impoverishment which can be had in a great many ways."

Some of the reviewers rejected Holland's model of reading but nevertheless praised individual readings. Erich Segal, still teaching classics at Yale before he resigned following the publication of *Love Story* in 1970, objected to the book's scriptural tone: "like any true believer, Holland is somewhat intolerant of those who do not share his orthodoxy." When Holland is less doctrinaire, Segal continued, he provides brilliant insights. Segal singled out Holland's superlative film criticism in *The Dynamics of Literary Response*. "Few critics have been as lucid as Holland in explicating the works of Fellini and other intellectual film-makers of our generation" (377). In the most thoughtful review, appearing in *The Journal of English and Germanic Philology*, Alan C. Purves faulted Holland for failing to distinguish between objectivity and subjectivity, the world of the text and that of the reader. "Holland admits that 'one constant problem in this book is subjective and objective'; unfortunately, he does not resolve that problem in his own writing" (562). Purves implies that no literary critic has solved this dilemma, and for that reason a reviewer must not be overly negative: "to point out such a failing and leave matters at that is to perform a disservice to its author." Purves concludes by praising individual readings and Holland's dictionary of fantasies.

Looking for Another Model

The Dynamics of Literary Response represents the beginning of Holland's efforts to create a new model of reading, one that would lead to a new literary approach: reader-response criticism. He still believed that literature "is an objective text but also a subjective experience" (108). He still believed that literature transforms readers instead of readers transforming literature. And he still believed that in one sense "it does not matter whether meaning is 'in' the text or whether the reader supplies it" (185). But he was already beginning to reject the model of reading offered in *The Dynamics of Literary Response*, not because it was ambitious but because it was not ambitious enough. As he admits in "The Story of a Psychoanalytic Critic," the model didn't adequately account for the wide differences in reading. He soon rejected the prevalent view that "texts did things." His new realization—that the reader, not the text, did the transforming—turned his intellectual world topsy-turvy. Meaning, he soon came to believe, lies entirely within the reader. "Looking at literature from the point of view of the reader required me to reverse completely the focus of my teaching and analysis" (252). And with that realization came his next two books, the beginning of reader-response criticism.

4

Developing a New Model of Reader-Response Criticism

Poems in Persons and *5 Readers Reading*

The Dynamics of Literary Response offers a transformational model of literary experience, and Holland's next two books, *Poems in Persons* (1973) and *5 Readers Reading* (1975), illustrate how this model works. Both books demonstrate that the transformation does not take place in literary works, as he had recently thought, but in those who read them. Just as the writer is the creator of a text, the reader is a remaker of the text. Readers construct meaning as part of their own reading experiences—their unique identity themes, a term inspired by the Prussian-born psychoanalyst Heinz Lichtenstein (1904–90). While studying at the Boston Psychoanalytic Institute, Holland began reading Lichtenstein's clinical essays on identity, which were not well known at the time, not even in the psychoanalytic community. The result for Holland was a eureka moment, an aha! experience.

Heinz Lichtenstein

After studying philosophy with Martin Heidegger at the University of Freiburg in Germany, Lichtenstein came to the United States in 1939. Trained at the New York Psychoanalytic Institute, he moved to Buffalo in the late 1940s, where he became a faculty member in the Department of Psychiatry at the University of Buffalo. As Lichtenstein notes gratefully at the beginning of his 1977 book *The Dilemma of Human Identity*, in the late sixties Holland and Schwartz invited him to participate in their newly created Group for Applied Psychoanalysis at Buffalo and in the Center for the Psychological Study of the Arts. It was an exciting interdisciplinary collaboration that enriched everyone. Holland and Schwartz provided Lichtenstein with a "most important stimulation and exposure to new dimensions of knowledge that have influenced my thinking in new ways" (x), as he writes in *The Dilemma of Human Identity*. Indeed, they were the catalysts behind authoring the book. Under Lichtenstein's supervision, Murray Schwartz was permitted, as part of his psychoanalytic psychotherapy training at the University of Rochester Medical School, to treat two patients at the SUNY Buffalo Medical School Clinic:

> As Lichtenstein's supervisee, what I most needed was help with questions of technique, and I benefitted greatly from his depth of experience. What impressed me most was his quick insight into my patients' unconscious fantasies and their transferential effects on our relationship. Who was I to them, and they to me? He helped me especially to navigate difficult moments in the therapeutic process, as when one young woman with a history of abuse at the hands of men repeatedly demanded signed gifts of my writings. ("Psychoanalysis in My Life" 143)

Lichtenstein's groundbreaking article "Identity and Sexuality," first published in 1961 in the *Journal of the American Psychoanalytic Association* and then included in *The Dilemma of Human Identity*, was the theoretical basis for *Poems in Persons* and *5 Readers Reading*. As Lichtenstein declares in *The Dilemma of Human Identity*, the "remarkable fact" that Freud did not write about the problem of personal identity has created a suspicion among many psychoanalysts that the concept may be used "to introduce surreptitiously 'culturalist' or 'existentialist' ideology into the legacy of Freud" (128). The statement bespeaks the closed-world insularity of orthodox psychoanalytic thinking at the time. To be sure, Erikson had written extensively on identity, but like Lichtenstein, he too was first regarded as an outsider. *The Dilemma of Human Identity* thus contains an unexpected irony: researching a subject that few in the profession were inclined to welcome.

Part of the problem for Lichtenstein, and later for Holland, was interpreting the repetition-compulsion principle that formed the basis for Freud's speculation in his 1920 book *Beyond the Pleasure Principle* of the existence of a "death instinct." Freud himself acknowledged the highly conjectural nature of his theory, though that hasn't prevented many analysts, particularly Melanie Klein and Jacques Lacan, from enthusiastically embracing it. Lichtenstein presents a compelling explanation of the repetition-compulsion principle that links it to the preservation of identity rather than to the desire for death. "It is my contention that the repetition compulsion is a manifestation of the necessity for maintenance of the 'theme of identity.' Identity, in man, requires a 'repetitive doing' in order to safeguard the 'sameness within change' which

I believe to be a fundamental aspect of identity in man" (103). These two sentences form the heart of Lichtenstein's theory.

Additionally, Lichtenstein postulated that "human identity is acquired very early in life as a thematic configuration, arising in the earliest, most primitive contact of the infant with the mothering adult." Relying upon ethological research, Lichtenstein suggests that an identity theme is an "imprinted configuration which from then on constitutes the invariant in the development of the individual" (251). Lest his theory sound too deterministic, Lichtenstein asserts that the identity theme "will be 'developed' in the course of life as an infinite variety of identity transformations, as a simple musical theme is developed into a symphony" (218).

Holland always gave full credit to Lichtenstein for the idea of an identity theme, mentioning him in book after book, a practice not always seen in other psychoanalytic thinkers. As Peter L. Rudnytsky notes, Heinz Kohut seldom acknowledged his indebtedness to Carl Rogers, John Bowlby, and D. W. Winnicott (*Psychoanalytic Conversations* 96). By contrast, Holland was so intellectually beholden to Lichtenstein's work that he wrote an obituary of him that appeared in the *International Journal of Psycho-Analysis*, the only death notice he wrote for publication. "At the heart of Lichtenstein's work is his theory of human identity," Holland writes,

> Other theories of identity deal with a sense of identity, a person's feeling of inner continuity and wholeness. Lichtenstein's idea is closer to a psychic structure, something in a person that psychoanalysts and others can observe. The most familiar version of identity is Erik Erikson's, a social identity: the me as creating and created by society. Lichtenstein's concept is deeper. Pre-social and pre-cultural, his idea attempts to answer the question: How does the unformed, animal-like baby become a person? How does a What become a Who? (528)

The obituary reads, in part, like an encyclopedia article, as when Holland observes that Lichtenstein's first article, published in 1935 on self and identity, received favorable notice from Freud himself. Apart from conveying the importance of Lichtenstein's theoretical work on identity, Holland captures the personal aspects of the man that were true of Holland himself, as when he writes, "he lived the subdued, reclusive life of a scholar, publishing a series of complex, erudite, and important papers on questions of identity and society" (527). Another characterization of Lichtenstein is a self-characterization: after listing the deceased's living relatives, Holland remarks that he is "also survived by his ideas, recently confirmed in unexpected ways" (528). In concluding the obituary with a prescient remark about Lichtenstein's legacy,

Holland was probably thinking of his own legacy: "In short, Lichtenstein was a clinician-philosopher who probed the deepest issues in psychoanalysis. His writings are like a psychoanalyst's best interpretations: we have not yet realized their full implications, nor are we likely to, even for many years after he has ceased to be with us" (529).

Monumental Research

Researching *Poems in Persons* and *5 Readers Reading*, Holland interviewed in the late 1960s several advanced undergraduate English majors from a nearby university; for a period ranging from eight to eleven weeks, they read a story or poem or watched a film or play. He then interviewed each one, taping the conversations. He asked the students in the interviews to talk about their free associations to each text. He avoided asking the students leading questions that would merely confirm his own presuppositions about what was happening during the act of reading.

Holland amassed an enormous amount of information, 200 pages of transcribed interview material for *each* student, which constituted the primary data for both books. In addition, each student agreed to take two different personality tests, a Rorschach inkblot test and a Thematic Apperception Test, both of which were administrated by a trained psychologist who interpreted the results. Finally, Holland gave the students the COPE test designed to elicit processes of defense or adaptation. He then pored over the results. He decided to focus on five students, two in *Poems in Persons*, Sandra and Saul, and the same two plus Sam, Shep, and Sebastian in *5 Readers Reading*. Holland sought to discover nothing less than the immutable psychological laws of reading, a discovery worthy of a conquistador. "No matter who the reader is or how he reads," he writes in *5 Readers Reading*, "what he reads will take the general form revealed by the model: a fantasy transformed by defenses and adaptations to give pleasure and unity and meaning" (40).

The subjectivity of the students' interpretation of literature stunned Holland. As he admits ruefully in *5 Readers Reading*, the less literary of the two books, it is "impossible to subtract the subjective elements in a reading from the objective, for each helps create the other." He felt lost in an unsettling paradox. "New Criticism turns out to have been Old Subjectivity. A reader finds something, certainly, but if one cannot separate his 'subjective' response from its 'objective' basis, there seems no way to find out what that 'something' is in any impersonal sense" (40).

Poems in Persons: Differences between the Two Editions

It is confusing to write about *Poems in Persons* because of the many changes, major and minor, between the first edition, subtitled *An Introduction to the Psychoanalysis of Literature*, and the second edition, published twenty-seven years later in 2000. The latter, published by Cybereditions, an online publishing venture designed to rescue out-of-print books, is itself no longer in existence, a cruel irony. The 2000 edition contains several typos. To give only one example, Holland writes, "I subtitled this second edition of *Poems in Persons*, *The Psychology of the Literary Process*. It is an ambitious title, but I will stand by it" (112; all page numbers to *Poems in Persons*, unless otherwise noted, refer to the 2000 edition). There is a world of difference between *The* Psychology of the Literary Process and *A* Psychology of the Literary Process, which appears on the title page of the 2000 edition. Recall Holland's (and my own) fondness of quoting Mark Twain's axiom, "The difference between the right word and the almost right word is like the difference between lightning and the lightning bug." In this case, *the* psychology is lightning, implying *the one and only model*.

Reading only the second edition of *Poems in Persons*, one would assume that most of the differences are those that Holland specifically points out. The major change, as we shall see, involved expanded commentary on the writer H.D., but there are many silent changes between the two editions, including Holland's modified view of the scientific credibility of psychoanalysis. He still maintains in the 2000 edition that the central theories of psychoanalysis have been confirmed, citing the landmark 1977 study *The Scientific Credibility of Freud's Theories*, by Seymour Fisher and Roger P. Greenberg, revised in 1996 as *Freud Scientifically Reappraised: Testing the Theories and Therapy*. But Holland then makes the following qualification. "Some of Freud's key ideas have fallen by the wayside, much of his theory of dreams, for example, or the basic idea that insight cures" (10). That is all he says about the old and now discarded belief, beginning with Socrates, that knowledge is power. Powerful yes, but not necessarily curative. As Fisher and Greenberg note in their 1996 study,

> Although psychoanalytic treatments produce positive effects, accolades need to be tempered by the continuing realization that briefer less orthodox variations of psychoanalytic techniques produce equally good results. Furthermore, other nonpsychoanalytic approaches very often achieve comparable (or sometimes even better) outcomes. Important post-1977 findings are beginning to clarify the role of interpretations

and insight in bringing about therapeutic gain. It appears very clear that verbal interpretations do not bring about changes simply or directly. The relationship context in which they are embedded and a variety of patient, therapist, and technique factors (patient interpersonal and coping styles, therapist skillfulness, and the accuracy and timing of interpretations) seem crucial for determining whether changes will follow. (264)

Some of the changes between the two editions are substantial, as can be seen in Holland's accounts of the spell cast over him by the New Criticism, the first passage from the 1973 edition, the second from the 2000 edition:

In short, the knowledge one brings to bear on a poem derives from a personal style just as much as preferences do. What is surprising to me—and troubling—is the discovery that my critical method, disciplined, professional, accredited, also acts out my identity theme. I *like* examining the verbal surface of a text, looking particularly for an "organic unity" in the way the parts all come together. From the very first evening I encountered it, the new criticism has exerted almost a spell on me. I found compelling and attractive the idea of analyzing the words on the page and them alone. The demand that one treat the poem as a thing in itself referring only to itself and hence that one pay no more attention than absolutely necessary to historical background, evaluation, or author's biography or intention suits me exactly. I took pride and pleasure in seeing this approach dominate more and more academic departments of literature, first in America, then in England, now on the continent. (112–13)

In short, the canons, the mode of interpretation, and the knowledge and skill one brings to bear on a poem are used in the service of a personal style just as much as preferences are. Interpretation is not "objective." That realization was once surprising to me—and unsettling. Yet now it seems second nature. My critical method, no matter how disciplined, professional, or accredited, also acts out my identity theme. I like examining the verbal surface of a text. I like projecting ways that the parts all come together. I like these things (I know) because of childhood experience. And I read accordingly. (92)

In the 2000 edition, Holland omitted the last sentence of the 1973 passage, perhaps because around the turn of the new century New Criticism no longer dominated English departments, as it had a quarter of a century earlier. What's puzzling about the passage in the 2000 edition is the enigmatic reference to the ways in which his childhood experience shaped his identity theme as a reader. If I were Holland's editor or a colleague reading the manuscript before he submitted it for publication, I would recommend that he either elaborate on the childhood experience or omit the sentence entirely.

Stung by an Unnamed Critic

Another difference is that the 1973 edition of *Poems in Persons* concludes with "A Polemical Epilogue and Brief Guide to Further Reading" that is absent from the 2000 edition. The 1960s was the "golden age" of psychoanalysis, when its power and prestige inside and outside the academy were at their peak. Mistrustful of the latest gurus—"'Existentialists,' 'third force psychologists,' 'encounter leaders,' Reich, Marcuse, Laing, Lacan, Perls," a statement that appears in the first edition of *Poems in Persons* (164) but not in the second edition—Holland dismisses them as seducers who treat their own therapeutic approaches as "quick, bright alternatives to a black magic fantasied about 'Freud' or 'orthodox psychoanalysis'" (164). By naming these dissidents, revisionists, or reductionists, Holland evidently doesn't mind antagonizing them. But there is one critic whom he refuses to name, consigning him to a long footnote in the first edition. "Long ago," writes Holland, "I was stung by a comment on psychoanalytic criticism made by a man both intelligent and sympathetic to psychoanalysis." He then quotes the unnamed scholar's hurtful critique:

> The obvious limitation of traditional Freudian literary analysis is that only one study can be written, since every additional one would turn out to say the same thing. Ernest Jones could do a beautiful job finding the underlying Oedipus complex in *Hamlet* but had he gone out to analyze *Lear* or *A Midsummer Night's Dream* or the *Sonnets* he would have found to his surprise that they reflected Shakespeare's Oedipus complex too, and, in fact, granting his theories, he would have made the same discovery about any other work of art. A criticism that can only say, however ingeniously, that this work is a result of the author's repressed Oedipal desires, turns out not to be saying very much.

To which Holland replies, wittily yet seriously, "Troubled by the misunderstandings this paragraph revealed, I resolved someday to write a book about psychoanalytic criticism in which the oedipus complex did not appear at all. This is it, and I have very nearly succeeded" (139–40).

The unnamed author was Stanley Edgar Hyman, who expressed this criticism in his 1948 book *The Armed Vision: A Study in the Methods of Modern Literary Criticism* (166). Hyman devotes a twenty-six-page chapter to psychological criticism, extolling the Jungian archetypal critic Maud Bodkin and frequently lambasting more Freudian-oriented literary critics. Hyman refers to the "loose band of social Freudian analysts and psychiatrists," such as Erich Fromm, Karen Horney, and Harry Stack Sullivan, as a "greatly promising school," but he characterizes them as "frequently at each other's throats" (161). By refusing to name Hyman, perhaps Holland signaled his wish to avoid being one of these bloodthirsty critics. Perhaps he knew Hyman and did not want to offend. For whatever reason, Holland must have assumed that no one would recognize the scholar in question.

Curiously, Holland omits the entire reference to the unnamed Hyman in the second edition of *Poems in Persons*. Instead, he now quotes Hyman by name in the second edition. "We readers re-create literary works so as to re-enact our own characters through a work of art. To paraphrase the late Stanley Edgar Hyman, readers poem their own poems, story their own stories" (76). The same sentence also appears in *5 Readers Reading* (4). Speak no ill of the dead, as the old adage goes. Hyman died in 1970 at age fifty-one, and now Holland enlists him as an ally. Even odder is that without naming the man who had once stung him, Holland now seems to agree with Hyman's criticisms. Admitting that he himself found earlier psychoanalytic criticism "mixed in quality," Holland concedes in *5 Readers Reading* that of the "developmental stages, only the oedipal was applied to literature. As a result, the psychoanalytic critic could only talk about narratives or dramatic works that had father-or mother-figures, not poetry or prose as such. These procedures gave psychoanalytic criticism a very bad reputation in literary circles, which, I fear, it has not overcome even today" (xi). Critical of psychoanalytic literary theorists in his first two books, *The First Modern Comedies* and *The Shakespearean Imagination*, and then praiseworthy, if not adulatory, in his next four books, *Psychoanalysis and Shakespeare*, *The Dynamics of Literary Response*, *Poems in Persons*, and *5 Readers Reading*, Holland now curbs his enthusiasm.

In the preface to the first edition of *Poems in Persons* (but absent from the second edition), Holland discloses that he has constructed the book around one particular fantasy: "the unconscious wish to undo, either lovingly or hostilely, one's separateness from a nurturing other" (ix). The nurturing other throughout Holland's psychoanalytic career was "Father Freud," from whom he never allowed himself to separate. Psychoanalytic theory "has already been built," Holland declares near the end of the first edition, "and it seems unlikely to me that the seventies, despite a more social emphasis, will produce any great theoretical departures from the comprehensive view of man achieved by psychoanalysis in the sixties" (166). It is an astounding pronouncement. In light of Holland's belief that psychoanalysis was entirely scientific and that scientific knowledge is always expanding, could he not foresee that psychoanalysis too would expand, rejecting some of its earlier theories in favor of later ones that could not yet be imagined? Nancy Chodorow's observation in *The Psychoanalytic Ear and the Sociological Eye* is apposite here. No scientist believes that the contributions of Einstein, Bohr, Fermi, or Heisenberg are the last words in physics. "So it should be with psychoanalysis and its founder" (169, n.2).

H.D.'s Analysis—and Perhaps Holland's

Chapter 1 of both the 1973 and 2000 editions of *Poems in Persons* focuses on H.D., Hilda Doolittle (1886–1961), an American poet, novelist, and memoirist who was psychoanalyzed by Freud and later wrote about the experience in *Tribute to Freud* (1956). H.D.'s writings, in Holland's view, "give us an unparalleled portrait of an analysis by the master psychoanalyst himself. In fact, I know of no account by an analysand that gives more details about his techniques or the analytic experience as it seems from within" (186). The opening chapter of the 1973 edition contains a discussion of H.D.'s identity theme based on all the information by and about her that was published at the time. The 2000 edition, by contrast, contains a sixty-five-page appendix in which Holland offers a slightly revised identity theme of H.D. based on the new writings by and about her published in the intervening years.

H.D. had two short analyses with Freud, the first one in 1933, for fourteen weeks, the second one in October, 1934, for five weeks. She called Freud "the Professor" and "The Master." The latter was also the title of a long poem she wrote in 1934 or 1935 about her analysis with him. She didn't want the poem published while she was still alive "lest her analysis with Freud be 'spoiled'" (164). The poem did not appear in print until 1981. Her two analyses with Freud would not today be called a "real" psychoanalysis, partly because they were so brief and involved time limits, and partly because they were many boundary violations or boundary crossings, such as the exchanging of books and gifts. Nevertheless, H.D.'s analysis with Freud was a transformative experience for her, leading to a burst of creativity. Holland describes her faith in Freud, despite her negative feelings toward him that she had difficulty expressing directly in analysis, as "Freudolatry," the same word I used earlier to describe his own lifelong idealization of Freud. Holland suggests that H.D. sought to fuse herself to Freud, whom she viewed as an omnipotent figure, in a mystical union. Holland's idealization of Freud may be similarly viewed as a wish to merge with an omniscient intellectual figure, though the union was secular, not mystical. Just as Freud encouraged H.D. to trace her idealization of him to its distant childhood origins, Zetzel presumably did the same with her analysand, tracing adult intellectual beliefs to unconscious needs.

Holland's guarded qualifications of the success of H.D.'s analysis with Freud are significant. In speaking to Freud about her conflicts, "she to some extent mastered them" (184), which is true of many people in psychoanalysis, including Holland himself. Another statement he makes about H.D. was almost certainly true of himself. Invoking Heinz Lichtenstein for support, Holland observes that her "basic character structure had not changed, and I am not surprised. I believe we can never change that even through a psychoanalysis" (184). Still another qualified endorsement of H.D.'s analysis with Freud likely characterizes his own analysis with Zetzel. "The analysis set her free in the limited sense that psychoanalysis does. That is, she became aware of her pattern. By understanding it and its sources, she could take conscious control of it" (185). The "pattern" was her identity theme. Part of what H.D. discovered was a paradox: "her gift of creativity came out of her fears as well as her desires" (185).

Using an expression borrowed from the title of the 1948 book by Theodor Reik, who himself borrowed it from Nietzsche's *Beyond Good and Evil* (558), Holland observes that in his analysis with H.D., Freud was "listening with the third ear." Holland then makes one of his few criticisms of contemporary psychoanalysts, a criticism that was evidently *not* true of his own analyst, Elizabeth Zetzel:

> To me, the "third ear" contrasts strikingly to the way modern therapists and analysts listen. Freud was observing *verbal behavior*. Influenced, I think, by object-relations theory, modern therapists pay attention to the relationships described, hence to the content of the language rather than the linguistic behavior at the surface. To me, such listening makes a major departure from classical practice and not necessarily a good one. I think it replaces observable behavior, the words the analysand uses, with either the analyst's or the analysand's sense of the events or relationships described. Freud, I think, interpreted to H.D. not so much from events or relationships, but from the language she used about them. (189)

Holland's criticisms reveal his mistrust of two-person analysis along with his skepticism of relational, interpersonal, and intersubjective psychoanalysis. He never publicly questioned Elizabeth Zetzel's conservative psychoanalytic approach or embraced the idea that psychoanalytic meaning is cocreated by the analyst and patient. Nor did he challenge classical drive theory, which has largely dropped out of psychoanalysis: Peter L. Rudnytsky cleverly refers to drive theory in *Psychoanalytic Conversations* as "creationism" (xii). Paul Mosher noted, in a 1998 article that examined the number of times *libido* appeared in the major psychoanalytic journals, that the word is used as often as "self" in the 1920s but steadily declines through the 1990s, suggesting that libido theory is all but dead. In *Off the Tracks* Paul Mosher and I cite Joseph Schachter's acerbic comment about the history of psychoanalysis: "discarded theories—like old generals—didn't die, they just faded away" (vol. 1, 417).

H.D.'s Identity Theme

Projecting himself into H.D.'s first-person voice, Holland offers in the 1973 edition of *Poems in Persons* his description of her identity theme. "*When I concretize the spiritual or mythologize the everyday, I create a perfect, timeless hieroglyph-world which I can be and be in. Or, I want to close the gap with signs*" (1973, 30; emphasis in original). A slightly expanded description of H.D.'s identity theme appears twenty-seven years later. "*I cannot tolerate gaps between me and the eternal, but when I make the spiritual material or mythologize the everyday, I create a perfect, timeless hieroglyph-world which I can be and be in. Or, abbreviated, I see fearful gaps, but I can make and be and be in perfect signs that close those gaps.*" Noting the similarity of his two expressions of her identity theme, Holland observes dryly, "The two phrasings seem to me much the same. That might suggest that I have not learned very much in the intervening years. More charitably, it suggests to me that my own identity, which shapes the interpretation, has not changed" (33). More charitably still, we might suggest that his perceptive early reading of her work was only reconfirmed by more information about her writings.

Spearless Athene

Holland felt no need in the 1973 edition of *Poems in Persons* to explain H.D.'s identity theme in terms of female psychosexual development, but he couldn't avoid the subject in the 2000 edition because of the 1981 publication of her poem "The Master" in which she angrily rejects Freud's belief that she was suffering from anatomical lack. Unlike the almost cavalier way in which Holland had written about penis envy in *The Dynamics of Literary Response*, he now writes far more cautiously and metaphorically about a subject that he knows will be unacceptable to many of his readers.

Penis envy arose during H.D.'s analysis when "one memorable day" Freud led her from the couch into his study to show her his favorite Greek figurine. He then held out a little bronze Pallas Athene that was "perfect," in Freud's words, "only she had lost her spear." In Freud's experience, Holland tells us, carefully choosing his words, "one of the irreducible difficulties in the analysis of women was the frustration and anger imposed by their strong unconscious wish to recapture a supposedly lost masculine power physically symbolized as the male organ" (141). Holland knows that this is an explosive issue, and he does his best to make it psychologically plausible.

> This moment in H.D.'s analysis, this showing of the spearless Athena, has become a *cause celèbre*. Even now, two-thirds of a century after he formulated it, Freud's claim that women want a penis angers feminists and women in general. In this respect, it is, like so many psychoanalytic ideas, like, for example, men's fear of castration, distressing, incredible, even repellent. (141)

Without explaining further, Holland begins the next sentence with "Penis envy, however, is not my essential theme" (142), but then he returns to the question four pages later where he gives what may be considered a cultural as opposed to a biological or psychological explanation:

> Physiology plays an obvious role here. A boy has a visible organ that gets bigger and smaller, playing out the drama that both boy and girl imagine of becoming big. A girl does not, and she may therefore see her difference as a lack. May. What she feels she has instead depends a great deal on her culture and her family. If they use femaleness as a reason for depriving women of avenues to various adult activities, then indeed a little girl is likely to feel that the difference between her and a boy is a plus for him and a zero or a minus for her. One can easily imagine cultures, however, in which women are given equal status with men in the workplace. (146)

But Holland is not yet finished with this awkward subject. After spending several more pages writing about H.D.'s hostile response to Freud's interpretation of the missing spear, agreeing with Arlene Kramer Richards's psychoanalytic view that Freud's interpretation succeeded because it reinforced H.D.'s need to be "perfect," Holland repeats his statement that "penis envy is not my cardinal concern. If I have spent this many paragraphs on it, that is because the topic has become so controversial" (167). Holland gives us the most positive spin to Freud's most problematic theory. Yes, one can say in response to Holland's argument, castration fear is disturbing, but it doesn't result in a weakened sense of morality for men, as Freud theorized penis envy produced in women. Feminist scholar Susan Stanford Friedman remarks in her two studies, *Psyche Reborn: The Emergence of H.D.* (1981) and *Penelope's Web: Gender, Modernity, H.D.'s Fiction* (1990), that although H.D. initially accepted Freud's theory of penis envy, she later rejected it in favor of a primal female erotic. Friedman makes no attempt to soften her criticism of Holland and his Buffalo colleague at the time, Joseph Riddel, for their approach to H.D. "Operating on the androcentric Freudian premise of female difference and consequent inferiority, Holland's and Riddel's reduction of H.D.'s search to penis envy is ridiculous at best and oppressive at worst" (*Psyche Reborn* 48). Using a Lacanian term, Friedman asserts in *Penelope's Web* that the "lesbian eroticism of H.D.'s resistance in 'The Master' explicitly challenges the patriarchal Law of the Father" (305).

It's surprising that Holland doesn't present the counterarguments to penis envy if only to acknowledge the extent of the controversy. Karen Horney, considered one of the four "mothers" of psychoanalysis (along with Helene Deutsch, Melanie Klein, and Anna Freud), came to reject Freud's phallocentric theory of female development. Summarizing Horney's views, her biographer, Bernard J. Paris—one of Holland's most dependable friends and colleagues—writes: "The psychoanalytic view of women's nature and development is the product of a male genius and a male-dominated culture" (70). Paris quotes a statement from Horney's 1926 essay "The Flight from Womanhood: The Masculinity Complex in Women as Viewed by Men and Women": if we "free our minds from this masculine mode of thought, nearly all the problems of feminine psychology take on a different appearance" (Paris, 70; Horney, 59). Holland was certainly acquainted not only with Horney's writings but also with Paris's 1994 biography, which he had read in manuscript.

Psychoanalytic feminists have either rejected or called into question Freud's masculinist bias. In her 1978 book *The Reproduction of Mothering: Psychoanalysis and the Sociology of Gender*, Nancy Chodorow asserts that "Psychoanalytic theory remains the most coherent, convincing theory of personality development available for an understanding of fundamental aspects of the psychology of women in our society, in spite of its biases" (142). And yet she persuasively shows the patriarchal distortions in Freud's—and his followers'—theorizings on female psychology. She offers example after example of how psychoanalytic theorists have implied that the pre-Oedipal development of girls is somehow inferior to boys' development. Implicit throughout Chodorow's book is the belief that we do Freud a disservice if we accept his claims unquestioningly.

Other scholars have explored the role of Freud's Jewish origins in the construction of his phallocentric theory. Sander L. Gilman, one of the world's leading cultural and literary historians, the author or editor of over ninety books, provides in his 1993 book *Freud, Race, and Gender*, a provocative explanation of Freud's reading of male and female anatomy:

> In 1926, Freud (in his essay on lay analysis) referred (in English) to female sexuality as the "dark continent" of the human psyche, the sphere less accessible to science: "The sexual life of adult women is a 'dark continent' for psychology. But we have learnt that girls feel deeply their lack of a sexual organ that is equal in value to the male one; they regard themselves on that account as inferior, and this 'envy for the penis' is the origin of a whole number of characteristic feminine reactions." In this phrase, Freud translates the complicated, pejorative discourse about the "dark" Jew with its suggestion of disease and difference into a discourse about the "blackness" (the unknowability) of the woman. The "Jewish" body (which in Freud's discourse is the body of the male Jew) becomes the body of the woman. (38)

Gilman shows how in Freud's mind (and writings) circumcision and castration are closely linked, both associated with Jewishness. "Circumcision is an early symbolic substitute for the castration of male children" (76). In Gilman's view, Freud's belief that the act of circumcision was primeval led to the construction of the universality of castration fear in men. I once heard Holland refer to Sander Gilman's work in the most admiring terms, but there are few references to Gilman's writings in Holland's books. Nor is it likely that Gilman's bold theorizings of Freud's construction of psychoanalytic theory influenced Holland's own thinking. Irvin Yalom has a different critique of castration fear, suggesting in his 1980 book *Existential Psychotherapy* that it masks a deeper fear with which Freud never came to terms: death anxiety, a fear that struck too close to home. Death was, in Yalom's words, "old hat, Old Testament," to Freud, an idea that would not lead to the eternal fame the psychoanalyst craved (58).

I suspect that Holland would agree with many of Gilman's and Yalom's critiques of psychoanalytic theory but nevertheless argue for its scientific credibility. He points out in the 2000 edition of *Poems in Persons* that Fisher and Greenberg's two books, which survey more than 2,500 experimental studies of Freud's ideas, present scientific proof of the frequency with which his ideas have passed empirical tests. Fisher and Greenberg, however, provide little to no support for penis envy in their 1977 study. "It can be immediately declared that Freud was wrong in his assumption that the average woman perceives her body in more negative and depreciated terms than the average man." If anything, Fisher and Greenberg conclude, women are more comfortable with their body experiences than are men: "consistent evidence exists that the female exceeds the male in general body awareness, sense of body security, adaptability to changes in body sensations and appearance, and the ability to integrate body experiences in a fashion meaningfully consistent with life role" (199).

On the other hand, Fisher and Greenberg conclude in their 1996 study that "one of Freud's most extreme and counterintuitive Oedipal formulations (also widely viewed skeptically) has stood up well to a number of empirical probes": the so-called penis-baby equation, the belief that a woman who gives birth has reparative fantasies of regaining a lost penis. "Far-fetched predictions, such as an increase in phallic imagery during pregnancy, have been affirmed in contexts of careful experimental control" (154). Fisher and Greenberg point out, though, that Freud's theory regarding the female superego is unsound. "Freud incorrectly assumed that females have a less strict and decisive superego than males. As noted, most studies find few or no quantitative differences between the sexes in this respect. The empirical data may even suggest slightly more strict superego standards in females than males" (166).

Sandra

Poems in Persons and the much longer *5 Readers Reading* are fascinating for many reasons. Holland's psychoanalytic interpretations of the five students' identity themes, as well as his own, are unprecedented: I know of no other scholarly work in which a professor attends so carefully to the nuances of students' language, both what they say and how they say it. Anyone who has attempted to summarize accurately and sensitively a single student essay, describing both its content and form, will appreciate the challenge of analyzing what amounts to a thousand pages of words—and then integrating these writings with responses to several different psychological tests. Holland's feat becomes more impressive when we realize that the interpreter is interpreting himself as well as five other people—and anticipating the seventh reader's response: ours. Holland's interactions with his students reveal much about his interviewing and teaching style. He has a novelist's gift for characterization, as we can see in his portrait of Sandra:

> She seemed to me to perceive the world as a kind of mystery; and sometimes by words like "trap" or "trick" she conveyed the feeling that

the mystery posed dangers. If it did, she would arrange to see it no longer, vision being crucial in the way Sandra approached the world. If she found a situation promising, however, she would try to see more of it, see it from closer up, touch or even merge with it. "Promising" had special values for Sandra: it meant an equalizing of differences, a flow of power from parent to child, older to younger, male to female, or, in general, from stronger to weaker. "Promising" also meant for her the simpler, earlier pleasures of nurture and food (associated, perhaps, with the stronger mother giving of herself to the weaker child). If I phrase my reading of her as an "identity theme," it is: *I want to see and approach more and more closely and even draw upon a source of power and nurture, but not to see its loss.* (46; emphasis in original)

I have written several books about the use of personal essays and diaries in the college classroom, and I appreciate the challenge of describing a student meaningfully in a few words. I marvel at Holland's ability to capture an aspect of Sandra's complexity. His interview questions allow her to open up about her thoughts and feelings regarding Fitzgerald's short story "Winter Dreams," Polanski's film *Repulsion*, and a poem by H.D. from her 1944 collection *The Walls Do Not Fall*. At one point, Sandra recites from memory a line, "Build thee more stately mansions, O my soul." Holland can't restrain himself from asking, "What's that from?" and when she replies, "Oliver Wendell Holmes," he exclaims in delight: "Oh, of course! 'The Chambered Nautilus'" (54). Reading their exchanges with each other, one senses their equality and harmony with each other. Both characteristics are part of Sandra's identity theme, which involved, in Holland's words, "the balancing and exchange of strengths" (50). They were sympathetic to each other, well matched, both emotionally and intellectually.

Saul

This was not true for Saul, which is apparent from Holland's opening description of him:

Saul seemed a serious young man whose impressive hairiness did not make me think he was defying anything: it simply demonstrated his concentration on the important things, instead of mere appearances. He conveyed an inwardness that had gained him a reputation among other students for scholarly intensity and intellectual commitment. Often speaking so softly no one else could hear him, he seemed focused on his own affairs, only occasionally becoming animated or involved with others. Toward me, the professor, the experimenter, he was very wary indeed, particularly when I would press him for easygoing, rambling talk about what he had read. Then he would turn back to the exact words in the text, reading them rapidly into his beard, as if to himself, to bear out the interpretation he was developing (although he rarely brought any of these interpretations to a final form). (64–5)

Holland never makes the connection, but Saul's troubled passive aggressive relationship with him conjures up Bartleby's fraught relationship with his employer in Melville's iconic story. When Saul, ignoring his interlocutor's request or perhaps order, reads "rapidly into his beard," he says to Holland, in effect, "I would prefer not to," the maddening words of the law-copyist, or scrivener, who refuses to do—or write—what he is told. Like the oppositional Bartleby, Saul is secretive, uncooperative, almost paranoid. "He constantly scanned his environment like a controller in an airport for anything big or vague that might pose the danger he had to avoid" (65). Holland was one of these dangers. "He fled any kind of relationship at all to the poem, just as he got angry at the first TAT picture" (68). And just as he got angry at Holland himself.

Holland may not see Saul as a modern-day Bartleby, but he certainly recognizes the tensions, even hostility, between teacher and student, interviewer and interviewee. "Irritated somewhat by his insistence that he had no reaction and no understanding of the poem, I gave him a testy, overbearing explication of a few lines, which led in turn to his flat rejection not only of the poem but of me. By his long silence he won, and all I could do was laughingly acknowledge that he had in fact won" (71). But Holland has also won, partly because he has not cherry-picked his data—a less scrupulous researcher might have refused to include Saul in *Poems in Persons* and *5 Readers Reading*—and partly because Holland's primary goal is not to demonstrate his teaching style, a work in progress, but to highlight Saul's identity theme, which is, as Saul himself has stated, citing the H.D. poem he read, "be indigestible, hard, ungiving," an indigestibility that Holland himself couldn't swallow.

Saul's closed-off qualities, or emotions, strikingly contrast Sandra's gift for relatedness. Holland captures the stylistic differences between the two students. Sandra was concerned with "balancing through mutuality and interpenetration"; by contrast, Saul was "less concerned with boundaries between people" than he was with his own boundaries with others (65–6). Holland does not comment on the Oedipal implications of his relationship with both students, how Sandra and Saul may have perceived him as a positive and negative father figure, respectively. In *5 Readers Reading*, he acknowledges the gender differences in his interactions with Sandra though he hesitates to attach too much importance to these differences: "she brought to both the stories and interviews a set of expectations and experiences not comparable to the male subjects', but this would be to treat her femaleness as though it were 'maleness-with-a-difference,' a very old-fashioned and clumsy way of thinking psychoanalytically about women" (101). Cannot gender differences be explained, psychoanalytically or any other way, without "maleness-with-a-difference" assumptions?

Transference and Countertransference in Reading

As Elizabeth Wright contends in her 1984 book *Psychoanalytic Criticism*, it's surprising that Holland doesn't explore the transference-countertransference dynamics of reading. "The novelty of Holland's model of reading-as-transference," Wright observes, "is that the text is the *analyst*, triggering off responses in the reader/analysand, although when Holland becomes the reader/analysand he is at the same time conducting self-analysis, examining his responses as a reader. He is both patient in transference and analyst in countertransference, examining his responses to his patient/self" (66).

It's also puzzling that nowhere in *Poems in Persons* or *5 Readers Reading* does Holland point out that the student-teacher relationship enacts the transference-countertransference dynamics that exist in the patient-therapist relationship. He was keenly aware of H.D.'s transferential relationship with Freud, yet he chooses not to bring in transference-countertransference dynamics with the two students. Why? It's true that Holland's conflicted relationship with Saul was primarily that of interviewer and interviewee, but it was also an implicit teacher-student relationship. In *5 Readers Reading*, Holland declares that he often found himself in the position of the analyst, seeking to interpret a patient's (or reader's) free associations (63). A discussion of Holland's troubled transference-countertransference relationship with Saul (and even more negative relationship with Shep in *5 Readers Reading*, as we shall see) would have been illuminating. Psychoanalytic literary critics have suggested that transference-countertransference plays a role in a reader's relationship to a text—readers projecting a lifetime of free associations onto a text, like patients projecting their transference onto the analyst. Holland probably doesn't want to equate the reader's projection with the patient's transference because he doesn't want to imply that a text can be active and therefore human. Nevertheless, I agree with Wright that a text functions as an analyst. Another reason for Holland's omission is that ego psychologists of the 1950s and 1960s were generally silent about countertransference.

Holland's Identity Theme

After offering Sandra and Saul's identity themes in *Poems in Persons*, Holland gives us his own. "I am, I believe, a person who would like to master the inside relationships of things by knowledge or vision but who, at the same time, feels his identity preserved in staying on the outside" (85). A few sentences later he elaborates, using more resonant language, "I see that I prefer images to which I can have an external, abstract relation over images which threaten to involve me in an inside where identities are engulfed or eaten." He soon elaborates again in a sentence that reveals the narcissistic implications of maintaining a healthy sense of self: "[M]y own identity theme has to do with preserving a sense of self and securing self-esteem by gaining power over relations between things, in particular, mastering them by knowing or seeing them from outside rather than being actually in the relationships" (91).

Holland's desire to remain on the outside, looking in, is so intense that we encounter similar statements elsewhere in his writings. In his 1981 essay on the science fiction writer Ursula K. Le Guin, for example, Holland remarks that while he was the director of the Center for the Psychological Study of the Arts at Buffalo, he remained "nevertheless obsessed with being on the outside of things." Reading Le Guin's *The Left Hand of Darkness*, he feels forced to "assert the essential, separate me-ness of me against the merger, the one-ness, the unisex of this novel. And it is not a friendly act" (133).

Without contradicting or qualifying Holland's perception of his own identity theme, I think we can add an important element to it. In many of his books he writes about *artists'* compulsion to create. "To the extent one particular activity (like writing in a particular style) functions as both satisfaction and defense for us," he observes in the 2000 edition of *Poems in Persons*, "we become committed to it, and it takes on the status of a permanent and preferred solution. Some of those preferred solutions prove so satisfactory as to give rise to the feeling many creative writers describe of being driven, as by an inner compulsion, back to the word processor" (38). The same inner compulsion drives *Holland* back to the word "processor," again and again, in book after book.

5 Readers Reading

Holland begins *5 Readers Reading* (1975) with a simple observation, the extreme variety of literary responses to the same work. How do we account for these conspicuous differences in reading? It was the same question he asked in *Poems in Persons*, but now he studies five readers in exquisite detail and depth. For the first time in any of his books, he refers to his professional life before becoming an English professor, explaining the reason for selecting the pseudonyms for his five undergraduate readers, all in their twenties: Sam, Saul, Shep, Sebastian, and Sandra. "The alliteration testifies to an ex-engineer's lingering nostalgia for the rigor of statistical work with objective Ss that so sternly commands attention in the psychological journals. But, in fact, I tried not so much to experiment as to empathize with and understand these readers' personal re-creations of the literary work" (44). Holland is the sixth reader, reading their identity themes through his own.

Holland's task is formidable, in effect, conducting an intense psychoanalysis of six different identity themes, including his own. He uses three canonical short stories as texts: Faulkner's "A Rose for Emily," Hemingway's "The Battler," and Fitzgerald's "Winter Dreams." To give only one example of his linguistic challenge, Holland was struck by the differences in the students' reactions to Colonel Sartoris, who "fathered" the edict requiring Negro women to wear aprons in the street in "A Rose for Emily." One would assume that the word has a fixed meaning, Holland observes, but it has different meanings to the students. To Saul, "fathering" meant merely "sponsored" because of his need to placate authorities. To Sebastian, "fathered" meant "fathering the women" in sexual intercourse between Southern whites and their black victims. To Sandra, "fathered" was a heroic word, viewing parents as sources of nonsexual strength and support (207).

Holland remains committed to classical psychoanalytic theory, which he argues offers the best way to understand individual responses to literature. He is most drawn to psychoanalytic ego psychology, which sees defenses as "necessary adaptations to inner and outer reality, not obstacles to pleasure but preconditions without which pleasure would not be possible" (116). As he disclosed in *Poems in Persons*, Holland is especially interested in the defense mechanism known as undoing, which Freud defines in *Inhibitions, Symptoms and Anxiety* (1926) as a form of "negative magic" in which one attempts to "'blow away' not merely the *consequences* of some event (or experience or impression) but the event itself" (*SE*, vol. 20, 119). In obsessional neurosis, Freud continues, undoing is an action that seeks to cancel another action, whereas, in reality, both actions have occurred. As James Strachey observes in a footnote on the same page, Freud had referred to undoing (and a related technique, isolation) in the case study of the "Rat Man," in which analysis revealed that the patient sought literally to make something unhappen. Anna Freud includes undoing in *The Ego and the Mechanisms of Defense* as one of the nine major methods of defense, and a tenth defense, which pertains to the study of "normal" (as opposed to "neurotic") behavior, sublimation (44).

One should point out, however, that contemporary analysts might say that these defenses can be either normal or neurotic depending upon the situation. Moreover, warmhearted feelings are not necessary defenses against cruelty, as Freud often implied. Simon Lesser voices the classical psychoanalytic view, which he softens slightly, that "Generosity may be a defense against stinginess, mildness a reaction-formation to strong aggressive feelings" (38). Holland makes a similar statement in "The Story of a Psychoanalytic Critic": we reverse aggression into its opposite, exaggerated kindness (249). Why should we assume, however, that cruelty is more instinctual than compassion? The existential psychiatrist Irvin Yalom cautions his patient Ginny not to dismiss her compassionate instincts as transformed vices, as she tended to do. "I in effect told her to stop this Freudian reductionism and accept generosity or gentleness as positive and important truths about herself which stand by themselves and don't require further analysis" (20).

Another Early Reader-Response Critic: Walter Slatoff

Early in 5 Readers Reading, while surveying the new interest in reader-response criticism, Holland agrees with Walter Slatoff's observation in his 1970 book *With Respect to Readers* that "we know almost nothing about the process of reading and the interaction of man and the book" (Slatoff, 188; Holland, 4). Slatoff was not a reader-response theorist, but he was unusually attentive to the ways in which the reader's experience, training, temperament, and biases affect the reading process. The last chapter of *With Respect to Readers* is appropriately called "Against Detachment" in which he expresses his attitude toward reading.

> We have an astronomical number of assertions that literature is not life and should not be confused with it; we have almost nothing to say about the danger of separating them, the danger of viewing literature in such a way as to make of it an object which we can manipulate instead of a force which can help to shape us. (188)

Slatoff was my favorite professor in graduate school[1] at Cornell; Len's suicide occurred at the beginning of the semester in which I was a student

---

[1] In rereading my PhD dissertation—a humbling experience—I came across the following sentence in the acknowledgments page: "Mr. Slatoff is that rare teacher and person who knows how to excite his students, and his vision of Conrad has profoundly effected me." Ouch. I always point out to my students the difference between affected and effected, and from now on, I must confess to them that I got it wrong on my doctoral dissertation.

in Slatoff's course on Conrad and Faulkner. I remember pouring out my grief over Len's suicide in Slatoff's office while he listened compassionately. It was in the same course that I began to write on Conrad and suicide; Slatoff later directed my PhD dissertation. Holland says little about *With Respect to Readers*, one of the earliest books on reader-response criticism. The two literary critics could not be more different. Whereas Holland sought to psychoanalyze a reader's identity theme, learning as much about the reader as possible, Slatoff emphasizes each person's unknowability.

> For one thing, real people are not quite so real and verifiable as we pretend for most practical purposes. Large parts of the lives even of those closest to us—wives, children, friends—are forever blacked out and unverifiable, even unknowable. Parts of our own lives are similarly unverifiable. Nor can we say of ourselves and others where we begin and end, what our limits are. Essentially our sense of a real person, like our sense of a fictional one, is a construction from a relatively limited number of observations of what he says and does. For another thing, we cannot really comprehend a novel or story without giving characters at least some of the attributes of living people, for much of the information we receive about them in the text itself makes it absolutely necessary to imagine that they have ongoing lives even when we aren't watching them. (15)

Ironically, despite Holland's belief in the knowability of a reader's identity theme, he admits next-to-nothing about his personal life until his penultimate book, whereas Slatoff, affirming unknowability, reveals a great deal about his personal life in *With Respect to Readers*. "When I read, for example, the self that responds is not quite Walter J. Slatoff, Professor of English, third-generation mostly assimilated Jew, aged 48, married, father of Joan and David, aged 18 and 16, soldier in World War II, etc., etc." (54).

Slatoff uses reader-response criticism much more personally than Holland does. Slatoff admits, for example, that because he is Jewish, he resents Hemingway's treatment of Robert Cohn in *The Sun Also Rises*. Slatoff does not call the novel anti-Semitic—though nearly all of the characters make disparaging statement about Cohn's Jewishness, and no one defends Cohn—but he was one of the first literary critics to call attention to this ugly aspect of the novel. I recall taking another course in graduate school taught by Arthur Mizener, F. Scott Fitzgerald's first biographer. In his lectures on Hemingway's *The Sun Also Rises*, Mizener didn't utter a word about the novel's virulent anti-Semitism. Reading the novel at the time, I remember counteridentifying with my Jewishness: I did not want to resemble Robert

Cohn, the emblematic hateful Jew. I felt the same Jewish self-hatred when the imperious Mizener lectured on *The Great Gatsby*; he never commented on the anti-Semitic portrait of Meyer Wolfsheim, whose cufflinks, made of human molars, symbolize the predatory Jew. Nor does Mizener's biography, *The Far Side of Paradise*, contain any comment about Fitzgerald's anti-Semitic caricature. Slatoff's reader-response criticism would encourage such discussion, showing how race, class, gender, or religion shapes one's "reading self"; by contrast, Holland's discussions of readers' identity themes generally avoid these cultural markers of identity.

There's only a hint in *5 Readers Reading* that one of the five students, Saul, is Jewish: both his Old Testament name and his "scholarly, Talmudic style" (77). By omitting any discussion of race, class, gender, or religion, Holland prevents us from seeing how these markers influence a reader's identity them. Erikson viewed ethnicity as central to the development of psychosocial identity, as he observed in *Identity and the Life Cycle*: "Men who share an ethnic area, a historical era, or an economic pursuit are guided by common images of good and evil. Infinitely varied, these images reflect the elusive nature of historical change; yet in the form of contemporary social models, of compelling prototypes of good and evil, they assume decisive concreteness in every individual's ego development" (18). Most reader-response theorists stress the role of ethnicity in identity, but Holland rarely mentions this in his elaboration of readers' identity themes.

"Literary Suicide: A Question of Style"

In the opening chapter of *5 Readers Reading*, Holland refers briefly to the tragic case of a patient of the Yale psychoanalyst Gilbert J. Rose, who committed suicide after watching a performance of Friedrich Durrenmatt's 1956 tragicomic play *The Visit*. Holland doesn't have much to say in *Poems in Persons* or *5 Readers Reading* about how authors may enact their identity themes when taking their own lives, but he writes about this in "Literary Suicide: A Question of Style," which was published in the first issue of *Psychocultural Review* in 1977, two years after the appearance of *5 Readers Reading*. The article appeared too late for me to use in my Conrad book, though I referred to it in *Surviving Literary Suicide* (1999).

Holland argues that we can understand suicide by looking at writers' self-inflicted deaths because they leave a written record of their lives and often foreshadow in their poems and novels their own deliberate endings. The essay is one of the first to apply identity theory to suicide. One cannot predict from a novelist's work that he or she will commit suicide—though

Philip Young did make this prediction, as he relates in *Ernest Hemingway: A Reconsideration*—but looking backward, one can see a pattern of suicide that unifies the work. If we find the "inside story" of their lives, Holland suggests, their "identity themes," we can see how they died in character. "The method of suicide, by definition, is the last choice in the series—it should, if anything, show the essential pattern *in extremis*" (291). Holland then discusses several literary writers who were self-destructive for much of their lives, including Edgar Allan Poe and F. Scott Fitzgerald, or who ended as suicides, such as Sylvia Plath, Yukio Mishima, Hart Crane, and Ernest Hemingway. Holland's discussion of Plath is especially perceptive, focusing on her massive inner rage: "she vilifies in others what she dislikes in herself" (298), an observation that helps us to understand the suicide of a key character in Holland's only novel, *Death in a Delphi Seminar*.

"Literary Suicide: A Question of Style" is dazzling in its psychological insights, enabling us to grasp the major lesson Freud taught us: the "rationality of irrationality" (285). Holland captures other paradoxes of suicide: a person makes a choice that ends choice itself. Suicide is an adaptive act that ends the possibility of further adaptations. He summarizes the many motives that suicidologists have postulated—the symbolic murder of another, the wish to be reunited with a lost loved one, the urge to return to the womb, the desire for revenge, the need for omnipotent self-control, the effort to avoid pain—and then he shows how these motives may influence an identity theme. Holland never allows us to forget the physical or mental suffering that may lead to suicide. Some suicides, he concedes, appear heroic, noting mordantly that he does not want Socrates "to escape the hemlock by bribing his jailors to let him sneak away" (287). Yet Holland never romanticizes or glorifies suicide, neither here nor elsewhere.

The two major ways to prevent suicide, Holland suggests, are by strengthening a patient's pre-existing successful adaptations and by expanding the patient's self-insight. His optimism over the possibility of therapeutic recovery is guarded, however: "an inner inevitability is in the nature of the illness: a functioning person sees customary strategies fail and finds self-destruction the only solution" (302). Holland ends the article with two eloquent sentences about our beholdenness to suicidal writers. "As we pay homage to the beauty they create by interpreting it and making it our own, we become indebted to them in another way. The same interpretation tells us a strategy for recognizing and preventing in others the solemn and tragic failure of adaptation that convinced these people they could sustain their true style only by choosing death" (302).

Tellingly, there are several omissions in Holland's article that characterize his later writings as well. There's no mention, for example, of the clinical fact that most people, writers and nonwriters alike, who attempt or commit suicide suffer from mood disorders. He touches on depression only twice, both times fleetingly, without elaboration. Depression was never a subject that preoccupied Holland in his writings, despite its impact on so many writers and students. He refers to suicide's irresistibility but doesn't mention that most people who make an unsuccessful suicide attempt never try it again. Nor does Holland write about physician-assisted suicide, rational suicide, and the wrenching aftermath of suicide on loved ones. There are no references in the article to suicide and the contagion effect: the ways in which one person's suicide may contribute to other suicides, a well-documented phenomenon. "Suggestibility" was not a subject he theorized.

"The Good Hysteric"

In *5 Readers Reading*, Holland agrees with Elizabeth Zetzel's statement in *The Capacity for Emotional Growth* that "Psychic development implies at all stages both progressive and regressive manifestations" (59, Zetzel, 268). There's another connection between Zetzel's book and *5 Readers Reading*. In her chapter "The So-called Good Hysteric," which begins with the Longfellow poem, Zetzel invokes the female "hysteric," surely one of the most problematic words in the history of psychiatry and psychoanalysis. So does the clinical psychologist of Children's Hospital (Buffalo), Dr. Andrew Corvus, whom Holland enlisted to help with the psychological testing of the five students. Sandra was the female, and Corvus characterized her, based on her responses to a Rorschach test, as a "good hysteric," to which Holland adds, perhaps attempting to soften the troubling word, "about as high a rank on the scale of normality as a clinician is likely to give—that is, someone whose fixations (on the body, typically) occurred sufficiently far along in development to leave only superficial, easily healed limitations" (103).

Unlike the expression "good neurotic," which analysts used a generation or two ago to describe patients ideally suited for psychoanalysis, "hysteric" has a vexed history, nearly always carrying misogynistic connotations. Freud's most antifeminist case study is *Fragment of an Analysis of a Case of Hysteria* (1905), the story of Dora, where he comes across as belligerent and vindictive. "I do not know what kind of help she wanted from me," he announces at the end, with only a trace of irony, "but I promised to forgive her for having deprived me of the satisfaction of affording her a far more radical cure for her troubles" (*SE*, vol. 7, 122). Once again, Holland misses the opportunity to distance himself from "hysteria," a dubious component of psychoanalytic theory.

A feminist *cause celèbre*, Dora has elicited much psychoanalytic commentary, particularly from two of Holland's Buffalo colleagues, Charles Bernheimer and Claire Kahane, who coedited *In Dora's Case: Freud—Hysteria—Feminism*, first published in 1985 and now in its second edition. Kahane, who taught at SUNY-Buffalo from 1974 until her retirement in 2000, authored *Passions of the Voice*, in which she used Freud's concept of hysteria to show how several female writers, including Florence Nightingale, Olive Schreiner, and Virginia Woolf, explored the crises arising from the breakdown of sexual difference. Kahane acknowledges, as Holland does not, that Dora "foundered as case, story, and case history precisely because Freud did not take into account the countertransference, the effects of Dora's voice on his desire and its articulations" (xiv). Madelon Sprengnether remarks in *Mourning Freud* that "what seems glaringly obvious to a contemporary reader is the inappropriateness of Herr K's advances to Dora, which border on child molestation" (3).

It's true that Corvus describes another student, Sam, in clinical terms as a "well-put-together, almost classical hysteric" (71–2), suggesting that the term can be used to mark both genders. Nevertheless, women, not men, have been victimized by the word. Holland uses another problematic word with sexist implications, referring to Sam's "feminine identification" arising from "being so passive" (69).

Returning, Obsessively, to His Own Identity Theme

Before sketching his readers' identity themes, Holland expresses his own. "I re-created 'A Rose for Emily' by means of a personality that combines a passionate desire to know about the insides of things with an equally strong feeling that one is, finally, safer on the outside" (39). In offering his interpretation of Faulkner's 1931 gothic vignette, which may be, he adds, "the single most popular short story in America" (20), Holland unexpectedly stops interpreting the tale "intellectually" and instead gives us his "gut" experience—literally:

> As I recite this litany of dirt, dust, and smell, I feel I am responding to the story, half-unconsciously, with a mixture of attraction and revulsion toward "dirty" body products. In any case, at an intellectual level, I recall that Freud identified a famous triad of traits: orderliness, parsimony, and obstinacy. All, he said, derive from holding on or letting go inner body "dirt" in response to outer demands. (25)

Holland then presents an original and compelling reading of Faulkner's story that emphasizes Emily's anal retentiveness (preserving the rotting corpse of her suitor); her cruel, dominating father whose behavior she recreates when she murders Homer Barron, whose name may suggest robber baron; and the prevailing issues of control and shame. Holland sees the story as revealing a breakdown of control in which repressive rules result in violence. "Given the familiar psychological association of the precious and the 'dirty,' I felt it fitting that some of what goes in and out is money" (26). The daughter's menacing father, who clutches a horsewhip, "evokes a child's feelings of fear and desire for him in Miss Emily—and in me" (26-7). Later Holland admits that, in contrast to Sandra, whose fantasies match those seen in the story, he found "A Rose for Emily" disturbing because his fantasies emphasize the need for possession and control of body products: "in short, fantasies from that stage in childhood when the child struggles with his parents over the lawfulness of that within him and the inner and outer pressures to give it up" (199). The controlling father in Faulkner's story produces a controlling masculinized daughter who commits a vengeful murder. "In my reading, the control through shame occasions the many, many references to watching in the story, mostly references to the peeping, whispering, gossiping townspeople as they comment on Emily's actions." Holland's next sentence contains a rare grammatical error. "This darkness and watching and shaming makes [sic] me nervous" (31). Nervous indeed!

The Anal Character

Holland makes only passing reference to the two short essays in which Freud explores the "obsessional personality." In "Obsessive Actions and Religious Practices" (1907), Freud describes the obsessional symptoms, common in religious rituals, that reflect an "unconscious sense of guilt"—the first time, James Strachey informs us, that Freud used the expression that would play such a noteworthy role in his later writings (*SE*, vol. 9, 123n.1). In "Character and Anal Eroticism" (1908), Freud elaborates on the triad of traits to which Holland refers:

> The people I am about to describe are noteworthy for a regular combination of the three following characteristics. They are especially *orderly, parsimonious* and *obstinate*. Each of these words actually covers a small group or series of inter-related character-traits. "Orderly" covers the notion of bodily cleanliness, as well as of conscientiousness

in carrying out small duties and trustworthiness. Its opposite would be "untidy" and "neglectful." Parsimony may appear in the exaggerated form of avarice; and obstinacy can go over into defiance, to which rage and revengefulness are easily joined. The latter two qualities—parsimony and obstinacy—are linked with each other more closely than they are with the first—with orderliness. They are, also, the more constant element of the whole complex. Yet it seems to me incontestable that all three in some way belong together. (*SE*, vol. 9, 169)

At least two of these qualities, orderliness and obstinacy, *in their positive intellectual form*, are present throughout Holland's writings. His passion for order, knowledge, unity, and control was unrivaled among literary critics of his generation—so much so that, after *The Dynamics of Literary Response*, he rejected the idea, held by almost every other literary critic, that a text could be active. No, he insists, the person acts on the text, not the other way around. "Most critics look at a text," he proclaims in the 2000 edition of *Poems in Persons*, "and posit a response to it. Wrong. That is to blind oneself to a key fact. A 'look at the text' is in fact an expression of one's own identity theme" (94). No less important is Holland's willingness to be an intellectual rebel, a disturber of the (literary) world's peace, like Freud, though he never rebelled against the master. Was the third component of the anal or obsessive personality, parsimony, also true of Holland? I suspected this was true but did not yet have any evidence.

Another characteristic of obsessional neurosis, one Holland often mentions though only occasionally applies to himself, is ambivalence. "According to psycho-analytic theory," Freud instructs the Rat Man in the 1909 *Notes Upon a Case of Obsessional Neurosis*, "every fear corresponded to a former wish which was now repressed" (*SE*, vol. 9, 180). Similarly, in several of his books Holland comments on the inseparability of fears and wishes. Throughout much of his life, the Rat Man is a "prey to an *obsession for understanding*" (*SE*, vol. 9, 190), a statement no less true of Holland, an example of his intellectualization. In one of his most insightful sentences in the case study, Freud maintains that compulsion "is an attempt at a compensation for the doubt and at a correction of the intolerable conditions of inhibition to which the doubt bears witness" (*SE*, vol. 9, 243). Holland, we recall, jokingly refers to his own ambivalence regarding his ongoing struggle between critical monism and relativism. Despite his rejection of text-active or bi-active models of reading in *Poems in Readers* and *5 Readers Reading*, he never overcame entirely his doubts.

In suggesting that Holland's writings reveal, from the beginning of his career to the end, two of the three characteristics Freud associated with the anal personality, orderliness and obstinacy (rebelliousness), I should point out, ironically, that he was characteristically ambivalent about character typology. Holland used it in some places while undercutting it in other places. "I tend to play down the usual psychoanalytic typologies (oral, anal, phallic, compulsive, etc.) in favor of a 'smoother' description based in a general principle of motivation" (5 *Readers Reading* 262). The "smoother" description, I suggest, is a more intellectually subtle description, making it more acceptable to academics like himself.

Significantly, Fisher and Greenberg report in both their 1977 and 1996 studies impressive empirical support for Freud's anal (obsessive-compulsive) character formulation. "Typically, anal clusters were identified that embraced such variables as orderliness, stinginess, concern about money, punctuality, interest in collecting things, rigidity, retentiveness, anxiety over loss of control, obsessional inclinations, conservation, hoarding, and attention to detail." With only a few exceptions, Fisher and Greenberg suggest, "the attributes in the anal clusters were apparently congruent with Freud's conceptualization of the anal character" (*Freud Scientifically Reappraised* [102–3]). The obsessive-compulsive personality, however, was not related to "measures of neuroticism, whereas obsessional symptoms are" (104). (Holland suggests in *Laughing* that "we are free, even if we live out an *inner* necessity, so long as we do not suffer an *outer* compulsion" [141].) Moreover, contrary to Freudian theory, there is no evidence to suggest that severe toilet training plays a role in the anal character cluster of traits. Interestingly, research subjects who tested high in anal characteristics were reluctant self-disclosers.

The anal character paradigm closely fits with a more current psychological construct called the "five-factor" model. Fisher and Greenberg cite one study that captures the essence of the five-factor model: "careful, fussy/tidy, hardworking, neat, punctual, scrupulous, thrifty, and well organized. . . . The other terms describe an abstemious, exacting, orderly, prudent, restrained, temperate person, a person who avoids excesses and pays close attention to detail" (114)—words that Holland's friends and colleagues would apply to him. Tellingly, Fisher and Greenberg point out, as have many other researchers, that the constellation of traits Freud assigned to the anal character is highly regarded in Western culture. "The investment in being self-controlled, industrious, and persevering fits well with what it takes to be successful in such societies. It is a bit of a paradox that a character type Freud depicted as fixated at an immature level should emerge as an example of what it takes to be successful" (115). Fisher and Greenberg conclude with an irony Holland would have appreciated: "in terms of Freud's paradigm, anality may actually represent the highest level of maturity attained by the modal individual" (116).

Shep

Of the five readers, Holland has the most difficulty with Shep. Holland's characterizations of him are the most judgmental. "Of all the readers, Shep most intrigued and most saddened me. I found him mixing in the most striking way, stereotype and original, morality and pathology, maturity and immaturity. He held forthright and progressive ideas but in a bitter, wronged way" (81). Holland is honest enough to admit that he found Shep's social and political radicalism unsettling. "I felt challenged and, in hearing or reading our interviews again, I often detected a testy note in my questions—as now I feel a distinct tendency to be defensive in writing about these discussions" (83). Yet he never tells us which of Shep's views he found sensible or silly. Nor does he explain how race, class, gender, or religion may affect his own or Shep's reading identities. Nearly every statement Holland makes about Shep begins with praise but ends with criticism. "As an adult, Shep showed in our interviews a warm desire to be a sensitive reader and teacher of literature coupled with an incomplete sense of self that sometimes helped him to be that sensitive reader and at other times gave rise to fierce aggressive impulses" (90). Incomplete sense of self? What does that expression mean? Anyone who receives that comment is likely to respond defensively.

Holland never tells us whether he showed the five students how he characterized them and interpreted their identity themes, but it's unlikely that he did, probably believing that by doing so, he wouldn't have the freedom to tell the truth, as he saw it. But how could he not see that many of his characterizations were censorious? He acknowledges later in *5 Readers Reading* what analysts would call countertransference difficulties. "I sensed in Shep a hostility just looking for something to pounce on. He seemed constantly to be tossing in baits to see if he could draw me into an argument of some kind" (159). Holland's metaphor of being baited by Shep, who is ready to pounce on him, recalls *in reverse* Freud's intellectually aggressive relationship to Dora, whom he describes in a letter to Fliess in 1900 as a case of an eighteen-year-old girl who has "smoothly opened to the existing collection of picklocks" (Fliess, 427). The earlier James Strachey translation of Freud's letters to Fliess is even more boastful: "the case has opened smoothly to my collection of picklocks" (325).

As I wrote in *The Talking Cure*, Freud's relationship with Dora "resembles a cat-and-mouse chase rather than a collaborative therapeutic alliance. There is more than a little arrogance here couched in an assaultive sexual image" (11). Holland never sensed how his own provoking statements and aggressive questions triggered Shep's hostility. What's striking about Holland's depiction of Saul and Shep is his limited empathy toward them. His characterization of

Shep's mistrust of empathy characterizes his own mistrust. "In effect," he was saying, "to be close, to empathize with someone, is to become the same body as that person or to be engulfed by him" (86).

Yes, one would like to say to Holland, empathy poses the danger of becoming too close to a person, of becoming burdened by that person's suffering, but one can learn to empathize without taking on another person's distress. Studies have shown that women tend to be more empathic than men. For this reason, it's not surprising that Holland characterizes Sandra as the most empathic reader of Faulkner's story. "Sandra saw the emotional overtones in the tableau [the young Emily standing in the background, with her father silhouetted in the foreground, holding a horsewhip] in a more subtle, empathic way than the four male readers, so that she, too, had her own version of the image" (4). Holland doesn't invoke penis envy to characterize Sandra, but he implies this when he describes her as being "rather in awe of male vigor, power, and protectiveness" (103). Is this why, in Holland's view, Sandra is empathic? Writing about Sam's "masculine dominance" (134), Holland reinforces Freud's belief that men are active, women passive.

And yet Holland could demonstrate keen empathic understanding, as we see in his 1978 essay "How Can Dr. Johnson's Remarks on Cordelia's Death Add to My Own Response?" Seeking to understand Johnson's belief that Cordelia's death is too painful to witness, Holland offers us an identity theme that helps to explain how the great eighteenth-century critic's lifelong struggle with depression shaped his reading of Shakespeare's play.

> Yet despite the magisterial writing, this perilous balance of assimilated danger and "merciless self-demand" could edge into excess: on the one hand, depression as a response to too much danger incorporated and now felt as within; on the other hand, "a morbid growth in the impulse to *correct* oneself and to keep on 'correcting' till the act of correction becomes an end in itself," as in Johnson's tics, "rollings," or counting compulsions. This correction could become "inevitable self-division and a savage turning of aggression against himself"—depression again. (27)

Holland doesn't suggest that depression catalyzed Johnson's creativity. Rather, depression heightened Johnson's need for self-control along with his belief in rationality and justice. Johnson's critical judgment that Cordelia suffered too much, in excess of what justice required, led him to reject the ending of *King Lear*. Unlike Johnson, Holland does not expect justice from the world, and, as he wryly puts it, he can tolerate injustice for the sake of poetry. Throughout the essay Holland empathizes with and understands Johnson's life and work as creative variations on the need to hold in check his fear of madness.

Sam's Homophobia

Writing at a time when homosexuality was still widely feared and stigmatized, Holland encountered Sam's homophobic reading of Hemingway's "The Battler." The story hints at a homosexual union between Ad, a former champion prize fighter, and Bugs, the African American man who cares for him. "My mind has been poisoned," Sam confesses to Holland, "by reading critics who tell me that the relationship between Ad and Bugs is essentially homosexual" (324). As a way to help the poisoned Sam overcome his anxiety of the story, Holland gives an alternative reading—an antidote. "Ad and Bugs are 'a pair of rather grotesque, and nightmarish parents,' Ad supplying the strength and money and Bugs doing the cooking and shopping and nurturing." Holland's interpretation revealed to Sam that "there was a way to nurture and be nurtured without being a homosexual" (211). If Holland were teaching "The Battler" today, one hopes he would see the story as affirming the possibility of nurturing and being nurtured in a homosexual relationship. Holland might also recognize that Hemingway is more of a countercultural novelist than he appeared to mid-twentieth-century readers. Holland characterizes the "homosexual" interpretation of "The Battler," formulated by Philip Young and others, as "psychological (or pseudopsychological)" (304), but there is both textual and biographical evidence to support a homoerotic reading.

An Early Glimpse of Delphi Teaching

In *5 Readers Reading*, Holland makes an implicit distinction between psychoanalysis as an explanatory system, capable of deciphering readers' identity themes, and psychoanalysis as a therapeutic system, used by trained professionals to improve a patient's health and well-being. He embraces the former as appropriate for an English teacher and rejects the latter as inappropriate for the classroom. Helping readers discover their identity themes requires "sophisticated students, ideally those with some insight into themselves arrived at in a clinical setting" (218). He points out that he has tried this kind of teaching only with advanced graduate students in a literature-and-psychology program. One must be "tactful and discreet," he rightly cautions. "Above all, one must avoid diagnoses or any use of terms that even slightly suggest psychopathology." The archaic "symbol-twirling that used to pass for psychoanalytic criticism is completely out of place" (218). Observing that the skills of the psychotherapist and the literary critic often coincide in their holistic method of analysis, Holland informs us that he served as an adviser to an internship program in a mental health clinic.

> I commonly see graduate students in English develop interpretations of "clients" that are at least as good as those of the social workers and medical students who are their fellow trainees. The study of literary texts provides to the physician and the paraprofessional alike a ready source of sharable and safe material on which to develop skills of psychiatric interpretation. (261)

Like Holland, I believe that the skills of the psychotherapist and literary critic often overlap. A fruitful cross-fertilization exists between psychological (which includes psychiatric and psychoanalytic) and literary education. But in using psychoanalytic theory in the classroom, can one disentangle the explanatory from the clinical? In a larger sense, can one make any meaningful psychological statement about others' lives that does not make them feel better or worse about themselves? Telling Shep that he has an incomplete sense of self is bound to be hurtful, provoking his hostility and defensiveness. Calling "Sebastian" a "complicated, engaging young man" who had a "sardonic sense of humor that made for lots of jokes and for amusing interviews" (90) is bound to make him feel good.

Published authors may receive a dozen glowing reviews of a book, but they are likely to obsess over the single negative review. As I discuss in *Mad Muse*, William Styron was always anxious about his writing and thin-skinned about negative reviews of his books: "He once said," reports his daughter, "he could remember every single word of some of his bad reviews, though almost nothing from the raves" (*Reading My Father* 104). A harsh review could derail Styron's work for days or weeks. If anything, students are more thin-skinned than published authors. Students often ruminate over a negative criticism expressed in a classroom even if the other comments are uniformly positive. Holland tries to be as fair as possible in his characterizations of the five students, and for the most part he succeeds, but it's difficult to make statements about a reader's identity theme, which is, after all, a part of that person's character, without conveying value judgments that have therapeutic or countertherapeutic implications.

DEFT

Holland reaches several noteworthy conclusions in *5 Readers Reading*. He expresses some of these conclusions aphoristically, as when he states that "character transforms characteristically" (122); fantasy projects fantasies" (117); and "style re-creates style" (201). His major insight strikes me as unassailable: "interpretation is a function of identity" (248). He maintains that one's identity cannot be essentially changed but that it can be modified. He leaves open the possibility of growth—through education, psychoanalysis, or reading. He celebrates difference, saying, perhaps with a deliberate pun, that it betokens "not a failure but the norm" (247). He disagrees with many of the interpretations of *Hamlet* expressed in the last 300 years but realizes he can learn much about himself and others by studying these disagreements. He urges a literary criticism that takes neither the text nor the self as the major object of inquiry but the relationship between the two: transactive criticism, a term used by fellow reader-response theorist Louise Rosenblatt (1904–2005) in her 1978 book *The Reader, the Text, the Poem: The Transactional Theory of the Literary Work*. Delighting in overarching generalizations expressed through analogy, he observes that "Unity is to the text as identity is to a person; or, you could say, identity is the unity I find in a person if I look at him as if he were a text" (259). In the 2000 edition of *Poems in Persons*, he uses the word "DEFT," an acronym (and mnemonic) that appeared for the first time in *Laughing*, to characterize the four principles of reading:

> Readers must be able to create their characteristic modes of adaptation or *defense* from the words they are reading.
> A reader brings characteristic *expectations* to bear.
> We project into the work a *fantasy* that yields the pleasure we characteristically seek.
> We therefore *transform* the fantasy we have projected into it by means of the defensive structures we have created from it to arrive at some aesthetic or intellectual or moral or political "point" to what we have read. (57)

But old habits are hard to overcome, Holland acknowledges, and sometimes in *Poems in Persons* and *5 Readers Reading* he finds himself lapsing into the discredited (for him) belief in a text-active model of reading. He uses in the latter book the archaic word "promptuary" (a crude sixteenth-century calculating machine) to describe how a story "acts as a ready reserve of structured verbal information from which the reader builds his fantasy as he did his defenses" (285). Holland uses the word again in *The I* (93) and in *The Critical I* (99), but it has never caught on, if only because the long-dominant tradition of a text-active model of reading is difficult to dislodge.

Reviews: David Bleich

Oddly enough, the sharpest (in both senses of the word) criticism of *Poems in Persons* and *5 Readers Reading* came from another reader-response scholar, David Bleich, to whom Holland had warmly acknowledged his indebtedness. In the preface to the 1973 edition of *Poems in Persons*, Holland writes, "David Bleich, by gently but persistently questioning my basic assumptions, has worked a major shift in my understanding of subjectivity" (x). Holland's praise of Bleich is even more effusive in *5 Readers Reading*.

> David Bleich has done outstanding work in this field on which I have drawn, but I am particularly indebted to him for his long and careful commentary on an earlier version of this book. He enabled me to make a transition I found extremely difficult: from a concept of reading as the reader's partaking partially of a process completely but potentially embodied in a text to reading as the reader's active re-creation of the text based on the materials he finds in it. (xv)

A few pages later, Holland commends Bleich for reversing the usual assumption of critics who believe that by analyzing the text, one can understand the response. Rather, Bleich shows how one can understand the text by analyzing what ordinary readers, such as students, find in it. "And he is right to do so" (12), Holland adds genially. Yet no such acknowledgment of help appears in the 2000 edition of *Poems in Persons*. What happened?

Bleich's first reference to Holland appears at the end of his 1975 book *Readings and Feelings*, where he observes that *Poems in Persons* and the forthcoming *5 Readers Reading* reach conclusions that are close to his own point of view. Yet in two brief notes published in *College English* in 1976 and 1978, Bleich spells out his criticisms of Holland's work. In the 1976 note, Bleich faults Holland for casting himself in *Poems in Persons* and *5 Readers Reading* as the "objective observer and his students as subjective respondents." In Bleich's view, Holland doesn't participate in either book in a genuinely intersubjective way. In applying his four principles to the act of reading, Bleich continues, "Holland rarely, if ever, considers such basic factors as the reader's interpersonal background, his affective response, and, most importantly, perhaps, his motive for reading on that occasion" (300).

I agree with many of Bleich's criticisms of the highly limited notion of intersubjectivity that we see in *Poems in Persons* and *5 Readers Reading*. I feel closer to Bleich's model of reader-response criticism than I do to Holland's. I also agree with Bleich's vision of self-disclosing teaching in his 1998 book

Know and Tell (which omits any reference to Holland's work): "Teaching through disclosure, which has grown out of self-consciously practiced subjectivist styles of teaching by some faculty members, reminds us that 'truth' includes the personal, the emotional, the ideological, and sometimes the irrational in each subject matter" (12).

Nevertheless, I believe that Bleich fails to appreciate Holland's major accomplishments in both books. Moreover, Bleich's strident tone, which can barely conceal his anger, is glaring. Reading Bleich's obsessive faultfinding with Holland, I feel as if I'm in the world of *Moby Dick*, witnessing Ahab's monomaniacal pursuit of the white whale. Bleich's 1978 book *Subjective Criticism* is startling in that he doesn't have a single good word to say about Holland. Witness, for example, the index in *Subjective Criticism* under Holland's name: "attempt of, to use pedagogical approach of subjective criticism; contradictory position of; epistemological problems in the work of; solipsism in thinking of." As if this isn't bad enough, Bleich continues his assault of Holland under the term "identity theme (Holland)": "epistemological problems with; failure of, to explain conscious initiatives; insufficient basis for use of, in Holland's work" (302).

I am not privy to "insider" information about their antagonistic relationship, and I have never met or corresponded with Bleich, but one senses his deep animosity toward Holland that cannot be explained entirely by intellectual differences, as when Bleich writes in the 1976 "Response to Norman Holland":

> In the five years of off-and-on discussion of his experiment with him, I had expressed many reservations and suggestions for changing his thinking. Holland has acknowledged my contributions on more than one occasion. Yet my thinking is developing and changing just as his is, so I would like him to forgive me for not mentioning sooner thoughts about which I was not altogether certain and which I could not offer at that time with full confidence. (300)

It is unusual for one distinguished scholar to ask forgiveness from another distinguished scholar, particularly when the issues at stake are so ambiguous. All one can say is that the thinking of both men continued to develop and change in ways that ended their professional relationship.

Jane P. Tompkins's even handed discussion of the differences between Holland and Bleich's approaches to reader-response criticism appears in her 1980 edited volume. "While Holland brackets the subject-object problem," Tompkins observes, "Bleich centers his theory on it because he views literary response as essentially an epistemological issue" (xx). Tompkins includes in her volume Holland's essay "Unity Identity Text Self," originally published in *PMLA* in 1975, and Bleich's essay "Epistemological Assumptions in the Study of Response," excerpted from *Subjective Criticism*. Revealingly, Tompkins editorially interrupts Bleich's discussion with the following bracketed words: "In material that has been omitted here, Bleich continues by criticizing at length and in detail Holland's experimental methodology in *5 Readers Reading* on the grounds that it is an extension of the objectivist epistemology that governs his conception of the text" (148)—the only time she makes this editorial decision in the nearly 300-page volume.

Another Crews Missile

Frederick Crews was not finished assaulting Holland's work, as we can see in *Out of My System* (1975). The title is apt, for Crews castigates a wide variety of thinkers, including Herbert Marcuse, Wilhelm Reich, and Norman O. Brown, for rejecting mainstream psychoanalysis in pursuit of their quixotic utopian agendas. By mobilizing against these Freudian ideologues, Crews is getting them out of his system, casting them off, like the body's immune system attacking a stubborn virus. Yet there is an unintended irony in the title, for in the larger trajectory of his career, Crews is only *beginning* to purge himself of Freudianism, a scourge that insidiously infects his thought, never completely out of his system. He acknowledges that all the essays in the volume "for better or worse, are internal dialogues between rebellion and caution." Crews then adds that his "vocation, it seems, is to be forever deciding that I would rather not be a fanatic of one sort or another" (xiv).

Yet Crews can't help himself, for in the last chapter, "Reductionism and Its Discontents," he disparages Holland's theory of a reader's identity theme. The tone of the chapter, Crews confesses in the headnotes, is jarring. "If my way of arguing, as usual, is somewhat negative, the purpose is affirmative: to renew appreciation of the criteria that enable rational, nonsectarian discourse about literature to occur" (165). But the tone of the chapter is more than "somewhat negative," and for whatever reason, the idea of a reader's identity theme remains threatening to Crews. He had denounced Holland's *The Dynamics of Literary Response* in "Anaesthetic Criticism," but he is openly hostile to Holland's *5 Readers Reading*. We don't go to criticism to discover students' or critics' identity themes, Crews asserts; rather, we go to criticism "because we hope to learn more about literature than we could have figured out for ourselves" (179). Crews dismisses the "subjectivism" that is both "in the air," like a pollutant, and in the idea of a reader's identity theme, a subjectivism that reminds him, unpleasantly, of the ethos of encounter groups.

Crews rejects not only *5 Readers Reading* but also those scholars who support Holland. "As one of Holland's supporters remarks of the new attitude, 'This in-mixing of self and other makes interpretation a potentially private affair, but it also can lead to a more inclusive sharing of emotional as well as intellectual dynamics than is now available'" (181). A footnote identifies the Holland "supporter" as Murray Schwartz. It may seem trivial that Crews doesn't mention Schwartz by name in the text, consigning him to a mere footnote, but it's noteworthy that Schwartz, one of Crews's own UC Berkeley graduate students and a contributor to *Psychoanalysis & Literary Process*, now becomes an enemy. Crews admits in the preface to *Out of My System* that intellectual rebels sometimes end up embodying the authoritarianism they spurn, a pattern that is true in many of his own writings.

Murray Schwartz observes, in his 1979 review of *Out of My System*, that Crews "enacts the ambiguity of its title repeatedly, with Crews both subject and object of his own systematic ambivalence, first absorbed in a system (an encoded, configurational totalization of reality) and then aggressively separating from that other through the power of language" (43). Additionally, Schwartz points out Crews's characteristic style, portraying issues in dichotomous terms, as Freud did: "One is either layman or priest, pious or skeptical, rational or fanatic, contained or released, infantile or adult" (44). Schwartz remarks in his intellectual memoir "Psychoanalysis in My Life" that "Crews's later furious combat against Freud and psychoanalysis, an obsession that continues to this day and is impervious to dialogue, has always registered for me as a deep disappointment and betrayal. All objections to his caricatures came to be treated as so many curve balls to be swatted out of the park" (135).

In retrospect, the optimistic title *Out of My System* has proven to be wish fulfillment, not reality, for Crews continues to revile and defile Freud in later books. Psychoanalysis has been reduced to an anodyne in *Skeptical Engagements* (1986), capable of numbing but not ameliorating the pain of existence. Those whom Crews has previously admired have betrayed him and are now summarily rejected. Erik Erikson has been from the beginning "less a sober clinical researcher than a virtuoso, mingling sensitive observations with a blend of Freudian dogma, conventional sentiment, and engrossing self-dramatization" (16). Literary critics whom Crews formerly praised in *The Sins of the Fathers*, such as Leslie Fiedler, are reduced to cruel caricatures. "He is like a bag lady permanently camped on the doorstep of criticism, muttering imprecations at the insiders and keeping warm by waving enthusiastically to oblivious passers-by" (209). In *The Memory Wars* (1995), Crews accuses Freud of fathering the satanic abuse phenomenon, an irony in that in *The Sins of the Fathers* Crews analyzes Hawthorne's ambivalent relationship to his Salem ancestors. Peter L. Rudnytsky's "Wrecking Crews," published in *American Imago* in 1999, highlights the greatest defect of *The Memory Wars*: "the proclivity to reduce complex issues to an either/or dichotomy in which one side is right and the other wrong." This outlook, Rudnytsky adds, "which precludes the possibility of genuine dialogue," is compounded by Crews's refusal "to interrogate himself, while impugning the character and motives of his opponents" (286).

In *Unauthorized Freud: Doubters Confront a Legend* (1998), Crews promises to "restore the mythified 'discoverer of the unconscious' to human size" (ix), but, in fact, he reduces Freud to Lilliputian stature. Crews grants that his book "incurs the risks of overkill" (xi), which is, no doubt, his intention. Crews continues his assault on psychoanalysis in *Follies of the Wise* (2006), the title of which does not refer to Freud, who was wise only for a few of Crews's misguided years. Having confidently predicted in his earlier books the demise of psychoanalysis, Crews is forced to concede the "continuing resilience of the Freud legend, which tends to snap back into shape at every point that is not under immediate pressure" (31). Unrelenting in his own pressure, Crews's strategy is to praise books that find fault with Freud. Crews's most recent book, *Freud: The Making of an Illusion* (2017), is a 746-page biography that emphasizes Freud's failures while ignoring his accomplishments. "Paraphrasing Voltaire," George Prochnik concludes in his *New York Times* review, "if Freud didn't exist, Frederick Crews would have had to invent him." One senses that Crews has never overcome the trauma of his early "seduction" by psychoanalysis, a narcissistic injury that motivates most of his scholarship.

The severity of that injury is painfully apparent in Adam Begley's article about Crews, "Terminating Analysis," which appeared in a 1994 issue of *Lingua Franca*. Begley interviewed Crews two months before his retirement as chair of the English department at UC Berkeley, where he had taught for thirty-six years. The article opens with a student's assertion that after reading one of Crews's essays, she was struck by the similarities between Freud and Hitler. To Begley's amazement, Crews enthusiastically agreed with the remark. Begley characterizes Crews as "quiet, unassuming, the kind of guy you just have to call mild-mannered." The only evidence of Crews's passion, continues Begley, "is his deadly polemical vendetta: He really hates Freud" (24).

The interview has a melancholy, elegiacal quality that cannot be explained entirely by Crews's impending retirement from teaching. He appears to be evaluating his life's work and, concluding that he has not been entirely successful in his profession, blaming the person responsible for his failure. "I feel I could have had a more productive career as an intellectual if I had never heard the word 'Freud'" (27). One thinks of Marlon Brando's line in *On the Waterfront*: "I coulda been a contender." But Crews was no washed-up boxer turned longshoreman; he was an academic superstar who still had plenty of books in him, all attacking Freud.

Begley offers a few details about his subject, but he coyly precedes these revelations with a beguiling warning: "Psychobiographers take note: Crews had a rocky relationship with his father, who wanted him to become a physicist or a mathematician. His father, says Crews, was 'extremely good at science'" (27-8). According to Begley, Crews "wolfed down" Freud when he was a graduate student at Princeton in the mid-1950s. His fascination for Freud was reignited when he wrote *The Sins of the Fathers*. "Crews was more than just a convert. He soon began to preach the gospel himself" in his oversubscribed Berkeley graduate seminars on psychoanalytic literary criticism. In the mid-1960s, at the height of his interest in Freud, he considered becoming a lay analyst, but he could not afford to pay for a training analysis: $10,000 a year for five years (28). Crews abandoned the plan to become a psychoanalyst "with real regret"—and then slowly turned against his intellectual hero in the same way that he was drawn toward him: through reading.

Crews freely admits in the interview that he exhibits "the God That Failed syndrome" (29), though he doesn't acknowledge how this syndrome has affected his ability to see Freud accurately. Nor does he acknowledge, as Murray Schwartz points out in his memoir, that by attacking psychoanalysis, Crews seeks to discredit Freud, the looming father surrogate in his life. Given the fact that Crews has become an influential authority in literary criticism, intolerant of those who disagree with him, Begley asks an obvious question: Is Crews himself "now trapped in the role of the Freudian father, trying to kill off his sons?" (29). Begley doesn't answer the question, allowing others to engage in psychobiographical speculations. Without remarking on the biographical ironies, Begley quotes one of Crews's most bellicose pronouncements in *Skeptical Engagements*: "Though Freud loved to sermonize about courageously opposing the human penchant for self-deception, it is no exaggeration to say that his psychoanalytic career was both launched and maintained by systematic mendacity" (Begley, 29; *Skeptical Engagements* 101). Part of the statement characterizes Crews: his literary career has been maintained by systematically opposing the mendacious Freud. There are other ironies in Begley's interview, including John Forrester's insight that Crews maintains a "highly idealized vision of what science does." Crews's UC Berkeley colleague Martin Jay agrees: "Virtually all science is methodologically inconsistent with its highest standards." To which Begley adds, "The gist of this agreement is that though Freud's methods fall short of the mark, so do almost everybody's; and valid results often follow from flawed procedures" (30).

Other Reviews

It's unusual for a reviewer to misrepresent or misremember his own earlier review, but this is true of Alan C. Purves. In his 1969 review of *The Dynamics of Literary Response*, we recall, Purves vowed not to be "overly negative," but in his 1974 review of *Poems in Persons*, he suddenly describes *The Dynamics of Literary Response* as a "masterpiece of systematized introspection," a book that "forced the best of Freudians, I think, to reconsider what they were doing (although few of them did)" (9). One can only wonder what was responsible for Purves's sudden appreciation of Holland's earlier work. Purves is guarded in his evaluation of *Poems in Persons*, criticizing Holland for presenting his data selectively—a strange criticism in that the amount of data in *Poems in Persons* and *5 Readers Reading* is exhaustive if not exhausting. Robert Mollinger ends his discussion of *Poems in Persons* published in *The Psychoanalytic Review* by noting that Holland is "exploring new ground and, though his theories might not always be convincing, they seem headed in the right direction" (185). Whereas Purves finds *Poems in Persons* "unsettling" (9), Paul Delany reaches the opposite conclusion in his *New York Times* review. Sounding like "one of Frost's New England farmers extolling the virtues of fences," Holland has a "cheery, informal style" that helps to "smooth over the more threatening aspects of his subject."

Holland's Cheerfulness

But not every critic has admired Holland's cheerfulness. Cary Nelson, for one, does not. In his essay "The Psychology of Criticism, or What Can Be Said," appearing in the same 1978 volume *Psychoanalysis and the Question of the Text*, edited by Geoffrey Hartman (in which Holland and Schwartz also have essays), Nelson finds himself "somewhat alienated by his cheerful form of self-representation," in part, Nelson confesses, because he is not a cheerful person himself. Moreover, Nelson finds Holland's public persona, that of a person who is "open, generous, and even innocent," hard to accept. Holland's statements about his identity theme, Nelson continues, "are so formulaic that they block any extended exploration of the guilt critics usually feel when they recognize, however obliquely, their wish to reconstruct a text and reorder it in their minds" (53–4). It is a shrewd criticism; only in his later writings does Holland expose the darker side of his personality.

5

Extending Identity Theory in the 1980s

"Re-Covering 'The Purloined Letter,'" *Laughing, The I and Being Human*, and *The Brain of Robert Frost*

"Re-Covering 'The Purloined Letter'"

The 1980s was a highly productive time for Holland. Having emerged as the leading American psychoanalytic literary theorist of identity, he began the decade with the publication of his wittiest and most playful essay, "Re-Covering 'The Purloined Letter': Reading as a Personal Transaction," published in Susan R. Suleiman and Inge Crosman's 1980 edited volume *The Reader in the Text*. The essay is fascinating for Holland's biographical self-disclosures and his eagerness to take on the two dominant French theorists of the age, Lacan and Derrida, both of whom he attempts to outsmart by offering a compelling model of reading that challenges their own.

Holland is iconoclastic throughout the essay. Witness the opening sentence: "Begin with the text, they say" (350). He does—but in an unexpected way. He recalls the 1940 Pocketbook edition of *The Great Tales and Poems of Edgar Allan Poe* he had read when he was thirteen. Now fifty-two, he contrasts his youthful reading of "The Purloined Letter" to that of a middle-aged professor. "Literature endures, while we change. Yet as we change we change it, so that this 'Purloined Letter' both is and is not the same 'Purloined Letter' I first read almost forty years ago" (350).

Holland's humor throughout the essay is never caustic or superior, and he must have had great fun writing it, for it displays his linguistic and scholarly talents:

> "Purloined," that lovely, artificial word, so typically Poe-etic; it comes from *porloignée*—Norman French or, if you like, Norm's French. When I studied French in school, my favorite province was, inevitably, Normandy. I feel protective toward that word *purloined*. It is not to be

confused (as Lacan, for example, does) with words meaning "alongside." This is truly *porloignée*, from *loin*, "far," hence, "to put far away." As the Minister D—does. As Dupin himself does. (350–1)

Having exhibited his enchantment with language and corrected a factual error of Lacan (a footnote explains that the French analyst misreported the word "purloined" in the *Oxford English Dictionary*), Holland calls into question Poe's basic premise in the story. "The Purloined Letter" is not about concealing secrets in plain sight—"One's secrets are always found out by the sheer bigness and brute force of government power" (352)—but about the nature of hiding. Reading the story as an adolescent, he had much to hide, sexually, but nothing like the implausible sexual interpretation of the early psychoanalytic critic Marie Bonaparte, whose 1933 book on Poe saw the story as expressing "regret for the missing maternal penis." Viewing the absent phallus as a "Bone-a-part," Holland suggests that like other readings from first-phase or symbolic Freudianism, Bonaparte's interpretation cost her nothing, unlike the sacrifice required for him to reveal his free associations to the story. "It cost me something to admit to you that I masturbated, even thirty-nine years ago and at an age when all boys do" (355).

Holland's more noteworthy free association, however, is that he loved to perform magic as a youth, making objects appear and disappear. He was the one in his family who knew secrets, not the adults. A decipher of texts, like Dupin, Holland thrilled in outmatching male authority, both then and now.

> How intelligent I thought myself when I was reading this story at thirteen; and I am not entirely over that vanity yet, as you can see by choosing to write about a story that two major thinkers have analyzed. They are able to be outwitted, all these fathers like the Prefect or the Minister, or, for that matter, Lacan and Derrida. (357–8)

Absence and Presence

Acknowledging his vanity may not endear him to his fellow literary theorists, but Holland comes across in the essay as a lover of literature who needs to know everything about Poe's "pure-loined letter," including the conjurer's belief in detection. "He holds a deep faith that there is some sort of thereness at the core of things, even if it be the beating of a murdered heart beneath the floorboards or the first feeble movements in the hollow coffin in the cellar of the House of Usher" (360). Poe's commitment to thereness, Holland continues, contrasts with Lacan's faith in absence. "I suppose it is the psychoanalysis in me, but I hear in that very preoccupation a longing for presence" (361). Lacan's assumption that the signifier signifies, that it has a "preordained trajectory," contrasts with Derrida's characteristic distrust. "In a world of deconstructions, the greatest intellectual sin is to try to take a fixed position. Derrida, I think, writes out of a need not to believe, a need to *dis*trust. Yet, as with Lacan, I feel the absence is itself a presence. Disbelief is itself a belief in disbelief" (361–2; emphasis in original).

Poe's 1845 short story inspired Lacan's 1956 "Seminar on 'The Purloined Letter'" and Derrida's 1975 "The Purveyor of Truth." Holland's contribution to the extensive theoretical discussion was to point out that the story's spatial metaphors reflect states of mind. "The concealed becomes the open, and the open becomes closed" (368). The statement allows him to bring in a variety of psychological themes—displacement, abreaction, transference, and repression—that demonstrate the importance of extratextual, extraliterary approaches to the story.

Holland uses his free associations—masturbation, magic, and outmaneuvering powerful fathers—to argue that his transactive model of reading is superior to Lacan's and Derrida's, both of which are based on a text-active or bi-active model. A bi-active model of reading is an improvement over the false text-active model, Holland concedes, but it has a major weakness: it requires two separate theories to explain it, a new theory of reader activity combined with the old discredited stimulus-response text-active model. Invoking the title of his earlier psychoanalytic book, Holland asks, "Is not a transactive criticism truer to the human dynamics of literary response than the linguistic glide of a Lacan or the deconstructions of a Derrida? Is it not better to have a literary and especially a psychoanalytic criticism that is grounded in the body and the family?" (364). Posing as a knight errant, Holland ends by suggesting that instead of eliminating interpretive differences, as old and new critics demand, the transactive critic celebrates different readings. "That way, we can re-cover the letter purloined by such abstract, intellectual readings as Lacan's or Derrida's" (370).

A Bitter Adversary

Holland's Poe essay appeared in the same volume as Jonathan Culler's "Prolegomena to a Theory of Reading." Susan Suleiman, coeditor of *The Reader in the Text*, noted in the introduction that Culler criticized Holland "harshly" (30)—an understatement in that Culler's attack is mean-spirited. Culler begins the essay, which was written for a 1976 session of the English

Institute at which Holland also spoke, by mischaracterizing Holland's position on reading. "Norman Holland, for example, would say that in our pursuits we attain no knowledge of literature but only exercise the self, as we sit in our studies hour after hour recreating our identity themes in one masterpiece or another" (46).

One can disagree with Holland's theoretical conclusions, but he always displays stimulating interpretations of literature. Contrary to Culler's claim, Holland *always* adds to our understanding of literature. Culler accuses Holland of speaking of personal identity as a given when, in fact, Holland takes pains to describe each reader's identity theme. The identity themes Holland discusses in his many books—those of novelists, poets, literary critics, or students—are always unique, not generic. Culler misses the central ambiguity in Holland's theory, namely, that identity is not "in" a person but somewhere between the interpreter and interpretee, in the realm of potential space. Nor does Holland "blithely" regard human behavior as the expression of a "consistent central human essence," as Culler opines. Rather, Holland maintains that people actively use language rather than, as the poststructuralists aver, are passively controlled by language. Culler can't resist a gibe at psychoanalysis. "This is, of course, the way of American ego psychology, which can be shown to be a vulgarized and sentimentalized version of the New Criticism" (55). Nor can Culler resist a parting shot at Holland's students. "Indeed, the behavior of Mr. Holland's five readers illustrates very nicely how much the activity of interpretation is determined by the codified commonplaces of a culture; his five undergraduates are most unlike one another at the moment when they proffer the clichés and codes of different cultures" (56).

Culler sees no value in studying a reader's free associations to analyze "competency," a judgmental word he uses throughout "Prolegomena to a Theory of Reading" as if he alone knows the difference between literary superiority and inferiority. "Far from discrediting a poetics focused on literary considerations, disagreements among readers make the need for it more apparent" (52). Culler's relationship to Holland is like Dupin's relationship to the mysterious D—in Poe's story: he is a bitter adversary. "Men of mind fighting with mind" (359), as Holland writes. The adversaries are, in this case, both literary theorists. Just as Minister D—in "The Purloined Letter" has, years earlier, done an evil deed to Dupin, for which Dupin now has his revenge, so will Holland reciprocate Culler's criticism, years later, in *The Critical I*, where he calls Culler's behavior "scandalous." For now, though, we can say that Holland cleverly places himself in relation to "The Purloined Letter," as Lacan and Derrida did before him, and by doing so, raises salient theoretical concerns.

Laughing

Holland begins *Laughing* (1982) with the sentence, "I like to laugh" (9). Always inquisitive, he then asks: Why do people laugh? To answer this question, which has provoked a wide variety of conjectures for more than 2,000 years, he surveys in Part I of the book nearly 200 theories, none of which offers a convincing unified explanation. In Part II, he interviews several students about why they laugh, using as texts seven cartoons by the American cartoonist B. Kliban (1935–90), whose lampoons regularly appeared in *Playboy* magazine. Holland selects cartoons not from Kliban's best-known collection, *Cats* (1975), but from the darker volume, *Never Eat Anything Bigger than Your Head & Other Drawings* (1978).

Laughing is a labor of love, as Holland admits in the preface. His challenge is to write engagingly, and often wryly, about a subject that can soon become dry and cerebral, thus antithetical to the nature of laughing. For half a dozen years Holland taught a course he called "The Comic Sensibility," though his students dubbed it "The Cosmic Sensitivity." One can imagine that the course was well received, though presumably it was academically rigorous, not entirely a laughing matter for the students.

Like his other books, *Laughing* gives us the impression that Holland has read everything written about the subject. As always, he wears his learning lightly. It is an easy and pleasurable book to read, not merely because it is laced with humor. My favorite Kliban cartoon, of the seven, shows a bearded man ordering dinner for himself and a monstrous mosquito seated across from him in an elegant French restaurant. "I'll have the gazpacho, leeks vinaigrette with shrimp, marinated zucchini, orange mousse, a bottle of côtes du rhne rôuge '59, and bring some shit for my fly" (118).

Aha! I exclaimed. How in character for Holland, who demonstrates repeatedly two of the three qualities of the anal personality, orderliness and obstinacy, to relish anal humor. I then turned excitedly to Fisher and Greenberg for empirical proof. Research indeed confirms, they report in their 1996 study, the prediction that "the greater the person's 'anal fixation' the greater would be his or her relative preference for anal jokes" (107)—true for females but not, alas, for males. So much for my theory. Perhaps I am only revealing, by singling out this particular Kliban cartoon, my own anal fixations!

Part II of *Laughing* focuses mainly on "Ellen," a 25-year-old graduate student at SUNY-Buffalo whom Holland interviewed in early 1978. She was a friend of the Hollands, and they would sometimes have dinner or watch films together. Holland asked Ellen what she found amusing about Kliban's cartoons, encouraging her to free associate, as he did with the undergraduates in *Poems in Persons* and *5 Readers Reading*. Holland theorizes, not surprisingly, that Ellen laughs when she recreates her identity theme. This is the general principle that he draws from his research, an overarching theory that he believes helps to explain all humor. Ellen "defts" Kliban's cartoons the way all people do, Holland maintains.

Holland ends the book by suggesting that the DEFT theory of laughing arises from the psychoanalytic model while at the same time embraces a more general model of the way we transact texts. "Identity and DEFT make Freud's theory more precise by turning the powerful lens of psychoanalytic interpretation on the laughter, when Freud looked only at the joke" (198). For the first time Holland suggests, suddenly transforming himself into a postmodernist, that identity theory decenters not only our knowledge but also our selves. "The center of me includes a not-me or a semi-me, the being who interprets me." It is, he suggests mirthfully, a "paradox, a most ingenious paradox" (198).

Fathers and Sons

Laughing is notable, biographically, because it contains Holland's first personal reference to something troubling about his childhood. He begins by recalling the iconic Herblock cartoon about Nixon, with his infamous five-o'clock shadow, climbing out of a sewer waving a brush. When Nixon complained indignantly to the cartoonist, who had created many unflattering drawings of the president, Herblock simply revised it without the shadow. (No stranger to controversy, Herblock coined the word "McCarthyism" to describe another reviled politician.) Observes Holland:

> I laughed by making Nixon into a father who had tried to smear others and ended up smearing himself. He had gone down and into a dirty place and been dirtied by it. By seeing him that way I attacked an authority who was "in" in several senses. The cartoon enabled me to assert such a father's private dirt against his public professions of probity. (173)

Discussing how his identity includes themes about "fathers private and public, inside and outside," Holland remarks cryptically, "I know they have played a painfully important part in my emotional life, going back to early childhood" (173). That's all he says about the subject, apart from admitting that these early childhood experiences have shaped his loathing of Richard Nixon and his own "malicious laughter" at Nixon cartoons.

For someone like Holland, who had, as we shall see, a stormy relationship with his own father, the patricidal implications of the Nixon cartoon are evident. Earlier in *Laughing*, he observes that central to the death-and-rebirth ritual is sacrifice: "a totem animal, a *pharmakos*, or a scapegoat (human or animal) is magically loaded with the sins of the community, then sacrificed by the community and mourned. The sacrifice rises to the gods and the community is 'reborn,' that is, cleansed" (35). Freud was the totemic father in the psychoanalytic community, the object of his rebellious followers' attack. Freud discusses this ritual in *Totem and Taboo* (1913), where he argues that the totem animal is a substitute for the father, who is killed and then mourned and worshiped as a god. "The ambivalent emotional attitude, which to this day characterizes the father-complex in our children and which often persists into adult life, seems to extend to the totem animal in its capacity as substitute for the father" (*SE*, vol. 13, 141). Holland, the dean of American psychoanalytic literary critics, sometimes played a similar totemic role, engendering widespread ambivalence from those who challenged his authority, particularly when he implied that those who had not undergone a personal analysis, like himself, were unqualified to challenge Freudian theory.

No Longer a Schematic Freudian

Without explicitly repudiating Freud's disparaging views of women, Holland does his best to distance himself from them. Ellen doesn't laugh at "The Nixon Monument" cartoon, which depicts people staring into a pit, mainly because she thought it showed something phallic missing. "Being a woman I would see that." Holland's response is revealing. "As the professor who felt responsible for her knowledge of psychoanalysis, I grumbled. In the seminars I teach, I try to get students past automatic symbolism or the theory that woman is a castrated man. But Ellen insisted on casting herself in the role of schematic Freudian" (164).

It is a significant moment in Holland's writings, when he heralds to the reader that he is no longer an orthodox—or schematic—Freudian. But it is a proclamation without fanfare, without an explicit or implicit admission that this represents a revision of his thinking. Readers who have not examined closely his earlier books are unlikely to notice a shift in his attitude. As we have seen, Holland would have responded differently to Ellen's statement earlier in his career.

How do we explain Holland's changed views? In a word, feedback. Not that he calls attention to his rejection of penis envy. Rather, he now begins to celebrate one of the great twentieth-century discoveries. "We humans have not used it for thinking about humans as much perhaps as we should: feedback systems" (176). He gives the example of steering a car on a highway that turns right, causing the driver to steer right. After telling us that behavior is the control of perception, and giving us a diagram of a feedback loop, he points out that feedback loops are not self-contained, as some psychology textbooks claim. On the contrary, feedback loops always refer to an outside source. "Somebody has to set the thermostat" (178). One of Holland's own feedback loops was the heated feminist rejection of his scholarship. How could he not have taken to heart Susan Stanford Friedman's withering criticisms of his emphasis on H.D's "lack" in *Poems in Persons*? Her censure must have been especially galling because he referred enthusiastically to her groundbreaking scholarship, observing in the 2000 edition that "Professor Susan Stanford Friedman has written more and probably knows more about H.D. than anyone" (32). Friedman's repudiation of Holland's interpretation of H.D. almost certainly affected his thinking about Freud's most problematic theory.

Laughing reveals much about what Holland finds funny and not funny.

> I don't mind jokes that suggest that professors are eccentric or absent-minded (I am), but I don't enjoy jokes that suggest we are impractical (I am not!) or that what we have to teach is not worth learning. Shaw said, "he who can, does. He who cannot, teaches," and I am not amused. I prefer "He who can, does. He who knows better, teaches." (189)

No one took teaching, reading, and writing more seriously than Holland, and whatever disagreements one may have with his theorizings, he always delights in knowledge. "A jokester is likely to be, as Hobbes pointed out, rather insecure" (49). Perhaps, but the jokester Holland succeeded in disguising his own insecurities in *Laughing*—resulting in a book that does much to explain why we find something funny. Or not.

The I and Being Human

Holland's synthetic imagination is best seen in his 1985 book *The I*, retitled (but not revised), with a new introduction, as *The I and Being Human*, published in 2011. Holland notes in the preface that *The I* began in the summer of 1975 as a coauthored project with Murray Schwartz, but the latter's departure from SUNY-Buffalo made collaboration difficult. "As it is," Holland writes, "in the chapters on symbolism and the first year of life, I worked from Murray's outline and notes, and throughout the writing, his comments, corrections, and suggestions have greatly enriched *The I*" (xiv). Holland thanks his other colleagues at the Center for the Psychological Study of the Arts and the Group for Applied Psychoanalysis in Buffalo. "In many ways this book does no more than summarize my fifteen years of cheerful talk with this gifted, inspiring group" (xiv). Significantly, for the first time he thanks Elizabeth Zetzel for being his analyst.

In extending identity theory to psychoanalysis, Holland shows how it can be applied to many aspects of human knowledge. He seeks nothing less than the unification of the sciences and humanities, or, as he says, "certainty and beauty, fidelity and desire" (326). Largely avoiding polemical or polarizing prose, Holland searches for unity even when it appears unlikely if not impossible.

Holland divides *The I* into four parts, each part building on the preceding one. Logical organization is characteristic of all his books. Part I, "The Aesthetics of I," focuses on how we can look at an I, a person, as a work of art, representing each person as a whole, a theme with infinite variations. He offers the identity themes of F. Scott Fitzgerald; Paul Lorenz (now known as Ernst Lanzer), Freud's famous "Rat Man"; "Anna S.," a patient of Heinz Lichtenstein; George Bernard Shaw; "Dr. Charles Vincent," a victim of Chinese brainwashing who was later studied by Robert J. Lifton; and (in a later chapter) Herbert Graf, Freud's "Little Hans." The next three parts explore the psychology, history, and science of I. *The I* is noteworthy for many reasons. The book contains Holland's first though by no means last critique of Jacques Lacan, the influential French analyst whose "return to Freud" Holland could never take seriously.

In the appendix to *The I*, Holland discusses how identity theory builds on the three earlier phases of psychoanalysis: a psychology of the unconscious, ego psychology, and a psychology of the self. He's particularly interested in showing how his concept of identity is consonant with Erik Erikson's. There are, however, two fundamental differences between the theorists' understanding of identity. Final identity for Erikson appears at the end of adolescence; identity for Holland, following Lichtenstein's theory, occurs much earlier, in infancy. Moreover, Erikson stressed how culture shapes identity, a question Holland largely ignored except in distinguishing his psychoanalytic views from Lacan's.

Holland quotes throughout *The I* creative writers and theorists who have remarked on the unity of the self. "I am conscious of myself in exactly the same way now, at eighty-one, as I was conscious of myself, my 'I,' at five or six years of age," Tolstoy wrote in the last year of his life (*The I*, x). "Each novelist writes one novel all his life," Bernard Malamud once told Holland (35). The French literary critic Charles Mauron argued that one can find a single *mythe personel* in each writer's work (357).

Then-I and Now-I

As in his earlier books, *The I* presents a few intriguing hints into Holland's personality, though in general he remains wary of self-disclosure. Holland quotes from a journal he wrote when he was twenty-three that ends with the following words. "I am glad to have kept this book, even sketchily as I have. Someday I shall look back, and when I do I daresay the then-I will wonder what the now-I was like, just as the now-I wonders about the then-I . . ." (284; ellipsis in original). Holland was fifty-eight when he used this entry for *The I*, and eighty-two when it appeared in *The I and Being Human*.

The most obvious statement one may make about the journal entry is that Holland's wondering about himself has never ended. Less obvious is the identity theme it discloses, which Holland describes using the third person.

> The passage proceeds by means of two sharply divided pairs, the now-I and the then-I, the then-I looking back to the past and the now-I looking forward into the future. At the same time, the prose doubles back on itself, as if to say, these seem different, but they aren't. The writer wants something that will resolve the dichotomy, an I or an end to wondering that will make the seeming two really one. The two mysteries he probes are time and the self, and the tactic that may provide an answer is *looking* at "this book." (285)

There's more that one can say about this journal entry and Holland's identity theme, as he acknowledges later in the book. "I *need* to know things," he admits, which is certainly not surprising, though the next sentences may be. "It is more than need. I hunger, I desire, I crave. I am an addict of ideas" (137). The need is so strong, in other words, that Holland is willing to pathologize it. Later he adds, "Not many people will 'need to know' as hungrily as I do" (144). Never before and never again will he express the need to intellectualize so dramatically—though he comes close a few pages later, when he derisively describes himself as the "relentless analyzer and knower who has hauled you through these theoretical chapters" (152).

Writing is Holland's preferred method of knowing, analyzing, hauling. Keeping a journal is a way to preserve the self for posterity, for a time when one will no longer be alive. A journal also implies a connection with a future reader. He doesn't mention the theologian Martin Buber, but he creates in *The I*, as in many of his other books, an intimate I-thou relationship with the reader. He writes to be understood and does everything he can to avoid being misunderstood. The first person to whom he pays tribute in the acknowledgments is the creator of psychoanalysis, but then, paralleling the analyst, who once said he was a Freudian but not a Freudist, Holland remarks that he is not a Freudian. "Using the discoverer's name that way, it seems to me, beggars psychoanalysis, making it less of a developed science and more the 'teachings' of Freud, as though he had created a dogma, a system of interpretations, or, as some French writers have suggested, a work of fiction" (xix–xx).

Parsimony

Until reading *The I*, I believed, on the basis of his earlier books, that Holland demonstrated two of the three traits Freud associated with the "anal" or "obsessive" personality, orderliness, and obstinacy. The orderliness is apparent everywhere—in the clarity of his prose, including its balanced rhythms, cadences, and parallelisms; his need to categorize, systematize, and theorize; and his temperamental demand for rationality, symmetry, and control. Anything that is out of order is disturbing, including typographical errors. *The I and Being Human* contains something one does not often see in the republication of an academic book, a list of errata from the original edition of *The I*, mainly minor typos that hardly anyone would notice.

If additional textual evidence is necessary to verify Holland's obstinacy or, more positively, his single-mindedness and persistence, he describes himself—after acknowledging that he found himself "marching up the ritual stages of assistant, associate, and full professor"—as an "unconventional college professor" who has "always taught in unconventional departments." He then adds, without further commentary, that being an unconventional professor in unconventional departments "implied still other rises and falls in my professional trek" (166). We know about Holland's professional rises, culminating in being an academic superstar, but what were the falls?

I could not say, until reading *The I*, whether the third quality of the anal or obsessive personality, parsimony, was true of Holland because I knew nothing about his attitude or behavior toward money. Imagine my surprise, then—and satisfaction—when I came across the following observation in *The I* about his need to find *one* rather than several identity themes in each reader.

> One could, of course, assume more than one theme and variations, let's say, one theme for Shaw's literary and political career and another for his sex life. One would lose parsimony and I do not see what one would gain, but in principle one could analyze a life by positing two, three, or a dozen themes with variations on them. (81)

Eureka! The third of the famous triad of anal or obsessive personality qualities has now been transformed into an intellectual trait. The principle of parsimony, which is the idea behind Occam's razor, suggests that a theory should offer the simplest explanation for a phenomenon. Having a single identity theme is more elegant—and parsimonious—than having many. Parsimony—frugality—characterized Holland's personal life, as we shall see in a comment made by one of his Buffalo colleagues.

Once again I should point out Holland's misgivings about characterology and typology despite his use of these terms. He is especially ambivalent about the anal or obsessive personality. For some reason, he renames the anal phase the "nomic," a term in science that refers to a law, not to be confused with "gnomic," a word that means enigmatic or mysterious. Perhaps he chooses "nomic" over "anal" precisely because the former has no pejorative connotations. Though he tells us that psychoanalysis quickly went well beyond the categorizing of mental illness to describe the dynamic causes of symptoms, he maintains that the nomic stage of development is undeniable, along with its adult transformations. He singles out "anal" writers like Ben Jonson and Nikolai Gogol. "The writers themselves show a strange restriction of the imagination. They can elaborate endlessly in some directions (odd habits, 'humours,' for example), but turn curiously vacuous in others (heroines)" (205–6). Holland then imagines an infinity of varieties on the nomic stage, all contributing to a growing I.

Veiled Self-Disclosures

The I is tantalizing, biographically, for other reasons. In describing his personal history beginning as a bachelor student and moving toward husband, father, professor, critic, and theorist, Holland refers cryptically to himself as a "would-be poet" (x). He now characterizes himself as a feminist, an identification that continues for the rest of his life. Describing Lichtenstein's patient Anna S., who supported herself through prostitution and then had a love affair with a man for whom she was willing to sacrifice her identity, Holland writes: "As a feminist, obviously I deplore such a renunciation or the merger of her own personality into her lover's. It is not for me to judge, however" (55).

Significantly, Holland is less judgmental and more empathic in *The I* than in *Poems in Persons* and *5 Readers Reading*. For example, he repeats his discussion of Sam's responses to Hemingway's short story "The Battler" without saying anything about the student's homophobia or his own alternative explanation of Ad and Bugs as a pair of grotesque and nightmarish parents, an interpretation I suspect he later regretted because of its evasiveness. For the second time, Holland refers to his pre-literature career as an engineering student. "Biologists of the 1980s accept all kinds of electrical procedures that biologists of the 1880s would have greeted with skeptical laughter. When I was an engineering student, we thought we were doing pretty well if we got within 10 percent of the answer we were supposed to get" (304). Holland's books abound in dizzying charts, diagrams, feedback loops, and flow charts, perhaps a consequence of his training as an electrical engineer.[1] Curiously, he was willing to admit that he majored in electrical engineering at MIT but not that he was a graduate of Harvard Law School—though one can see the value of a law education for a literature professor, as the rise of the interdisciplinary movement law and literature shows. (Holland's fellow reader-response theorist Stanley Fish held appointments at various schools of law.) Holland's most self-disclosing moment in *The I* occurs when he informs us that he rejected most of his parents' values when he was in his twenties (341), a statement that he doesn't expand upon until *Meeting Movies*.

Holland does acknowledge, however, that it is hard for him to accept the paradoxical nature of identity theory. "That which is most our own to have or to be, our essential wholeness, is not our own, because the minute we review that wholeness, either we must divide ourselves into an observing self and a self observed and so cease being whole, or our supposed wholeness is something someone else must provide us" (287–8). Identity theory simultaneously gives him control and mastery but also controls him—a disturbing paradox. "That is, I feel helpless as I try to work with the between-ness of a self I once thought autonomous. I feel weakened by intrinsic limitations to science and human knowledge. I feel split if one me is really two, a self I feel immediately and a represented self" (288). We are once again reminded of Holland's struggle between critical monism and relativism.

Jacques Lacan

"Possibly I am being American in my response to Lacan's intense Frenchness" (94). Apart from Sander L. Gilman, who has written several books on how

---

[1] Robert Sprich, Holland's former student, told me that "at MIT he would put 'road maps' on the blackboard to connect the central elements of literary works. A number of students commented that these road maps looked like electrical circuits. None of them knew that Norm had, in fact, studied electrical engineering!"

Freud's racial identity as a Jew influenced the construction of psychoanalytic theory, it is unusual for a theorist to describe how nationality or culture affects the formation of his or her own theory or response to another person's theory. But Holland emphasizes the "Frenchness" of Lacanian theory. Lacan uses an identity theme to describe the Rat Man, but he limits the identity theme to Ernst Lanzer's "neurotic" self rather than finding an identity theme that applies to his entire life, as Holland prefers. A stronger criticism is Lacan's emphasis on the baby's "alienation" when encountering otherness rather than experiencing what Holland prefers to call, more positively, "community." Crediting Murray Schwartz for the insight, Holland points out that "what makes Lacan so hard to understand is that he uses the words and concepts of early psychoanalysis to state the ideas of much later psychoanalysis" (221). What is even harder for Holland to understand is Lacan's high prestige among literary theorists, producing a flood of published articles and books on the French analyst each year.

Lacan's infamous use of puns—which Holland counters with his own memorable pun, "French Fried Freud," to which I had referred in my 2007 celebration of Holland's work, only exacerbates the problem of understanding the punster. Holland notes, for example, that Lacan's expression *le nom du père* can mean the "name," the "noun," or the "no" of the father. Nor does Lacan refer to a specific historical or personal father but rather to a metaphorical one. Lacan's symbolic order privileges the father, Holland observes, but largely ignores the mother, who may have even greater power in influencing the child's development. Lacan's emphasis on the "mirror stage" (*le stade du miroir*), where babies perceive an illusory bodily unity that is later shattered, has no clinical support. "Unfortunately for the theory," Holland quips, "babies do not behave this way with mirrors" (178).

Holland concedes that there are similarities between Lacan's ideas and his own. In Lacan's theoretical system, the child's struggle to understand the bewildering world of signifying networks corresponds to the theme-and-variations aspect of identity. For Lacan, the child's awareness of lack corresponds to Holland's notion of feedback, which highlights the differences between the individual and society. For both Lacan and Holland, the most we can discover about ourselves is knowledge, not truth. There is also a blurring between fantasy and reality.

Yet these similarities pale in contrast to the radical differences between the two psychoanalytic systems. Perhaps the major difference is that whereas Lacan believes that language alienates, confuses, and seduces with the promise of understanding, an idea the French analyst conveys through obscurantist prose, Holland maintains that language, while always imperfect and often misleading, can lead to genuine insight and self-mastery. Lacan's language is often impossible to understand, and Holland is always uncomfortable with figures of speech that mask human activity. Lacan's apparent elimination of the mediating role of the ego, along with the concepts of defense mechanisms, distresses Holland:

> Hence, I think Lacan is kidding when he claims a "return to Freud." Poor dignified Professor Doctor Freud. Lacan's ministrations make him look as though, on his morning constitutional around Vienna's Ring, he had stepped into a clothing store, and the clerk sent him on his way in purple espadrilles, a cowboy hat, and wraparound sunglasses. Surely the clerk ought not also to proclaim, "See? This is the *real* you!" Lacan is more a Freudian prophet than a Freudian fundamentalist. (360)

Earlier I argued that Holland *largely* avoided polemical or polarizing prose in *The I*, but this passage is the conspicuous exception, the only moment when he uses caricature to disagree with an intellectual opponent. For the most part, Holland avoids relying on ridicule—one can only speculate on whether his law school training involved learning rhetorical techniques to overcome an adversary—but occasionally he gives way to this temptation. Even as an untenured assistant professor, Holland was willing to state that the vast bibliography on Restoration comedy was a mountain that has brought forth a mouse, but now he takes on the leading figure of continental psychoanalytic literary criticism and his many disciples in American universities. One's judgment of this passage will largely depend on his or her judgment of Lacan, but regardless, one must acknowledge that during the 1980s Lacan's prestige in the academy was at an all-time high.

William Kerrigan and Andrew Gordon

Holland's withering criticism of Lacan occurred years before William Kerrigan's 1989 essay "Terminating Lacan," which marked the end of Kerrigan's five-year intellectual love affair with the French analyst. Kerrigan, former president of the Milton Society of America and professor emeritus at the University of Massachusetts, Amherst, doesn't cite Holland in the bibliography, but he criticizes Lacan for many of the same reasons, including the French analyst's dependence upon Saussure's and Roman Jakobson's linguistic systems. Like Holland, Kerrigan argues that Lacanian psychoanalysis has no empirical confirmation or clinical utility. "To me it looks more and more like a pretentious, personless, metaphysically inspired variation on psychoanalysis, caught up in absolutist styles of thought and insufferably nationalistic polemics" (997). Again like Holland, Kerrigan faults Lacan for pretending to be an all-knowing master. "Few readers of Lacan doubt that whatever else may be said of the imperial expositor enthroned in his texts he is, for sure, to put the language of the street on it, a sonuvabitch" (999). Kerrigan is more abrasive than Holland, though, in criticizing fellow psychoanalytic literary theorists (such as Jane Gallop, Shoshana Felman, and Robert Con Davis) who have placed their faith in Lacan, an "exorcist who identifies with the demon" (1007).

Andrew Gordon, Holland's Florida colleague and friend, reaches a similar conclusion in a 1997 article. Calling Lacan the "pied piper of the intellectuals," Gordon concludes: "I cannot understand a psychiatrist who seems so anti-humanistic, who establishes a sadistic stance toward others, and who seems to have little use for people. I am sad and angry to see so many fellow critics falling for this Music Man, this Lacan man." Gordon concludes that Lacan has nothing to teach him and that he would never want to be in therapy with the French analyst.

Holland calls into question Lacanian theory for similar reasons, yet he goes out of his way in the preface to *The I* to thank two Lacanian scholars, Robert Silhol, professor of American Literature at the University of Paris VII, and Ellie Ragland-Sullivan, for their help. I have attended many PsyArt conferences in Europe where Silhol gave Lacanian presentations that were always witty but formulaic and reductive, fathomable only to those conversant with Lacanian theory. Silhol and Holland remained on good terms despite their fundamental differences about French psychoanalysis.

Holland repeats his criticisms of Lacan in later writings. In "The Story of a Psychoanalytic Critic," he adds another objection. In 1971, Holland attended Lacan's clinical case presentation at the Hôpital Sainte-Anne, and he found the French analyst's behavior toward mentally ill patients "brutal and deceptive" (254). Given the unsoundness of Lacanian thinking, Holland remains baffled by its popularity in the academy. "I can only wonder at my literary colleagues' enthusiasm for it."

In Thrall to Lacan

Lacan's cruelty to patients appears in Élisabeth Roudinesco's biography. Despite her assertions that Lacan never used his "transferential power to exploit anyone who was handicapped or mentally ill" (387), she cites examples to the contrary. She quotes a remark made by the Canadian psychiatrist and medical historian Henri F. Ellenberger, author of *The Discovery of the Unconscious*, that Lacan demonstrated "aristocratic arrogance" toward his patients. "His barbs always struck home, and he didn't spare even his patients. I remember him saying of someone, 'He's very well thought of . . . by his concierge'" (17–18). Roudinesco cites the following statement by Houda Aumont who was in analysis with Lacan shortly before his death in 1981:

> Lacan let patients come every day and then threw some of them out again. Sometimes he got into terrible furies and even punched people. Sometimes they were only "sham rages." Then he got so that he couldn't bear me not to say anything. I would be lying down, and he would come over, his face stiff with anger, and pull my hair. "Say something!" he would order. I would be shocked and feel I had to defend myself against such behavior. Then the same evening he would telephone to apologize and insist that I go over and carry on with my sessions. (394)

Lacan's cruelty as a clinician may also be seen in Catherine Millot's 2018 memoir *Life with Lacan*, which describes her affair with him during her eight-year analysis. Untroubled by Lacan's egregious sexual boundary violation, Millot, now a Lacanian analyst, still appears to be in thrall to him, as when she writes: "Lacan had no psychology; he had no ulterior motives; he did not try to second guess the other" (36). Yet she conveys incidents that would horrify most readers:

> He didn't let his [medical] audience delude themselves into thinking there was any hope for the therapeutic future of the patients. In the discussions which followed the presentation, after the patient's departure, Lacan did not hesitate to assert that one man was "fucked." He would even sometimes tell the patient this himself, which surprisingly had the effect of relieving the patient. (54)

Stuart Schneiderman is no less in thrall to the French analyst in *Jacques Lacan: The Death of an Intellectual Hero* (1983). Schneiderman left Buffalo and his career as an English professor to study with Lacan in Paris from 1973 to 1977, the only American to train with Lacan. I found myself reading Schneiderman's book oppositionally: the more he defended Lacan's role in the psychoanalytic world as an enfant terrible, the more critical I became. In what is surely an understatement, Schneiderman notes that Lacan "seems to have gone to great lengths to prevent people from finding out what he had to say" (vi). Schneiderman returns to Lacan's inscrutability a few pages later with an anecdote. "One day at his seminar Lacan was trying to explain his impenetrable prose style: if they knew what I was saying, he offered, they would never have let me say it. This has a slightly paranoid tinge, but that does not mean he was wrong" (11). Slightly paranoid? Lacan's only flaw, Schneiderman concedes, was hubris, which, he insists, was not grandiosity, though Schneiderman's readers may not see the difference.

Schneiderman doesn't deny that Lacan, who acted like a "Zen master, becoming himself a splendid enigma" (81), exerted autocratic control over his students and disciples. Schneiderman agrees with Lacan's belief that the ego is the "enemy," and he justifies Lacan's rejection of "scientific psychology" (in Schneiderman's words) "as alien to his enterprise, as a product of what he saw as the worst tendencies of American life" (109). Schneiderman viewed Lacan as a modern Lear, betrayed by his family (his brother-in-law, Jacques-Alain Miller) and followers. Schneiderman became a Lacanian analyst and practiced in New York City for many years, but according to his website, he has become a life coach, mainly because, he says, his clients want not interpretation but guidance.

Notwithstanding Holland's caricature of the Lacanian Freud in *The I*, he tends to build rather than detonate bridges between opposing systems of thought. That's what he does with deconstruction in *The I*. Admitting that deconstruction "looks for—and proves—disunity," he argues that "to look for disunity, one must presume a unity against which to see the 'dis-.'" His neat conclusion is unlikely to convince deconstructionists. "Similarly, applying a theme and variations strategy, one is constantly aware of thrusts away from the unity being sought or imposed. One could think of any given variation on an identity theme as either the construction of that theme or its deconstruction. A variation is, after all, both" (49).

Revising Psychoanalytic Theory

Holland also seeks to integrate classical drive theory, emphasizing biological instincts, with British object relations theory, highlighting relationships and psychic adaptations. In the same way, Holland affirms theorists like Nancy Chodorow, who shows in her 1978 book *The Reproduction of Mothering* how gender affects parenting. Holland cites Chodorow several times in *The I*, particularly her observation that mothering reproduces itself: mothers create women who will be mothers and men who will resist being mothered. Holland postulates a new developmental psychosexual stage, the "intrusive" stage, which he finds less problematic than the phallic stage, though he doesn't return to this idea in his later writings. In *The Psychoanalytic Ear and the Sociological Eye* Chodorow identifies a new American psychoanalytic tradition, intersubjective ego psychology. Holland would have certainly embraced ego psychology, but he remained skeptical of intersubjectivity, believing in one-person, not two-person models of psychoanalysis.

Holland continues in *The I* his subtle revision of classical psychoanalytic theory, without mentioning that decades earlier he had unquestionably accepted it. "The little girl may feel the absence of a penis as a traumatic lack that must be compensated for, as in the classical idea of 'penis envy.' Yet the wish for a penis does not seem today as biologically determined as it once did. The wish may be exaggerated or tempered or, indeed, nonexistent" (210). Freud's ideas about women and female development, Holland now recognizes, reveal more about Freud and the Viennese culture in which he lived than about female development. Throughout *The I*, Holland places more emphasis on culture's role in the formation of psychological theory than he had done years earlier. Yet he is unwilling to give up the ideas of castration anxiety and penis envy, and one wonders whether he realized the pun in the last word of the following sentence. "To be sure, in Freud's culture and our own, castration anxiety and penis envy are probably the norm" (223).

A Muse for Theorists

Paradoxically, penis envy continues to serve as a muse for theorists, as can be seen in Mari Ruti's delightful 2018 book *Penis Envy and Other Bad Feelings*. Ruti engages playfully with Freud's misogynistic idea, observing that when she came across the theory in college, she declared that Freud's a "fucking idiot," but she later came to realize that in a society that confers on the possessor of the penis obvious political, economic, and cultural benefits, "women would have to be a little obtuse not to envy it" (ix). A distinguished professor of Critical Theory and of Gender and Sexual Studies at the University at Toronto, Ruti offers in her book a critique of what she calls "neoliberal heteropatriarchy," but the most exuberant elements of her study are the personal moments, as when she writes about her encounters with a flaccid penis. Sitting in a Finnish sauna with her father when she was seven, she asked him whether he was going to die. "Startled, he said, 'Why do you ask that?' 'That tumor between your legs looks pretty bad,' I responded. So much for penis envy" (xiv).

Holland, I suspect, would have enjoyed Mari Ruti's witty book despite his likely rejection of her curious defense of impenetrable prose. "I routinely explain to my students that many postwar European thinkers saw their unintelligible writing style as part and parcel of their critique of Enlightenment rationalism" (194)—which explains, in part, her pleasure in reading Lacan: "if rationality leads to violence, then whatever is the antithesis of rationality—in this case, ambiguity, nontransparency, indecipherability, and unintelligibility—seems to counter violence" (195).

I DEFTly ARC

In *The I*, Holland elaborates upon and refines the identity theory he had propounded in his earlier psychoanalytic books. He discusses another important idea for his reader-centered approach: feedback. "Things don't just impinge on us. We impose schemata on things to assimilate them to our minds. . . . Presumably inside out and outside in and bottom up and top down all work together in intricate feedback loops at different levels" (114). As part of his DEFT model, he uses the anagram ARC to describe identity theory and the concepts upon which it is built: agency, consequence, and representation. "I DEFTly ARC" (or I ARCing DEFTly) conveys the complexity of the I:

> Identity (an agency, a consequence, and a representation as theme and variations) governs the if-thens and correlations of our bodies and our cultural values as they function in feedback loops when we feed actions into the world and it feeds responses back to us. Ultimately what decides what we will accept as truth is how that feedback feels: clear or muddied, congenial or dissatisfying, culturally coherent or bizarre. (325)

Holland admits that identity theory does not necessarily rest on the claim that identity is a theme and variations but rather on the proposition that one can *represent* a person's identity as a theme and variations. Unlike Lichtenstein, who argued that primary identity is *in* a person, a preverbal identity that can never be put into speech, Holland maintains that a statement of identity is a representation of a person and a representation of the "representer's identity." Expressed differently, identity can be perceived by the person in question, "the one 'inside' the identity"; and identity can be perceived by another person, the one "outside" (334). The distinction between inside and outside, self and other, is crucial for Holland, in part because his own identity theme involves looking intensely inside while remaining safely on the outside. He acknowledges that in his early books he had a "powerful curiosity about the self as it related to literature but an equally strong inhibition against entangling myself with that self" (285).

Holland's belief that identity is a "function of the interpreter as well as the interpretee" (354) is consonant with postmodern theory, which is skeptical of "objective reality" and "grand narratives." We can never be certain whether our identity theme for another person is correct because we all see differently. "By the very act of interpreting someone, a representer of identity does something which thereby becomes part of the representer's style or identity. 'Identity' thus has the same ambiguity as 'history.' It claims to say how things actually were, but it is necessarily someone's account of how things actually were" (36). The more identity themes we have of another person, the more knowledge, and perhaps truth, we have of that person—and ourselves. Consensus is possible, but seldom if ever does it lead to complete agreement.

In keeping with contemporary psychoanalysis, Holland argues that identity is a relational term. "Identity is between people, and because identity consists of words between people, identity presupposes a cultural realm of shared ideas and shared ways to represent them—language" (283). No matter how different identities may be, Holland suggests, one can see how converging identities exist in a community of selves.

"The Promising Writer"

How persuasive is Holland's identity theory? Of the various literary figures Holland writes about in *The I*, I'm most familiar with F. Scott Fitzgerald. Here is Holland's description of Fitzgerald's identity theme:

> How can I phrase Fitzgerald's life style? I see three basic polarities within which he interpreted his world. First, I think, he saw situations in terms of bigger powers and lesser powers, in particular, his own self and the much bigger world he resolved to conquer. Second, he tended to divide things into those which were magical and infinite as against those which were separate and broken. The most important such dualism involved himself and the world: either he magically participated in the world, or he was his stoically resolute, separate self at the risk of being emptied and broken by it. Third, actions for him took the shape of giving and being given unto as against not giving, not being given unto, and therefore being—in that world which he came back to over and over again— "broken." His great imaginative gift was that he could project all these inner ups and downs onto an infinite plane outside, as a child might.
>
> If I try to put into a single sentence a Fitzgerald-ness based on these three complex polarities—giving and being given to, big and small powers, being part of a magical world and having a separate, broken self—I come out with this: *By giving myself, I show I am part of a world*

that magically gives me infinite supplies of talent and grace; but by not giving I show I can stand alone, even at the risk of being broken. (30; emphasis in original)

Scholars have written scores of books on Fitzgerald's life and art, but Holland's brief identity theme illuminates the inner struggles of the novelist's three major male protagonists: Amory Blaine, the bildungsroman hero in Fitzgerald's first novel, *This Side of Paradise* (1920); James Gatz, who reinvents himself as Jay Gatsby in Fitzgerald's most famous novel, *The Great Gatsby* (1925); and Dr. Richard Diver in his last completed novel, *Tender Is the Night* (1934). The three male protagonists find "promising" women who ultimately disappoint, reject, or betray them.

Of the three men, Amory is the only one who is not broken at the end, but the romantic hero is disillusioned with the alluring women he has met, all variations of his highly narcissistic mother, Beatrice. Gatsby pursues the American dream in the form of Daisy Buchanan, but the closer he gets to the woman he intended to marry and her glittering world, the more the dream turns into a nightmare, as the novel's narrator, Nick Carraway, realizes. Dick Diver, a psychiatrist who is more of a writer than a clinician, like Fitzgerald himself, sabotages his life and career when he marries a mental patient, Nicole Warren, a fictional portrait of the novelist's wife, Zelda. In all three novels, the hero enters a magical world of infinite hope and promise, but in each case the hero is either unmoored, broken, or bereft at the end. Holland captures much of this complexity in two paragraphs.

Ambivalence in Fitzgerald's Identity Theme

An identity theme, Holland remarks in *Laughing*, "makes no more than the opening statement in an explanatory conversation. To formulate an identity theme is to ask for feedback and dialogue" (138). I'm struck by the perceptiveness of Holland's identity theme for Fitzgerald: nearly all the details in Fitzgerald's fiction converge on the centering theme of the "promising writer." Holland devotes scarcely more than ten pages to a discussion of Fitzgerald's life and art, but he expresses a central unifying pattern. Holland might have quoted one of Fitzgerald's most indelible observations, from the posthumously published *The Crack-Up*: "The test of a first-rate intelligence is the ability to hold two opposed ideas in the mind at the same time and still retain the ability to function" (69). Fitzgerald's insight into the nature of ambivalence holds a special place in the history of psychoanalytic literary criticism: Lionel Trilling cites the quotation in *The Liberal Imagination* (238), as does Simon Lesser in *Fiction and the Unconscious* (84). Throughout his life, Fitzgerald struggled to live with his conflicted feelings of love and hate toward women, desire, money, success, and fame, an ambivalence that informs his portrayal of his fictional characters—and, as Holland notes, his self-representation. Trilling's belief that Fitzgerald "seemed to feel that both love and art needed a sort of personal defenselessness" (239) is consistent with Holland's identity theme for the novelist.

While many novelists betray profound ambivalence toward their characters, Fitzgerald is perhaps the most striking. I would include heightened ambivalence toward self-knowledge as part of Fitzgerald's identity theme: a tension between seeing and not seeing, knowing and not knowing, learning and not learning. At his best, Fitzgerald is able to see his characters' ambivalence, as Nick demonstrates in his shifting attitude toward Gatsby. Too often, however, Fitzgerald's characters will proclaim, with the novelist's apparent blessing, that they understand themselves when, in fact, they do not, as with Amory Blaine's last words in *This Side of Paradise*: "'I know myself,' he cried, 'but that is all'" (282). Of all Fitzgerald's major characters, Nick is the only one with a first-rate intelligence, yet throughout *The Great Gatsby* he makes statements that reveal his close-mindedness and smug superiority, as when he remarks, casually, that "Dishonesty in a woman is a thing you never blame deeply" (63), or when he says, "I am one of the few honest people that I have ever known" (64). Robert Penn Warren's insight in *All the King's Men* regarding the double-edged nature of self-awareness—"the end of man is knowledge" (9)—is true in Fitzgerald's world. One never knows whether knowledge will be the "end," or goal of life, or whether knowledge will lead to one's "end," or death.

And Ambivalence in My Own Identity Theme

In writing about Fitzgerald's need to recreate through art traumatic losses and then reversing and triumphing over them, Holland exposes something similar in his own identity theme. "In the same way, the types of art that I prefer allow me to imagine risks that are real risks for me, reverse them, and come out triumphant" (231). This observation resonates in me because I, too, feel a need in my teaching and writing to return to traumatic losses, recreating and temporarily triumphing over them, all the time recognizing that repetition implies unfinished business. Understanding these losses, and returning to them throughout my adult life, has taught me to appreciate ambivalence—which is why, no doubt, I often quote Fitzgerald's words from *The Crack-Up*.

Indeed, I used the quotation in my 1971 PhD dissertation, *Joseph Conrad and the Self-Destructive Urge*. In describing Marlow's ambivalence toward Kurtz, "the nightmare of my choice," I was unconsciously describing my ambivalent relationship to Len (an instructor in the English department chaired by Holland), whom I saw as a Kurtz figure, whose last words were a blood-curling "The horror! The horror!"

I use the word "ambivalent" so often in my teaching that, a half-century ago, one of my Cornell students gave me a sign, elegantly hand-written in Gothic-style calligraphy, "Be ambivalent clearly." The white cardboard on which the words are written has turned yellow with age, but it holds a prominent position on the bookshelf in my university office, a reminder of the importance of living with sharply conflicting thoughts and emotions. In reflecting on the ways in which Holland's identity theory applies to my own life, I see striking patterns that have remained consistent in my life, giving special meaning to Holland's words "no loose ends" cited in *The I* (11) and elsewhere.

"Two Hollands"

Holland's identity theme of George Bernard Shaw is less successful, as the UCLA psychoanalytic literary critic Albert Hutter complained in a 1989 review published in the *International Review of Psycho-Analysis*. "His discussion of Shaw is alternately enlightening and remarkably reductionistic and ahistorical" (122). Hutter bemoans the repetition of DEFT and DEFTing, which strikes him as unconscious self-parody. Another criticism is Holland's oversimplification of other literary movements—a criticism Holland seems to acknowledge in "The Story of a Psychoanalytic Critic" when he confesses to his "fatal habit" of oversimplifying structuralism (245). Hutter begins and ends his review of *The I* with high praise, but he points out that there are "two" Hollands in the book:

> one is inspiringly ambitious as a theorist and, above all, as a synthesizer of theories and as a reader who loves to read; but, growing out of this first "identity," is another kind of thinker and writer, too committed not just to summary and overview but to occasional over-simplification of the ideas of others as to a constant reification of his own concepts. Whenever we are able to break through the jargon we always find ourselves in the presence of an exceptionally sensitive critic. Indeed, Holland is not only a sophisticated literary critic: he is a pioneer in the application of transference and countertransference phenomena to the psychology of reader response. (123)

The Brain of Robert Frost

"Obviously, I owe my first and weightiest thanks to Robert Frost himself," Holland observes slyly in his acknowledgments at the beginning of *The Brain of Robert Frost* (1989). "He has played the perfect gentleman throughout, obligingly demonstrating again and again the wisdom and truth of the assertions I have made about him and his brain. I trust that wherever he is, he grins his wonderful grin as he contemplates our interplay" (v).

The reader, too, may grin, for Holland's playful beholdenness sets the tone for his next book, one of his briefest, which is more about brains in general than Robert Frost's brain. *The Brain of Robert Frost* has the distinction of being the first book to show how psychoanalysis and the new discoveries of cognitive science bear upon literary criticism. Building on the identity theory of *The I*, Holland turns to one of the country's most beloved—and controversial—poets to show how our emerging knowledge of a three-pound lump of what looks like a soft avocado or cream cheese can create miraculous art.

The tone of *The Brain of Robert Frost*, however, is not always mirthful. Two-thirds of the way into the book, after expressing pride that literary critics and theorists have moved from a "genteel, somewhat snobbish 'appreciation' in the early 1950s of a canon (primarily white, English, and male) to a challenging intellectuality of interpretation, questioning, and theory," Holland reveals his darker thoughts about the profession: "My disappointment comes from the unwillingness of most of my fellow professors to question the simple text-active model" (130). Throughout *The Brain of Robert Frost*, Holland insists, as he has in his earlier books, that literary critics and theorists should base their assumptions of reading and writing on the "best psychology," that is, the most up-to-date science. Once the literary profession does this, Holland promises, the classic text-active model of reading, and a more contemporary *Rezeptionsästhetik* bi-active model championed by the German reader-response theorist Wolfgang Iser, will seem hopelessly out of date. Holland hopes, additionally, that Ferdinand de Saussure's theory of linguistics, which heavily influenced Lacan and Derrida, will be replaced by Noam Chomsky's more scientific model of psycholinguistics. Holland's growing disenchantment with literary criticism is striking in his later books, but it is palpable here, when he accuses his reader-response colleagues of not being brainy enough about cutting-edge scientific research.

The opening chapter, "Thoughts about Brains," introduces ideas upon which Holland elaborates in later books. Describing himself as a "layman" in brain research, he tells us that the brain first develops rapidly in infancy and then "ungrows" in early adolescence, when, from the ages of eleven to fourteen, the metabolic rate rapidly falls. "In effect, nature first grows and then prunes away vast numbers of neurons, axons, and synapses in the course of bringing a mammal from infancy to childhood" (7). No one knows whether personal identity is hard-wired in the brain, but a brain that changes so dramatically from infancy to adolescence may have an identity inscribed in it. Even if an identity theme is not *in* a writer, Holland asserts, he can represent it with his own identity theme. The crucial point is that there is no way to know identity except through another identity. The most far-reaching insight Holland derives from brain research is feedback—"an assumption we can safely embody in literary thinking, because it is unlikely to be upset by future researches" (12). It is through a feedback system sanctioned by cognitive psychology, not by a stimulus-response system, that Holland proposes to study Robert Frost's brain—and, more to the purpose, his identity theme as a poet, his "Frost-ness."

Chapters 2 and 3 focus on "Reading Frost" and "Frost Reading," a neat symmetry that demonstrates Holland's characteristic delight in parallelisms. After discussing Frost's poem "Once by the Pacific," he turns to the iconic "Mending Wall," a poem about the making and breaking of walls—one, I might add, that has chilling relevance to the time in which I write, late 2019, when "Build a Wall" has become a political battle-cry to demonize the other. Noting that Frost is both the speaker and neighbor in the poem, Holland contributes to the vast commentary on "Mending Wall," which he dutifully cites in the footnotes, by viewing the poem as about the establishment of a sense of self. "The wall stands, on the one hand, for separateness and identity, on the other, for one's relatedness to other humans" (27). Expanding this insight, Holland suggests that "boundary and eating and identity and the ability to deal with reality all go together. A failure to keep one's boundaries marks the most severe mental disorders" (30). The collapse of the wall betokens nothing less than the collapse of identity. Holland's conclusion is that the "warm spring-like (but dangerous) walls-down feeling corresponds to a poet's wish for a cozy but risky return to some original one-ness" (31).

From an analysis of "Once by the Pacific," "Mending Wall," and Frost's extensive correspondence, Holland offers the following identity theme: "*to manage great unmanageable unknowns by means of small knowns*" (38; emphasis in original). Holland sees a continuity between the poet's childhood and his efforts near the end of his life, while traveling in the Soviet Union, to treat Nikita Krushchev, first secretary of the Communist Party and leader of the country throughout the Cold War, as another farmer, like himself. Holland uses this identity theme to trace not only the contours of Frost's life and art but also his suicide attempt in 1894 when, at age twenty, rejected in love, he drove from Boston to North Carolina and tried to drown himself in the aptly named Great Dismal Swamp. "Surely this is a devious way to kill oneself," declares Holland. "It is remarkably characteristic of Frost, though, if one thinks of him as submitting himself to a big, mysterious entity" (40).

"The Miller's Wife and the Six Professors"

After describing Frost's identity theme, Holland devotes the next chapter, the pivotal one in the book—"The Miller's Wife and the Six Professors"—to a reader-response study of Edwin Arlington Robinson's "The Mill," a haunting 1920 poem of suicide that never once uses the word. Holland is interested in the same reader-response questions he had explored in *Poems in Persons* and *5 Readers Reading*. Now, however, instead of analyzing undergraduates and their free associations, he focuses on a workshop he taught at a large midwestern university, probably the University of Iowa, where he had spoken about the research culminating in the present book.

Referring to himself in the third person as the "Visiting Fireman"—presumably to extinguish incendiary scholarly debates but more likely to ignite one—Holland asked a group of workshop attendees to respond to five questions about "The Mill" that ranged from the most objective to the most subjective. In designing the questions, Holland sought to address the objections to his reader-response methodology offered by Jonathan Culler, who claimed in "Prolegomena to a Theory of Reading" that the main differences in Holland's students were when they "proffer the clichés and codes of different cultures." The intention behind the questions, which Holland did not share with the participants at the time, was to determine the model of reading that shaped their responses to "The Mill": a text-active model; a bi-active model where the text sets limits but readers arrive at their own interpretations; or a transactive model where readers control the response.

The results of the forty-four questionnaires, submitted mainly by English professors, "faculty wives" (apparently there were no faculty husbands), and graduate students, confirmed the extraordinary variety of responses Holland's undergraduates demonstrated years earlier. There was widespread agreement on the two factual questions about the poem, corroborating Stanley Fish's notion of an "interpretive community," but on the other questions, such as the most important word in the poem, what the miller's wife looked like, and of whom the wife reminded the reader, there was little agreement, thus undercutting the validity of either the prevailing text-active or Iser's bi-active model of reading.

One can only conclude that the responses to these three questions support a transactive model of reading in which the reader is active, the text reactive—precisely what Holland had seen in *Poems in Persons* and *5 Readers Reading*. The respondents used a two-level feedback system, an "objective" lower-level one that processed the simple reading of letters, words, and sentences, and a "subjective" higher-level one that shaped highly individual interpretations. Both levels, however, are part of the same feedback system. Holland then analyzes in depth the responses of six questionnaires and formulates a theme or themes that characterize each set of five answers. "The professors read 'The Mill' as a function of their identities, and I interpret the professors' questionnaires in terms of mine" (68). Analyzing Frost's own reading of "The Mill," Holland shows how his mind "moves in a constant rhythm of small to large to small to large, the small somehow managing to stave off or cope with or survive within the large" (45).

In the next two chapters, "We Are Round" and "Reading and Writing, Codes and Canons," Holland discusses how brain scientists confirm the idea of a central organizing principle, similar to an identity theme that governs feedbacks. These feedback loops influence our reading and writing. A feedback system, which Holland defines as the active testing of hypotheses, helps to explain the combination of sameness and difference, "objectivity" and "subjectivity," that is part of reading. He subdivides internalized cultural feedback loops into codes and canons. Codes, which are "cognitively impenetrable," govern reading, providing us with the rules by which we interpret the shapes of letters and numbers. Canons, by contrast, are highly variable, representing the forces that result in individual differences. Holland reaches three conclusions in these chapters: interpretation involves a feedback process; the feedback occurs in a hierarchy; and higher-level processes govern lower-level ones.

Murray Schwartz: Holland's Feedback System

In tracing the reading identities of the six professors who responded to Robinson's "The Mill," Holland offers his own reading identity. First, though, he discusses how his closest colleague, Murray Schwartz, views him. "Murray Schwartz knows me about as well as anybody does. He described my identity theme as a 'delight in individual differences' combined with a 'genius for unifying diverse materials.' 'Freedom and variety within the sameness of identity are the hallmarks of Norm's life.'" Adds Holland, "Surely, by this time in this book, you can see the sense in Murray's reading, for this book 'reads' me, Frost reads me, you read me" (109).

Citing Schwartz's praise here, Holland implicitly identifies his most stalwart colleague as a vital part of his own feedback system. Although he might not appreciate my next comment, Holland implies that Schwartz is, in Kohutian terms, a mirroring selfobject. Before elaborating, I should point out that Holland had many doubts about the validity of Kohutian self psychology. In *The I*, he called Kohut's contribution to psychoanalysis a "category theory, very diagnostic" (236), lacking in the logical developmental stages seen in classical psychoanalysis. Holland believed that Kohut's observations of grandiosity, mirroring, and idealization occurred mainly in transference relationships, dependent on the analyst's empathy, and thus a "far cry from the directly observable miserliness or dependency that mark classical anality or orality" (236). Holland took a wait-and-see approach to Kohut's work. "Most of all, I want to see how the theory fares in therapy over the next decade—that is the only test I know for a psychoanalytic theory, and the best" (236).

Kohutian theory has indeed fared well in the three decades following the publication of *The Brain of Robert Frost*, and it has been integrated into mainstream psychoanalytic theory. Kohut's most profound insight, in my view, is the recognition that everyone needs mirroring selfobjects to maintain the experience of continuity, coherence, and well-being. Kohut's example of a mirroring selfobject is the gleam in a parent's eye—or, I would suggest, another scholar's consistent approval. According to Kohut, people live in a matrix of selfobjects from birth to death. "He needs selfobjects for his psychological survival, just as he needs oxygen in his environment throughout his life for physiological survival" (478). Holland cites Schwartz's characterization of *The Brain of Robert Frost* as a "utopian project, like psychoanalysis, in its desire for full awareness." Holland agrees: "True. I would like us to share Nietzsche's awareness that our findings of goodness, beauty, or truth express our own need to make our world understandable. I regard his likening this book to a psychoanalysis as a still greater honor and compliment, even if no book can possibly live up to it" (169). The Holland-Schwartz collaboration was based on unwavering empathic support.

In using Kohutian theory to explain the significance of Holland's collaboration with Murray Schwartz, I don't mean to imply that either was highly "narcissistic" or "grandiose." Kohut's work is as much about healthy self-esteem as it is about wounded narcissism. Both Holland and Schwartz were highly attuned to and respectful of the boundaries between self and other, never viewing the other as merely an extension of oneself. One doesn't see in Holland's writings the shifting between the extremes of overidealization and devaluation that is a characteristic of narcissistic personality disorder, as defined by the *DSM*. Nor do the other symptoms of pathological narcissism appear, such as entitlement, the need for excessive admiration, or exploitation of others. One can regard oneself, consciously or not, as a disturber of the world's sleep, or, in this case, a master identity theorist, without having unrealistic expectations of the singularity of one's work. Holland could always count on Murray Schwartz for insight, friendship, and support. Regardless of whether they lived near each other in Buffalo or thousands of miles away from each other, they knew how to preserve closeness without identity loss. Both understood the truth of the speaker's neighbor in "Mending Wall": "Good fences make good neighbors."

The remaining chapters in *The Brain of Robert Frost* explore the implications of a transactive model of reading. In "A Digression on Metaphors," Holland refers to George Lakoff and Mark Johnson's 1980 book *Metaphors We Live By*, a classic study of the rhetorical figures of speech that shape our everyday perception of the world without our conscious awareness. A feedback model of reading requires us to acknowledge the reader's agency—not easy to do, Holland concedes, when our entire literary training has taught us to say "the poem implies" rather than "I infer from the poem." Holland finds himself slipping back into text-centered language, suggesting the challenge of changing lifelong habits. In "Literary Process and the Personal Brain," Holland states that identity theory based on a theme and variations does not lead to determinism. "Identity is constantly being created by the very feedback loops that identity governs. Also, because identity is a representation (a fiction, if you like), it is always de-centered. It is always between an interpreter and what is being interpreted" (151). And in the final chapter, "Hearing Ourselves Think," Holland emboldens us to use metaphors that express the mastery and artistry we bring to reading and writing.

Pedagogical Insights

Holland makes several intriguing suggestions in *The Brain of Robert Frost* for the heightening of emotional intelligence in the classroom. Just as students have hands-on experience in the chemistry classroom, he asks, why shouldn't they have hands-on emotional experience in the literature classroom? "Why should that be any more of a private matter to be excluded from the classroom than the bodily practice of heating test tubes, writing to floppy disks, or training mice in mazes?" (146). Sander L. Gilman makes a similar statement in *The Fortunes of the Humanities* (2000), suggesting that teaching students how to record and analyze their own dreams "becomes as strongly empirical an experience as the work in the chemistry or genetics laboratory" (53).

Holland's transactive model of reading implies a transactive model of *teaching*, in which the educator plays a more permissive role in the classroom. The teacher knows that students' differences in canons will result in differences in literary interpretations. In the following paragraph, Holland contrasts a text-centered model, which implies right-or-wrong answers, to a transactive model, which invites a variety of responses:

> In our script, the teacher asked, "What is the effect of Robinson's saying only indirectly what happened to the miller?" That question looks as though it were asking students for their feelings. Actually, however, the teacher has distanced the personal response, because the question assumes a uniform response, "*the* effect." The questioner did not ask, What is the effect on *you* of Robinson's method? How do *you* feel? And, of course, the word "effect" assumes a cause-effect, stimulus-response, text-active model. Contrast a teacher's asking, "What do you make of Robinson's saying only indirectly what happened to the miller?" (144)

What's impressive, finally, about *The Brain of Robert Frost* is Holland's openness to new ideas: the integration of literary criticism and cognitive science. He remains a paradoxicalist, fascinated by the dialectics of sameness and difference, separateness and relatedness, stasis and change. He describes, not prescribes or proscribes, how people read texts, and he doesn't privilege readings that emphasize unity over disunity. He recognizes that transactive models of reading and teaching are ideal for the classroom, narrowing the distance between teacher and students.

Yet honesty compels Holland to admit his discomfort over crossing or transcending walls, and near the end of the book he acknowledges his conflict over boundaries. "Consciously, I want to see the walls come down. Yet I know that, deep down, I feel more secure with boundaries firmly drawn.... Perhaps that ambivalence toward boundaries is why I feel so drawn to the feedback picture" (177). This is, we might say, *creative* ambivalence, an example of Holland's first-rate intelligence. Despite his fear that literary criticism will remain wedded to antiquated assumptions, Holland's lifelong search for unity is remarkable—and within character. He remains hopeful about the future: "The brain scientists are offering literary critics a utopian picture, the sciences and the humanities united round a concept of the human brain" (89).

6

Speaking in a Lone Voice among the New Cryptics

Holland's Guide and *The Critical I*

Holland's Guide to Psychoanalytic Psychology and Literature-and-Psychology (1990) contains a list of essential writings in the field, a "tendentious list," the author unapologetically admits, "designed to give you whatever knowledge reading can of how to apply clinical psychoanalysis to literature and the other arts" (4). Written mainly for undergraduate and graduate students, *Holland's Guide* is unique in that, unlike other bibliographies, it shows how psychoanalytic theory may be applied to literature. Holland is not shy in revealing his candid opinions on the best and, if not worst, least authentic psychoanalytic literary approaches. He authored the book around the time he felt he was a lone voice in an academic world dominated by Lacanians and poststructuralists who rejected humanistic conceptions of the self. Perhaps that was the main reason he wrote *Holland's Guide*: to steer students in the direction of "real" psychoanalysis.

Holland's tendentiousness starkly contrasts the more evenhanded discussion of "Literature and Psychology" by Murray Schwartz and David Willbern in the 1982 Modern Language Association publication *Interrelations of Literature*, edited by Jean-Pierre Barricelli and Joseph Gibaldi. Schwartz and Willbern don't take sides when discussing Anglo-American and French approaches to psychoanalytic literary criticism. "French psychoanalysis has been especially effective in challenging the positivist reductions of some American criticism, while contemporary American and British writing derives from new concepts of narcissism and identity that account for the relational, rather than objectivist, meanings of experience" (217). In his 1978 essay "Critic, Define Thyself," Schwartz observes that there are "psychoanalys*es* today; there is no psychoanalysis," adding sardonically, "there are schools in which psychoanalytic theorists make love and war, like critics" (2). Nevertheless, he remains hopeful that psychoanalysis will adapt to the future. The title *Psychoanalyses/Feminisms*, edited by Peter L.

Rudnytsky and Andrew M. Gordon, also foregrounds the manifold nature of both movements.

The Science of Human Subjectivity

Holland's Guide, an intellectual roadmap to psychoanalytic studies, reflects the author's familiar themes. Psychoanalysis is the "science of human subjectivity," but a reading knowledge of psychoanalysis is not enough (2). He acknowledges the widely held present view that psychoanalysis is not a science but a hermeneutic, a system for interpreting texts, but in his opinion, this approach denies the scientific credibility of psychoanalysis. Holland rarely if ever implies that psychoanalysis has its roots in both art and science, as does John Bowlby in "Psychoanalysis as Art and Science," the title of his 1978 article that locates the talking cure in the humanities and social sciences. Thrice repeating the credo that "all knowledge is personal knowledge" (59, 66, 71), Holland rejects philosophical approaches for excessive theoretical abstraction. He is blunt in his criticism of French poststructuralism. After the Second World War, "French intellectuals decided that an autonomous self was a bourgeois, capitalist fiction. Even mentioning 'identity' or such concepts can get you into trouble among the French and their American disciples" (67).

Freud's greatest achievement, in Holland's view, was the discovery of free associations, allowing insight into unconscious thoughts, feelings, and behavior. One problem with Lacanian theory, according to Holland, is that it minimizes the importance of an analysand's actual free associations. Another problem is Lacan's belief that ego psychology merely perpetuates neuroses and self-deception. "Therapy should aim," Lacanians insist, "not to strengthen the ego (as in American ego-psychology) but to recognize the split, de-centered self, which is 'the truth of the subject'" (46). No Lacanian himself, Holland enlisted the help of Ellie Ragland-Sullivan to authenticate his representation of the French analyst's views.

Holland continues to distance himself from psychoanalysis's early antifeminist theory, quoting the anthropologist Margaret Mead who "cannily pointed out that Freud's theories about women were those of a six-year-old boy" (11). True, we might add, but Holland was much older than six before he challenged Freudian thinking about female psychology. "Happily," he declares later in *Holland's Guide*, "Freud's boyish theories on women do not pass muster" (62). Declaring himself a feminist, as he had done in *The I*, he is suspicious of Franco-American psychoanalytic feminist criticism, which has resulted in a "paper feminism" (52), losing sight of real oppression in women. It's likely that these unnamed authors—Shoshana Felman, Jane Gallop, Luce Irigaray, and Ellie Ragland-Sullivan, all of whom are cited in *Holland's Guide*—would find this statement offensive. Holland promises to tell the truth as he sees it, but he characteristically discloses little about himself except for one puzzling comment. Searching for the truth, he tells us, is a key component of his identity theme "because of a childhood with a lot of unreality in it—or things I wished were unreal and didn't really know whether they were or not" (59). It is the most mystifying personal remark that appears anywhere in his published writings. Holland doesn't reveal whether he explored this unreality in his personal analysis. Indeed, he has nothing to say about therapy or therapeutic techniques, a subject he felt was far from the literary aims of *Holland's Guide*. Another reason for the omission, I suspect, is his rueful recognition that psychoanalysis is not as effective a therapeutic strategy as he once believed. Recall his statement in the second edition of *Poems in Persons* that some of Freud's ideas have "fallen by the wayside," such as the belief that insight cures (10).

The Dodo Bird Effect

Had Holland included a brief section on the therapeutic efficacy of psychoanalysis, he might have discussed the "dodo bird effect." In 1976 Saul Rosenzweig published an article with the colorful subtitle: "At Last the Dodo Bird Said, 'Everybody Has Won and All Must Have Prizes.'" The subtitle comes from Lewis Carroll's 1865 novel *Alice in Wonderland* in which all the contestants who run around a lake are judged to be winners. Rosenzweig's counterintuitive conclusion was that all forms of psychotherapy lead to beneficial outcomes. As Bruce E. Wampold and Zac E. Imel note in *The Great Psychotherapy Debate* (2015), common factors— "hope, expectation, relationship with the therapist, belief, and corrective experience" (33)—are far more important in therapy than a particular theoretical approach. The Dodo bird effect, also called the common factors theory, remains highly controversial. Some studies have concluded that treatments like cognitive behavioral therapy produce better outcomes for particular disorders, such as anxiety, than other treatments. Nevertheless, Wampold and Imel argue that dozens of meta-analyses used to compare multiple evidence supported treatments confirm Rosenzweig's thesis. The differences among treatments, Wampold and Imel maintain, are small or nonexistent. "The Dodo bird conjecture has survived many tests and must be considered 'true' until such time as sufficient evidence for its rejection is produced" (156).

In his magisterial *The Noonday Demon: An Atlas of Depression*, Andrew Solomon cites the classic 1979 study by Hans Strupp and Suzanne Hadley concluding that *any* form of psychotherapy is effective provided certain criteria are met. In Solomon's words, the criteria included "that both the therapist and the patient were acting in good faith; that the client believed that the therapist understood the technique; and that the client liked and respected the therapist, and that the therapist had an ability to form understanding relationships." Adds Solomon, the experimenters "chose English professors with this quality of human understanding and found that, on average, the English professors were able to help their patients as much as the professional therapists" (111).

Holland might have said that the psychotherapies spun off from psychoanalysis provide merely symptom relief rather than deep structural change. He concedes in *Holland's Guide* that psychoanalysis may no longer be the treatment of choice, but he nevertheless maintains that it remains necessary for a mental health professional's education. "I find it hard to imagine anyone who intends to practice a 'talking cure' who does not need the special insight into self and others the experience of psychoanalysis gives" (74).

Mistrustful of Philosophy

"I reject a philosophical, really a magical, version of psychoanalysis," Holland admits in the *Guide*, "because I think it confuses words and things. I want some proof of what psychoanalysis asserts, something the mind can rest on more securely than the reasons one might believe, say, Nietzsche or Saint Augustine" (61).

Holland's rejection of philosophy, which he oddly associates with magical thinking, is puzzling for at least two reasons. Freud acknowledged that the poets and *philosophers* had long ago discovered the unconscious; moreover, Nietzsche profoundly influenced Freud's thinking, as Ronald Lehrer points out in his 1994 book *Nietzsche's Presence in Freud's Life and Thought*. Jonathan Lear, a member of the philosophy department at the University of Chicago and a distinguished psychoanalyst, reveals in his 2017 book *Wisdom Won from Illness: Essays on Philosophy and Psychoanalysis* that his life as a philosopher has helped him as an analyst: "Over time, I have come to see that the unconscious functions not unlike a philosopher. I would not have been able to see this if I had not spent my life in philosophy" (4). Philosophical inquiry, Lear insists, lies at the heart of psychoanalytic technique. "Even in the minutest here-and-now moment of a psychoanalytic session, how can we evaluate it properly if we have only the vaguest sense of what we are aiming for—or why we are aiming for that rather than something else?" (157).

Bernard J. Paris

Holland's Guide refers often to Bernard J. Paris (1931–2019), the former director of the Institute for Psychological Study of the Arts at the University of Florida. Paris authored more than a dozen books on the intersections of literature and psychology, including *Karen Horney: A Psychoanalyst's Search for Self-Understanding*, a biography that was a *New York Times* Notable Book in 1994. Paris was especially interested in Third Force (humanistic) psychology, which includes such figures as Horney, Abraham Maslow, and Carl Rogers, all of whom believed that an evolutionary constructive force motivates us to strive for our potentialities. No psychologically oriented literary critic was more gifted in analyzing fictional characters than Paris, as two of his books demonstrate: *Conrad's Charlie Marlow* (2005) and *Dostoevsky's Greatest Characters* (2008). Both Holland and Paris supported each other's work and read each other's manuscripts before publication, but they practiced different forms of reader-response criticism. Whereas Holland looked at the identity themes of various readers, Paris analyzed his own vastly different responses to the same novels over time.

In "No Longer the Same Reader," the opening chapter of *Rereading George Eliot*, published in 2003, Paris compares his current literary responses to those in his 1965 book (based on his Johns Hopkins PhD dissertation), *Experiments in Life: George Eliot's Quest for Values*. Like Holland, Paris credits the experience of being in therapy for deepening his understanding of literature; but unlike Holland, he discusses specifically what he learned about himself. While writing his dissertation, which was directed by J. Hillis Miller, Paris subscribed to "George Eliot's Religion of Humanity," which gave him a humanistic value system he desperately needed at the time. He convinced himself that the highest good was self-sacrifice, living for others, as she claimed. Paris championed her philosophy, he admits ruefully, with a proselytizing fervor. After completing his degree, however, he unexpectedly lost enthusiasm for Eliot's writings. As he recounts in *Imagined Human Beings* (1997), while in therapy in the early 1960s, he pursued psychoanalytic theory in the hope of reaching life-transforming insights:

> I did not connect it to the study of literature until one memorable day in 1964 when I was teaching Thackeray's *Vanity Fair*. Again it was Horney

who helped me to understand what was mystifying me. While arguing that the novel is full of contradictions and does not make sense thematically, I suddenly remembered Horney's statement that "inconsistencies are as definite an indication of the presence of conflicts as a rise in body temperature is of physical disturbance" [Horney, *Our Inner Conflicts* 35]. In the next instant I realized that the novel's contradictions become intelligible if we see them as part of a system of inner conflicts. I have been unfolding the implications of that "aha" experience ever since, with profound effects on my view of literature. (4–5)

The eureka experience enabled Paris to realize that what was most important to him was what Abraham Maslow calls self-actualization, a discovery that allowed him to reach a deeper understanding of both himself and George Eliot. Paris began to see in her fiction a struggle, of which she was almost certainly unaware, between a mimetic portrait of character, where her protagonists struggled boldly to achieve fullness of life, in all its richness and complexity, and the rhetoric surrounding each character, the devices a novelist uses to influence readers' moral and intellectual responses. "Mimetic characters are almost bound to subvert a work's formal structure, because literary form and realistic characterization involve canons of decorum and universes of discourse that are incompatible" (*Rereading George Eliot* 14).

Paris developed a psychological approach to mimetic literature that offers an answer to the question that Holland agonized over for decades: Can we treat fictional characters as if they are real? Paris answers the question affirmatively with the following qualification. Realistically drawn characters "are not flesh and blood creatures, of course, but are imagined human beings who have many parallels with people like ourselves" (*Imagined Human Beings* xi). He argues convincingly that exploring the behavior of fictional characters in motivational terms, using the best psychological theory, is not only possible but also necessary.

In his 1991 book *Bargains with Fate: Psychological Crises and Conflicts in Shakespeare and His Plays*, Paris explores the psychodynamics of trying to control fate by living up to its presumed dictates before our wishes are granted. The terms of the bargain, he points out, are shaped by our predominant defensive strategy—similar to ego psychology though with an emphasis on the ambiguities of self-idealization. "Bargaining is a magical process in which conforming to the impossibly lofty demands of our neurotic solution (which Horney calls 'a private religion') will enable us to attain our impossibly lofty goals" (2). Notwithstanding their different approaches to reader-response criticism, both Paris and Holland are keen anatomists of human character, demonstrating the interrelationships among literature, theory, and self-understanding.

A Synthetic Study

Despite its partisan nature, *Holland's Guide* reveals his best efforts to synthesize various approaches to psychoanalytic literary criticism. After describing the three chronological phases of psychoanalysis, Holland argues that each phase incorporates what preceded it. His "break" with David Bleich does not prevent him from citing four of his fellow reader-response critic's books. Moreover, he credits Bleich for helping him examine the "real responses of real readers" (56). Holland enlists the help of the Jungian psychoanalyst Paul Kugler to write brief descriptions of both classical and modern Jungian criticism. Holland cites Frederick Crews's 1970 book *Psychoanalysis & Literary Process*, though he doesn't remark on the UC Berkeley critic's rejection of psychoanalysis in *Out of My System* (1975). Citing his own research on identity theory and feedback loops, Holland insists that real psychoanalysis rests on observation and testing, admitting that he becomes "uncertain and troubled" (61) when theorists stray too far from couch, clinic, or laboratory.

Seeking Holland's Approval

Academics rarely admit in public that they are flattered or hurt when their writings are cited or ignored by renowned scholars. Imagine my delight, then, when I came across a reference to my 1985 book *The Talking Cure* in *Holland's Guide*. I felt like I had been invited to one of Gatsby's fabulous parties, with Holland's beaming face conferring long-sought scholarly approval, as Nick felt in the presence of his host: "It was one of those rare smiles with a quality of eternal reassurance in it, that you may come across four or five times in life. It faced—or seemed to face—the whole external world for an instant, and then concentrated on *you* with an irresistible prejudice in your favor" (*The Great Gatsby* 52). It's true that Holland devoted only one skimpy sentence to my book, a sentence that was merely descriptive, not evaluative: he notes that I "collected and studied" dozens of novels about psychoanalysis (78). I would like to believe, of course, that *The Talking Cure* cannot be adequately interpreted and evaluated in under 362 pages, which is the length of the book. Nevertheless, I couldn't help grinning when I saw my book listed in *Holland's Guide*, which suggests, apart from the vanity of all things, my need for his recognition and approval. Much has been written about the analyst's recognition of the patient, but a teacher's (or scholar's) recognition of the student (or younger colleague) is no less important.

The Critical I

The Critical I, published in 1992, is Holland's final attempt, before the fictional "A Cyberreader Defends" and *Death in a Delphi Seminar*, to convince his fellow academics that they have gone astray in privileging texts over readers. The book represents a punning "I-ing" of contemporary literary criticism. *The Critical I* is Holland's most polemical book, betraying Swiftian indignation over the state of literary criticism. He presents a potent corrective for what he believes to be a disease of the intellect: the annihilation of the self.

Part One, "I-ing an Audience," focuses on three viewers' responses to the 1975 Franco-German porn film *Story of O*, directed by Just Jaeckin. The film was based on the 1954 novel of the same name, written by the French author Anne Desclos, under the pseudonym Pauline Rage—though the author's identity was not disclosed until after the publication of *The Critical I*. "Norm" is one of the three viewers, and he treats the film, a story of sadomasochistic female sexual submission, as an intellectual puzzle to be solved. In Holland's words, "Norm re-created the film around the idea of a person's achieving domination by possessing rules. He could possess or master this movie or woman or world by solving abstract, intellectual puzzles of the kind he felt comfortable with" (14–15). In centering his reading of the film around the idea of learning the rules, or laws, of the world, Holland omitted disclosing that his lifelong impulse to "master the strangest, most disturbing things, making them ethically coherent," initially led him to become a lawyer, which he gave up in favor of literature.

The Kuleshov Effect

Reaffirming the model of reading he had advanced recently in *The I* and *The Brain of Robert Frost*, Holland examines the "Kuleshov effect," a 1929 experiment described by the Russian director and theorist V. I. Pudovkin. In the experiment, a young painter or theorist, Lev Kuleshov (1899–1970), took non-expressive close-ups of the Tsarist matinee idol Ivan Mosjukhin and then inserted them into three different scenes in a film, the first showing a plate of soup on a table, the second portraying a dead woman lying in a coffin, and the third depicting a little girl playing with a toy bear. Unaware of the director's secret, the audience believed that Mosjukhin looked differently in each shot, praising his acting ability when, in fact, his expression was the same and had nothing to do with the film. "The public raved about the acting of the artist," Pudovkin effused in 1942. "They pointed out the heavy pensiveness of his mood over the forgotten soup, were touched and moved by the deep sorrow with which he looked on the dead woman, and admired the light, happy smile with which he surveyed the girl at play. But we knew that in all three cases the face was exactly the same" (*The Critical I* 42).

In Holland's view, the Kuleshov effect demonstrates how high-level canons use low-level codes. The audience appears to react automatically to the film, as if the film is controlling them, but, as cognitive psychologists would point out, we are applying hypotheses to what we see. The audience, Holland explains, was using different sets of codes relating to soup, death, and desire. "The feedbacks by which I read Mosjukhin's expression continue and build on the feedbacks by which I see a cut from a bowl of soup to a man's face as different angles on one event" (45). The Kuleshov effect thus reveals the extent to which viewers (or readers) project their own feelings and identities onto a film (or text). The theory behind the Kuleshov effect is not stimulus-response, Holland concludes, but projection. Additionally, Holland calls into question the influential "suture" theory of film response, in which the spectator is passively sewed or sealed into a film, forced into the position of seeing what the camera sees. The suture theory implies either a text-active or bi-active approach that is less convincing to Holland than a spectator-active or reader-active model.

The Kuleshov effect has passed into mythology, but it's not clear, Holland concedes, whether the experiment took place, largely because the original film footage was destroyed during the Second World War and because Kuleshov made contradictory statements about the film near the end of his life. Nevertheless, the Kuleshov effect has been repeatedly confirmed. A 2016 behavioral and eye tracking study conducted by Daniel Barratt and his associates showed that the thirty-six participants who looked at twenty-four sequences of neutral faces across six different emotional conditions made the appropriate choice more frequently than the alternative options. A 2017 study by A. M. Baranowski and H. Hecht demonstrates the auditory implications of the Kuleshov effect: music significantly influences emotional judgments of facial expressions.

"Thirty Days Hath September"

Part Two, "I-ing Critics," begins with the analysis of an unusual "poem": "Thirty Days Hath September." Holland recalls Theodore Spencer's 1943 burlesque, which highlights "excepting," followed by various poststructural critics whom Holland enlists. He pseudonymously calls the first professor "Adrian Ade," who deconstructs, as would Jacques Derrida, the usual binaries in the poem; "Ben Bee," another Derridean scholar who views the poem as the basis for the creation of an aftertext; "Cecil Cee," a film critic who privileges iterability, the "volatility/mobility" of all signs; and "Daniel Dee," a British critic who compares the poem to a rugby game. Daniel Dee alone senses the hidden agenda in Holland's request to analyze the poem. In Holland's words, Daniel Dee "concludes that 'Norm is getting exactly what he wants . . . Material for his article,' while his own motive is 'To impress Norm. Touchè'" (81). The response earns Holland's silent assent.

As a psychoanalytic critic, Holland felt like "something of an odd duck" among literary theorists or, changing metaphors, someone "outside the fray" (82). The situation makes him uncomfortable, particularly because two years earlier he had authored the *authoritative* guide to literature-and-psychology. In a later chapter, he discusses two psychoanalytic critics, "Eli Ede," who recalls, to his embarrassment, that he could not correctly identify the number of days in each month when he was a student; and "Fred Fay," who maps Lacanian theory onto the poem. Fred Fay's wife, who is also a professor and Lacanian, presents her own interpretation of the poem, pointing out "the very interesting and true observation that it is in leap years (i.e., when February has its peculiar 29th day) that women are, exceptionally, permitted to propose marriage to a man. In Lacanian terms, one could say that February's love-cum-relationship specialness succeeds in subverting or at least inverting the Symbolic Order" (95).

We can identify the real Fred Fay and his wife. In his acknowledgments early in *The Critical I*, Holland expresses gratitude to Henry Sullivan and his wife, Ellie Ragland-Sullivan, a prolific and well-known Lacanian scholar who taught at the University of Florida and then at the University of Missouri-Columbia, where she was professor of English and honorary French professor and edited the Lacan journal *Newsletter of the Freudian Field*. Reading Ellie Ragland-Sullivan's seven books on Lacanian theory, one realizes the truth of Holland's following observation.

> In the Fays' associations to "Thirty days," as in all Lacanian criticism I have read, the associations tend to be abstract, intellectual, cultural, or etymological rather than personal. If they are "free associations," they do not lead to the Fays' work or family. There is, then, a distinction to be drawn between Lacanian psychoanalytic criticism and other kinds as to what is an "appropriate response." (102)

I suspect Holland knew that acknowledging his gratitude to Henry Sullivan and Ellie Ragland-Sullivan would compromise their anonymity in *The*

Critical I, but it's unlikely that his characterization of their associations to the poem disturbed either of them.

After discussing poststructural responses to "Thirty Days Hath September," Holland gives his own response, based on his rich free associations to the poem, which he had to memorize for Mrs. Guiney, his middle school teacher. "Dear Mrs. Guiney," "I failed you," he confesses, and then he explains how he never succeeded in learning the days of the months when she taught her seventh- and eighth-grade pupils mathematics and penmanship "with a vengeance." Holland was lucky enough to be one of her favorites, and he remembers her affectionately despite her severity. He associates his teacher with two other elderly women who favored him: his wife Jane's aunt, who with her husband made possible his psychoanalytic education, and his grandmother. He then offers the most self-disclosing statement that appears in any of his publications prior to *Death in a Delphi Seminar*. "Let me stop and, in the manner of psychoanalytic work (as I do it anyway), try to hear (with, as psychoanalysts say, the third ear) what these associations are saying. Elderly women of whom I was a little afraid, because they were aggressive, strong, even fearsome, but who favored me" (88).

There's nothing sensational about the self-disclosure, nothing that will surprise Holland's supporters or critics. He doesn't explore the Oedipal implications of his attraction to older women nor any possible tension with their husbands, whom the son-figure might desire to conquer. It's hard to imagine someone as precocious as Holland failing to remember how many days there are in each month of the year, though his next statement piques our curiosity: he never learned the days of the year "until many years later when I got involved with investments, financial reports, and interest payments" (88), a possible reference to his unhappy experience as a lawyer. In explaining how his associations to the poem evoke three older women who were initially threatening but who nonetheless favored, even loved him, he notes how the crucial rhyme on "ember" in three of the months has a double meaning to him: "one, the importance of having or being a bright, glowing 'ember' or a 'member,' the other the 'embers' I associate with the dying of a fire or the dying of a year in September and November and December" (89). There is another meaning of "ember" apart from Holland's rem*ember*ing. Only a rigid Freudian, or a Lacanian obsessed with sexual puns, would point out the phallic meaning of member. However strained this reading may be, it is consonant with Holland's own reading of his identity theme, as revealed by his interpretation of the poem. "I would talk of infant separating from (fearsome) mother, the young and growing from the old and dying, and male boy from female mother. I would wish for the parceling out of goodies to that favored boy: love, psychoanalytic training, fame, long life" (89).

War on the I

Part Three, "I-ing Theorists," is the longest and most consequential. Having attended a 1980 conference titled "Self and Other," Holland realized gloomily that the I is in big trouble. "The best literary theorists of today seem to have declared war on the I or the self, and *you's* and *I*'s are vanishing wherever you (if you will still allow me that pronoun) look" (107; emphasis in original).

Holland's frustration is evident throughout the final part of *The Critical I*. In using the agonistic metaphor *war* to describe these literary critics, Holland surely knew, as Lakoff and Johnson point out repeatedly in *Metaphors We Live By*, that combative metaphors only heighten tension, in this case, in scholarly debates. Whereas in his earlier books Holland sought to build bridges between American psychoanalytic theory and European-imported deconstruction and Lacanian analysis, now he perceives the futility of his efforts. Dismayed that Derridean and Lacanian text-active models continue to be taught in the academy, silencing or ignoring reader-active models of identity like his own, he throws up his hands in consternation, but his exasperation, paradoxically, energizes his writing.

As an example of his vexation, Holland cites unnamed friends, more sympathetic to Barthes and other French poststructuralists than he is, who offered an historical explanation for the disappearance of the self in France. "After the undistinguished performance of most French people during World War II, postwar existentialists like Sartre, Camus, or de Beauvoir laid a heavy weight of responsibility on the individual. Work like Barthes' tries to vanish that postwar guilt by vanishing the individual" (174). French poststructural supporters would counter that Holland's belief in ego psychology and a self capable of making intelligent choices is illusory, an example of American naivete. "Yes," I can imagine Holland saying, "but I would prefer to believe in the future of an illusion than its alternative, nihilism."

Unlike the American psychoanalytic literary critics who study the relationship between self and text, the French poststructuralists, Holland bewails, are awash in a sea of language, swept away from human reality. Labeling poststructuralists like Roland Barthes, J. Hillis Miller, Jacques Derrida, Paul de Man, Michel Foucault, and Jonathan Culler as the "New Cryptics"—a satirical expression he was the first to coin—Holland argues that they resemble the old New Critics. The poststructuralists, Holland insists, are fatally attracted to Saussure's fundamentally defective theory of linguistics, which Noam Chomsky rendered obsolete. In a rare moment of reconciliation, Holland attempts to show how Lacanian theory has elements in common with his own theory, but he is not hopeful he will make any converts.

Holland devotes separate chapters to the poststructuralists who claim that the concept of the self as a recognizably stable subject, capable of rational choice, has never existed. These figures include Jacques Derrida (two chapters), Roland Barthes, Michel Foucault, Umberto Eco, and Jacques Lacan. Holland also returns repeatedly to other prominent poststructural theorists such as J. Hillis Miller and Jonathan Culler. These theorists use a conduit metaphor to describe text-active models of reading. "The speaker puts ideas (objects) into words (containers) and sends them (along a conduit) to a hearer who takes the ideas/objects out of the word/containers" (*The Critical I* 114). Holland also devotes chapters to Saussure and Chomsky, quoting the cognitive linguist Mark Turner's statement that Saussure's theory was "Wrong on a grand scale" (141), mainly because the abstraction of Saussure's system cannot account for the historical changes in language, the creation of new words, or the context of what is being said.

Holland's Counterattack

A mind-boggling number of articles and books have been written by proponents and opponents of a "humanistic self," but suffice it to comment briefly on Holland's rhetorical strategy in *The Critical I*. He takes his opponents' arguments seriously and, in my view, represents their positions as fairly as possible within a few pages. ("It would be a superhuman task to try to read all of contemporary literary theory, and it would be tedious beyond belief" [209].) Holland's sardonic voice in *The Critical I* recalls D. H. Lawrence's thunderous jeremiads in *Studies in Classic American Literature* (1923). Whereas Lawrence asserted that the "proper function of a critic is to save the tale from the artist who created it" (2), Holland seeks to save the self from the theorists who would write it out of existence. Never trust the teller, only the tale, Lawrence exhorts his readers; never trust the norm, only the norms, Holland urges *his* readers.

Foucault, though no deconstructivist, seemed to be gleeful about the self's eventual disappearance. "It is comforting, however, and a source of profound relief to think that man is only a recent invention, a figure not yet two centuries old, a new wrinkle in our knowledge, and that he will disappear again as soon as that knowledge has discovered a new form." To which Holland responds, "Oh, my. Here I was just getting used to being around on this planet. Foucault may have found the disappearance of man comforting, but I don't, particularly when I think about the blunderers in the white house with the red telephone" (108)—one of Holland's few political barbs. Using a biblical metaphor, he claims that literary critics who base their theory on Saussure's linguistic system are hopelessly conservative. "They trot out Saussure against psychology or reader-response the way fundamentalist preachers quote the Bible to cry down evolution or family planning" (146). Saussure's system is finally for Holland a "flat earth theory" (155).

Calling Derrida a "prestidigitorial" theorist, one who makes the self disappear upon command (166), Holland uncharacteristically turns to Foucault, who, according to experts, decided near the end of his life that his separation of language from human agency was a grave error. "He learned from his mistakes, they say, as he followed his central themes: how human beings constitute themselves as subjects; how they treat one another as objects; ultimately, how the individual is supposed to constitute himself as a moral subject of his own action. Good for Foucault. He rescued the I from the death-grip of Saussure's linguistics" (178). Linguistics, Holland could have added, remains fiercely contested in the academy. "It is soaked with the blood of poets, theologians, philosophers, philologists, psychologists, biologists, and neurologists, along with whatever blood can be got out of grammarians," writes Russ Rymer in *The New Yorker* in 1992. Later Holland quotes a statement by Anthony Wilden, one of Lacan's earliest commentators, who noted "Lacan's logical view of the subject as the 'empty subject'—a subject defined only as a locus of relationships." Holland's reaction? "Abracadabra, the self itself has vanished!" (200).

J. Hillis Miller awakens Holland's strongest ire. He satirizes Miller's pronouncement that the "self is a figurative construction—a metalepsis." Mocking lit-crit jargon, Holland then uses a word known by even fewer readers. "In case you are not up on the cacozelic terms of modern rhetoricians, rather like Hamlet's parody of Osric, 'metalepsis' is the figure of speech that attributes a present effect to a remote cause" (107–8). (Technically, metalepsis is a word used in a new context.) Most of us will need to google cacozelia to find out that it is a "stylistic affectation of diction, such as throwing in foreign words to appear learned" (*Wiktionary*). Holland has it both ways here, satirizing Miller's highly specialized rhetorical vocabulary while using a more recondite word. One recalls Hemingway's biting observation that anyone who pulls the erudition or education on you hasn't any. Like Miller, Culler evokes Holland's angriest criticism. He finds it "astonishing, not to say scandalous" (149), that Culler's chapter in his 1982 guide written for "non-specialists, particularly students," published by the Modern Language Association, does not even mention the linguistic revolution following Chomsky's work. In a later chapter in Part Three, Holland enlists the help of fellow reader-response critic Stanley Fish, an intellectual maverick whose idea of interpretive communities resembles Holland's notion of canons. He notes that his own views on reading resemble Fish's despite differences in theoretical language. Holland then makes a comment I have never seen before. "I almost never find a statement by Fish with which I disagree. That, of course, has the unhappy result of leaving me much to applaud but little to say about him in a polemical discussion like this" (191).

A Thorn in His Side: Lacan

By contrast, Holland has much to say about Lacan, most of it disapproving. Because Lacan is a fellow psychoanalytic theorist who insisted he was returning faithfully to Freud, he remained a thorn in Holland's side, a prickly figure Holland could not ignore. What must have been especially galling to Holland was Lacan's enormous prestige in the academy, prestige that seemed to increase as a result of the inscrutability of his writings.

Lest he be accused of misreading, Holland wisely relies on Lacanian scholars to tease out meanings from the notoriously mystifying French analyst. Holland has done his homework in surveying the vast field of Lacanian scholarship, quoting from, among others, John P. Muller and William J. Richardson's *Lacan and Language: A Reader's Guide to Écrits* (1982), Ellie Ragland-Sullivan's *Jacques Lacan and the Philosophy of Psychoanalysis* (1986), and Bice Benvenuto and Roger Kennedy's *The Works of Jacques Lacan: An Introduction* (1986). Holland goes out of his way to praise these scholars, calling Muller and Richardson the "authors of an excellent study" (197), commending Ellie Ragland-Sullivan's "fine study of Lacan" (197), and lauding Benvenuto and Kennedy for their "especially lucid explication of Lacan" (198).

Holland argues that Lacan was wrong in two major ways. First, Lacan relied uncritically on Saussure's outmoded signifier-signified conception of language. One can understand Lacan's error in the 1930s, before the Chomsky revolution that began with the publication in 1957 of *Syntactic Structures* swept away Saussure's beliefs, but contemporary Lacanians, to Holland's horror, continue to accept Saussure's thinking. Second, Lacan reinscribes Saussure's theory into psychoanalysis, converting linguistic concepts into psychological ones. Lacan assumed that language, the process of signifying, denies the possibility of agency or choice. The signifier thus dominates and overwhelms the subject, rendering it into a slave, a position that Holland categorically rejects. He objects to other aspects of Lacanian theory, particularly the "mirror stage," which is central to his notion of child development. Most contemporary literary theorists remain unaware of the growing body of empirical studies that show no evidence of young children regarding their image as "unified" when looking into a mirror. Nor is there evidence that infants feel "jubilation" when looking at a mirror, as Lacan claims. Besides, Holland adds, how can we know what infants are thinking?

Daniel N. Stern's landmark 1985 study *The Interpersonal World of the Infant: A View from Psychoanalysis and Development Psychology* provides strong empirical evidence that "some senses of the self do exist long prior to self-awareness and language" (6). Based on close observations of early mother-child interactions, Stern argues that infants begin to experience a sense of an emergent self from birth. "They are predesigned to be aware of self-organizing processes. They never experience a period of total self/other undifferentiation. There is no confusion between self and other in the beginning or at any point during infancy" (10). Stern refers to Lacan only once, cautioning that mirroring is a misleading clinical term because it suggests "complete temporal synchrony" (144) that doesn't exist.

Lacan's mistrust of empiricism has carried over to Lacanian analysts, as Nancy Chodorow reports in a fascinating footnote in *The Psychoanalytic Ear and the Sociological Eye*:

> At the 2000 Delphi psychoanalytic conference, a French analyst assigned to introduce and chair an American infant researcher's presentation announced that she did not believe in empirical research and then walked off the stage and left the room as the American was presenting. In France at a conference two weeks earlier, an American empirical researcher on psychoanalytic process had been booed off the stage as he tried to present. In my own limited experience, I have not seen or read of such dismissal—though of course I have seen and read radical disagreements—going in the other cultural direction. (70, n.17)

Chodorow doesn't refer to "French Fried Freud," as Holland does, but she shares his insistence that psychoanalysis must rest on scientific support.

> In the academic humanities, we find that psychoanalysis is thought to begin and end (with the exception of Lacan and related theorists) with Freud. As a result of militant opposition to ego psychology, moreover, academics often write as though Freud's contribution ended in 1922, just after the death drives but before the structural theory, which has been of central importance to most approaches to clinical practice. (169, n.2)

Holland does not dismiss all of Lacan's observations. The French analyst was right to emphasize the importance of language in psychoanalysis, and he even hints at the role of feedback loops representing the external world, the "Other," though Lacan's emphasis on the "alien" and "repressive" goes against Holland's belief in the possibility of rational understanding and control. We use language imperfectly, Holland concedes, invoking T. S. Eliot's haunting words in *Four Quartets*: "And so each venture / Is a new beginning, a raid on the inarticulate / With shabby equipment always deteriorating" (*The Critical I* 206; Eliot, 128).

Hope for the Future

The Critical I has a two-part conclusion, "Looking Backward" and "Looking Forward," a pairing that showcases Holland's fondness for symmetry. In the former, he dismisses the deconstructive claim that its interpretations are politically radical, citing Andrew Gordon's quip that it's hard to believe the president of General Motors trembles whenever Derrida uses his word processor. "What current literary theory badly needs," Holland adds, "is less theory, more irony" (213). In the latter, he expresses hope that in the future literary theory will avoid self-imprisoning binaries. On the penultimate page of *The Critical I* he declares that unlike the poststructuralists who assert that language is the only reality, he believes in the self, not an autonomous entity that acts independent of reality, but a self that acts endlessly through higher and lower feedback systems. "It is a field very like the endless sea of intertextuality, but the players on my field are not texts but people. Imperfectly, flickeringly perceived, but people nevertheless" (219). He ends cheerfully, optimistically. "In short, we need not lock ourselves into the stifling either-ors of today's literary theory. We can have it both ways, several ways, indeed many ways. So let's" (232).

"A Must"

I located only one review of *The Critical I*, written by Nicolae Babuts, a French professor at Syracuse University. "Holland's book is a must for anyone interested in literary theory and criticism. Brilliantly written, cogently argued and fast-paced, it captures the excitement of the theoretical confrontation between those who believe in the existence of the I and those who try to make it disappear" (310). Babuts's only criticism is that unlike Holland, he believes Lacan's statement that the unconscious is structured like language is a rich concept. "Lacan's error," Babuts suggests, "is not so much in assigning a dominant rule to signifiers but in generalizing this dominance, taking it to an extreme and neglecting the wider dynamics of our cognitive processes." He ends his review by agreeing with Holland's "invitation to accept a world-view supported by data from interdisciplinary sources, a world-view whose time has come" (312).

7

Penning Fiction

"A Cyberreader Defends" and *Death in a Delphi Seminar*

Holland's science fiction story "A Cyberreader Defends" appears in Daniel Rancour-Laferriere's 1994 edited volume *Self-Analysis in Literary Study: Exploring Hidden Agendas*. I was at the time general editor of New York University Press's Literature and Psychoanalysis series, and I had invited Professor Rancour-Laferriere, a well-known Russian scholar who has authored many books on psychoanalytic literary criticism, to assemble the volume. Holland's essay, one of eight psychoanalytic studies in the volume, is the only work of fiction—and the most unusual. "A Cyberreader Defends" is the least self-disclosing essay in the volume, but it offers a glimpse of Holland's personal psychoanalysis and his lingering doubts over the validity of his life's work, identity theory. The short story is also a warm-up for his novel, published one year later.

"A Cyberreader Defends" takes place in the "Buckydome" bar in a time distant from the "Gutenberg" era of the printed page. We overhear two English professors in the same department, "Norbert," a crusty 65-year-old academic given to theoretical rants, and his young feminist colleague, "Norma," worried that her scholarly research on films of the 1960s and 1970s will sabotage the possibility of tenure. Something dreadful has befallen Norbert, and Norma finds herself trapped into hearing his woeful story. He reminds her of a "real Ancient Mariner with the genuine hunted look. Or do I mean haunted?" (85). "A Cyberreader Defends" recalls Coleridge's "The Rime of the Ancient Mariner," but in Holland's version, an unspeakable crime has undermined the hoary professor's most cherished beliefs. The crime is not as visible as those that appear in *Death in a Delphi Seminar*, but its consequences are momentous for the troubled Norbert.

A Severed Lifeline

It turns out that Norbert's confession is not that he has killed an innocent albatross but that he has almost lost his bearings as a result of an encounter with a Lacanian who has tried to cut his "lifeline." Norbert growls that the Lacanian *barre*, the line the French analyst used in reference to Saussure's concept of the sign that separates the signifier from the signified, threatens his connection to the real world. Holland reminds us that although fictional characters cannot be treated like real people because they do not exist outside of a text, they are real in another way. "Hamlet has everything a real man would have except for location in space and time. Same with events, places, settings. Real life but without location—except in textspace. Not really real at all—but real another way" (89). Norbert further contends that texts cannot "do" anything on their own. Additionally, he vents his anger at "W'Iser," Wolfgang Iser, the German reader-response critic who advocates a bi-active model of reading that Holland regards as wrongminded. "They tried to change the model on me," Norbert grumbles to Norma. "If you believe the text is hard, that it walls some things off from you, then it will. Wall-ness becomes part of the hypotheses you bring to bear in textspace. You look for walls, so you find walls" (101–2).

The fun of reading "A Cyberreader Defends" lies in Holland's delightful wordplay and his creation of two impassioned academics who are at different stages in their careers. The story is filled with neologisms: "Cyberreader," "textspace," "Barthing" (a computer server whose name puns on Holland's Buffalo colleague, the novelist John Barth), "wrinkly" (old person), "moodlight," and "phallicity," along with expressions like "thank goddard," an allusion to the French filmmaker Jean-Luc Godard. Reading conventional print occurs in the "Gutenberg Zone," and free associations become "mindsurfing."

"A Cyberreader Defends" is narrated from Norma's point of view. As the story opens, she regards Norbert as a "grumpy old geezer," particularly since he calls her, patronizingly, "little Norma," a "pretty young thing" (84). Another reason she is uncomfortable speaking with Norbert is because he is a "three-step full [professor]" who is likely to be on her tenure and promotion committee. Through her perceptions of Norwood, Holland pokes fun at his own physical appearance. "Norwood was always losing it, out in the Zone. He was a thin man, ascetic-looking, very tall but humped over, spidery hands, classical features, shaved head, although you could see there hadn't been much more than a fringe to shave" (85). If this weren't enough to evoke the reader's laughter, Norma observes that he "rolled his billiard ball of a head around for a minute or two, as if he were trying to work a stiff neck out" (86).

Norma grouses throughout the story about Norbert's "damned digressions," something one doesn't detect from Holland's writings, but in his conversations with colleagues—who knows? Holland captures the power inequality between the two academics. Surfacing sector 17-C, "late Willie," Norbert admits that he can do scholarship for fun, "not like you, not for tenure," a thoughtless statement that angers Norma. "That made me mad," she tells us. "I wanted to say I did it for fun, too, but he might have gotten the wrong idea" (87). Their bantering has erotic overtones, as she admits in a passage charged with linguistic if not libidinous energy.

> It was no bad thing that he liked to talk to me, but wrinklies like Norwood sometimes get the wrong idea, because we smoothies at the U talk pretty gamy. I could tell he was not averse to a little flirtation, but I figured I could keep it within bounds. And besides, I sometimes wondered what it would be like to do it with a famous old guy like him. (85)

Holland knew he was taking a chance here, risking professional censure; but it would have been riskier had Norbert expressed sexual desire for Norma.

The age difference between Norbert and Norma betrays shifting attitudes toward women. Norbert begins cursing the Barthing server, expressing a nostalgic wish for the past. "Whatever happened to the beautiful cocktail waitress in a leather mini and net stockings?" Norma responds indignantly, "she went the way of 'my girl will call your girl.'" Norbert apologizes and then, invoking his age, begins to praise the past when she cuts him off. "The bad old days? When there was sexism built into all your cybering?" (92–3). Norma has the last word here, expressing the authorial point of view.

Seeing a Merlin

A riskier self-disclosure occurs in another passage when Norbert confesses to Norma that his anguish over Lacanian theory has compelled him to consult his Merlin:

> He was sixty-five if he was a day, and I gasped. "You still use a Merlin?"
> "And damned glad I do. Otherwise I'd never have gotten out of this."
> "Wait a minute. What kind of Merlin?"
> "A regulation WOP."
> I winced. "We don't use that word."
> "Sorry. A WOM. An old timer. 1964 issue."
> "A WOM?"

"Wise Old Man. Haven't you learned your acronyms?"
"It's been a long time since I needed a Merlin. Mine was a WOW. I terminated psychoanalysis a good five years ago."
"*Twenty* years ago for me! But I sure as hell needed one this afternoon."
(97; emphasis in original)

Holland is willing to go only so far here, and instead of offering readers his real psychoanalyst's name, Elizabeth Zetzel, he refers to seeing "old Threik," a reference, he explains in the acknowledgments, to Theodor Reik. Norbert doesn't travel through time to speak to Threik; instead, he summons the analyst's wisdom through an introject, an internalized image. "He saved me," Norbert exclaims, and when Norma asks him how, he responds, "Shrinkery. Tie the now to the then with the lifeline." Through analysis, Threik takes Norbert all the way back to adolescence, where he recalls a brown-haired girl who "dumped" him. The figure evokes his first love, also with brown hair, his mother, who represents to him *Paradise Lost*, which happens to be one of Norbert's, and Holland's, favorite poems, cited throughout the story. "The Merlin had reestablished all the sinews," Norbert enthuses. "Mother tongue. Mother land. Threik cast off and rocketed to wherever he lives. I started to cyber back" (97–8). Rarely has psychobabble sounded so inventive.

The Narcissism of Minor Differences?

One can only imagine what old Threik would have discussed with Norbert. Would he have reassured Norbert that his identity theory remained valid regardless of a bi-active or reader-active model? Would the analyst have added that because the controversy can never be resolved scientifically, why fret over it—particularly since both models preserve reader agency? Would the classically trained Threik have encouraged Norbert to reflect on Freud's evocative theory of the "narcissism of minor differences," expressed in *Civilization and Its Discontents* (1930) and elsewhere, the "phenomenon that it is precisely communities with adjoining territories [or adjoining theories?], and related to each other in other ways as well, who are engaged in constant feuds and in ridiculing each other" (*SE*, vol. 21, 114)? How would Norbert have responded to this clinical insight? One can only wonder.

Apart from embodying gender and age differences, Norbert and Norma reveal the contrasting pedagogical and playful aspects of Holland's personality. This explains why he has given the two characters his own names. Norbert quotes effortlessly from *Paradise Lost*, instructs Norma on poetic scansion and the use of the caesura, and lectures her on the etymology of the word "buxom": "Indo-European *bheug-*, to swell, or bend, bow, elbow, bight, and so on" (87). Norbert's pedantic lecturing of Norma reminds me of the time Holland lectured me during my disastrous meeting with him in his office. Unlike me, Norma can hold her own, and, amid his rants, she knows how to pique his curiosity by offering psychoanalytic insights into *Paradise Lost* that he had not seen before, such as Milton's portrayal of women as lack, the centrality of the father-son relationship, and the primal scene imagery. She's not afraid to offer her opinion of the Miltonic Adam who questions why God created women: "this fair defect / Of nature, and not fill the world at once / With Men, as Angels, without feminine." Norma's response? "Weird is our J-M. Sick. Really! These dead white European men!" (94).

"A Cyberreader Defends" is academic without being boring. Holland succeeds in conveying his *ek-statis* for reading. Probing a long stretch of text, Norbert compares the experience to looking at fractals. "Deep in or far out—the same configurations, but varying" (90). An allegory of reading, the story rejects both the classic text-active and the recent bi-active models in favor of Holland's transactive approach.

Norma proves to be a fast learner, understanding everything Norbert has tried to teach her. She repeats his lesson so that readers will understand Holland's truth. "You're saying you have to connect both to your lifeline and the textspace. Otherwise you get flipped into these other models and lose the allness of it" (103). Grinning in agreement, Norbert adds a new metaphor, comparing reading to sailing. "You don't just slue around in wind and wave. You can't see wind, you can't define a wave, but you work with them, you shape direction and purpose out of shapelessness" (103). At the end of the story, Norbert recognizes in Norma a dependable colleague, smart, feisty, outspoken, fearless. His final words to her reflect his professorial judgment: "And listen, little Norma. You've got my vote and a lot of other people's. Quit worrying" (110).

Self-Analysis in Literary Study

"A Cyberreader Defends" is thoroughly entertaining, but Holland's anxiety that Lacanian psychoanalysis has severed his lifeline pales in contrast to the anxieties and fears expressed by the other seven contributors to *Self-Analysis in Literary Study*. In his introduction to the volume, Daniel Rancour-Laferriere quotes Jane Tompkins's observation in "Me and My Shadow" that she is tired of avoiding personal matters in her professional discourse.

"I think people are scared to talk about themselves, that they haven't got the guts to do it" (Rancour-Laferriere 24; Tompkins 25). The contributors to *Self-Analysis in Literary Study* would agree that while self-disclosure is always risky, exposing one's vulnerability if not narcissistic injury, there are many benefits: "self-analysis can be a boon to other-analysis, including psychoanalysis of literature" (29).

Therapist self-disclosure has been a noteworthy development in contemporary psychoanalysis, particularly the analyst's disclosure of countertransference, as Theodore J. Jacobs pointed out in 2019. "Today its exploration as a way of obtaining valuable information about the self and others is widely accepted and highly valued. In 1970, I could not imagine ever seeing this day arrive" (160). The day arrived earlier for clinical psychologists and counseling psychologists. A 2001 study by Marna S. Barrett and Jeffrey S. Berman found that "clients receiving psychotherapy under conditions of heightened therapist disclosure not only reported lower levels of symptom distress but also liked their therapist more" (597). Therapist self-disclosure improves both the quality of therapy and the outcome of treatment. A 2014 meta-analytic review by Jennifer R. Henretty and her associates of the impact of counselor self-disclosure showed similar results. "[C]lients/participants had favorable perceptions of disclosing counselors and believed themselves more likely to disclose to a disclosing counselor" (197).

Many of the contributors to *Self-Analysis in Literary Study* write about gut-wrenching experiences. David Bleich, in "How I Got My Language," discusses how his parents' Yiddish language and culture, of which the German-speaking Kafka was part, highlight the ever-present perils of German culture. Bernard J. Paris, in "Pulkeria Alexandrovna and Raskolnikov, My Mother and Me," explores one of the major issues of his therapy.

> My obsession with academic success and my anxieties about it were disrupting my relationships and putting me under so much pressure that writing was a torment. I did not attribute these difficulties entirely to my mother, but she had played and continued to play a major role, and one of my objectives in therapy was to free myself from her influence. (113)

Barbara Ann Schapiro, in "Attunement and Interpretation: Reading Virginia Woolf," admits that she couldn't understand Woolf's ambivalence toward her maternal characters until she understood her own. "Twenty years ago it was too threatening for me to see these characters as anything other than strong and heroic. New dimensions opened up after I was able to analyze my narcissistic anxieties and to understand and empathize with my own mother's fragility" (185). In "'The Grief That Does Not Speak': Suicide, Mourning, and Psychoanalytic Teaching," I acknowledge the central role of the repetition-compulsion principle in my life as a result of my mentor's suicide. "By converting a passive situation (standing helplessly by as a friend committed suicide) into an active one (becoming a psychoanalytic critic and doing research on self-destructive writers), I have gained a degree of control over a frightening situation" (43). All of these self-disclosures are far more personal than the ones we see in "A Cyberreader Defends."

And yet it would be unfair to minimize Holland's self-disclosures in the story. Nothing less than his life's work, his reputation as a theorist, was at stake. It was not easy for him to admit in public, under the veil of fiction, that the Lacanians had thrown him into a crisis, resulting in his "hovering" (98), or vacillating, unmanned by his own indecisiveness. How could he not feel threatened when the leading literary theorists of the age claimed that his language was not his own and that his understanding of psychoanalysis was not, as the Lacanians would say, authentically Freudian? Viewed from this perspective, Holland's confession in "A Cyberreader Defends" was bold and risky, though nothing like those seen in his novel.

Theory as Unconscious Autobiography

Curiously, Holland was never interested in the extent to which a theory reveals hidden aspects of the theorist's personality. Nietzsche was the first to formulate this provocative idea. "It has gradually become clear to me," he writes in *Beyond Good and Evil*, "what every great philosophy up till now has consisted of—namely, the confessions of its originator, and a species of involuntary and unconscious autobiography" (386). Every theory thus bears the theorist's signature—and unique identity. Without crediting Nietzsche, Robert D. Stolorow and George E. Atwood develop this idea in *Faces in a Cloud: Subjectivity in Personality Theory* (1979). As an example, Stolorow and Atwood show that the

> defensive operations which Freud employed to protect the idealized vision of his mother from invasion by a deep unconscious ambivalence conflict fatefully left their mark on his theory of psychosexual development and its central metapsychological reifications, in which the sources of evil were internalized, hostility was displaced onto the father, and the split-off bad maternal image was relegated largely to the psychology of the girl. (68–9)

As evidence, Stolorow and Atwood point out a discovery Elizabeth Zetzel made in *The Capacity for Human Growth* (216–28): the stark contrast between Freud's few references to the Rat Man's mother in the published case study and the more than forty references to the highly ambivalent mother-son relationship in Freud's original clinical notes.

Death in a Delphi Seminar

Once I started reading *Death in a Delphi Seminar*, I had difficulty putting it down. Indeed, it consumed much of a weekend, and when I finished, I wanted more. The book is fascinating, completely accessible even as it deals ingeniously with the most arcane lit crit jargon (what Holland has wittily called elsewhere the language of the "New Cryptics"), and accurate in its characterization of postmodern theory. Plus it is witty, clever, ironic, allusive, and sophisticated without being pretentious.

It should come as no surprise that the two antagonists in Holland's 1995 novel are in thrall to the New Cryptics. Nor is it a surprise that Holland portrays American reader-response criticism engaged in a life-or-death struggle with Parisian-dressed theory. The big surprise is that the dean of American psychoanalytic literary criticism has written for the first and only time a novel to advance his ideas. SUNY Press asked me to evaluate *Death in a Delphi Seminar* when the manuscript was submitted for publication, and the above comment, which appears on the book jacket, was my conclusion. I feel the same enthusiasm for the novel a quarter of a century later. Now, however, I have a deeper understanding and appreciation of how the novel fits into the entirety of Holland's work as a theorist and teacher.

"Inside every critic is a frustrated writer" (48), observes "Norman N. Holland" in the novel. The quotation marks surrounding the English professor's name suggest that he is, like the other characters in this double murder mystery set in 1984 at SUNY-Buffalo, an invention of the author of the same name. And yet anyone who is familiar with Holland's publications will recognize his kinship to the fictional professor. Holland has written a metafictional whodunit that cleverly dramatizes the major ideas he developed in his long career as a psychoanalytic theorist.

Death in a Delphi Seminar is both a mystery and a *roman à clef*, but it reads like nonfiction. Some readers may believe that Holland is describing an actual murder that took place in one of his literary seminars. Holland has constructed a suspenseful plot that holds the reader's interest from beginning to end. In searching for the solution to two puzzling crimes, the reader is initiated into the often-arcane world of contemporary literary theory, a world profoundly influenced by Lacanian and Derridean ideas. *Death in a Delphi Seminar* may be considered a "theoretical thriller" in that it dramatizes the challenges to traditional humanistic scholarship posed in different ways by Holland, Jacques Lacan, and Jacques Derrida. Although the fierce theoretical disputes of the academy may not be of much interest to those outside its ivy towers—the reason academic politics is so vicious, Henry Kissinger, a former academic himself, has sardonically observed, is because nothing is at stake— Holland's story confirms that these battles have far-reaching consequences.

As *Death in a Delphi Seminar* opens, we learn that a female student in "Holland's" graduate seminar on reader-response criticism has been murdered, presumably by another member of the class. The narrative arises out of the conflicting texts surrounding Patricia Hassler's death: transcripts of police interviews, student essays, department memos, newspaper accounts, the professor's private journal, and the inner musings of Detective Lieutenant Norman "Justin" Rhodes, who is in charge of solving the murder. All eight members of the Delphi seminar are suspects—the seven students plus an untenured assistant professor who is sitting in on the course to learn more about Holland's distinctive psychoanalytic approach to literature.

Hassler was an obnoxious student, disliked by everyone in the seminar. "Holland" himself is a suspect in the murder, for he has, like the others, the "motive, means, and opportunity" (197), an expression that Holland took from reading the indispensable how-to book *Mystery Fiction: Theory and Technique* (37) by Maria J. Rodell, whose help he acknowledges at the end of the novel. He learned from Rodell how to maintain dramatic suspense as long as possible. What happens in a mystery should always be considered before it happens, Rodell advises: "Carpentry composes one-half of the work" (9). In constructing the novel, Holland proves to be an expert carpenter. Hassler's strident views alienate everyone in the seminar. Before the murder is solved, a second corpse appears, that of an ominous interloper who has been secretly disrupting the seminar by writing hate letters to the other students. Lieutenant Rhodes's task is to solve these two perplexing crimes. Rhodes succeeds, largely by enlisting the help of Holland's controversial theory of reading.

The Delphi Seminar

To appreciate the pedagogical force of the novel, the reader needs to understand the workings of the actual Delphi seminar that Holland pioneered. In 1975, Holland published an article in *College English*, cowritten with Murray Schwartz, on "The Delphi Seminar." The article became the basis for a book with the same title published in 2009. Focusing on the Delphic Oracle's injunction, Know thyself, the seminar used psychoanalytic techniques to enable students to analyze their personal style of reading and writing. In the first half of the course, students write about their free associations to various poems and stories. These free associations, which the students then circulate to their classmates, resemble those of a patient in psychoanalysis. In the second half of the course, the students analyze their own reading styles. In doing so, the students arrive at their own reading identities. Murray Schwartz's influential reader-response article "Where Is Literature?" appears in the same issue of *College English*, arguing that all literary interpretation is a "coming together between the opposition of subject and object, here and there, me and you" (764).

A Unique Collaboration

Holland's long and fruitful collaboration with Murray Schwartz remains unique in the history of psychoanalytic literary criticism. As Schwartz recounts in his lively essay "Psychoanalysis in My Life: An Intellectual Memoir," published in 2018 in *American Imago*, of which he is now editor, he arrived in Buffalo in 1970, the year Holland founded the Center for the Psychological Study of the Arts, which Schwartz directed from 1970 to 1979. For the next thirteen years, until his departure to the University of Massachusetts at Amherst, Schwartz worked closely with Holland to establish the Buffalo English Department as the country's leading center for psychoanalytic studies. The "Buffalo" school of criticism was never as famous as Yale's, and there were few if any "Hollandians," unlike the many Lacanians and Derrideans, but several graduates went on to become notable psychoanalytic literary critics, including Dianne Hunter, Richard Wheeler, Joel Fineman, and Christopher Bollas.

Holland warmly expresses gratitude to Schwartz in nearly all of his books. Schwartz does not mention *Death in a Delphi Seminar* in his intellectual memoir, but his description of the process closely matches what we see in the novel. "The Delphi method built upon trust," Schwartz writes, "encouraging the greatest possible consciousness and tolerance of differences in reading to explore the recurrent patterns of response we each bring to the literary transaction" (139). Citing Erik Erikson's notion of trust in his 1963 book *Childhood and Society*, Holland and Schwartz express the same need for trust in their 1975 *College English* article: a student in a Delphi seminar "must risk a little, and to do that he must trust" (791).

Holland and Schwartz were good friends, sharing a love for Shakespeare and psychoanalysis, but they were temperamentally different, as we can see in a comparison of their intellectual memoirs. Holland never explains in "The Story of a Psychoanalytic Critic" what led him into analysis. Schwartz does:

> I had not arrived there only to learn about analysis, but to cope with powerful mixed feelings about my precocious professional life. Why had I taken on so much, and so fast? Why was I so frequently angry with colleagues when they seemed to inhibit my sense of autonomy? After all, was I not striving to fulfill my "mission" in life, to be first among equals, to create new interdisciplinary opportunities, to make happy families? Why, as a colleague once put it, to my chagrin, did I need to "have a finger in every campus pie"? (144)

Both Holland and Schwartz were interested in building bridges between psychoanalysis and the academy, but whereas the former was primarily concerned with writing, developing a comprehensive theory of reading based on the reader's identity theme, the latter turned to academic administration to advance psychoanalytic teaching and research. While continuing to teach and write, Schwartz was a university administrator for nearly thirty years. Following his departure from Buffalo, he became dean of Humanities and Arts at the University of Massachusetts, Amherst. In 1991, he became the provost of the Claremont Graduate University, and in 1997 he moved to Boston where he became vice president for Academic Affairs at Emerson College.

Schwartz's candor here and elsewhere is compelling. He is not afraid to describe his working-class Sephardic Jewish family, his competition with his identical twin, and even his Freudian slip when referring to his younger non-twin brother, Jerry, who was born with a severely clubbed foot that required painful operations in infancy. "I vividly remember his screams when scars were cauterized during hospital visits, though he also learned quickly to use his cast (at first I typed 'caste') as an effective weapon" (127). He also describes in detail his dreams, including his fear/desire of "going too far" professionally. Like Holland, Schwartz tells us that analysis did not fundamentally change his identity but rather helped him understand himself. Unlike Holland, Schwartz discloses that since his first analysis in Rochester, New York, he has returned to analysis at transitional moments in life for "help in navigating the emotional complexities of inner and outer crises" (145). Again unlike the polarizing Holland, Schwartz has always desired to "mediate conflict" (126), a goal that made him an outstanding academic administrator.

Teaching Psychoanalytically: Fact and Fiction

It is during the second half of the semester that the Delphi seminar becomes challenging—and problematic in the novel. Each week a different student is "it," as in hide-and-seek: the student receives interpretations of his or her identity theme from the other students and must react to their interpretations. Although Holland tells his students to censor highly personal material—they are to disclose abstract themes in their lives, not actual events—some students may become angry or defensive. Self-disclosure is, of course, difficult and fraught with peril; psychoanalysis, as Freud well knew, often brings out the worst in people. It is not clear whether any of Holland's seminars in Buffalo, where he taught for close to twenty years, and at the University of Florida, where he founded the Institute for Psychological Study of the Arts and taught from 1983 until his retirement in 2008, at age eighty-one, was emotionally explosive. Holland and Schwartz report no untoward events in their 1975 *College English* article. The fact that Holland successfully taught the Delphi seminar for so many years indicates his ability to avoid serious problems.

In the novel, however, a fatal problem arises, not so much because of the seminar itself but because of the instability of two students: Hassler and Christian Aval, a young Frenchman who first met her at Yale, where they studied literature together and came under the influence of Yale's preeminent English Department, with its French poststructuralist approach to literature. After the breakup of a stormy love affair with Hassler, in which each accused the other of plagiarizing an honor's essay, Aval followed her to Buffalo, where they enrolled in "Holland's" seminar, despite the fact that their Franco-American beliefs about literature clashed with his Anglo-American views.

"There's Nothing outside the Text"

Ironically, the students' instability accurately reflects their deconstructive belief that everything in language is built along a series of linguistic differences and that, consequently, every text reveals internal inconsistencies. Taking deconstruction to its most nihilistic conclusion, Hassler and Aval assert that nothing exists outside of language. Echoing one of Derrida's most controversial claims, Hassler exclaims, "*Il n'y a pas de hors-texte*," which she then translates as "There's nothing outside the text" (306), though a more accurate translation would be "there is no outside-text." Language, Hassler and Aval insist repeatedly, is inherently duplicitous. In the novel's brief and admittedly schematic account of postmodernism, Nietzsche argued that the subject is only a fiction or construction; Foucault came along and proclaimed that the author is merely a projection of how we think about literary texts; then Roland Barthes followed with the claim that the reader is a composition of other texts of linguistic codes. In such a postmodern world, neither writers nor readers exist, only language. Gone, too, is the human self. Holland has expressed these criticisms in the books preceding *Death in a Delphi Seminar*—*The I, The Brain of Robert Frost, Holland's Guide*, and *The Critical I*—but now he imagines the consequences of these ideas in real life.

In seeking to exorcise the specter of poststructuralism, which he regards as both excessively theoretical and theoretically unsound, Holland insists on the danger of any totalistic philosophical system that abrogates autonomy and free will. When Rhodes asks Aval to identify himself and acknowledge that he is being tape recorded, he betrays the absurdity of his deconstructive credo: "I would make the claim that I cannot be recorded in the mode you indicate. That is, language flees, leaving behind only the traces of disparate and destabilized meanings. No effort to fix it can succeed" (22). Aval is right, in one sense, when he says that he is always a "shifter"; he is also shifty. By novel's end, he acknowledges that at Yale he plagiarized Hassler's senior honor's thesis—plagiarism was paradoxically his "one authentic act" (325). Hassler's death turns out to be suicide, consistent with her identity theme, that of someone "who's preoccupied with turning things against herself or against others" (260). Her massive inner rage recalls Holland's description of Sylvia Plath's identity theme discussed in his 1977 article "Literary Suicide." Hassler's self-inflicted death, along with Aval's murder of the interloper and subsequent disappearance and probable suicide at the end, suggests the bankruptcy of any philosophy that does not affirm humanistic values.

Despite his critique of the more radical assumptions of postmodernism, Holland agrees with its basic premise that we cannot perceive a real, true, or objective reality. It is for this reason that each character in Holland's fictional Delphi seminar sees Patricia Hassler differently: there are as many different interpretations as there are interpreters. The difference between Holland and other postmodern literary theorists is that whereas many of them privilege language over readers, he affirms that readers create interpretations based on their characteristic identity themes. And whereas many postmodern theorists seem to be dismissive of lived experience, preferring to see reality as they wish, not as it is, Holland examines real readers by studying their interpretive responses to literary texts. Holland would certainly agree with Freud and Charcot that theory is good but it doesn't prevent facts from existing—facts that each reader perceives differently.

Unlike Lacan, Holland maintains that we control our language more than it controls us. He also believes that the ego can reconcile the competing claims of the id and superego. Holland is in the tradition of Heinz Hartmann and Ernst Kris, both of whom emphasized the adaptive, integrative functions of the ego. In further contrast to Lacan, Holland has created a psychoanalytic model of identity that is consistent with the findings of cognitive psychology and neurophysiological research into the functioning of the brain—a psychoanalytic model that is as scientific as possible. In all his writings, Holland has argued that if psychoanalysis is to progress, it must be based on empirical observation and scientific testing, discarding those elements of its theory that are not verifiable—although as we have seen, he was slow to criticize classical psychoanalytic theory.

Some readers will take issue with Holland's critique of postmodernism and his faith in the future of psychoanalysis. Other readers will enjoy his satirical attack on the New Cryptics, whose obscure language has produced so many unreadable academic texts. Whether one agrees or disagrees with Holland's ideas, he is never guilty of linguistic mystification. (He would be dismayed by the fashionable belief that clarity is merely an ideological position.) Literary and psychoanalytic theories come alive in *Death in a Delphi Seminar* in ways that they seldom do in textbooks or in the classroom. I suspect that an increasing number of graduate students and professors would secretly agree with the statement of a member of the Delphi seminar who, exasperated by the dominance of theory in the academy, yearns for a return to the study of imaginative literature: "What I didn't anticipate was that the study of literature wouldn't be the study of literature. It would be this dreary 'theory.' That's why I'm taking this seminar. It has to do with real people reading books" (223). *Death in a Delphi Seminar* does not ring the death knell for theory, which flourished in the academy in the last quarter of the twentieth century, but it reminds us of the enduring power of literature, which can never be reduced to ideology.

Holland's Wordplay

Holland must have had fun writing *Death in a Delphi Seminar*. There are many in-jokes, some obvious, others not. The former includes the name of Detective Yorrick ("Alas, poor Yorick! I knew him, Horatio," laments Hamlet); the offices and classrooms reserved for faculty "with pull" located in Fiedler Hall (named for Holland's colleague Leslie Fiedler); and the name of the medical examiner, Dr. Welder (recalling the Viennese psychoanalyst Robert Waelder, whose 1936 essay "The Principle of Multiple Function:

Observations on Over-Determination" Holland cites in many of his writings). The interloper's name, Felix Kulper (*felix culpa*, Latin for "happy fault"), evokes his twisted mordant humor in writing anonymous seminar squibs to the Delphi students and his culpability in disrupting the class. Some of Holland's provocative puns demonstrate Freud's belief that humor allows one to express veiled (or, in this case, unveiled) aggression, as when a member of the seminar uses the word "Decockstruction" (38). Other puns are in questionable taste, such as the name of Sgt. Herman Gehring, evoking the Nazi leader Hermann Göring, head of the Gestapo. Some of the puns are overly clever, as with the name "Abe Poria," suggestive of the deconstructive word "aporia," popularized by Derrida to express an irresolvable impasse or contradiction in a text. A student apartment building is located on "Masling" boulevard, the name of a University of Buffalo psychology professor, Joseph Masling. Some of the novelist's statements reveal anxiety over his new career as a fiction writer, as when "Holland" observes, "I'm pretty good at reading identities, but I'm not sure I could write a novel or a play" (72).

Twinning

In creating his cast of characters, Holland included academics whom he knew personally. Apart from "Holland" himself, there is another faculty member of the seminar, Wally Sisley, who has an identical twin. "In one of the responses he wrote for the seminar, he said he felt in the shadow of his older brother, his twin" (20). "Holland" is intrigued by the idea of twinship. "I find his account of being a twin fascinating, and it suggests to me a confusion about his identity (a comedy of errors that wasn't funny at all)" (147). In *Laughing* Holland remarks that Freud answered Pascal's question, why do we find something funny in identical twins? Because, in Holland's words, "Experience tells us that each living being is different and demands a considerable amount of effort to understand. When we see identical twins, we have that effort, and the extra goes off as laughter" (50). In his novel, Holland displays the twins' tricks, showing how Sisley's twin appears in the seminar without anyone noticing the difference.

Without disclosing that Holland used this aspect of his identity in *Death in a Delphi Seminar*, Schwartz admits in his intellectual memoir that his life was shaped by his identical twin, Albert, who was "born to (re)join me after nine minutes" (127). The "twins," as he called his brother and himself, were fiercely competitive, graduating from their large high school "first (Al) and second (me), for once reversing the usual order" (128). Central to Murray Schwartz's identity was twinship: "After all, my twin was quite literally a reflection of myself, and his success was also mine, his shortcomings a source of my shame, my advantages and triumphs a guilty pleasure" (129). Interestingly, though Schwartz does not comment on this in his intellectual memoir, his remarks in the coauthored *College English* article reveal his twinship identity theme. "I find an I," he states in his response to the writing of another member of the Delphi seminar, "that protects against merger and is defined by the desire to lose itself in merger, a dilemma, being oneself without the inside/outside boundary" (Holland and Schwartz, 797).

Raymond Federman

"Holland's" day begins badly when he receives a rejected manuscript in the mail and an advertisement for a rival's book. Hassler attempts to drive "Holland" crazy with envy by constantly praising another colleague's graduate seminar. "Phil Feder's Theory of Fiction," she enthuses—"now *there's* a seminar. I've scarcely begun to digest it all. Phil can recite reams of *Finnegans Wake*, theorize any critical position, analyze rock and roll, problematize pro wrestling, for God's sake—he can do *anything*" (114; emphasis in original).

Feder is based on Holland's celebrated colleague Raymond Federman (1928–2009), a Franco-American novelist and academic who taught at SUNY-Buffalo from 1973 to 1999, where he was distinguished professor of English and Comparative Literature and director of the Creative Writing Program. Holland was almost certainly aware of Federman's essay "Critifiction: Imagination as Plagiarism" appearing in his 1993 book *Critification: Postmodern Essays*. Had Aval decided not to kill the interloper and remain alive, bad-mouthing "Holland," he could have enlisted Federman's defense of plagiarism, which the experimental postmodern novelist calls "pla(y)giarism." Rejecting the assumption of writers in the romantic period of a single creator-proprietor of a text, Federman insists that "language belongs to everyone in the same measure, that language is democratic, and therefore *plagiarism* is the stuff of literature." Federman, a provocateur, does not appear to be speaking hyperbolically, for in the next sentence he writes: "Or as it was once proposed quite seriously: *plagiarism is not only admissible in literature, it is advisable*" (57; emphasis in original). Aval might have further taunted "Holland" by citing Federman's contemptuous dismissal of the talking cure:

> Psychoanalysis uses oedipal reduction and substitution to have the patient believe that he is going to speak in his own name, but it is a trap. He will never speak his own personal words, he will never be allowed to speak his own original words. He will only repeat the words put in his

mouth.... As long as this imposture works it is called a neurosis, but if the patient cracks, if he refuses to say the words put in his mouth, then it is called a psychosis. (59)

If fiction-making, or metafiction, what Federman calls "surfiction," is mainly about its own self-creation, and does not attempt to mine a deeper unreality, or unconscious, which does not exist, then psychoanalysis can be of no use to the novelist. This was also the position to which the novelist John Barth, Federman's (and Holland's) colleague, subscribed. As Doris L. Eder pointed out in a review of Federman's 1975 book *Surfiction: Fiction Now . . . and Tomorrow*, "New fiction leaves psychoanalysis of the individual to psychologists and the study of group behavior to sociologists. Most contemporary writers mistrust psychoanalysis and no longer believe in the integrity of the self" (156).

Deconstruction and Psychopathology

Federman's mistrust of psychoanalysis and rejection of an irreducible individual self have their counterpart in Holland's mistrust of deconstruction in *Death in a Delphi Seminar*, but the novelist is on dangerous ground when he implies that Hassler's psychopathology is both a cause and effect of her pursuit of deconstruction. "There were times when she seemed to me what the psychiatrists call a borderline personality," the English professor writes in his journal, "someone whose boundaries between self and others are very shaky and often tangled up with control and anger" (116). Hassler's lack of boundaries seems to be exacerbated by deconstruction's subversion of boundaries. "Holland" compares Hassler to Alex (Glenn Close) in the film *Fatal Attraction* (an anachronism: the film appeared in 1983, three years *after* the novel takes place), suggesting that her devotion to deconstruction is based on the belief that language is duplicitous. There's no evidence, though, that Lacanians or Derrideans are more conflicted than anyone else. There are plenty of clinical psychologists, psychiatrists, and psychoanalysts of all different theoretical orientations who have harmed their patients: a partial list of transgressive psychotherapists appears in the two-volume book Paul Mosher and I coauthored: *Off the Tracks: Cautionary Tales about the Derailing of Mental Health Care*.

The Double

Holland tries to distance himself from his fictional counterpart through some of Detective Rhodes's statements. Rhodes, who comes from a wealthy family that has contributed generously to the university, knows nothing about literary theory, but he shares Holland's aggressive rationality. Rhodes is, by avocation, an off-Broadway playwright, just as Holland is, by avocation, a novelist and, as a youth, an aspiring poet. Rhodes is as rational as Holland, using his combative intellectuality to understand human behavior. Rhodes has chosen not to go into his father's business, a decision that has resulted in becoming the black sheep of the family—the same position in which Holland found himself, as we learn in his next book, when he decided not to become a patent lawyer, like his father. Like both the real and fictional Hollands, Rhodes believes in organic unity, no loose ends. The technique of criminal detection, he instructs "Holland," is "fitting facts together to form a cohesive whole" (260). Readers may find themselves sharing Rhodes's early skepticism of "Holland's" theory, as when he states that it's "so relativistic" (132). Some of Rhodes's statements to "Holland" may contain more truth than the novelist intended, as when the detective urges the English professor to "[o]vercome your retentive tendencies" (290)—a statement that reminds us how parsimony, or stinginess, is one of the "anal" qualities.

Rhodes and "Holland" have an excellent working relationship, combining criminal detective work and literary sleuthing. Holland uses Poe's method of hiding in plain sight in "The Purloined Letter" to good effect. Just as Poe's astute thief hid a stolen letter, which he disguised by turning the envelope inside out and writing a different address on it, a mystery solved by Dupin, the interloper hid his copies of the seminar squids in piles of colored typing paper, a mystery solved by "Holland." Both Rhodes and "Holland" are masters of reading character.

"Holland" is less self-assured than Holland is in his other books, but that's because the fictional English professor is a suspect in a murder—and also because what's at stake in the novel is nothing less than the legitimacy of the Delphi seminar, in which Holland has invested his entire reputation. Rhodes occasionally makes statements critical of "Holland," as when he muses about the English professor, "You can't draw a line between intellectual disagreements and personal attack" (48). It's obvious that Holland gives Rhodes his own first name to suggest a connection between them. Despite Rhodes's criticisms of the English professor, there is little narrative distance between the real and fictional Holland; any statement about the latter is likely to be true of the former.

Unlike the students, who reveal much about their lives in the second half of the semester, "Holland" discloses little about his own life, apart from his long marriage to Jane. Holland's persona in the novel closely resembles the one he portrayed throughout his scholarly writings—an erudite, affable, witty scholar passionately devoted to literature and psychoanalysis. Liberal in his social and political views and conservative in his lifestyle, he is wholly committed to the life of the mind. If there is a darker side to his character, as there is in everyone, he keeps it carefully hidden. In one of the most autobiographically revealing statements in the novel, "Holland" observes about his own identity theme: "I think my own motivation is, if I go deep enough, that I'd like to know what makes people tick, but I don't want to get close enough to find out" (140). Neither the real nor the fictional Holland discloses anything about his life that might have been painful or shameful: no major regrets, failures, or traumas.

"About Me"

On one occasion, Holland revealed his darker side to the real graduate students taking his Delphi seminar. I know this from a startling document he wrote, "About Me," sent to me by David Willbern, Holland's Buffalo colleague. Holland never discussed in any of his books or articles the specific details of his psychoanalysis or his feelings about his analyst, but he shared some of this information with his students on October 22, 1975. "About Me" is fascinating for what it both reveals and conceals. I quote it in its entirety:

> I am confident you will all arrive at appropriate themes from my responses: sees the world in dualities, aggressively converts people into things, has lots of anger, needs to control and dominate, approaches the world through knowing and seeing, etc. At the same time, I worry a bit that you may also surprise me, that you will somehow get past my defenses to something I don't want you to see or know. Nevertheless, because I feel confident that you will all say the "right" things about me, I don't feel a need to do so myself. Besides, I've stated my "identity theme" or some of it, at least, in *Poems in Persons* and *5 Readers Reading* and various lectures—I've been there, and that's perhaps why I have this impulse not to talk about my responses at all, but just to talk about myself, to enjoy the curious and unusual luxury of being able to indulge myself to a more or less willing audience in one or many pages just talking about myself—my wishes, fears, pleasures, exculpations, and so on. And perhaps this is why, ever since this tactic first occurred to me (on Tuesday, before our last meeting), I (sort of) knew I would write about the only other place in my life where I could (sort of) simply talk about myself—my analysis.
>
> Partly, I think you might be interested in the differences between analysis proper and the kind of thing the seminar does. Partly I feel I'm being show-offy and razzle-dazzle: "*I've* been analyzed." (A satisfaction

tempered by guilt: Jane's uncle helped me financially with it, and now I can't seem to give him anything.) Partly I think I'm titillating and seducing you: "Secrets of an Analysis," *True Confessions*, October 1975. Partly I think I'm warding you off: I already know everything you could tell me—and more. And partly I think I'm trying to come to groups (oops!) grips with various ways of experiencing oneself, myself.

What can I say, though? I learned a tremendous amount about myself. At first I insisted that the analysis (required in my training) was useful for my personal life, but as for literary criticism and other professional applications of psychoanalysis—I knew all that already. One of my great and most difficult insights was that the two were inseparable. I learned, for example, that I didn't really believe in unconscious processes. (No one does, I think, until your own mind forces you into it. I learned it from some striking forgettings and dreams.)

My case was special, perhaps, in these more advanced days when character disorders and object relations are the thing, in that there was a particular phenomenon in my childhood of overwhelming importance. We "recovered" it over my strong repression (another telling instance of the power of "the unconscious") until I could establish by external evidence that it had to be so. I never cease to be astonished at the ramifications in my life of that one pattern. I don't exactly feel resentment at my parents for doing it to me—they didn't know any better, I guess. I do feel, though, a kind of awe at the role of the unimportant and fortuitous in the development of people's characters. I am impressed by the marked vulnerability of children to certain kinds of seemingly mild stress (yet from things that are not easily changed)—the seductive or the missing or the unloving parent. I am equally amazed at the extraordinary strength children show in the face of other kinds of stress (some of which can be softened by social reform): economic deprivation, physical cruelty, bodily handicap. Truly, there is a deep logic and a deep illogic, a deep determinism and a deep chance in our development. There is both so much and so little we can do. I feel it is very dangerous to alter the established patterns of child development for either uncaring or ideological reasons. I have great hopes of socio-economic improvements, but I have the gravest doubts about social or individual programs that tinker with the familiar and intuitive shape of children's growth, and I have them from painful personal experience.

Curiously, I and my traumata exist in "the literature" as a case history or, more precisely, one of a group of related cases. I remember my analyst asking me if she could use me in a paper she was writing, and I said (rather pleased), "Sure." But then I never saw or heard anything about the paper. I wondered about it for a bit but never found it, not even in her *Collected Papers*. Then, one day last spring, I sort of stumbled on it—an idle hunch paid off. I was surprised to read phrases I had used, that were very important in the analysis, startled and a bit hurt to hear me described in the harsh terms of clinical exactitude. Yes, all very accurate—too accurate. I am afraid that anyone seeing that report would recognize in it the (to me) shameful (although it was not my fault) sources of my deficiencies as a person and as a professional literary critic. I very much don't want you or anybody else looking (key term) at my weaknesses.

I am safe in the sense that this report is so buried in the clinical literature it would be well-nigh impossible to find it, even if you knew my analyst's name. At the same time, I have been having this impulse to spell it all out (or a muted version of it, anyway) as part of a collection of essays I am working up. You see, it is the best way I know of what seems so hard for even my psychoanalytically oriented literary colleagues to understand: that one's most advanced and "objective" thinking (secondary autonomy and all that) is still a function of infantile experiences (in the old characterology; identity theme in the new one). I realize too that my exhibitionistic impulse is also a way of saying, "Here I am. Look at me. What a wise, courageous fellow I am to be able to reveal myself this way. I'm *okay*!" And all for *your* benefit, of course.

I learned a lot in analysis. Esalen [a reference to the Esalen Institute in California that played a key role in the human potential movement in the 1960s] says, "Understanding is the booby prize in the game of life." Maybe so—certainly every time I am tempted by a pretty woman I know what they mean. But for me understanding and knowing were and are tremendously satisfying modes. I tended to treat my own analysis as primarily an affair of understanding. People have analogized psychoanalysis to an education—its results are objectively elusive but subjectively intense, it is interminable, it takes a long time, there are no short cuts, etc. I think the comparison is apt: education (as we practice it) is the study of "out there," and psychoanalysis is the study of "in here," and, for me, any kind of study is deeply gratifying. To know the truth. Me'n Siggie.

At first, I was very uptight on the couch, lying there, arms folded, stiff as a board, coming out with one- and two-word associations. I got over *that*, but I was never easy. I always felt it as a defeat, somehow, that I was there, an admission of weakness. I would assert myself by intensely *knowing* what was going. I always had a bit too much of the "observing ego" carefully watching the "participant ego" to see that things didn't get out of hand. It was hard for me to relax and just let things flow. I tended to bring in too much material, I now think, from current hassles with my department, wife and kids, publishers, editors, parents, etc. I think I was afraid to go back, down, in.

I was always doing my own interpreting (as you've seen me do in these responses) rather than letting her do it. I tended to intellectualize a lot. In fact, I chose my analyst because, as I told her, she had "a mind like a steel trap." Also a great belly—from what? From sitting behind a couch all those years?

I wondered about her—that was and is my style—and I wonder now about "the transference." I'm not sure I had much of one. I'm not sure I *ever* felt much love or hate or jealousy or dependency toward her. I think I tempered my feeling with knowing. The last time I saw her she seemed very distant, even hostile. I think she was surprised to see me—it was at a psychoanalytic meeting in San Francisco. Had I not paid a bill? Had I failed her somehow? We had both worried after I terminated in 1966 that I would "close up" again. I was afraid I had. The years in Buffalo had been full of all kinds of stress. I had sent her a copy of *Dynamics* with an inscription full of foolish certitudes. She never acknowledged it.

She died that autumn, an incredibly easy death: heart failure while sleeping off a Sunday dinner. It was not until sometime later that the *International Journal* came out with the customary obituary. I was in Paris in the funny little library of the Paris Psychoanalytic Institute when I read it. The family and professional friend who wrote about her remarked on her shyness and how difficult it was to get to know her even after years of companionship. I felt a great surge of relief. It wasn't just me—others too. It wasn't just me!

After she died and especially after reading that obituary (I still turn to it for comfort—and yet, looking it up this minute, I find tears in my eyes, too) . . . Ever since her death and obituary, anyway, my analysis had become an open thing for me. It had felt, after I had terminated and moved to Buffalo, "done." That was that, and I did not feel it had anything to do with my new and taxing life here. After her death, though, I began re-working the whole thing in my mind. I found I was consolidating what I had learned and what we had worked through. Moreover, I could carry what I had learned into new situations.

Perhaps the most puzzling thing, though, was the way I began to be more aware of my feelings and associations and more able to use them in directing myself. An analytic proverb: The greatest part of a psychoanalysis takes place after it is over. At the same time (and I'm not sure if the two are related), I became more involved with therapeutic activities here. At first it was the very medically oriented Student Health Service, where I took on a couple of clients and attended clinical conferences. The first time I ever did anything like therapy. My supervisor was a remarkable woman (my alter-analyst?) who emphasizes feelings almost to the exclusion of conceptual understanding (although she, too, has had psychoanalytic training). I then became involved in the much freer Student Counseling Service and the T-group for the 67S staff; my English students got into it, too. The result of all this was a long two-year weaning of me away from my tendency to concentrate almost exclusively on insight and intellectual understanding.

Conceptually I think of both my activities and the clients' as "corrective emotional experiences." Such are not considered by psychoanalysts adequate substitutes for insight, and I would agree—they are two completely different things. On the other hand, for me, at least, they can complement one another beautifully. Insight makes it possible for me to know why it is so hard for me to risk myself in the feelingful setting and then I *can* risk myself, knowingly (that's important for me). The pay-off from that emotional gamble then provides, as it were, the capital for further emotional change. I can be different from what I am, to do new things, yet continue to be the same me. I can, in short, grow.

I am not a religious man, but if I believed in a deity I would thank her/him for what seems to me a very precious chance I have been given. As I look around at my agemates, damned few of us get the chance to grow at forty-five and after. Yet my writing and thinking took a new and very exciting direction in 1972. I found a whole other way of understanding literature and my (and others) relation to it. This kind of seminar stumbled into being as part of this process. I've developed new kinds of friendships and a different feeling about students. My politics are more radical. I even got into TM. And now I feel I am working on psychological and philosophical questions of grand importance.

Last year was a bit of a relapse for me: I was on leave, writing about theoretical issues in a most intellectual way without the motional give-and-take of a seminar like this or the various therapeutic settings I had been into. So I closed off again, and, as some of you have noticed, it has taken me a while to open up the seals. I'm not sure they're open yet, but I do know where I'm trying to go: to a state of mind where knowing (of a very sophisticated kind—it would have to be for me) and feeling go together, each fulfilling the other. Or to state it in terms of what is, more or less, my identity theme: to know and so control the way knowing and feeling go together.

What shall we say about this extraordinary revelation—or confession? Did Holland consider using it years later for *Self-Analysis in Literary Study*?

"About Me" reflects familiar Holland themes: the need to remain in control, the fear of being financially beholden to another person, the tension between knowing and being, the use of intellectualization as a defense. Holland's keen disappointment that his analyst never thanked him for his gift to her, a copy of *The Dynamics of Literary Response*, demonstrates the importance of the professional relationship.

Characteristically, Holland enacts throughout "About Me" the role of both analyst and analysand, and he dares his students to point out anything about himself that he doesn't already know. (Does he realize his hunger for approval? His ambivalence toward self-disclosure?) One is reminded of his statement in "Re-Covering 'The Purloined Letter'": "One's secrets are always found out."

Traumatic Repression

After reading "About Me," I began to wonder where Zetzel's case study was published. I couldn't find it in her 1970s book *The Capacity for Human Growth* or in her coauthored *Basic Concepts of Psychoanalytic Psychiatry*. Paul Mosher helpfully sent me a list of Zetzel's publications indexed in PEP-Web (www.pep-web.org), the online bibliographical tool that archives the major journals in the field. I dutifully began reading Zetzel's journal articles, but few of them contain any case studies. Just when I was ready to give up, I came across an article published in a 1968 issue of *Revista de Psicoanálisis*, the official publication of the Argentine Psychoanalytic Association. With the help of *translate. Google.com* and other online translation services, I may have found it.

"Repression of Traumatic Experience and Learning Process" ("Represión de la Experiencia Traumática y Proceso de Aprendizaje") contains a discussion of two patients, a woman and a man, one of whom appears to be Holland. Nearly everything Zetzel says about the male patient appears consistent with what we know about Holland. Both patients, described as similar in many ways, were affected by the early and repeated witnessing of the primal (translated as "primary") scene. The male patient was "very intelligent" and "talented," an "excellent" student who "despite certain neurotic symptoms" was "able to perform extremely effectively, especially in the intellectual field." He had made a good marital choice and had children before beginning analysis. "He attributed exaggerated importance to achievements related to active learning," felt the need to control knowledge, and had manifested a "certain compulsion about memorizing" (922). The patient was "currently attending specialization courses [which I infer as being in psychoanalytic training] and seemed destined to become an outstanding professional" (921). Before analysis, he had "attached fundamental importance to external achievement, status, exhibitionism, and active dominance" (924)—again, like Holland, as he spells out explicitly in *Meeting Movies*.

Deeply motivated as a patient, he "manifested considerable conflict lying on the couch"—just as Holland describes in "About Me." Zetzel adds, "It was often important for him to look at me and/ or say a few words at the beginning or end of the session." The description of her patient's parents matches what we learn about Holland's parents from *Meeting Movies*. "As his analysis progressed," Zetzel writes, "it became apparent that he viewed the father as an omnipotent individual and his mother as a helpless and undervalued being." The authoritarian father and submissive mother "reinforced his envy of the penis and helped mobilize active defenses against underlying passivity, during dormancy and adolescence" (924). Holland describes himself and his mother in *Meeting Movies* as having to "toe the line" (88).

Zetzel's patient entered analysis because he could not "easily open up," "relax," or allow a "passive enjoyment" of language, literature, and art. "Thus, his appreciation of poetry, the visual arts, and subtle nuances, remained at a significantly lower level than his ability to understand, conceptualize, remember, and organize" (924). The patient's desire to know, Zetzel implies, inhibited his ability to *feel* and *enjoy*:

> He could not spontaneously share the pleasure that certain books, radio shows, or movies brought him. After making some active efforts to achieve this, he came to the conclusion that there was really nothing to understand, and that all that was needed was to examine and master the written or spoken manifest word. In the early stages of his analysis, he demonstrated enthusiastic acceptance and also prior knowledge of psychoanalytic symbolism, despite which he tended to give such symbols an anagogical meaning of a general nature or to resort to the generalization of universal conflicts. (924)

"About Me" never reveals the specific traumatic childhood experiences that affected Holland—his parents "didn't know any better"—but I suspect he was referring to the primal scene. Zetzel points out that although her patient did not share a room with his parents, his crib was in a nearby room, and the door was usually left open. (Recall Holland's statement in *The Dynamics of Literary Response* of growing up in a one-bedroom apartment.) During these primal scene experiences, Zetzel explains, he "perceived as castration the change in the paternal penis before and after experience," resulting in his fear of his mother's genitals, which seemed "dangerous and destructive" (923). This is consistent with Holland's more vivid description of primal scene fantasies in *The Dynamics of Literary Response*: the child "may regard his mother's body as a trap, a Hell or darkness or sulphurous pit which engulfs that precious organ" (45). Holland attaches great significance, as we have seen, to primal scene imagery in "Dover Beach." Moreover, in his discussion of *Children in Paradise* in *Meeting Movies*, Holland observes that "Psychoanalysts think that primal scene fantasies, evidenced by a fixation on looking, underlie a later preoccupation with theatrical performances and movies" (130). In his analysis of *Shakespeare in Love* he describes how a child "may fearfully fantasize about disappearing body parts" as a result of witnessing the primal scene (151). One page later he admits that he discovered in analysis that primal scenes "were an important part of my childhood" (152).

Zetzel mentions two of her patient's early traumatic events that I cannot confirm. "At the age of three he had not only been separated from a babysitter who until then had taken great care of him, but also suffered a rather serious physical illness that led to his separation from the entire family for a considerable period" (925–6). Nor can Holland's children confirm these events. Kelley Holland is unsure whether the case study describes her father, who, in her view, always took pleasure in literature, and never was interested in sports, as Zetzel's patient was.

The patient's analysis was successful, Zetzel informs us near the end of her article, because of the profound changes in his understanding of literature and art. He was able, in her words, to "read with a more calm and open attitude and be moved by literature. For the first time in his life he was able to read some poems and appreciate the concrete words and the visual and auditory images that they stimulated" (926). In short, Holland—"something of a Puritan"—discovered the pleasure principle, an element that became increasingly important in his work.

One of the ironies of "About Me" is that even as Holland states his new interest in the affective realm, as opposed to the world of cold intellectuality, he remains heavily guarded about emotion. Cannot one disclose vulnerability without sounding like *True Confessions*? Cannot the expression of vulnerability be a strength rather than a weakness? Self-disclosure is a gift that encourages others to reciprocate with their own gifts. It took Holland ten more years to disclose in *The I* the name of his analyst, perhaps because of the fear that someone would locate her published case study of him. He could have disclosed it himself—with justifiable pride that he was teaching his students something important he had learned about himself. He would be, after all, elaborating on his identity theme. We can only assume that the continuing shame of his childhood prevented him from further self-disclosure to his students.

I don't know how Holland's students responded to "About Me," but I saw him in a new light. I felt protective toward him, grateful that he allowed me to have a deeper understanding of him. His expression of vulnerability is endearing, helping to narrow the distance between teacher and student. We can identify with his disappointment over his analyst's failure to acknowledge the book he inscribed to her. We can also appreciate the risk he took in teaching a class like the Delphi seminar. I was especially moved by his statement that the preceding year was a "relapse" for him, when he found himself closing off again. In revealing that he is human, all too human, he allows his students, past and present, to make the same observation about themselves. The Delphi seminar was a daring, even revolutionary pedagogical experiment, one that few teachers, then or now, are willing to make.

Dangerous Empathy

"Holland" tells his literary agent that he has written a book about "not knowing what you know" (3), like the foundational paradox of psychoanalysis, self-knowledge based on the assumption of not knowing. We suspect, though, that he doesn't know the extent of his irritation with Hassler, who gets under his skin. When speaking to Rhodes about her sad history in a "strict and tiny southern town, a Bible-thumping, flag-waving, gun-totaling family" (47), "Holland" seems offended by every aspect of her culture, including her fundamentalist upbringing, conservative politics, and working-class roots. "I could be sorry for her, if she weren't so damned irritating" (47). The novelist's judgmental attitude toward her is only slightly more censorious than Holland's remarks about some of the students in *5 Readers Reading*. The most visible physical detail about Hassler is her obesity. "She was god-awful fat" (32), one student comments, reflecting the novel's aversion to her appearance. In *Poems in Persons*, Holland describes his reaction against anything "flabby, amorphous," and "fleshly" (85), which is exactly how Hassler appears.

Holland never associates his identity theme with a mistrust of empathy, a word that *never* appears in the index of any of his books. He felt that excessive empathy was dangerous, and in the relationship between self and other, he preferred remaining on the outside, looking in. His discussion of "Mending Wall" in *The Brain of Robert Frost* reveals the importance of firm boundaries. Empathy dissolves the distance between inside and outside, leading to precarious fusion or merging. Not only does the failure to maintain boundaries lead to mental illness, it betokens to Holland "either a regression to the earliest stage of infancy or a failure to develop out of that oral stage"

(30). Holland hears the neighbor in "Mending Wall" saying, "If there is no wall, craziness will break through" (30).

Holland's wariness of empathy appears in his portrait of Amy Lemaire, the most empathic—and vulnerable—character in the story. A "particularly likable person" who is in her mid-thirties, she has the best empathic understanding of her classmates. "When students say uncomfortable, risky things, she's always the one who comes up with the right support and reassurance" (19). "Holland" tells us that Amy is a "born teacher, maybe because she's a born mother" (19), perhaps suggesting his belief that some people are empathic by nature. There may be a pun on her surname: "mère" is "mother" in French, and "la mer" is the "sea," the source of all life. As Holland writes in *Meeting Movies*, "water in a Freudian sense . . . is one of the powerful symbols for mother" (42). Amy likes to take care of people, and she offers the most insightful analysis of Hassler's situation:

> She needed support, but we didn't give it to her. We couldn't. She wanted us to hate her, and we did. We couldn't help it, and she played on that. I think she felt that if we hated her, then she was justified in hating us and being as nasty to us as she was. We shouldn't have, but I don't see how we could help it. That's why I say we all killed her. And Trish herself, most of all. (41)

There are several ironies surrounding Amy Lemaire's character. Holland suggests that because she's so trusting and dependent, she's a "compulsive giver" (222), as she herself confesses. For that reason, Amy gives too much to Hassler, sharing a dark secret about her earlier life, when she was a prostitute. (Lichtenstein's patient Anna S., we recall, supported herself through prostitution.) Hassler uses the secret to blackmail her. Amy becomes so enraged by the threat, which would have ended her dream of becoming a teacher, that she vows to kill Hassler. For this reason, Amy becomes a prime suspect in the murder. Empathy is perilous in Holland's world because it leads to a breakdown of boundaries between self and other, heightened vulnerability, betrayed trust, and loss of self-control.

Freud wrote little about empathy, nor was empathy one of his strengths. Following Freud, the early figures in the psychoanalytic had almost nothing to say about empathy. Beginning in the last quarter of the twentieth century, Otto Kernberg and Heinz Kohut became the leading theorists of empathy. As I discuss in *Narcissism and the Novel* (1990), Kernberg and Kohut could not have been more different in their visions of narcissism or in their clinical approaches. Kohut was the more revolutionary of the two thinkers, creating a new movement, self psychology, based on a radically different paradigm of therapeutic cure, in which the analyst's unwavering empathic support is used to heal narcissistic disturbances. Showing little enthusiasm for Kohutian theory, Holland remained wary of Amy Lemaire's gift of empathy.

Pedagogical Questions

Despite "Holland's" inability to scale the empathy wall in *Death in a Delphi Seminar*, the novel raises intriguing pedagogical questions about overcoming mistrust. I know from my own experience with reader-response diaries and personal essays that special precautions must be taken to minimize the possibility that students may be inadvertently harmed in the self-disclosing classroom. "Holland" is right when he tells Rhodes that students "tend to be protective of their maimed colleagues" (119). Did Holland worry that students might be harmed by dredging up their free associations to literature? Was he concerned that, despite his fictional professor's protestations to the contrary, critics of Delphi teaching would accuse him of practicing psychotherapy in the classroom? Did he worry that he would be burdened by his students' self-disclosures?

One can only guess whether "Holland's" adversarial relationship with his department chair, Romola Badger, is based on real life struggles with academic administrators. She badgers him throughout the story, objecting to his controversial teaching. Motivated mainly by the desire for power and public image, not by the wish to encourage authentic teaching or groundbreaking scholarship, she does everything she can to discredit him. "They will say that he was doing a kind of psychotherapy for which he was not qualified and that one of these students broke down in the process and committed murder" (186). Both the real and fictional Hollands take this charge seriously, realizing that the Delphi seminar is fraught with danger. The novelist does everything he can to defend himself from these criticisms when "Holland" observes in his diary, "So far as my teaching is concerned, I've had psychiatrists sit in on the class and okay it. I've written this method up, and people all over the country are emulating it" (228). As Holland and Schwartz write in their *College English* article, "To avoid getting into any kind of group therapy, we encouraged privacy and, if necessary, periphrasis, so that people felt easy with what they were saying about themselves" (790). One can imagine, however, a student becoming deeply disturbed by a frightening free association that is then shared with classmates and teacher.

I've never had a student regret a self-disclosure in a reader-response diary or personal essay, but there's no question that *Risky Writing*, the title of my 2001 book, leads to "risky teaching" for students and teachers alike.

If a student in a traditional college course suffers a breakdown or commits suicide, the professor is not held accountable, but if that student is taking an emotionally charged course taught by a "maverick" professor (as Badger brands "Holland") who encourages self-disclosure, then the professor may worry that something in the course triggered the student's breakdown or suicide. These worries become even greater as a result of the contemporary crisis in youth suicide, as Jane E. Brody announced in the *New York Times* in 2019. "In October, the Centers for Disease Control and Prevention reported that after a stable period from 2000 to 2007, the rate of suicide among those aged 10 to 24 increased dramatically—by 56 percent—between 2007 and 2017, making suicide the second leading cause of death in this age group, following accidents like car crashes." Brody quotes the director of an Ohio poison control center saying that "Suicide attempts by the young have quadrupled over six years," adding, "and that is likely to be an undercount."

In light of the author's acknowledgment in *Holland's Guide* that he has omitted one major topic, therapy and therapeutic techniques, it's curious that the embattled student in the novel appears to suffer from borderline personality disorder, a diagnosis that has become, we learn in *Holland's Guide*, "highly influential among American therapists" (11). Given the norms of teaching reader-response criticism to a group of graduate students who are subjected to a classmate's out-of-control behavior, how does a professor maintain civility and decorum while encouraging free speech? This is only one of the questions we are left with at the end of the story.

Envenomation

In an effort to frame Aval, whom she cannot forgive for stealing her work, Hassler disguises her suicide as a homicide, sitting down in the seminar room on a thumbtack on which she had placed a deadly nerve toxin. "Envenomation took place through a small puncture wound, about one milligram in diameter, on the right buttock on the dorsal surface nearest the hip joint" (34). The improbable plot device represents, psychologically, Freud's classic view of suicide, internalized rage that is symbolic murder of the other.

But Hassler is not the only character in the novel who suffers from envenomation: her hateful words poison everyone in the seminar, especially the professor. Indeed, as Holland's writings in the 1980s and early 1990s reveal, particularly "A Cyberreader Defends," he found his "lifeline" imperiled by Lacanian and Derridean ideas. It is possible that Hassler's toxic denunciation of her professor is a metaphor of Jonathan Culler's venomous criticisms of Holland. Language becomes lethal in the novel, driving nearly everyone to murderous thoughts. Holland never wrote about the contagion effect, the extent to which emotions may become as infectious as germs, but Hassler's words contaminate everyone in the Delphi seminar. "Holland" has difficulty remaining good natured and upbeat amid the onslaught of her verbal abuse.

The New Cryptics' Response

Like *The Critical I, Death in a Delphi Seminar* is not likely to win converts among the New Cryptics and their supporters. A case in point is Michael Greaney's *Contemporary Fiction and the Uses of Theory*, a 2006 study of fictional portrayals of literary theorists. Openly acknowledging his bias toward the "word from Paris," Greaney finds nothing mirthful or humorous in Holland's postmodern mystery. He faults Holland for skewering deconstruction as a "misanthropist's theory of choice, a heartlessly dehumanizing celebration of pure textuality at the expense of literature's historical origins, experiential content and affective power" (128). There's some truth in this criticism: even non-deconstructionists would acknowledge Holland's use of caricature, though they might appreciate his satirical humor. Holland limits his hermeneutics of suspicion to Lacanian and Derridean ideology, exempting his own equally controversial theoretical approach, reader-response criticism, from the same scrutiny. But satire is, by its nature, exaggeration: Holland humanizes his own theory while dehumanizing, even demonizing, other theories. Greaney finds Holland's novel doubly unnerving, as may be seen by his typo: *Death in a Deadly Seminar* (160).

A More Positive Review

A more positive evaluation of *Death in a Delphi Seminar*, by the eminent Princeton professor of comparative literature Theodore Ziolkowski, appears in a 1997 issue of the *American Scholar*. Commenting on several novels that fictionalize philosophy, including Jostein Gaarder's 1991 *Sophie's World* and Steven Lukes's 1995 *The Curious Enlightenment of Professor Caritat*, Ziolkowski characterizes *Death in a Delphi Seminar* as a "remarkable murder mystery" (558) that succeeds in explaining to a non-specialized audience the workings of literary theory. Unlike Greaney, Ziolkowski is not a New Cryptic. "Holland satirizes the commitment to post-modern theory that has seized almost dictatorial control of many English departments and reduced enrollments in literature courses" (561)—a statement with which both the real and fictional Hollands would grimly agree. Ziolkowski ends his review with another statement worth quoting:

> The "linguistic" turn in the university, the "dehumanization" of the humanities, the "hegemony" of theory have in recent years come under frequent and sometimes uncomprehending attack by critics outside the academy. These fictions suggest that professors within the institutions are now addressing the same concerns in a manner at once more knowledgeable, more playful, and, in a word, more humanistic. (561)

Denise Levertov (1923–97) offers another positive comment. The members of the Delphi seminar write their interpretations of her 1958 poem "To the Snake," and "Holland" then studied these interpretations to arrive at the students' identity themes. Holland thanks Levertov for allowing him to reprint her poem in the novel. Her praise appears on his website. "The book was such fun—riveting! How much the novel entertained & engaged me during the 2 days when I spent every free moment with my nose in its pages!"

Death in a Delphi Seminar is not a great novel, nor does it pretend to be. The characters for the most part embody theoretical positions, and Holland's psychoanalytic profiles of his seminarians are sometimes formulaic. The overly neat resolution of the major questions at the end of the story underscores the aesthetic criterion of "No loose ends," as Holland observes in *Laughing* (136), and as Rhodes often repeats. Like most novels of ideas, *Death in a Delphi Seminar* does not contain psychologically complex characterization. Hassler's suicide is in character but Aval's is not; the novel would have been richer, aesthetically and psychologically, had he become a deconstructive or Lacanian literary critic, disparaging Holland's theory as naïve and sentimental, as have Holland's opponents.

Death in a Delphi Seminar remains one of the few novels in which we see a leading thinker bring his theory to life, showing how our styles of reading reflect our inner identities. "Thinking as teachers," Holland and Schwartz argue at the conclusion of their *College English* article, "the two of us believe a Delphi seminar would work with any combination of students, graduates, undergraduates, or even schoolchildren, and in a variety of subject matters—provided the group is willing to chance the Delphi method" (800). That optimistic, perhaps utopian statement is qualified in *Death in a Delphi Seminar*, which acknowledges that the art of teaching depends upon trust that cannot always be achieved.

8

Exposing the Film Critic's Free Associations

Meeting Movies

"We want the truth about ourselves to be known by those who love us," Simon Lesser remarks in *Fiction and the Unconscious*. "We long to be accepted as we are, *to tell the bad and still be loved*" (92). Holland could have used this observation as the epigraph to *Meeting Movies*. Published in 2006, when he was seventy-nine, *Meeting Movies* is his most personal book, filled with stunning self-disclosures that do not appear in his earlier publications. There are, of course, limits to these admissions. Unwilling to intrude on the privacy of living people, Holland understandably avoided any revelations about his wife, children, friends, or colleagues. He reveals little about sex or money, which he wryly refers to as life's "big secrets" (179). "I love gossip, the more scandalous the better," he confesses, but he reveals none himself.

The "usual critical essay has become wearisome" (156), Holland complained to himself upon being invited to give a talk on film at a Harvard conference. He may have felt the same way about writing another "usual" book about the New Cryptics. Instead, he decided to write a most *un*usual book. *Meeting Movies* is not "The Key to All Mythologies," the title of the dry-as-dust Edward Casaubon's unfinished scholarly tome in George Eliot's masterpiece, *Middlemarch*. Nevertheless, *Meeting Movies* casts much light on Holland's earlier books, helping to explain his fierce intellectual aggressiveness, his "phallic" strivings, his concealed impulse toward sentimentalism, his need for boundaries, and his wariness of empathy. As he acknowledges in the afterword, the book is "part confession, part intellectualizing, partly sincere but necessarily defensive" (179). He discloses for the first time his conflicted relationship with his father, his anxieties as a child and adolescent, his struggle between becoming a patent lawyer, as his father was and wanted him to become, and his desire to be, first, a poet, and when that proved impossible, a literary critic. We can see what he learned about himself—and what he might not have learned, or at least what he was not willing to share with his readers. *Meeting Movies* was a risky book to write, exposing his anxieties, fears, uncertainties, and vanities, a book that was both in and out of character. The decision to use in the title the word "movies" instead of "films," which most academic specialists would use, emphasizes the book's personal nature.

The Film Critic

While he was an assistant professor of English at MIT, Holland's program *The Film Critic* appeared from June 1957 to June 1959, fifteen minutes weekly, on WGBH-TV in Boston. It's fitting that he returns near the end of his career to his provenance as a film critic. He revisits his early reviews of such classic films as Michael Curtiz's *Casablanca* (1942), Marcel Carné's *Children of Paradise* (1945), John Huston's *Freud* (1962), Federico Fellini's *8½* (1963), Ingmar Bergman's *The Seventh Seal* (1957) and *Persona* (1966), and Hitchcock's *Vertigo* (1958). He also discusses a contemporary film, John Madden's *Shakespeare in Love* (1998). The difference between his old and new reviews of these films is that now he shares his free associations of each film with his readers, showing how he goes "inside" each film, and the film inside him. These free associations expose for the first time his vulnerability, which hitherto he had kept safely hidden. When he reviewed these films in the 1960s, he was a New Critic, believing that the themes and fantasies were in the films themselves. Now, over four decades later, as a reader-response critic, he believes the themes and fantasies are inside his psyche, which transforms the film in ways characteristic of his identity theme.

Each of the eight films evokes free association that enables us to see key aspects of Holland's identity. Admitting that much of *Casablanca* is "hokum," a word he uses three times in the chapter, he nevertheless loves the film's portrayal of American goodness and nobility. He readily acknowledges his sentimental side—and now for the first time he returns to his jarring assertion in *The First Modern Comedies* that he is a sentimentalist. Recalling the legendary quotes from *Casablanca* that he has downloaded, he confesses that "sentimental tears still come to my eyes" (26). Noting that *Casablanca* is a war film without any scenes of war, a movie about infidelity without any infidelities, Holland adores the film despite its triumphant evasions and denials. He similarly relishes *Vertigo* for its inhibitions. "Scottie denies the unreality of someone like Madeleine and so limits and subverts his chances at real love" (53). *The Seventh Seal* recalls his religious cycle of belief-disbelief-belief-disbelief that lasted until graduate school. John Huston was an all-powerful figure in Holland's childhood; *Freud* implies that people are "endlessly substitutable": human life is an "endless series of displacements from what we really and originally desire and seek" (92–3). Holland admires but does not enjoy watching *Persona* because it threatens to dissolve the boundaries between self and other. He views *Children of Paradise* as a film about ambitions, reminding him of the beguiling nature of fame. *Shakespeare in Love* delightfully portrays the bard's early writer's block—and the limits of Holland's own creativity. And 8½ reminds him of something he resisted when he first reviewed the film in 1963: we don't change as much as we like to believe.

Holland refers repeatedly to Harvey R. Greenberg's 1975 study *The Movies on Your Mind*. Greenberg, a New York City psychoanalyst and pop culture critic, was a "moviemaniac" long before he became an analyst. "Cinema is a supremely valid source of free associations, a powerful touchstone into the unconscious" (3). Unlike Holland, however, Greenberg doesn't offer his own free associations to the films he discusses. Greenberg notes in passing the three great stories within the past century of old men who moments before their death experience cataclysmic emotional epiphanies and growth: Leo Tolstoy's *The Death of Ivan Ilych*, Thomas Mann's *Death in Venice*, and Bergman's *Wild Strawberries*, for which the Swedish *auteur* wrote the original screenplay. Tellingly, Holland did not have much to say, even late in his life, about the sting of mortality: none of the films he analyzes explores aging, existential anxieties, or preparing for death.

Throughout *Meeting Movies* Holland rejects simplistic psychiatric explanations of films, "cookbook psychiatry" (49), as he dismissingly calls it. The psychiatrist in *Vertigo* who describes the tormented hero's breakdown as "acute melancholia together with a guilt complex" offers a meaningless label. "Psychiatric explanations are worthless," Holland reminds us, "because the problem is deeper" (49). He prefers second- and third-phase psychology to over-obvious first-phase psychology, "id psychology," which he often describes as "crude." Many of Holland's film interpretations depend upon Freud's repetition-compulsion principle, the need to repeat a traumatic act to achieve mastery over it. Holland cites his original 1958 interpretation of *Vertigo* centered around the theme of Scottie's need to bring the dead mother back to life. Hitchcock's worldview, Holland suggests, involves the attempt to evade undeserved guilt, which underlies the director's insistence on as much control over his films as possible.

"Report: Focus Group on Revisionism"

One can never predict a film's popularity, Holland asserts near the end of his discussion of *Vertigo*. "That's why the movie people take their nearly finished films to focus groups and test audiences" (35). Focus groups fascinated him because they represent feedback systems that are central to identity. Holland's gift for academic parody may be seen in an article published in *New Literary History* in 1998, eight years before *Meeting Movies*. He creates in "Report: Focus Group on Revisionism" seven fictional academics—he is the eighth—who meet to consider how literary studies may be revised for the new millennium.

Holland revels in poking fun at all the discussants, including himself. When a physicist recalls fondly a course he took years earlier at MIT in which the Shakespearean scholar was a "little nuts" on the subject of "organic unity," the aggressive feminist caustically responds that the professor "*wasn't* talking about how Gertrude and Ophelia are treated as the property of the men" ("Report" 178). Nor was the professor, we might add, criticizing Freud's view of women. The academics reach no conclusions in the focus group apart from agreeing that revisionism aims to find and not find the truth. The conclusion prompts Holland to remind the group of the classic psychoanalytic insight that fears and wishes are inseparable, an insight he traces to our first experience of mother. "We love her but we also fear and hate her. And ever after that, desire is ambivalent" (192).

Holland and Holland

The greatest surprise in *Meeting Movies* is not that Holland's parents wanted him to follow in his father's footsteps but the bitter, protracted intensity of his conflict with them, as he confesses in the most searing self-disclosure found anywhere in his publications:

> All through my childhood both my parents took it for granted that I would become a patent lawyer like my father and take my place in his firm. Holland and Holland. So I was encouraged to go to engineering school and labor mightily at it. Indeed, I could see no alternatives. (To be fair, I rather liked the science for most of the time.) But then, after I developed dreams of literary glory in my senior year, the pressure began. I was to go to law school, the next step toward that law firm, or out on the street, working as an engineer, which by then I surely did not want to do. So law school it was, and a pretty miserable time for three years until I finally got up courage enough to get into graduate school in literature, working in a patent law firm, ironically, to pay my way out of the profession. By the end of it, when I was twenty-nine, it seemed as though I had been in school all my life, as indeed I had, ever the dutiful student. (87)

Exposing the Film Critic's Free Associations 199

One would assume that after their son spent so many years pursuing the wrong career, his parents would have relented and supported his new goal, that of becoming a college professor. It's not like he decided to become an ax murderer—or a dropout. Holland became, after all, an academic superstar who was one of the first reader-response theorists. He couldn't patent the theory, but he wrote book after book guaranteeing that his name would always be linked to his work. Holland casually mentions in his discussion of *8½* that "in this country we always need a lawyer" (169). Could he not have convinced his parents of a need for literary scholars?

I don't know much about Holland's father, but Laura Keyes Perry, who was a doctoral student at Buffalo, kindly provided me with some information about the two Hollands:

> Norm's father's achievements were impressive. He came from a rural Maryland background. The 1900 census lists his father as a farmer in Somerset County, Maryland, which is on the Eastern Shore, on the Chesapeake Bay. (It is still very rural, the second-least-populated county in the state.) At that time Norm Sr. was four years old, not the eldest, and his father was 49. When I mentioned to Norm that his father did not come from a privileged background, Norm said it was very strange visiting the relatives in Maryland. To a boy who lived on Riverside Drive in NYC, it must have been another world. They were mostly farmers, although I believe there was an uncle who was a barber and lived in town.

Adept at genealogical research, Laura sent me a copy of the April 6, 1940, census statement that gave information about the three Hollands: "Norman," age forty-two, a lawyer in private practice, was listed as "head" of the family; "Harriette," age thirty-eight, was listed as "wife"; and "Norman," twelve, was "son." Laura also sent me information about Holland's father's obituary that appeared in the *New York Times* on November 29, 1981. The obituary fails to mention that the older Holland died at age eighty-five:

> HOLLAND—Norman N., patent lawyer, died Saturday, November 28, at his home in Manhattan, after a brief illness. Mr Holland, a founder and Senior Partner of Holland, Armstrong, Wilkie and Previto and predecessor firms, and past president of the NY Patent Law Association, was also active in national and international patent law associations. Mr Holland, who will be buried in Princess Anne, MD, is survived by a son, Norman, and two grandchildren, Kelly and John.

Laura at first thought that Holland had written his father's obituary, but then she thought not, mainly because his daughter "uses her mother's maiden name, Kelley with an E." Laura revealed another detail about Holland's relationship to his father. "I remember once that Norm joked about having a father who was a high-powered patent lawyer. 'And his office was in the EMPIRE STATE BUILDING.' We were taking his literature-and-psychology course, and we got it."

Curiously, Holland never discloses in *Meeting Movies*, or anywhere else, for that matter, that his mother, Harriette, was also a lawyer. I would not have known about this detail had it not appeared in an obituary of Holland published in "Howling Pixel." But why would Holland conceal this information? To focus his anger exclusively on his father, not on both his parents? To preserve his love for the good parent? To avoid the pain of acknowledging that *both* his parents failed him? The answer is anyone's guess.

Holland never did receive parental approval. Once he made the fateful decision to pursue literary studies in graduate school, his father cut off financial support—although, as we shall see, John Holland finds it understandable that his grandfather eventually ended financial support. Cutting off emotional support, however, was more ominous. "My resentment permanently changed our relationship. From then on, my father was something to be coped with, not someone to be admired or loved. A problem, not a solution" (*Meeting Movies* 87). Like Baptiste's father in *Children of Paradise*, "mine used to expect a great deal and to belittle what I did accomplish, as though he expected nothing. He never really accepted my being a college professor instead of what he had planned for me" (116). He reports tersely on having the identical name of his father, Norman Norwood Holland. "I was a little 'Norman junior'" (21), reflecting his parents' wish for him to be a second edition. He portrays his father as Kafkaesque, a menacing authoritarian figure who brooked no opposition. "He earned the money, as he never tired of reminding us. He bought the car. He drove the car. He would throw his temper tantrums, and my mother and I would toe the line" (88). Had we known that Holland's mother was also a lawyer, we might have had greater reason to wonder why she, like her son, was forced to submit to her husband's authority.

Holland's characterization of the troubled father-son relationship raises many questions. How did he avoid becoming another version of his hated father? One does not need to be in psychoanalysis to realize that the more we vow to be different from a disappointing or feared mother or father, the more we may unconsciously resemble that parent. This has been one of my own struggles, as I admit to my students. Throughout my life I sought to counteridentify with my ornery, negativistic father, but the few times Barbara and I had serious arguments during our thirty-five-year marriage, she would reduce me to tears with the words, "You're just like your father!" She was right. I counteridentified with my father while he was living and dying, but he is in me, for better and for worse. Was this not also true for Holland about his own internalized father? In his various roles as husband, father, department chair, and professor, how did he deal with the inner father who demanded unquestioning obedience? In *Of Woman Born*, Adrienne Rich uses the word "matrophobia" to describe a daughter's fear of becoming her mother (235). Did Holland worry about patrophobia, becoming like his father? Theodor Adorno and his colleagues noted in their classic 1950 sociological study that a "basically hierarchical, authoritarian, exploitative parent-child relationship is apt to carry over into a power-oriented, exploitatively dependent attitude toward one's sex partner and one's God" (971). Was this a problem for Holland?

Meeting Movies contains several statements that Holland could have explored in more depth. Describing the brash actor Frédérick Lemaître (played by Pierre Brasseur) in *Children of Paradise*, Holland admits that he is fascinated by the type: "a self-promoter, a boaster, a seducer; worldly-wise, a rogue riding roughshod over husbands and creditors—and eminently successful. Unfortunately, that's a type I'm drawn to. I admire them and enjoy their getting away with it. I have had so many friends like that. . . . I suppose I am, in psychoanalytic jargon, identifying with the aggressor" (116; ellipsis in original). Holland is often most serious when he admits to using psychoanalytic jargon, perhaps suggesting an insight gleaned from his personal analysis. This is the only time in the book when he speaks about identification with the aggressor, a defense mechanism popularized by Anna Freud in *The Ego and the Mechanisms of Defense*, where she speaks about a boy who "identified himself with the teacher's anger and copied his expression as he spoke, though the imitation was not recognized" (110). Holland's use of ellipses when referring to his identification with Frédérick betrays his uneasiness with this line of thought.

Insofar as Holland himself was eminently successful in his profession, not as a seducer or a rogue but as the leading American psychoanalytic literary critic of his generation, a position that required presenting oneself in the public arena through writing and speaking as an original thinker, bold, sophisticated, and smart, how did he avoid further identifications with the aggressor? He writes about his intense intellectuality but not about his fierce combativeness with the New Cryptics. What does he mean when he says that he could have "profited more from self-promotion" (116)? I doubt any of Holland's supporters or detractors would understand this self-criticism.

Know Thyself

Supremely gifted with intelligence and memory—he could remember, years after taking a graduate course with the great Shakespearean scholar Alfred Harbage, some of the lectures almost verbatim—Holland must have realized early in his analysis that his intense intellectuality represented a need for control and mastery. This remains one of the major biographical insights of *Meeting Movies*. To intellectualize is to control, to master, to dominate. He cultivated not the heart but the brain: the word appears in two of his book titles as well as in his epilogue, "A Brainy Afterword," published in Vera Camden's 1989 edited volume *Compromise Formations*: "If you will permit the pun, this is heady stuff" (241). He desired not an ordinary brain but a supersized one—"I will have the bigger, better brain" (33). Holland's belief in the Delphi Oracle's injunction, know thyself, may be seen throughout ancient and contemporary literature, as James Atlas observes in *The Shadow of the Garden*, a 2017 study of his lifelong interest in the biographical arts:

> *Know thyself.* Juvenal and Plato, among others, had suggested this might be a good idea if one were to live effectively in the world, but when it began to crop up in Renaissance biographies, it resonated with a kind of pre-psychoanalytic insistence. Boccaccio, in his book on Dante, remarked, almost as an aside, "In this world it is of great importance to know yourself." And Vasari said of Brunelleschi: "He knew himself." Why did these cautionary words so affect me? They suggested that insight into one's own motives and character was the key to self-autonomy—that in knowing yourself, you could control your fate, if such a thing is possible. It was out of that struggle that all the interesting dramas in life emerged—and out of those dramas come biography. (108)

Know thyself was central to Holland's identity theme. As *Meeting Movies* suggests, he regarded intellectual writing as sublimated sexual potency. Few literary critics of his age were more prolific or influential. Holland was certainly aware of the Oedipal implications of his intellectual desire, but I'm not sure he realized how alienating this intellectual domination could be to someone who didn't share his views. He loved to play the role of the good father, and that was how I came to experience him, but the bad father was never far away, as I suspect he realized. Lawyers are by training if not temperament contentious, and Holland used his aggressive rationality to his advantage. He acknowledges in *Meeting Movies* that seeing *The Seventh Seal* again helped him realize his "old and always problem, relying on reason and rationality to the exclusion of everything else," repeating what the campus beauty queen told him when she dropped his course: she could not stand "the relentless analysis" (67).

Holland's relentless hyperrationality recalls Susan Sontag's sardonic statement in *Against Interpretation* that "interpretation is the revenge of the intellect upon art. Even more so. It is the revenge of the intellect upon the world" (7). But Holland could never embrace Sontag's erotics of art. (Nor could she, for that matter: years later she came to realize that interpretation is as necessary as metaphorical language, which she had also previously rejected.) Better to be cerebral than emotional, in Holland's view. And better to be active than passive. In analysis when he first saw *8½*, he recalls feeling at the time that "To be passive would be feminized with all the fantasies and stereotypes that that implied to someone who grew up in the 1930s and '40s. To be active, in control of literary works, that was the masculine thing" (175). Equating active with masculine and passive with feminine was not uncommon in the 1960s, but he still holds to this fixed binary forty years later, viewing *8½* as dichotomizing the "male tendency toward abstract ideals" and the feminine defined as "full of life and love and sex, passive, nurturing, subservient—and dangerous" (176-7).

Family Secrets

Another surprise in *Meeting Movies* is Holland's shame over his father's relatives, who lived on "the Eastern Shore" of Maryland; his use of quotation marks contains a hint of mockery of his family's pretensions. His father's relatives were "rough, patriarchal farm people who frightened and repelled me" (88). The description may remind us of Patricia Hassler's southern rural roots in *Death in a Delphi Seminar*. Holland's Protestant parents were not fundamentalist, as Hassler's parents were, but he came to despise every element of his religion, which represented to him, as he reveals in his discussion of *The Seventh Seal*, a source of embarrassment and guilt, "particularly sexual guilt—and ignorance and repression" (68). Interestingly, he does not refer, as an example of sexual guilt, to masturbating as a teenager, a detail he discloses in his 1980 essay on "The Purloined Letter."

Some of the childhood scenes he recalls in *Meeting Movies* are more traumatic than anything Hassler experiences. He recalls sitting with his father in the front seat of a "rattletrap truck" while his paternal uncle "took out his pecker (a word I probably learned on that occasion) and pissed all over a head of lettuce at the corner of the field. Har, har, har! I was disgusted, thinking of city dwellers like me, buying such a head of lettuce in the grocery store." The situation became Dickensian in its evocation of a child's fear, indignation, and helplessness. His uncle took out his penknife and threatened to cut off his nephew's penis. "He opened the blade, and I screamed and cried, terrified. He and my father thought that was a great joke" (91). In later years, Holland wondered why his father thought the "joke" funny and did not rush to his son's defense. One can only imagine Hassler's response had "Holland" told her that he understood her shame and rage over her background because it resembled his own. One recalls Hans Loewald's felicitous distinction between ghosts and ancestors. "Those who know ghosts tell us that they long to be released from their ghost life and led to rest as ancestors. As ancestors they live forth in the present generation, while as ghosts they are compelled to haunt the present generation with their shadow life" (249). Holland never tells us whether his father remained a haunting specter in his life.

Shame is not a central word in Holland's vocabulary, though we recall his rare grammatical error in his discussion of Faulkner's "A Rose for Emily," when he observes, "This darkness and watching and shame makes me nervous." We also recall his reference to shame in "About Me." The psychoanalyst Léon Wurmser has written about the three aspects of shame: *shame anxiety*, the "fear of disgrace," the "anxiety about the danger that we might be looked at with contempt for having dishonored ourselves"; *shame affect*, feeling ashamed for being exposed; and *shame as a preventive attitude*, as in the expression "Don't you know any shame?" (67–8). All three components of shame appear in Holland's discussion of his family secrets.

Did Holland reveal these family secrets to his relatives or friends? In her 1992 book *Family Secrets and the Psychoanalysis of Narrative*, Esther Rashkin discusses how shameful family secrets are often transmitted without the sender's or receiver's conscious awareness of their transmission. Relying upon the work of the Hungarian-born French analyst Nicolas Abraham (1919–75), Rashkin uses the word "phantom" to describe how these shameful secrets are kept alive. In light of Holland's revelations about his dark family secrets in *Meeting Movies*, one has a sense of the phantoms that he disclosed publicly only near the end of his life.

As Nancy Chodorow remarks in *The Psychoanalytic Ear and the Sociological Eye*, several female analysts, including Karen Horney, Ethel Person, and Jessica Benjamin, have pointed out that humiliation is more closely related to masculinity for men than femininity for women. Indeed, Chodorow suggests that the "humiliated, rageful warrior Achilles may be a more apt mythic model than Oedipus" (43). This provocative insight strikes me true of Holland, who sought to liberate literature from what he perceived as the tyranny of a text-active model of reading.

Holland's maternal relatives were, by contrast, German, having immigrated to the United States near the beginning of the twentieth century. The German heritage represented a different problem for Holland. "My mother was halfway convinced that much of the news all through World War II, even the pictures of the concentration camps near the end, were just more of that old baiting of Germans. 'Germans are good people. They wouldn't do that.' Our feelings about the war got even more complicated because my father and mother fiercely hated Roosevelt" (21). It's likely that Holland's embarrassment over race, class, nationality, and religion prevented him from revealing how they contributed to his identity theme as a reader. This is one of the many questions he *fails* to raise in *Meeting Movies*. Writing in an age that saw the birth of cultural studies as an academic discipline, Holland disclosed nothing, prior to *Meeting Movies*, about how his own family culture shaped his thinking.

Holland writes much less about his mother than about his father. After referring to his "rivalry" with his father, he then mentions his "lost love" for his mother (134), but he doesn't elaborate. Was this the kind of lost love that is inevitable with Oedipal rivalry, when the son must relinquish his exclusive claims on the mother, or was it because she failed to come to her son's defense during her husband's temper tantrums? Holland never expresses a single specific criticism of her, but given his many battles with his father, his silence about his mother is puzzling. Zetzel states in her case study that her patient's mother was a "helpless and undervalued being"; one can only assume that his long and fulfilling marriage to Jane was the opposite of his parents' marriage. Holland refers to his parents throughout *Meeting Movies* as a unit, never as two people who might disagree with each other over how to raise their only child.

Renunciation of forbidden love is a central element in Holland's interpretation of films. Giving up the "mother-woman" is central to his identity while watching *Casablanca*. He understands, intellectually, while viewing *Vertigo* that Scottie's fantasy woman, Madeleine (Kim Novak), is connected to the cozy, motherly woman, Madge (Barbara Bel Geddes). "To hell with that" exclaims Holland (51), wishing to preserve the mysterious goddess. Yet he also knows that such desires are best enjoyed in fantasy, not reality. No one needs to convince him that inhibitions result in civilization and its discontents.

"The Sparrow"

Still another surprise in Holland's revelation is that he wanted to become a poet but couldn't write poetry. His candor and wit are endearing here.

"What I wanted was to 'be a poet,' not to write poetry. I could not get past the clichés" (133). Reflecting on John Updike's elegant prose, he wonders, "Where do those surprising but right words come from? Adjectives to die for" (133). Not many literary critics admit that they wanted to be creative writers but lacked the requisite creativity. Acknowledging that he suffered from writer's block when he attempted to be a poet, Holland doesn't tell us that when he was twenty-eight he published a poem in *The Hudson Review*, "The Sparrow," based on the Anglo-Saxon prose of Bede's *Ecclesiastic History*, completed in 731. Holland chooses an incident when the Bishop Paulinus seeks to convert Edwin, the king of Northumbria, to Christianity:

> This life, O king, it seems to me beside
> That time we know not of, as though in storm
> Of winter, you, your earls and thanes all sat inside
> At banquet, fire crackling and hall warm,
> While outside, wind swirled hail and sleet and snow—
> And should a sparrow come, fly through your hall,
> Swiftly in one door, out the other: lo,
> In that time he feels no snow fall,
> But that time is an instant, an eye's wink
> Warm between winter and winter. So do I think
> This life of men on earth, instant. What goes
> Before, what comes behind it, no man knows;
> If this new lore speaks anything more fit,
> Or certain, surely we should follow it.

The sonnet, with its unusual ABAB CDCD EEFFGG rhyme scheme, deftly evokes the early Christian symbolism of the sparrow, an icon of God's love for the smallest of creatures. The monosyllabic diction conveys the stark power of Anglo-Saxon prose. Holland's gift for the musicality of language is striking, especially his use of alliteration and assonance in the sibilant line "While outside, wind swirled hail and sleet and snow." There's also the artful symmetrical pairing, "What goes / Before, what comes behind it." Apart from its genre, the poem is unusual in that Holland does not often dwell on the theme of mortality or the possibility of an afterlife. The conversion poem never becomes proselytizing or polemical: the final couplet leaves us in uncertainty.

Holland's "The Sparrow" was in good company: the same issue of *The Hudson Review* contained poems by two distinguished American poets: Joseph Warren Beach and James Wright. The *un*certainty of "The Sparrow" may remind us of "The Journey of the Magi," by T. S. Eliot, one of Holland's favorite poets. I detected in *Meeting Movies* two allusions to "The Love Song of J. Alfred Prufrock": "the face we put on to meet the faces that we meet" (13) and "I am not Lord Freud [or Prince Hamlet], nor was meant to be, am an attendant lord, one that will do to swell a progress, start a scene or two" (87). Both allusions came easily to Holland, who probably assumed that his readers would have no difficulty appreciating them.

Holland's blockage compelled him to admit in his discussion of *Freud* in *Meeting Movies* that he felt in competition with the artists about whom he writes. Notwithstanding the blockage, he came up with the following rationalization to make himself feel better. "They may be gifted, but I'm smart. I can see complexities and subtleties in their work that they had no idea of" (93). The insight that he craved the creative writer's perceived prestige and glamour but could not summon the imagination or risk failure proved life-transforming. "Once I said it out loud, I scarcely needed the good doctor. I was over it. I had made my own breakthrough" (146). Ironically, Freud also wanted to become a poet but turned pragmatically to another profession where he could earn a living. "I am a scientist by necessity, and not vocation," he told Giovanni Papini in 1934. "I am really by nature an artist. Ever since childhood, my secret hero has been Goethe. I would have liked to become a poet, and my whole life long I've wanted to write novels" (99).

Fear of Closeness

Other breakthroughs, of an affective nature, were harder to achieve. Part of Holland's lifelong identity theme is the fear of emotional closeness, which leads in his view to humiliation, as he admits in his discussion of *Persona*, when the nurse-caregiver Alma overidentifies with the mute actress Elisabet and finds the boundaries between self and other disappearing. "No way could I do what Alma does," Holland confesses, "tend to another person like a mother. Nor could I tolerate this closeness. It feels all wrong to me, not my nature. To be a good psychiatrist, I believe, one has to be able to care and nurture. One has to have a strong mother-identification, and that's not me" (100).

Just as Holland never theorized the gender implications of a father's humiliation of a son, he never pointed out that the fear of merging is more common among men than women. To cite Chodorow again in *The Psychoanalytic Ear and the Sociological Eye*, "Seeing the self as not the other, defining the self in opposition, does not seem developmentally or dynamically as important to women as to men, nor does merging seem as threatening. Insofar as ideologies of self and identity are involved, then, it makes sense that women would not feel as endangered as men by threats to cultural selfhood" (42).

Of all the films Holland cites, *Persona* awakens his greatest anxiety. "As far as I am concerned, Bergman portrays a pathological regression, and he achieved one—in me. In *Persona*, I think, he succeeded not just in communicating, but creating a psychic state. For me it is an uncomfortable one" (110). Holland quotes his psychoanalyst uncle-in-law, G. Henry Katz, as saying that "It's good to be a little psychopathic" (91). Was Holland himself a little psychopathic—perhaps embodying the trio of "anal" traits that appear in all his writings?

Katz may have been thinking of what the early psychoanalytic art historian and critic Ernst Kris (1900–57) called "regression in the service of the ego," the ability to overcome one's defenses to tap into the power of the imagination, including unruly aggression and sexuality. A related idea is Keats's Negative Capability: "When man is capable of being in uncertainties, Mysteries, doubts, without any irritable reaching after fact and reason" (261). Negative Capability may be good for the poet, Holland concedes in *The Brain of Robert Frost*—to "put one's own identity aside and imagine oneself into the things and persons of the world outside the self" (29)—but he felt it is bad for nearly everyone else. Seeing *Vertigo*, Holland admits to relishing his denials, even though he knows that these denials can lead to "serious mistakes, the failure of relationships, dangers, even death" (53).

Holland's discomfort with regression, a loosening of one's defenses, may help us understand why he avoided theorizing certain subjects related to suggestibility. He tells us in *Laughing* that Ellen, the graduate student who took several literature-and-psychology courses with him at Buffalo, was "susceptible to suggestion" (148), but he doesn't explain how reading may have weakened her defenses. Nowhere in any of his books does he confront literary contagion: the possibility that reading certain books may drive a reader to suicide. If he did discuss this dark subject, he would express it differently than I did. He would reject the stimulus-response language of text-oriented criticism, "container" metaphors, and instead use reader-response language. Readers susceptible to literary contagion would, to use Holland's language, project their darkest feelings into a book and, seeing the worst confirmation of their fears, act out a fictional character's suicide. But whatever language or model of reading we use, the effect is the same: a book that glorifies suicide may compel a reader who is already at risk to overidentify with a suicidal character, with lethal results. I discuss numerous examples of this phenomenon in *Surviving Literary Suicide*. Holland had little to say about many subjects explored by other psychoanalytic literary theorists, including trauma and the therapeutic implications of reading, writing, and teaching.

Nor did he write about the emerging discipline of narrative medicine. In the latter part of his career, he was far more interested in cognitive science than in clinical research on mood disorders, mourning, and bereavement.

Empowering the Reader

What Holland did write about, in book after book, was reader-response criticism, an idea he loved as much as he revered *Casablanca* and perhaps for the first reason. He reads the Second World War film as identifying patriotic bravery both with "goodness-as-nobility and nobility-as potency" (24). Just as the film celebrates American democracy, freedom, and power, extolling the common (and uncommon) man and woman, so does Holland's vision of reader-response criticism affirm the individual reader. The reader acts, transforms, controls the text, not the other way around. It may be fanciful to view Holland as a resistance fighter on behalf of the reader, attempting to overcome the tyranny of text-oriented readings, but I think this is how he viewed himself, especially near the end of his career. His wish, as he states near the conclusion of *Meeting Movies*, is to "liberate my profession of literary criticism from its laborious, jargon-ridden lucubration" (176). This is another reason for citing an unnamed friend in *The Critical I* to explain the disappearance of the self in Barthes's writings: the attempt to eliminate French postwar guilt by vanishing the self is antithetical to both *Casablanca* and reader-response criticism, both of which celebrate the self, the *American* self. The poststructural effort to abrogate human identity, freedom, and autonomy must be resisted. Not that every reading is equally valid, as he wryly admits near the end of *Meeting Movies*. As a reminder of how much he now disagrees with his 1963 review of *8½*, he has a cartoon tacked up on his office door that shows a professor addressing a student in class. "There are no wrong answers, but if there were, Mr. Jones, that would be one" (176).

Viewing the entirety of his career, Holland believes he hasn't changed much. He still analyzes films, though the analysis has changed. So have some of his values. "The old polarity is reversed. What was positive is now negative. What I thought was bad I now think is good" (176). Sophisticated film critics may laugh, he admits, at his "middlebrow" taste in films (114), but he always brings uncommon insights into his discussions. Holland recalls Proust's observation that "we age into parodies of ourselves" (68), but *Meeting Movies* presents us with a gifted film critic whose lifelong love for the cinema appears on every page. In a review published in *Psychology of Aesthetics, Creativity, and the Arts*, Danny Wedding observes that although he was trained as a behavior therapist and has little interest in psychoanalytic approaches to art, he enjoyed *Meeting Movies* and found Holland's discussion enlightening. "Holland is well versed in psychology and especially psychoanalytic approaches, and his criticism of these eight films is consistently interesting. His willingness to self-disclose makes this book all the more fascinating. The book will be rewarding for anyone genuinely interested in the interface of psychology and film" (49).

Despite his vaunted hyperrationality, Holland doesn't come across as an egghead or snob. He could have titled his book "Fantasizing Films," but that would have been more academic than the simpler "Meeting Movies." Most readers will believe, as I do, that Holland fulfills Horace's injunction that the poet—and, by implication, both the filmmaker and the film critic—should enlighten and delight. He maintains an intimate voice throughout the book, using the second-person pronoun whenever possible. "Why do I feel so relieved? Why do you, perhaps, feel the same way?" (30). In writing *Meeting Movies*, Holland traveled far out of his comfort zone. He credits his loyal colleague and friend Bernard J. Paris for the existence of the book. "It was his enthusiasm, moreover, that finally persuaded me to publish something I had thought too private" (182). Holland ends *Meeting Movies* with the paradox that he sees dramatized throughout 8½. "We can't quite accept that we can't quite accept ourselves as we are" (177–8), a paradox that enables him to complete the book. The film critic may be "handmaiden to the muse," as he ruefully admits, but readers of *Meeting Movies* will enjoy the handmaiden, too, who never disappoints.

9

Venturing into a New Field

Literature and the Brain

Among Holland's many goals in his final book is to ground traditional ideas about literature, such as character, meaning, distance, and form, in brain science, showing how the brain both empowers and limits our responses to literature. *Literature and the Brain* is divided into four parts, "The Questions," "Being Transported," "Enjoying," and "The Big Questions." Two questions dominate the last part: "is literature innate?" and "why literature?" A twenty-six-page appendix includes technical information about the physical brain and its functioning. Holland's fondness for drawings and diagrams is apparent. The appendix includes color figures of the brain in the skull, the brain's lobes, typical neurons, neurotransmission, a Brodmann map relating brain functions to regions, and the brain's left hemisphere.

Literature and the Brain is genuinely interdisciplinary and synthetic, demonstrating how literary theory may be compatible with brain research. Holland recognizes both the similarities and differences between the sciences and the humanities. Knowledge in the sciences is cumulative, leading to truths that can be confirmed or disconfirmed. Knowledge in the humanities is not cumulative, at least with respect to interpretation. The humanities offer a "continuing conversation" (271) to which *Literature and the Brain* makes a noteworthy contribution.

The point of *Literature and the Brain*, Holland reminds us at the beginning and the end, is *"not to change what we do and feel about literature, but to change how we think about what we do and feel"* (9; emphasis in original). He offers us neuroscientific explanations of why we accept cognitively the fact that we cannot change a work of art by our own actions, how we shut off parts of the brain to gain pleasure from reading, and why we become "absorbed" by a story. Our ability to shut down brain systems imbues us with what Coleridge calls "poetic faith." At the end of the book, Holland summarizes in a single sentence the governing principle of neuroscientific research on reading: "*When we are experiencing literature, we turn on and turn off brain systems in ways that we do not in ordinary life*" (349). Holland is well aware of the limits of our present understanding of the brain. "I have not tried to relate particular literary works to the brain, because I do not think that it is possible at this stage of neurological knowledge" (352). Avoiding over-reaching, he signals the direction for future research on literature and cognitive science.

A prolific author's final book holds special interest to a scholar, particularly if the writer knows it's his last book, as Holland did when writing *Literature and the Brain*, published in 2009, when he was eighty-two. Final books allow authors to sum up what they have learned from life and perhaps speculate on how their work will impact the future, when they are no longer alive. *Literature and the Brain* achieves both aims, an impassioned summary of what Holland has learned as a literary critic and a prescient hint of how new brain research will affect our future understanding of literature.

Late Style

The early-twentieth-century German philosopher Theodor Adorno used the expression "late style" to describe Beethoven's final compositions. Inspired by Adorno, the Columbia University postcolonial scholar Edward Said (1935–2003) then explored artistic lateness in *On Late Style*, published posthumously in 2006. Said focused on an artist's inability or unwillingness near the end of life to resolve, reconcile, or harmonize inner tensions. As I discuss in *Dying in Character*, Said was interested mainly in a form of late style that involves, in Said's words, a "nonharmonious, nonserene tension and above all, a sort of deliberately unproductive productiveness going against . . ." (Said 7). But Said refers to another form of late style that reflects a new spirit of reconciliation or serenity not found in the artist's earlier works.

Written in a spirit of reconciliation if not serenity, *Literature and the Brain* reflects Holland's late style. His language conveys his curiosity, playfulness, openness to experience, and passion. The book abounds in whys and hows. Holland writes like a much younger person, in awe of the beauty and mystery of life. He still relies on dry irony, but more often than not, he uses it to poke fun at himself, not at others. He may be more educated than his neighbors, he implies at the beginning of the book, but he often reacts in the same way they do, as when he describes seeing the "fine old weeper" *Love Story* in rural Florida. "And there we were: the rednecks and the Ph.D., tears rolling down our eyes because Jenny Cavilleri, newly married Radcliffe girl, is dying of leukemia" (3).

Holland revels in jokes of all kinds. Noting that psychologists and linguists have spilled much ink trying to figure out how we process ordinary discourse, he recounts that when his wife asks him, "Can you take out the trash?", he provides a one-word answer, "yes," followed by a question to us: "How do I know that my wife wants more than just a statement of my abilities?" (172). He cracks jokes that take us a few seconds to figure out, as when he recalls the four Fs of the medical students' old quip: "feeding, fighting, fleeing, and sexual reproduction" (28). A lifelong professor, he knows how *not* to write like an academic, as when he says about our rapt absorption in a story, "the literary work feels really, really real to us" (52). In a far-ranging discussion that moves quickly from the stock market to literary value to glamour to political charisma and then to psychotherapy, he senses that he may appear to be "scatterbrained" and then adds, "that is a possibility not to be lost sight of" (318–19).

Tunneling

Along with a lucid prose style, Holland's language is richly metaphorical. He begins the chapter "The Alp of Mind" with two lines from Gerard Manley Hopkins's 1885 sonnet "No Worst, There Is None": "O the mind, mind has mountains; cliffs of fall / Frightful, sheer, no-man fathomed" (10). He then describes how the neuroscientist and the humanist are like two small miners energetically tunneling in from opposite sides of an immense Alp:

> Although the neuroscientists on their side of the Alp do not listen much to sounds of digging from the humanists on the other side, some humanists, those concerned with the brain's role in the arts, listen very closely to what the neuroscientists on the other side are saying. We draw hopefully on a great many researchers. . . . We hope for answers from them to the questions that bother us. The neuroscientists and we of the human sciences, even if we are divided into two groups, share the same hope. Although dwarfed by the mountain, we hope our diggings will meet in the middle of that huge Alp, and there we will discover this mysterious, magical treasure, Mind. We hope. (11)

C. P. Snow argued famously about two cultures dominating the intellectual life of Western society, the sciences and the humanities. Holland conveys this division in the metaphor of boring through the Alps, but he also suggests, without naivete, that the two cultures may be united through a common recognition of goals. Holland is one of the tunnelers, and he reminds his readers, most of whom are likely to be fellow humanists, of the value of attending to the scientists whose research illuminates the arts.

Eric Kandel

Holland's commitment to psychoanalysis as a scientific theory of the mind, validated by the latest research on cognitive science and neuropsychology, is as strong as ever. He invokes for support the Austrian-born American psychiatrist-biochemist Eric Kandel, who won the Nobel Prize in Physiology or Medicine in 2000 for his research on memory storage in neurons. Holland quotes Kandel's 1998 statement that psychoanalysis "still represents the most coherent and intellectually satisfying view of the mind" (Holland, 15; Kandel, "A New Intellectual Framework for Psychiatry," 505). In his 2006 book *In Search of Memory: The Emergence of a New Science of Mind*, Kandel returns repeatedly to the biological validity of Freud's theory of the unconscious. Kandel is more specific than Holland in acknowledging how analysis has helped him understand and improve the quality of his life:

> I am often asked whether I benefited from my analysis. To me, there is little doubt. It gave me new insights into my own actions and into the actions of others, and it made me, as a result, a somewhat better parent and a more empathic and nuanced human being. I began to understand aspects of unconscious motivation and connections between some of my actions of which I was previously unaware. (182)

One can only wish that Holland elaborated in more detail in his publications—in *any* detail—what he had learned from his long analysis with Elizabeth Zetzel more than half a century earlier. Did he become, like Kandel, a more empathic and nuanced person? Holland includes some information about his analysis in "About Me" but not whether it improved his relationships with his family and friends. Did he discover the truth of Nietzsche's aphoristic admission: "When one hasn't had a good father, it is necessary to invent one"—a statement that Harold Bloom cites in *The Anxiety of Influence* (56)? Did he realize in retrospect how conservative psychoanalysis was in the early 1960s when he was analyzed? Did he question *any* of the conclusions he had reached about himself in analysis?

The Freud Wars

Holland mentions for the first time in any of his books the fierce "Freud wars" that began in the 1960s, including his debate with Frederick Crews.

Holland repeats in *Literature and the Brain* the two major points he had first made in his debate with Crews. "First, there is in fact a good deal of *experimental* evidence about psychoanalytic theory. Sometimes it does not confirm Freud's ideas, but oftener it does. Second, the critics have failed to appreciate that psychoanalysis relies, not on experiment, but on participant-observer method and holistic reasoning" (16), the same approach that psychoanalysis shares with the social sciences and some of the hard sciences in which experimentation is difficult if not impossible.

Unlike Crews, who is often nasty and peevish when disagreeing with the defenders of psychoanalysis, Holland avoids ad hominem attacks. In an article published in *The Scientific Review of Alternative Medicine* in 2006, Holland reminds Crews that experimental and observational studies of psychoanalysis are more specific and accurate than philosophical and historical studies, which are, by contrast, more removed from empirical data. Neuroscientists are also validating key aspects of psychoanalytic theory. "What emerges is not Freud exactly, but something that's close enough to give the psychoanalytic theory of mind a long-wished-for basis in hard science. Professor Crews should have a look, and, one can hope, an unprejudiced one" ("Response to Crews" 30).

Holland is never polemical, defensive, aggressive, or mocking in *Literature and the Brain*, as he sometimes is in his earlier books. For example, in *The Critical I* he characterizes the deconstructive literary critic J. Hillis Miller, whose work he found highly problematic, as one of the New Cryptics. There is no mention in *Literature and the Brain* of the sarcastic expression; moreover, Holland precedes both of his references to Miller with the words the "distinguished" critic and theorist. He uses the same word, "distinguished," to describe Roland Barthes, Jacques Derrida, Michel Foucault, and Wolfgang Iser, adding that they are "critical luminaries" who believe in the autonomy of language (313). He refers respectfully to Lacan, noting that the French analyst's expression *pleine parole*, "full speech," corresponds to Freud's *Wechsel*, "switch words," words that have double meanings with which our minds can begin two unrelated trains of thought, such as "clasp," which can refer either to an embrace or part of the binding of a book (193). One suspects that Holland's respectful characterization of these scholars with whom he disagrees so forcefully is not simply a rhetorical strategy to win his readers' support but a recognition that intellectual disagreement is inherent in the search for truth. Written in a spirit of reconciliation and reparation, *Literature and the Brain* may not heal old wounds, Holland's or his critics', but it is written in a genial, spirited tone, suggestive of a scholar who enjoys what he's doing and knows that he doesn't want to waste his remaining time by engaging in fruitless contestation.

Like his previous books, *Literature and the Brain* gives us the impression that Holland has read, digested, and synthesized everything written on the subject: hundreds of monographs and articles. One can read a scientific journal article that abounds in citations but without a single word of commentary. By contrast, Holland patiently explains the new research, some of it bewilderingly technical, but which he is always able to express in highly readable prose that is rarely reductive. Theories of emotions, he reminds us, all have their "plusses and minuses" (83). Sometimes he'll make an observation or speculation and then say, "but this is simply my guess" (150). Unlike the admittedly tendentious list of readings that appears in *Holland's Guide*, he quotes findings in *Literature and the Brain* that do not always confirm his own model of reading. Yet Holland's judgments of brain research are always reasonable, and for neophytes like myself, who know next-to-nothing about the latest (or, for that matter, the earliest) neurological research, the book offers compelling insights into why we read.

Folk Beliefs

Brain research demonstrates, Holland points out early in the book, that we cannot know the world directly. Rather, we know external reality through our senses. Neuroscientists refute the idea, held by New Critics and postmoderns alike, that what we see in a text is free from the activities of our brains and sense organs. Without referring to the New Cryptics, Holland uses the term "folk theory" to describe the mistaken belief that "*what we see simply is*" (35; emphasis in original). He returns to this idea a few pages later. "The folk belief that our perceptions simply equal whatever is 'out there,' be it text or brain, is alive and well in literary circles" (39). He repeats in *Literature and the Brain* the core ideas of his earlier books: his preference for a reader-active model, his belief in a reader's identity theme, and his emphasis on feedback loops, codes, and canons. But he breaks new ground by showing how we use literature to create a hunger within ourselves that is then fulfilled through reading.

The Binding Problem

Holland refers several times in *Literature and the Brain* to Mark Turner's 1991 book *Reading Minds: The Study of English in the Age of Cognitive Science*. Turner's 1996 book *The Literary Mind* is no less relevant in showing how the central issues for cognitive science are those for the literary mind. "We expect our phenomenology to indicate the nature of neurobiology," Turner asserts (110; emphasis in original), but the opposite is true. Turner, a Case Western Reserve University cognitive scientist and linguist, is best known for his theory of conceptual blending. The image of a horse, for example, may seem unified, not piecemeal or fragmented, but research indicates that the brain blends various fragments of the image, located in different parts of the brain, into a coherent whole. How is it, Turner asks, that if different regions of the brain process the form, color, and motion that are all attributed to a horse, they are all blended into a single image? This problem, known in neuroscience as the "binding problem," represents part of a larger problem, integration, which continues to mystify neuroscience researchers.

Building on researchers like Turner, Holland offers many intriguing observations about the nature of creativity, including the seldom-realized insight that creativity rests on value judgments that always change. "When we say a literary work is good, we are predicting that it will please many and please long. We do not award the accolade 'creative' unless we think the work has value, and that decision depends on what uncountable numbers of brains do now and in the future" (8). Another perceptive observation is that literary genres that do not allow readers to feel transported or enraptured seldom become popular. Holland's example is hypertext, generated through the advent of computers, where readers must choose their own paths through a story or poem. "The world cannot evaporate, nor can we feel transported into the world of the story. Instead, we are busy at the computer. I suspect that is why hypertext has never caught on with the reading public. We want the trance-like experience" (41).

SEEKING

In Holland's view, the recent efforts to revive through brain research Freud's original hope for a neurological basis of psychoanalysis are among the most exciting psychological developments in memory. Of all the brain researchers, Holland is most intrigued by the work of Estonian-born Jaak Panksepp (1943–2017), the coiner of the term "affective neuroscience." Panksepp showed through the use of electrical stimulation that all mammals, including humans, have a similar emotional system embedded in the brain. Panksepp, who taught at the Washington State University's College of Veterinary Medicine, identified seven primary-process affective systems that motivate behavior. He called the most important of the systems SEEKING. (He used capital letters to signify a specific scientific meaning associated with brain systems and the neurochemicals that are part of the system.) "The mammalian brain," Holland quotes Panksepp as saying, "contains a 'foraging/exploring/investigation/curiosity/interest/expectancy/SEEKING' system that leads organisms to eagerly pursue the fruits of their environment—from nuts to knowledge, so to speak" (86). Noting the intersections of Panksepp's research and his own, Holland argues that through SEEKING we "give narratives and poetic language coherence and significance. We also bring in our personal unconscious concerns" (7). In writing the present book, Holland adds, he is SEEKING; we are also SEEKING when we read and enjoy literature. Panksepp relates SEEKING to the Freudian theory of libido. Holland further links SEEKING to both Freud's pleasure principle and Erik Erikson's notion of basic trust.

Mirror Neurons

The discovery of mirror neurons captivates Holland. He begins by summarizing the import of the research. "Generally, when we watch someone else doing something, our mirror neurons fire as if we ourselves were doing the same thing. Because we are acting (in imagination) like the other person, we will feel the same emotions as the person in the situation we are watching" (95). He sees a connection between mirror neurons and what the early psychoanalytic literary critic Simon Lesser calls "analogizing" in his 1957 book *Fiction and the Unconscious*: "we recall or invent episodes involving ourselves which parallel a story or various parts of it" (Lesser 148). Holland then agrees with the literary theorist Suzanne Keen's suggestion that mirror neurons may be the basis for identification in our experience of literature. Holland characteristically—and generously—pays tribute to past and present scholars whose research has made possible his own. When we watch someone doing something, he remarks, our mirror neurons fire as if we ourselves are doing the same thing. "Could it be," he then muses, "that the *sight* of faces and bodies is why most people find movies and plays more arousing than written texts?" (96).

A Poetic Ear

Holland may not have been able to become a poet, but he had a poet's ear. Noting that literary language surrounds us everywhere, not merely in the genres of fiction, drama, and poetry, he singles out a sentence written by the *New Yorker* film critic Anthony Lane about the difficulty of understanding Jean-Luc Godard's 2001 movie *In Praise of Love*. "My wish to relate the events of this second half is slightly thwarted by my inability to work out what they are." Most of us, myself included, would not have lingered lovingly over this sentence to remark on its musicality, but Lane's linguistic virtuosity beguiles Holland:

> This is a sentence about being stopped in one's tracks—thwarted. The first half has several *s* sounds: "My wi*sh* to relate the event*s* of thi*s s*econd half i*s s*lightly. . . ." And it has several sounds that I feel in my mouth as lasting a bit of extra time, as continuing, like those *s sounds*: "My wi*sh* to re*l*ate *events of* this second ha*lf* is *sl*ig*h*tly. . . ." Together these give me the feeling in the muscles of my mouth of a continuous moving, a lengthening of time. Then I come to the double dentals of "thwar*ted.*" Bump. I hit a wall (the wall of my teeth?). And the dentals are followed by "*by . . . bi*lity . . . work . . . what." (242)

Because I read faster than I type (I am, alas, a two-finger typist; only nonacademic students took keyboarding when I was in high school), it was only when I began to type slowly Anthony Lane's sentence that I appreciated its aural power. Many theorists are tone deaf; Holland, by contrast, has a keen ear—and eye—for poetry and poetic prose.

Returning to Old Questions

Holland is not afraid to change his mind about issues he felt strongly about in his earlier writings, such as the question whether we should treat fictional characters as if they were real people. "I know," he declares, "the instant that I think about it, that Little Nell is a figment of Charles Dickens' imagination. Yet in some ways I regard her as a real person. And even sophisticated literary critics treat fictional characters like real people" (107). These sophisticated critics include Bernard J. Paris, who argues that complex mimetic characters enable us to ask the same questions about their motivation that we ask about real people. After summarizing the centuries-old debate between literary critics who treated fictional characters like real people, the "realists," and those who rejected this approach, the "formalists," Holland explains how brain research helps us to solve this conundrum. It turns out that sensory information from our eyes and ears travels along two different neural systems, a "what" path and a "where" or "how" path. In life, the "what" and "where" pathways confirm each other, but in reading a book about a fictional character, the "what" and "where" pathways separate. "Our 'what' knowledge that we are reading a book rules out a location for characters and events that are part of that 'what' knowledge. And our 'where' system does not supply one" (119).

What would Holland have said, we wonder, if we reminded him how vociferously he maintained the opposite position earlier in her career, namely, that fictional characters are only a figment of their creators' imagination? He might have simply said that new scientific information about the brain has allowed him to change his mind. Or he might have said, very well, then I contradict myself. I am large, I contain multitudes.

Another surprise is Holland's response to the question whether we should treat literature as a problem to be solved, rather, than, for example, a mystery to be appreciated without seeking a rational explanation. In *Psychoanalysis and Shakespeare*, Holland agreed with Lionel Trilling's rejection of Ernest Jones's belief that *Hamlet* represents a "mystery" to be "solved" (184). But now Holland admits in *Literature and the Brain* that his favorite literary works are those that he can approach as a problem with a solution. "I find myself treating literary works as like jig-saw puzzles where my aim is to fit all the parts together in a rational way.... For me, literature is a puzzle, a puzzle that I have been trying all my professional life to solve" (269). The metaphor of a jigsaw puzzle implies an organic wholeness in which all the pieces fit neatly, recalling Holland's instincts as a New Critic. Although the jigsaw metaphor suggests that a text has a preexisting meaning, which is antithetical to reader-response criticism, Holland uses it to show his journey from the writer's text to the reader's brain, where the meaning of a work exists somewhere *between* us and world.

Holland's delight in his work as a literary critic is palpable throughout *Literature and the Brain*, but he ruefully recognizes that not everyone appreciates the value of literary criticism. He singles out the Israeli novelist Amos Oz's petulant statement about the "literati" who ruin literature. "They analyze everything *ad nauseam*, techniques, motifs, oxymorons and metonyms, allegory and connotation, hidden Jewish allusions, latent psychological keys and sociological implications, and archetypal characters and fateful ideas and whatnot. Only the pleasure of reading do they castrate." Holland doesn't deny that there may be a tension between the creative artist and the literary critic; instead, he simply says, "We enjoy our work—at least I do" (267). Holland's joy in his work is infectious. As an octogenarian, he could have long ago stopped working, but he can't because he works to live and lives to work.

Colleagues and Students

Looking back on his long career, Holland recalls affectionately his teachers, colleagues, and students. His Harvard professor Walter Jackson Bate, "the very model of a professional critic," influenced him in graduate school. Bate affirmed the "moral imagination," not surprising because he was a Keats scholar, "surely the most moral of the romantic poets." Bate also regarded Dr. Johnson as a font of wisdom, as did Holland (and Harold Bloom). Holland's colleague Leslie Fiedler (1917–2003), an intellectual maverick, could not have been more different from Bate. "Leslie liked to stand conventionality on its head. His great theme, the one that runs through all his work, was bringing whatever was marginal, whatever was outside the mainstream, into the mainstream. Indeed he would replace the mainstream with what was marginal—until he came along" (268–9). Fiedler's *Love and Death in the American Novel* (1960) remains one of the great early cultural studies of American fiction, particularly the chapter "Come Back to the Raft, Ag'in, Huck Honey!" which uncovers the homoeroticism in Mark Twain's celebrated novel. While not a systematic psychoanalytic critic like Holland, Fiedler used Freudian and Jungian archetypal criticism to explore classic American literature.

Holland also refers to Christopher Bollas, calling him a "leading contemporary analyst" (198). Before becoming a psychoanalyst and a British citizen, Bollas received a PhD in English at SUNY-Buffalo, where he worked with Holland, Fiedler, and Murray Schwartz. The author of several psychoanalytic books, including *The Shadow of the Object* (1987), Bollas is best known for the theory of the unthought known, the "reliving through language of that which is known but not yet thought" (4). In *Being a Character*, Bollas refers to both Harold Bloom and Holland. "Harold Bloom, the literary critic, has argued that literary history is a tradition of creative misperception, as poets and novelists distort, alter, and misread the works of their master. Norman Holland's research of ordinary readers' responses to literature convincingly demonstrates how we misread the literary object" (186). Ironically, Bollas's characterization of Holland's work is itself a creative misperception, insofar as once Holland became a psychoanalytic critic, he never suggested there is a single correct way to read a text. One can only assume, from a Bloomian viewpoint, that Bollas was creatively misperceiving Holland, his former Buffalo professor! Bollas silently corrects the error in his next book, *Cracking Up*, where he argues that Holland shows in *Poems in Persons* (1973) that "no critic can divorce his reading from the peculiar effect of the text upon his identity, so there will be neither two identical readings of a text nor a final, correct one" (23).

Holland has much to say about the mystique of literary creativity, including its "compulsive" quality. "Creative people, not just writers, are driven" (277). He quotes many artists on their need to create, including Picasso ("I could not live without devoting all my hours to it"), Sylvia Plath, Ernest Hemingway, Salman Rushdie, and Chekhov. "Writers *have* to write," Holland asserts, and then he explains why: "It's something they have to do, *or they're not themselves anymore*" (278–9; emphasis in original). He cites Hemingway's fear of writer's block: "It is facing the white bull which is paper with no words on it" (264).

Madness and Creativity

Having written about Hemingway and Plath in his 1977 essay "Literary Suicide: A Question of Style," Holland returns to the question of a possible connection between mental illness and creativity. He cites John Dryden's often-quoted line, "Great wits are sure to madness near allied" (*Literature and the Brain* 283). Holland considers a possible link between creativity and mood disorders: "Perhaps creativity requires a brain more subject than most to depression or bipolar disorder" (301). Yet the most he is willing to say is that "depression might co-occur with creativity, not cause it" (296). He references in a footnote literary theorists and mental health researchers who have probed the relationship between mood disorders and creativity, including Nancy Andreasen and Kay Redfield Jamison, but he doesn't examine their work in detail. He leaves us with the impression that the "mad" artist is largely a stereotype. True, one might respond, but Jamison has shown in her 1993 book *Touched with Fire: Manic-Depressive Illness and the Artistic Temperament* how mental illness is often the driving force behind creativity, conferring advantages to creative writers that allow them to investigate states of mind less accessible to ordinary consciousness. Jamison discusses many twentieth-century poets afflicted with mood disorders, including Robert Lowell, about whom she later wrote a magisterial biography. Lowell asked in a late poem, "Is getting well ever an art, / or art a way to get well?" (Jamison 170). Holland would have appreciated Lowell's mordant quip in his poem "Since 1939": "if we see a light at the end of the tunnel, / it's the light of an oncoming train" (qtd. in Jamison, *Robert Lowell* 131).

I suspect that Holland was skeptical of the link between mood disorders and creativity largely because it went counter to his belief in the order, control, and self-discipline required in art. Yet there is much clinical and empirical evidence to support a causal connection, particularly with respect to Freud. George Pickering argued in his 1976 book *Creative Malady* that psychological illness may sometimes be an aid to creative work, "indeed essential" (17) in the writers he studied, including Freud. The historian of dynamic psychiatry Henri Ellenberger suggests in *The Discovery of the Unconscious* (1970) that Freud suffered from a creative illness in the 1890s, a thesis that Freud's most recent biographer, Joel Whitebook, accepts fully. "[E]verything Ellenberger describes—the dedication to an ideal, the intense suffering, the outward normality of everyday life, and the presence of a shamanistic mentor—fits Freud's experience during the Fliess years to a tee" (180).

As in his earlier books, Holland does not discuss the contagion effect, perhaps because it implies a text-active model, where a story or film has the power literally to sicken a reader or viewer. Even when readers confront love and loss, he maintains, they don't themselves suffer. "We can have the pleasure of the emotions that accompany loss or injury while remaining certain that [we] will suffer the real effects of neither" (57). But as I have suggested, the contagion effect rules out such certainty. Recall Holland's extreme discomfort in *Meeting Movies* seeing *Persona*, in which he found himself experiencing a pathological regression.

The Compulsion to Write and Teach

Curiously, Holland doesn't apply the recognition that writers must write to *himself*. Many literary scholars, like the novelists and poets they study, must keep writing to maintain their identity. This is certainly true of me: writing and teaching define my identity—so much so that I end my 2009 book *Death in the Classroom: Writing about Love and Loss* with "A Teacher's Self-Eulogy," *my* self-eulogy:

> Jeff Berman's fantasy came true yesterday when his body was found in his office minutes after teaching the final class of the semester. For decades the popular English professor had disclosed to his students that he wanted to expire teaching, dying in harness. The bizarre wish came true. He was eighty-two years old and had been teaching at the University at Albany for fifty-four years, longer than any other faculty member in that institution's history. The news stunned his devoted students, though one expressed the hope that his teacher had submitted final grades in the course before passing on. (219)

The sharp distinction Holland makes in *Literature and the Brain*, *Meeting Movies*, and elsewhere between artists and scholars is more ambiguous than he wants us to believe. Freud also erred in making this firm distinction. Freud was jealous of creative writers who, he believed, were able to intuit truths that investigators like himself had to arrive at scientifically; yet ironically, the only major award Freud received was the Goethe Prize for *Literature*. Freud was, like the other examples of creative individuals Holland cites, a compulsive writer, as was Holland himself. Never short on ego, Holland was reluctant to group himself with the creative writers. Thus he makes statements like "Most of us lack this compulsion to create, this driven quality" (282). Yet Holland demonstrates throughout the course of a long life the insight, imagination, and literary style worthy of the poets and philosophers.

The Pleasure Principle

Holland wisely leaves the "big questions" unanswered in *Literature and the Brain*. We still don't know whether literature is innate and whether it confers evolutionary advantages. He does suggest, however, that literature depends upon metarepresentation, the ability to "think about our own and others' mental states" (326). He acknowledges that many people prize literature as a "Good Thing," but the trouble is, he adds quickly, "we don't know that any of this super-Darwinian claim is true. We don't know that literature enhances our brains' vital capacities. We might like to think that literature does all these good things, but do we have any proof?" (335-6).

Holland's final answer is that we read for pleasure, which is the only reason we need. We turn to literature "because we get pleasure from it, just as we get pleasure from all our SEEKINGs (at least when they succeed)" (353). The man who described himself in *The Dynamics of Literary Response* as "something of a Puritan" (222) happily ends his career by acknowledging pleasure as the major reason he turned to literature to which he devoted his entire life. "We do literature simply because we enjoy it" (333).

Doing literature mainly for pleasure doesn't blind Holland to the practical considerations of teaching literature, especially in public institutions. "We are unprofitable humanities professors," he remarks dryly, "who are competing in our universities' budgets with scientists who bring in grant and contract money. What we do sometimes seem to the legislators and trustees who manage our universities, arcane, frivolous, unmanly, or useless. We need some kind of convincers that what we do is worthwhile" (334). He understands the need for these arguments, which may involve the belief that literature heightens our moral power (though he reminds us that English departments are not populated by sages or saints), or the evolutionary claim that literature confers certain survival benefits. But he never loses sight that we read literature mainly for pleasure.

Three Reviews

The Maryland psychoanalyst Joseph R. Silvio's review of *Literature and the Brain* is largely a summary, but he concludes with a qualified endorsement. We read literature mainly for literature, he states, but reading Holland's book was work. "Unfortunately, the pleasures derived from Dr. Holland's book do not come so effortlessly, but the active effort of working through it does bring considerable rewards" (377). Describing *Literature and the Brain* as a "magnum opus," Nicholas O. Pagan suggests that "Holland may be given credit for being the first to try to relate the distinctive features of the two hemispheres to literary response" ("Evolution of Feeling-Dominated Response" 126). Pagan repeats Holland's cautionary reminder that left brain/right brain dichotomies are not absolute. Both brain hemispheres remain interconnected in ways that continue to challenge researchers. "If the key to unlocking the mystery of literature's appeal has to do with emotion," Pagan writes, "this may even be compatible with the Delphi seminar's creed 'Know thyself'" (126).

Patrick Colm Hogan, an English professor at the University of Connecticut who has written several books on the cognitive and affective aspects of literature, restates at the beginning of his review in *Style* the enthusiastic endorsement he wrote when he read an early draft of *Literature and the Brain*. "It is the first work I know of that systematically treats current neuroscientific research and a broad range of fundamental theoretical issues in literary study" (445). Hogan then recalls his history of "productive disagreement" with Holland, listing the ways in which he believes Holland misrepresents his own research on appraisal theory, the dominant account of emotion in cognitive science. He faults Holland, in particular, for the failure to see how appraisal theorists treat grief over death—a canny criticism in light of Holland's larger unwillingness to theorize loss and bereavement either in literature or life. Despite these criticisms, Hogan ends his review by reaffirming the value of *Literature and the Brain*. "Holland's book is challenging and stimulating on virtually every page. It brings together a breadth of reading, poses important questions, and provides provocative arguments" (450).

A Sharper Focus

Literature and the Brain was Holland's last book, but he continued to write, creating *A Sharper Focus*, an online resource that features his essays on over 200 films. He makes a distinction between film reviewers and film critics. "Film reviewers, by and large, treat films as entertainment, and that's what their readers want. Film critics, as opposed to reviewers, treat films as works of art, write about them as such, and encourage their readers to see films as art. That's what I do on *A Sharper Focus*." A theorist to the end, Holland observes that although it is more convenient to watch a film at home on a DVD or streamed to a television, iPhone, or iPad, there is a loss. Seeing a film in one of the palatial theaters of the past, one is part of a large audience: "you turn over part of your mental functioning—your defenses—to that collective mentality." The result is a loss of control that intensifies the viewing experience. There's another reason why it's better to see a film in a theater than at home. Because the theater and the projectionist control the viewing, the film rules. "You have to give yourself to it or leave. That is the important reason nothing substitutes for the theatrical experience."

Younger viewers (and older ones like myself) are unlikely to know that although watching a movie at home is technologically sophisticated, the progress is an example of back to the future. "Curiously, that was the way Edison created for seeing films when movies were first being invented. You were to look, one viewer at a time, into his Kinetoscope, like one of those viewers you still see at amusement parks where you peer through a peephole eyepiece as photographs that flip past, creating the illusion of motion."

Endings

Literature and the Brain never betrays any anxiety over aging, suffering, or death, the existential fears that the elderly often experience. Holland does make several observations about dementia, a topic that is more likely to conjure dread in older rather than younger people. He quotes Oliver Sacks's insight that style is the "deepest part of one's being" and "may be preserved, almost to the last, in a dementia." In Holland's words, Sacks "pointed to letters Henry James wrote in a delirium that show signs of the delirium but also James' distinctive prose style" (214). Holland never expresses the fear of losing his own cognitive ability, though he does tell us, without elaboration, "I am sorry to say that sometimes elderly professors suffering from dementia can speak whole lectures, because they have repeated them so often they have become rote" (134–5).

A chapter in *Literature and the Brain* is called "Endings," although it is not, counterintuitively, the end of the book. The real end of the book is worth quoting:

> What this book has shown, I hope, is how, when our brains work in special ways to create or re-create a literary work, we can freshly sense our selves and our world, relish our language, and confront our feelings

toward one another. Fully engaged with and thinking through works of literature and the arts, we uncover our own individuality. We open ourselves to the largest truth of who we are, who we have been, and who finally we will be. In the last analysis, understanding a literary work means understanding our own humanity. That was the foremost command of the Oracle at Delphi: Know thyself. That is the wonder and joy we get from literature—and the thoughtfulness—that our brains create. (359)

It is a perfect ending, combining feeling and thought, heart and mind, emotional and intellectual intelligence. "That's so like Norm," we want to exclaim. The words "I hope" have a double meaning, expressing Holland's intention in writing the book and his faith in the future. He uses strong, active verbs—"relish," "confront," "engage," as well as other verbs, such as "uncover" and "open," which convey his efforts to capture truths that may lie beneath the surface. The rhythm and cadences of the third sentence capture the temporal nature of human identity, past, present, and future. "In the last analysis" conjures up psycho*analysis*, his lifelong passion. The paragraph bespeaks generativity (as opposed to stagnation), the seventh of eight stages of Erik Erikson's life cycle, "the concern for establishing and guiding the next generation" (*Identity: Youth and Crisis* 138). The penultimate sentence alludes to the titles of two of his books: *Death in a Delphi Seminar* and his coauthored book with Murray Schwartz: *Know Thyself: Delphi Seminars*. The last sentence embodies the theme of *Literature and the Brain*, perhaps reminding us of the haunting line from an Emily Dickinson poem that he recites earlier, a line befitting a prolific author's final book: "There is a finished feeling . . . A leisure of the future" (238).

And Gratitude

Holland never theorizes gratitude in any of his books, but he always acknowledges his beholdenness to friends and colleagues at the beginning or end of a book. After listing his gratitude to many colleagues and friends who helped him with *Literature and the Brain*, he mentions two deceased individuals: his uncle-in-law, G. Henry Katz, who paid for his analysis, and Elizabeth Zetzel, his analyst. And, of course, he thanks the most important person in his life. "My heart warms especially when I think of all the things my wife Jane has contributed. I have tried to list them in the dedication, but there are always more" (361). One cannot imagine a more heartfelt sentence.

10

Contemplating Endings

Holland and I were never colleagues, but we became trusted friends, seeing each other at PsyArt conferences. After I received tenure, I reminded him in a telephone conversation about the rocky beginning of our relationship, about which he had completely forgotten. He had only a vague memory of Len's suicide, which occurred after Len had left Buffalo. In September 1999, sixteen years after he had moved to the University of Florida, Holland telephoned me, and, without disclosing he had been diagnosed with lung cancer, which was surgically removed in 1991[1]—I later found out about this from a mutual friend—he asked for my view of "rational suicide." We had a long telephone conversation, the details of which I cannot remember, and he then sent me a letter to which I responded with my own:

Dear Norm,

Thanks for your letter: it's always a treat to hear from you. I felt glad while reading the first paragraph and sad while reading the second. I hope that the question you posed is still an academic one, though I realize that one can't live forever. I do hope you're in good health and remain that way for a long, long time. I wish that I had the brain power in my 50s that you have in your 70s.

I've thought a great deal about the question you raise—both for myself and for others. I can't give you advice. But I can share with you my thinking—realizing, of course, that one can never predict one's feelings and thoughts while confronting the immediacy of death.

I used to feel, when I was younger (before Len died), that suicide was a viable option, particularly "rational suicide." I still believe that one should try to remain in control of one's destiny as long as possible, and that suffering is generally not ennobling, despite Tolstoy's *The Death of*

---

[1] In his review of the quasi-documentary 2005 film *Good Night and Good Luck* (appearing in his online film resource *A Sharper Focus*), about the television commentator Edward R. Murrow, who criticized the demagogic Joseph McCarthy, Holland points out that Murrow is always shown with a cigarette in his hand. Holland then adds, "In the 1950s I was, like most of my friends, puffing away, and it was only decades later that the evidence became so clear to us that we all had to quit."

Ivan Ilych. Moreover, I hope that my own dying is not prolonged, which would be excruciating for my family. Suicide becomes attractive because it is a way to control one's life, even though at the same time it annihilates all control. It also seems attractive if one believes that one is making it easier for one's family, even if they may not view it that way.

But what worries me about rational suicide is the signal it gives to our loved ones. If, for example, people are encouraged to commit suicide when they are terminal, then sooner or later their children and grandchildren might well feel similar pressure when they are in that situation. That is, I can imagine people thinking, "My father killed himself when he had terminal cancer, and now that I'm in the same situation, perhaps I should do so too—my gift to my family." I think that the expectation might then be to commit suicide as an alternative to burdening one's family. Within a few years those who do not commit suicide when terminally ill might be viewed as selfish.

I say this because of the contagious nature of suicide. It is well documented that when one person in a family commits suicide, the other family members are at risk. Suicide becomes a deadly seed that takes root, crowding out other more life-preserving plants, and no one can predict where and how it will grow. Already there are instances of people who took their own lives because they thought they had a terminal illness, when in fact they were not seriously ill.

About a year and a half ago, my father died of prostate cancer. He was not supposed to die—that is, all of the doctors assured us, first, that he did not have prostate cancer, second, that although he had it, it was treatable and had not spread, third, that although it did spread, he would have many more years. Well, he died within six months of being diagnosed. All the doctors were shocked, as we were. No one can explain why he succumbed so quickly, but I suspect that my father's negativity did him in. He was the most ornery person I ever knew, and once he realized he had cancer, I think he decided that he didn't want to be a patient. "The story is over," he told me, when he was still relatively healthy. I was angry at him for not being a fighter and kept imploring him to take his medicine and food and do his exercises, lest he die of pneumonia. The last few weeks were horrible. The irony was that even as *we* knew he was dying, his doctors (all excellent, from Sloan-Kettering) kept insisting that he had many more years. At a certain point his suffering was so awful that we wanted him to die, to end his and our suffering.

Yet I would not have wanted him to commit suicide. I don't regard suicide as an act of courage or cowardice, selflessness or selfishness, but rather as an act of hopelessness. Throughout my father's life he was an unpleasant, hopeless person, treating my mother very poorly, and for as long as I can remember, I counteridentified with him. I counteridentified with him when he was living, and I counteridentified with him when he was dying. For example, not once during his illness did he thank my mother for being such a good caretaker. He just assumed that she would do everything for him. Nor did he tell her that he loved her or was appreciative of their life together. If and when I'm in my father's situation, I hope I will be able to express my love and thanks toward my family: they are the ones who matter to me, and I believe that I can make their suffering easier not by committing suicide but remaining committed to life to the very end.

As you can see, my argument against rational suicide lies with its aftermath on family and friends. We may not be in a position to give our loved ones a good death, but at least we can try to avoid burdening them with the guilt and stigma that almost inevitably accompany suicide. You mention the Japanese as an example of a culture that doesn't stigmatize suicide, but even they were horrified by Mishima's suicide.

My opposition to suicide does not preclude the possibility of a dying patient having an understanding with his or her physician or family to "pull the plug" when the time comes or to receive a fatal dose of morphine. I don't view this as suicide but rather as pain management. To be sure, there are many ambiguities surrounding this situation, but I think that these are ambiguities that one can live—and die—with.

I've never expressed these thoughts before in writing, and in trying to answer your question, I'm clarifying my own thinking. I'm honored that you asked for my point of view.

Holland, who read deeply in literature and psychology, was almost certainly familiar with Albert Camus's bold assertion in *The Myth of Sisyphus*: "There is but one truly serious philosophical problem, and that is suicide. Judging whether life is or is not worth living amounts to answering the fundamental question of philosophy." Less well known is Camus's unequivocal answer to the question: "It is essential to die unreconciled and not of one's own free will. Suicide is a repudiation" (41). Everything I have read suggests that most terminally ill people who raise the suicide question do so for psychological rather than philosophical reasons: the dying wish to be reassured that they will not be forced to endure unendurable suffering.

Barbara was in great pain in the final weeks of her life, despite massive amounts of morphine, and near the end she asked me if I would give her *all* of her morphine. As I admit in *Dying to Teach*, her question was horrifying, reminding me of Len's suicide decades earlier, despite entirely different circumstances. I'll never know whether Barbara was in her "right mind" when she asked me the question—she was taking so much morphine that she was not thinking clearly. Nor will I know what she would have wanted me to do if I had answered the question positively. I could not fulfill Barbara's request, if that's what it was, and I learned only after her death that sometimes, with a patient's or family's approval, a physician will prescribe enough morphine to ensure death. Barbara's suicide question haunted me for years, and I still don't know the right answer to the question. Kierkegaard observed that we can understand our life only backward, but we must live it forward—but some questions remain torturously ambiguous even in hindsight.

Holland wrote me back immediately, and while I don't have his permission to quote his letter, I don't think there's anything in it to which he would object. There's nothing personal about the letter: indeed, given his question about suicide, it's striking that he never explains the reason for raising it:

Dear Jeff,

I've been mulling over your wise letter with its characteristically personal and human touches. I hear and appreciate what you're saying about the effect on family. I would hate to think that anything I did to shorten suffering urged anyone I love on the same path.

You make a strong point about the uncertainty of diagnoses. Yes, that is troubling. Yet, is life in the prolonged old age that is common now so fine that one cannot afford to lose days, months, or even years of it? I suspect that's a question that I answer one way now and I might well answer the other way four or five years hence. That's a hard one and I don't have an answer—I suspect it depends on what you feel at that time.

Yet the question of family and loved ones leaves me with a further question. Suppose the decision were all very open and everyone agreed on it. I'm thinking about the Kevorkian situations, where loved ones accompany the sufferer and are present at the act. Or as described in Derek Humphry's books, where the loved ones accompany the sufferer and are present at the act. Or suppose the sufferer simply said on repeated occasions before the question arose, This is my philosophy, this is what I'm going to do, I don't want you to worry, I prefer it this way, it's a purely personal decision, nothing you need take as an example, just my preference. Those are two possible ways one might obviate negative effects on the survivors. The second, clearly, is more problematic than the first.

Your account of your father's life and death was saddening. It's hard to think someone living such negativity.

Your letter was a long one and I hate to be troubling you again—except that I think we are both interested in thinking these questions through as best we can in our present circumstances, where the issue is moot. I suppose it is foolish of me, but I keep thinking of those noble acts of suicide in Shakespeare: Brutus, Cassius, Cleopatra. They do seem noble to me, yet I have to say there are others that don't: Romeo, Portia. And is literature relevant here? It's complicated.

Anyway, thanks for your letter. I do appreciate it, and I do not wish to overburden you with this second round, yet I do value very much your thinking.

Holland comments on the "characteristically personal and human touches" of my letter, but without being overtly self-disclosing, he reveals his own characteristically personal and human touches: the wish not to burden anyone with his suffering, the need to think through complicated questions, the ability to read carefully one's arguments and then make compelling counterarguments, the recognition that literature may or may not be helpful when making difficult existential decisions. He ends the letter with an expression of gratitude, which I greatly valued, the reason, no doubt, I have kept his letter for two decades. We never spoke about the suicide question again.

There isn't a hint of Holland's cancer diagnosis in any of his writings, but I wonder if his heightened awareness of mortality motivated him to write "The Story of a Psychoanalytic Critic," published around the same time he wrote to me about the suicide question. If so, that may explain the essay's puzzling last sentence. After describing the central insight he had gleaned from psychoanalysis, the inseparability of fears and wishes, he observes, as if he is writing good-bye: "Had I not lived the story you have just read, had I not known that wish and fear both as theme and as insight, I could not now go on to another chapter" (258–9).

Jane Holland's Death

Many people are too distraught to write about a loved one's recent death, but Holland sent an email to the members of the PsyArt listserv on June 11, 2015, one day after his wife's death:

> I am very sorry to tell you that my wife of 60 years, Jane Kelley Holland, died early Thursday morning. She had been ill for quite a while, but she died peacefully. Hospice made it possible for her to take her last breaths with her head on my shoulder. Both our children, Kelley and John, were in the room. Jane lived to find the world a wonderful place and leave it even better.

She was a dedicated and enormously influential advocate for women's freedom of choice and health, serving in leadership positions with Planned Parenthood in both New York and Florida and creating networks for caregivers to improve their reach to women and children in both states.

Jane, a redhead till the end, also traveled the world and devoured literature, opera and classical music, movies, and theater. She was a prodigious punster with an encyclopedic vocabulary, rattling off words like "salubrious" even in her last days. She never said no to a Maine lobster, a dozen Wellfleet oysters, or an organization working to help women anywhere in the world.

She leaves behind her husband, her children, four grandchildren, and many, many grateful women. All of us will miss her.

After Jane's death, I sent my condolences to Holland, and we had several email exchanges. He must have spent hours and hours patiently writing to colleagues and friends. He appreciated letters of condolence: "At a time like this," he wrote to me five days after Jane's death, "thoughts like yours are a great comfort." I told him in an email that although I had the pleasure of meeting Jane only a few times at PsyArt conferences, she was always witty and warm. "I've never read a writer who devoted more books to a beloved spouse than you; your dedications to Jane were always an example of showing instead of telling." Later, when writing a book about Irvin Yalom, I discovered that he, too, wrote deeply moving dedications to his wife in each of his many books.

It's curious how I associate Holland with Len's and Barbara's deaths. I recall the lovely summer day Barbara and I met the Hollands for lunch in Cooperstown, New York, where they were attending a performance at Glimmerglass Opera. I remember the date, August 11, 2002, our thirty-fourth wedding anniversary. Barbara hadn't been feeling well, and when the Hollands asked us how we were, she said that she had minor stomach discomfort. Barbara was not given to complaint, and there was an uneasy silence for a few seconds. The next day she was diagnosed with pancreatic cancer.

For decades I had sent "print" holiday cards to the Hollands, and during the last decade or so they responded with virtual cards. He knew that five years after Barbara's death, I began dating Julie, whom I married in 2011. Julie and I attended eight PsyArt conferences together, but this was after the Hollands had stopped attending them. In his emails, Holland often expressed the desire to meet Julie, whom he referred to as the "mystery woman." On December 29, 2016, Holland emailed me from his retirement community, telling me about a "special friend" he had met whose husband died shortly after Jane. "I think of you and Julie as models." I wrote back immediately, expressing my delight that he was doing well:

It's always great to hear from you—and hear that you are doing well despite your beloved Jane's absence. Yes, I hope that Julie has the pleasure of meeting you. You have been such an important person in my professional life. Though I've never become a reader-response critic, like you, your work has been inspirational to me, and I can never thank you enough for your support when I came up for tenure in the 1970s. Your letter was crucial; without it, I might not have received tenure.

I'm happy to hear about your special friend. I suspect that each of you is an unexpected gift to the other, something you could not have imagined years ago. When I was researching my 2015 book *Writing Widowhood: The Landscapes of Bereavement*, the best quotation I came upon was Eleanor Bergstein's observation to Joyce Carol Oates [who had recently lost her husband of forty-seven years, Raymond Smith]: "Though you loved Ray, very much, and could not imagine living without him, you will begin to discover that you are doing things that Ray would not have been interested in doing, and you are meeting people you would not have met when Ray was alive, and all this will change your life for the better, though you might not think so now."

I'm just finishing a book on the existential psychiatrist and novelist Irvin Yalom. I'm sure you have heard of him and probably read some of his books, perhaps *Love's Executioner* or *When Nietzsche Wept*. I sent him the manuscript, and he graciously read and commented on it. He's 86 and has just completed his memoirs. Have you thought about writing your own memoirs? If so, I would love to read it.

"Thanks, Jeff," Holland wrote back on December 31, "for your encouraging email, as always humanly wise. I'll think about memoirs. At the moment, I'm having a lot of fun doing close readings of classic movies. 136 so far. www.asharperfocus.com. Best to Julie and let's both of us keep on living."

The Rest Is Silence

I learned of his death from Murray Schwartz's eloquent posting on PsyArt on October 4, 2017:

> Norm died on the morning of September 28 while he was peacefully asleep. His passing marks the end of a long and wonderfully productive and generous life. Without him, this message would not be reaching you. Without him and Jane, the PsyArt Foundation would not exist. Without him, the field of psychoanalytic study of the arts would be a much less

rich and varied part of the intellectual history of the past and present centuries.

In an obituary published in *The Gainesville Sun*, Deborah Strange cited several of Holland's Buffalo and Florida colleagues who paid tribute to his life. "He was certainly the single most important figure of American study of psychoanalytic literature," Murray Schwartz observed. Richard Brantley, a retired Florida colleague, stated that he took an "old fashioned history of ideas" approach to literature. "But when I talked to Norm, and when I read his many books on the subject, I gradually learned to be less old fashioned and to include a personal and humanizing element in my intellectual histories."

A brief obituary of Holland appeared in *PMLA*, the leading journal in the field of literary studies. Written by Nicholas O. Pagan, of the University of Malaya, it describes Holland's major writings, noting that his more recent books are not as widely known as those from the late 1960s and the 1970s:

> This may be partly because Holland had moved further and further away from any attempt to provide fresh insights into works of literature. He was always more interested in human nature than in hermeneutics. Indeed, his sustained concern for "the human" might help explain why some of his writings have been translated into so many languages, including Japanese, Korean, and Mandarin. Ultimately, Holland may best be remembered as a literary theorist, some of whose writings will never relinquish their global appeal because they invariably focus on the relation between reading literature and human identity. (1270)

Conclusion

Norman Holland's Legacy

Holland's final years demonstrate what Erik Erikson calls "ego integrity," the eighth and final stage of his theory of psychosocial development, the time when people contemplate their accomplishments and prepare for death. "Only in him who in some way has taken care of things and people," Erikson writes in *Childhood and Society*, "and has adapted himself to the triumphs and disappointments adherent to being, the originator of others or the generator of products and ideas—only in him may gradually ripen the fruit of these seven stages" (268). Admitting that he lacked a clear definition of ego integrity, which is the opposite of despair, Erikson pointed out that it includes the ego's "accrued assurance of its proclivity for order and meaning" (268), a statement that would resonate strongly with Holland's lifelong identity theme. Ego identity, Erikson adds, "implies an emotional integration which permits participation by followership as well as acceptance of the responsibility of leadership" (269).

Creating a Psychoanalytic Community

Apart from bequeathing his writings, a major part of Norman Holland's legacy, in Erikson's terms, the responsibility of leadership, was his creation of PsyArt, the online forum. Started in 1993, the discussion group encourages the exchange of ideas about the psychological study of literature and the arts or about psychoanalysis or psychology generally. A message posted on the listserv goes to all the members. Holland moderated the listserv until his death; Murray Schwartz now moderates it. The number of subscribers has decreased, but the listserv still remains a valuable discussion group. Although conversations on PsyArt have on rare occasions been contentious, reflecting the heated controversies that have bedeviled psychoanalysis from its inception, the discourse has remained remarkably civil and friendly, a testament to both Holland and Schwartz.

A typical exchange: on the day I began writing this chapter, in late October, 2019, an Israeli clinical psychologist posted a message asking whether there are any PhD programs, preferably in the New York City area, where she could study psychoanalysis from a humanistic perspective. Claire Kahane, one of Holland's Buffalo colleagues who is now a research associate at UC Berkeley, suggested several northeast universities with psychoanalytic literary programs. Murray Schwartz responded with additional suggestions. A day later Martin Gliserman, former editor of *American Imago*, offered other recommendations. "Thank you for these ideas," the psychologist wrote, "which are very helpful for me to begin my search for a studies program."

Two weeks later a more scholarly thread began when Caragh Wells, a senior lecturer in the Department of Spanish, Portuguese, and Latin American Studies at the University of Bristol, UK, sought information about the 2004 book *Peut-on appliquer la littérature la psychanalyse* by the French analyst Pierre Bayard. Within a day came responses from the French psychiatrist Yves Thoret (whose help Holland acknowledges in *Death in a Delphi Seminar*), Peter L. Rudnytsky, Daniel Rancour-Laferriere, and the British writer Meg Harris Williams. Murray Schwartz followed with the recommendation to read Rosemary Rizq's essay "The Figure in the Carpet: Psychoanalysis and Ways of Reading" and Norman Holland's *The Critical I*.

Holland also created the PsyArt Foundation, to which he and his wife made a generous financial contribution. PsyArt hosts an annual summer Conference on Psychology and the Arts at the University of Florida that occurs usually in a different European city each year. The thirty-sixth International Conference was held in Vienna in 2019, sponsored by the PsyArt Foundation, the Sigmund Freud University, and the University of Vienna. Papers deal with any application of psychoanalysis—including Freudian, Jungian, and Lacanian approaches. No less welcome are approaches to the arts based on cognitive psychology and neuroscience. The conference is small (with a maximum of seventy-five papers), convivial, and draws scholars from around the world. The PsyArt Foundation offers up to three Norman and Jane Holland Travel Fellowships for outstanding graduate student papers. To honor the memory of Andrew Gordon, who directed the Institute for the Psychological Study of the Arts at the University of Florida and organized the annual Conference on Literature and Psychology, two Fellowships are offered for PhD students who participate at the conference for the first time.

PsyArt: A Hyperlink Journal for the Psychology of the Arts has been in existence since 1997. A free, open access journal for submissions of any type of psychology to all forms of art, it publishes up to fifteen articles a year. All articles are peer reviewed by two experts in the field; authors and reviewers do not know each other's names. Holland was the founding editor-in-chief until 2000, followed by Murray Schwartz (2000–11) and Camelia Elias of Roskilde University, Denmark (2011–17). The current editor-in-chief is Samir Dayal, professor of English and Media Studies at Bentley University.

Holland's books were published by the country's most prestigious university presses, including Columbia, Cornell, Harvard, Oxford, and Yale, as well as the country's leading commercial publishers, such as Macmillan, McGraw-Hill, Norton, and Routledge. He chose the PsyArt Foundation to publish his last book, *Literature and the Brain*, an indication of his commitment to the foundation he created.

Importance in One's Domain

Many psychoanalytic scholars expressed their gratitude to Holland, beginning with Murray Schwartz, who wrote to me when I told him I was beginning this book.

> I am always amazed at his ability to read texts, and though we had many arguments about identity theory over the years, he was a very important figure in the history of psychoanalytic criticism and theory, and a very generous colleague and teacher. Have I told you that his partner in his last year sent me his [edition of Freud's] *Standard Edition*, which I donated to Hampshire College? (My *Standard Edition* was a gift from the Buffalo graduate students.)

Affecting Eternity

"A teacher affects eternity; he can never tell where his influence stops." To understand the truth of Henry Adams's insight, which ironically belies his frustration as a new assistant professor of history at Harvard more than a century ago, I sent a posting to PsyArt in December, 2019, asking members to comment briefly on Holland's influence on them. I received an outpouring of responses, too many to include, but the following are representative. Of all the people who responded, Robert Sprich, professor emeritus, English and Media Studies at Bentley University, knew Holland the longest:

> Norm Holland was my freshman advisor at MIT (1956). That was about the time that he started the program at the Boston Psychoanalytic Institute. Of course, I took all of his courses (Introduction to Literature, Shakespeare, Comic Sensibility) and became interested in "psychological" criticism. At Norm's suggestion I joined the Boston Group for Applied Psychoanalysis in 1963. (I gave a paper on *Jude the Obscure*.) I kept in

touch with Norm after his move to SUNY-Buffalo. In the spring of 1976 I was appointed a Visiting Fellow there and enjoyed taking courses with Norm and Murray Schwartz. In 1977 Richard Noland and I edited a collection of Simon Lesser's essays titled *The Whispered Meanings*. Norm wrote a Preface. I did a piece on Norm's reader-response criticism: "Pressed Flowers/Fresh Flowers: New Directions in Psychoanalytic Criticism," published in *Colby Library Quarterly* in 1977; Norm said, "Let's hope the flowers continue to bloom!" I joined the PsyArt Network and attended the summer conferences in Italy, Denmark, and Germany. In 1996 I hosted the International Conference on Psychology and the Arts at Bentley University, which Norm said was one of the best. Thereafter Norm and I communicated by email. I was glad that I was able to put into words how important he was to me. He spoke of the value of long term friendships.

Claire Kahane, professor emerita, SUNY-Buffalo, and a graduate of the San Francisco Center for Psychoanalysis, was one of a handful of female faculty members in the sprawling Buffalo English department, but she immediately felt at home, partly because of Holland's welcoming presence:

I first heard about Norman Holland from Fred Crews when I was a grad student in his [Berkeley] psychoanalysis and literature course. In those pre-apostasy days, Crews informed us that the best and most insightful advocate of psychoanalytic criticism was Norman Holland and that we should read *The Dynamics of Literary Response*. I rushed to get a copy and was blown away by Norm's astute use of psychoanalytic theory to unravel those dynamics. A year later, when I was on the job market, I was lucky enough to be offered a position at SUNY-Buffalo, where Norm had organized a Literature-and-Psychology sub-group in the English Department called the Center for the Psychological Study of the Arts.

It was an amazing time at Buffalo, its intellectual ferment and academic experimentation a treat for a new assistant professor. Although I was a woman in a department predominantly male—the ratio of men to women at the time was 70 to 5—the Center was very welcoming to me, with Norm very supportive of my feminist projects. And I learned so much from him. Norm's and Murray Schwartz's Delphi Seminar, which put into practice their assumption that readers interpret literature through their own unconscious conflicts and concerns by having us interpret our own literary responses to texts, proved an eye-opener as soon as I discovered that my interpretation of Macbeth focused on his relation to Cordelia and reflected my own relationship with my father. And then, in 1980, Norm used his Chair in the department to fund my conference, "The Creative Use of Difference," one of the first feminist conferences to bring together feminist-psychoanalytic critics from around the country. In the years following, he and Murray instituted the International Conference on Psychology and the Arts that began in 1983, again a pioneer gathering of psychoanalytic critics in Pecs, Hungary, that has continued, as you know, in different venues to this day. In Buffalo, Norm was always a genial social presence as well, he and Jane opening their home for occasional social gatherings that made us truly a community. When he left Buffalo for Florida, he left a huge gap in my departmental life.

David Willbern, professor emeritus at SUNY-Buffalo, was Holland's colleague for more than a decade, and he offers both praise and criticism of Holland's reader-response approach to literature. David's weekly responses to the actual Delphi seminar he attended in the 1970s give us a vivid first-person account that we do not see in Holland's novel. I smiled when I read his comments about Holland's penchant for diagrams and charts, few of which, I must admit ruefully, had any impact on me:

I knew Norm reasonably well from 1971 to 1983, when we were colleagues at SUNY-Buffalo. After that we kept sporadically in touch via correspondence and conferences to 2017, his last year. At Buffalo, I sat in on seminars with Norm and Murray Schwartz. Through Murray I learned about object-relations psychoanalysis (especially Winnicott), and through Norm I encountered Heinz Lichtenstein, a European psychoanalyst practicing in Buffalo, whose ideas about identity formation were central to Norm's notions of readers forming "transactive" relationships to literature. Norm refashioned Lichtenstein's concept of unconscious instrumental identity into ideas of "Identity Themes" in individual writers and readers. The idea was important and helpful for Norm, but not so much for me. His first published work on identity themes, I believe, was for the poet H.D. (who was analyzed by Freud): "To close the gap with signs." For me, the phrase evaporates into generality: What is language itself but closing gaps with signs? I should add that the essay, published first as an article and then as Chapter One in *Poems in Persons* (1973), is a superb blend of biography and literary analysis. For me the identity themes distillation adds little.

At Buffalo I participated in the "Delphi Seminar"—described in Norm and Murray's book *Know Thyself: Delphi Seminars* (2009). These seminars were of unquestionable value in revealing personal styles of reading. In them I would sometimes argue with Norm about the extent to which subjective cognition constrains perceptions of objective reality. Gradually I began to understand for myself that the fact that individuals had personal styles of cognition did not obviate the brute fact of (scientifically measurable) external objects, *aka* the "real world." I would also argue with Norm about the value of naïve (undergrad) literary responses, and the larger question of "right" or "wrong" readings. For me it was a pedagogical question: What are we teaching, literature or psychology? (Yes, I know: both.)

Some of my arguments—and some of the flavor of the Delphi Seminar—are in copies of my weekly responses that I've kept from over forty years ago. I quote four instances. The first is my response to Norm's shift away from literary study and analysis—what is "in" the text—and into personal psychology (student responses)—what a reader brings to a text. (This shift was later intensified when Norm moved into brain science.)

(1) "I knew you so well on paper, and now that I know you in person I'm finding the stranger parts. Years ago, when I stumbled onto Lit&Psych (as a field of study), and then your Shakespeare books and *The Dynamics of Literary Response*, I could feel my eyes being opened. 'This is all so strange,' I would think, 'so weird and so true.' You helped me put a body (mine) back into literature, and exemplified for me a way of reading that paid attention to everything: sound, texture, shape, image, presence, absence, even meaning. Your work examined what others denied. Encountering your paper person was liberating for me. Now I've discovered that you've liberated me into a box you've just climbed out of. 'Wait for me, Norm,' I want to say. 'I'm still back here, where you were, not sure that I've checked it all out.'"

On Norm's penchant for diagrams and charts as a defense against what he called "groupiness and peopletude":

(2) "You would chart us, box us in your crystal-set diagrams—Christ, how you schematize!—and yet you would befriend us, apologize to us for being an engineer and not a poet. That tension in you. People vs. Charts. Like all those polarized identity themes you thought up: you're in that 'vs': a versus, a verse, turning now this way, now that. Janus-faced: the scientist and/or the humanist. Both sides can be a refuge from the other."

On Norm's position as director/participant/observer in the seminar:

(3) "You are the person in the center: center-maker, center-finder. 'One person at the center,' you write. 'All the others circle around him. They

focus on him, or he acts on them.' Elsewhere you write, 'He has seized the center.' I recognize that your discovery of Central Themes is an analogue of your own wish for centrality: a literary image of a personal stance. The convergence method."

On my objection to identity themes:

(4) "Your urge to encapsulate and schematize is an aspect of your interpretive genius, but I find it reductive. . . . You seem to have some skepticism about your schemata. In your recent talk on 'Identity and Its Uses'—a nicely utilitarian title—you spoke of the identity theme as 'a handy-dandy marvelous concept, a way of grasping the essence of another person.' I flash on a fast-talking snake oil salesman or foodmill pusher. 'Step up, ladies and gents, and get yours while they last! Guaranteed to solve any essence. Distill the loved ones of your choice!' I'll listen to the spiel, but I'm not sure what I'm buying. Grasping, but no touching. You're very tactful, but I wonder how tactile. How to be DEFT (Norm's acronym for four categories of reader response, Defense, Expectation, Fantasy, Transformation) with (Look, Ma!) no hands."

Norm's centering was extensive. At Buffalo he created the Center for the Psychological Study of the Arts, the Group for Applied Psychoanalysis, the annual May symposia for Literature and Psychology, and the annual International Conference on Psychology and the Arts, which has endured now for almost forty years. The Symposia and the Conferences were a lively and casual blend of intellectual and social interactions, like the summer parties at Norm's pool in the Buffalo suburbs.

Norm's wife, Jane, was at those parties, sharing in the conviviality and the intellectual conversations. The couple shared an intimate partnership: a marriage of true minds, as Shakespeare wrote. They bought identical cars (Toyota Tercels as I recall). They had identical suitcases, which once led Norm to miss a flight to an international Lit&Psych conference, when he grabbed Jane's suitcase instead of his own (she had packed to join him later), discovering at the airport that he had no passport, nor clothes he could consider wearing.

Norm was bright, curious, affable. He was intellectually and emotionally generous to me and his colleagues. He was also quite frugal—a trait that could shade into parsimony. His business sense eventually produced a large treasury in his largest orbit: IPSA (Institute for Psychological Study of the Arts) at the University of Florida, that with the help of his colleague Andy Gordon (now also sadly deceased) continues to support conferences and PsyArt, the online forum and journal initiated by Norm.

Richard P. Wheeler, professor emeritus of English and emeritus dean, University of Illinois at Urbana-Champaign, was a graduate student at SUNY-Buffalo when Holland arrived along with Murray Schwartz and C. L. Barber. Reading Holland's early books was a transformative experience for him:

> As someone stumbling around with only three certainties in my intellectual life—I knew I wanted to study Shakespeare, and I knew I wanted to study Freud, and I knew I wanted to connect them somehow—I could not have been luckier. Through all of the maddening complications and struggles that have faced anyone interested in psychoanalysis and literary criticism over the last half century, the deep and wonderfully clear grounding provided by Norm's *The Dynamics of Literary Response* has been a godsend. And his *Psychoanalysis and Shakespeare* set out a whole new field of possibilities, with Norm as reliable, generous guide. I have admired and benefited from much of his subsequent work, but these two early books were more or less hard-wired into my system, equally useful when I found myself in agreement and when I saw things differently.

"I could write a chapter myself on what Norm meant to me and how much he affected my life," declared Burton Melnick, who as a doctoral student at the University of Lausanne enlisted Holland's help and then went on to teach English at the International School in Geneva. Like the other former students or examinees who responded to my PsyArt posting, Burt implies that Holland was not only supportive but also protective:

> When my doctoral dissertation on Jane Austen was approaching completion, we needed to appoint a third member to the jury. The requirements were that this person would be a specialist in lit-and-psych and would come from somewhere outside of French-speaking Switzerland. My director and I approached some people from nearby countries but without success. I then wrote to Norm, whom I didn't know personally, to see if he could suggest someone. He did, and the person, who lived in southwest Germany, was an excellent choice—except that he couldn't free himself from his analytic practice to be able to come to Lausanne at the necessary time. When I wrote back to Norm to ask for another recommendation, he simply volunteered himself to come, despite the distance. His comments on the dissertation were extremely helpful and constructive.
>
> At the defense I got the impression that he didn't know the European traditions about such an event. The custom is to go out of your way to give the candidate an ostentatiously hard time. It is a matter of show. The

candidate, of course, knows this and so can remain relatively unruffled. But Norm, with his kind nature, couldn't hide how disturbed he was by the pretty brutal and apparently stupid attacks on me that the man from Geneva was making. (The director, a scholar and a gentleman and something of a politician besides, said very little and quietly pushed all the right buttons.) After the defense Norm took me aside and said something like, "Who *is* that guy? He comes on like a Mack truck." The quotation isn't perfectly accurate, but the part about the Mack truck is. I think it was at the party after the defense that Norm invited me to join PsyArt and encouraged me to come to the conferences. He later invited me to become one of the editors of the PsyArt Journal.

Wendy Creed's experience with her dissertation was not traumatic but nerve-wracking, and Holland characteristically came to her defense. I suggested earlier that Holland's beaming face had a Gatsby-like quality, which in Nick's words "concentrated on *you* with an irresistible prejudice in your favor." Wendy makes a similar observation:

> I am looking at the photograph of Norm on the back cover of *Death in a Delphi Seminar*, and I am instantly transported back to the first time I encountered him. The moment when he graciously answered an email from an overexcited Master's student (me) working on her dissertation on the reader and gothic. I had only recently discovered his writing, specifically, *5 Readers Reading*, which lit a fire in my brain that has yet to extinguish. He answered all my queries (which he must have heard so many times before in many guises) with patience, good grace and humility. When PsyArt came to Greenwich in 2003, John Williams and I had the pleasure of hosting the conference. Watching him talk was fascinating. He held his audience captive, every pause, every nuance carefully chosen for maximum effect. He made it look effortless and left you wanting more. I thought long and hard about his affect and concluded that above all else Norm was a seeker of knowledge who liked nothing better than to share what he had discovered.
>
> When it was time to have my Ph.D. examined (reader response to the book as a physical object), who else would it be but Norm? Having read my thesis, he flew to the UK and one sunny Greenwich day I stood before my examiners and answered questions they put to me. I was nervous, shaking, and to add to my tension, my IT demonstration refused to work; but a quiet calm voice just said "Breathe, take your time," and he smiled, and after that the discussion flowed. That single, succinct phrase sums up my memory of him, calm, encouraging, approachable but most

of all open. All delivered with that cheeky smile, a smile that began from his eyes.

I was lucky enough to meet Jane too, such a complementary "marriage of two minds." She was a woman of strong social conscience, and together they were a formidable intellectual pair. On one of their visits, we went to George Bernard Shaw's house, and, stopping for a foaming pint and a rambling conversation at the local hostelry, we talked and talked and laughed. They loved the house, and they enjoyed this idiosyncratic piece of Englishness, tucked away in the Hertfordshire countryside. I can still see them in my mind's eye, arm in arm walking through Shaw's garden, complete and happy.

I guess what I take from knowing Norm (and of course Jane) is that it is less what he said but how he made you feel. It was as if you had known him forever, that you were so very special to him and of course you were, because this seeker of knowledge was listening to you. To quote Newton, "If I have seen further than others, it is by standing upon the shoulders of giants." Norm *was* such a giant.

Holland was the director of Laura Keyes Perry's dissertation committee at Buffalo, and she was struck by how careful a reader he was, "able to follow one's arguments and make suggestions or corrections without condescension." Laura, who later taught at DePauw University in Greencastle, Indiana, was impressed by Holland's many acts of kindness, as the following example shows:

When I started applying for jobs, he suggested that I come to his house to use his computer to write letters of application. Using a form letter would save me a lot of typing and time. Now, Norm really liked computers. I think his first one was from Radio Shack, which gives you an idea how early he became a fan. I remember that before AOL, he had a gadget that entered numbers for access to the internet, so that he did not have to enter about 30 digits every time.

In his enthusiasm, he overlooked the fact that I had never used a computer before. Apparently I was a slow learner, too; I remember that I kept hitting Enter at the end of lines, as one does with a typewriter, instead of letting the software deal with that. My first draft looked very strange. The afternoon wore on, and eventually it was time to eat. Instead of leaving me upstairs swearing at the computer, Norm's wife, Jane, graciously invited me to join them for dinner.

They were both kind people. They made me feel welcome and special. Maybe they found graduate students occasionally amusing, but who wouldn't? They were open, tolerant, caring, and generous to us.

Considering how much time I spend using a computer these days, I think I should be grateful to Norm for teaching me that, too!

Holland's misgivings regarding Lacanian theory did not affect his collegial relationships with French clinicians and scholars, as can be seen in the following statement offered by Yves Thoret, an associate professor of psychopathology in the University of Paris-10-Nanterre, psychiatrist in hospital practice, and a "regular" at the International Conferences on Psychology and the Arts:

> Thank you for offering to collect souvenirs of the PsyArt members about this late great figure of Norman Holland. During one of his comings to Paris, we organized with Robert Silhol a conference of Norman about his fantastic researches about the links between literature and performing arts on one side and psychoanalysis on the other side. It took place in an amphitheater of the Sainte-Anne psychiatric hospital in Paris, as a major conference of the CREF, "centre de recherches et d'études freudiennes" belonging with its leader Professor Roger Dorey to the Paris-10-Nanterre University.
>
> He was brilliant as ever and always very finely friendly. He mentioned my interest to the PsyArt Research group with a reference to the famous French film, *Le Ballon Rouge* by François Truffaut. He liked to use some sentences in French and his presentation of this research was most brilliant and appealing. We were admirative of his keen reference to the French analytic schools, considering their specific conflictual ambition to be properly French. For many members of our research team, it was a wonderful discovery of such a rich interest about the deep links between clinical practice, psychoanalysis, literature and performing arts.
>
> We appreciated as well his great culture about French analysts, writers, and also, our good food and wine.
>
> After this brilliant conference, I drove Jane and him, with Robert, to their hotel and it was the day when, once a year, we all celebrate music, "la fête de la musique," as if Paris was offering to Jane and him a musical homage all spread around Paris city, so well deserved by them.
>
> Such events leave in my souvenir a very strong reference and example. This souvenir was the strongest one I could evoke now as a funeral homage.

Nearly all of the respondents commented on Holland's approachability and inviting presence, appreciated greatly by graduate students and new assistant professors. Cecilia Beecher Martins, a faculty member at the English Studies

Department of the School of Arts & Humanities, Universidade de Lisboa, first met Holland at the twenty-fifth International Conference on Psychology and the Arts in Lisbon in June, 2008. She had read his essay "The Mind and the Book" and *Meeting Movies*, both of which she felt would be helpful for her dissertation on how readers can be affected by getting lost in a book or a film. She hoped to meet Holland at the conference but feared he would be too busy to hear about her dissertation:

> I wondered if I could talk to Norm, but how? After all, he was a highly acclaimed and recognised scholar; I was beginning my doctoral project. Moreover, as I attended sessions, I saw how those presenting their papers always wanted Norm's feedback, and during coffee breaks there was always a queue of people waiting to talk to him. So, I reconciled myself to the fact that I would not get to talk to him, but I would hear his keynote lecture and the sessions were very relevant and interesting.
>
> However, I need not have worried. Towards the end of one of the coffee breaks, as I was standing beside the coffee pot, a warm, youthful voice greeted me, "Well, Cecilia, what are you doing here?" I was completely taken aback; there was Norm himself, asking me by name (of course, he had read my name tag) what I was doing at the conference. I managed to explain very quickly, and he said, "how fascinating, we must talk more about this after this session, will you wait for me?" Well, my answer was of course a no brainer, and I haven't a clue what the next session was about, but after it we talked, Norm asked me to send him my dissertation proposal and said he would "look over it for me." His assistance was vital as he helped me structure my thoughts, and over the next four years Norm offered me constant support and advice. He became my Ph.D. co-supervisor on my doctoral project which, among other things, looked at how using free associative film analysis could help people understand their narrative of self, correct erroneous perceptions of self, and in some cases develop coping strategies to deal with anxiety. He also enlisted other scholars, namely, Murray Schwartz and Keith Oatley, to advise me. What can I say? His support and deep knowledge of and grounding in literature, film, psychoanalysis, and neurobiology were fundamental to my work. I am eternally grateful to the generous man and talented scholar that Norman N. Holland was.
>
> Today, I continue to use free associative film analysis in both my research and teaching at the University of Lisbon. Also, because of the European Erasmus Student Mobility Program, students from Portugal, Spain, the UK, Greece, Denmark, and Germany have been introduced to it. Thank you, Norm, from the bottom of my heart.

Other scholars praised Holland for similar reasons, singling out his new approach to literature and enthusiastic support of their developing careers. "I met Norman Holland when as a graduate student of English I enrolled in his Literature and Psychoanalysis course at SUNY-Buffalo in 1968," commented Dianne Hunter, professor emerita at Trinity College in Hartford, Connecticut. The author of many articles on literature and psychoanalysis, she was one of the first literary critics to embrace Holland's reader-response criticism. "Norm had a profound and lasting influence on the way I thought about and taught literature."

The British author Meg Harris Williams, who has written extensively on literature and psychoanalysis, cited Holland's personal and practical help in getting an article published.

I believe his work on reader-response really marked a seismic shift in the kind of link that psychoanalysis could make with the arts—it was certainly very important and encouraging for me in my own work. And of course the PsyArt forum is something quite unique, and in welcoming serious debate from everyone, it makes a wonderful change from so many psychoanalysis-related organisations which have a tendency to be doctrinaire and hierarchical.

Teaching in the Department of Psychiatry at Harvard Medical School, Emily Fox-Kales met Holland at the International Conference on Psychology and the Arts in Arezzo, Italy in 2002:

I was immediately charmed not just by the setting but by the way Norm and Jane welcomed me into what soon became a thriving interdisciplinary community of creative colleagues. After earlier experiences at behavioral neuroscience and clinical case conferences in my graduate and postgraduate years, it seemed like a warm and welcoming place indeed.

Norm and I very quickly discovered that we were both cinephiles. I cherish his *Meeting Movies* and continue to share his thoughts on *Vertigo* in that work with my students. His generosity in writing a blurb for my own 2011 film book *Body Shots: Hollywood and the Culture of Eating Disorders* was for me yet another expression of his boundless capacity for encouragement and enlivening the conversation of ideas.

Kathy Bahr, professor of English at Chadron State College, first met Holland at a Freud conference in Washington, D.C.:

He had invited a group of PsyArt members to gather for lunch. Most of us knew each other only through our posts on the PsyArt list. I was a newbie to the field, an assistant professor of English at a small, rural Nebraska college, teaching full time and writing my dissertation. To me, Holland was a legend in psychoanalytic criticism. However, he seemed genuinely pleased to meet me and the others, asked about our work, and followed up with online correspondence both on and off the list. He encouraged me to submit my work on Matthew Arnold to the PsyArt Journal and actually read and critiqued the article before I submitted it. Far from resting on his "greatness," he exhibited a rare generosity towards people in my lowly position. He wrote a recommendation letter for my promotion and tenure portfolio and invited me to give a paper to his Group for the Study of Psychology and the Arts. Through Norm, I learned that a truly great scholar is not egotistical but eager to learn from and help others, no matter what their relative positions in the academic hierarchy.

Nelly G. Kupper, professor of French and Russian at Northern University Michigan, first met Holland at the International Conference on Psychology and the Arts in Cyprus in 2002. "He was a very impressive man to a recent Ph.D. graduate that I was at the time." Her early scholarship benefited from his constructive feedback during her presentations at several PsyArt conferences. Holland was the first to read the manuscript that culminated in her 2018 book *Gaze, Memory, and Gender in Narrative from Ancient to Modern*. "He passed away during our communication about it, in mid-sentence, as it were. It was devastating to lose him. His contribution to the world of knowledge will be enduring, as will be the memory of his interpersonal, gregarious manner. He was a great, magnificent, and generous man."

The above testimonies affirm Henry Adams's insight that teachers affect eternity. Teachers live on through their students, and by becoming teachers themselves, pass on new discoveries that are revised by future generations. "Individual immortality is neither possible nor desirable," Sander L. Gilman observes in *The Fortunes of the Humanities*, "but the need to function as educated men and women in a world such as that of higher education makes us part of an immortal undertaking, part of a long chain not of genes but of knowledge" (121–2). Janus-faced humanist and scientist; fast-talking snake oil salesman; reliable, generous guide; seeker of knowledge: all of these expressions convey colleagues' and students' impressions of a complex teacher-scholar who was part of an immortal undertaking.

Norman Holland's Children

After completing the manuscript, and following Peter L. Rudnytsky's excellent suggestion, I sent an email to Holland's two children, John Holland

and Kelley Holland, asking if they would be interested in reading about their father's work and sharing their impressions with me. Both kindly offered to do so, and they told me much about their father that I had not known. As with many families, they had strikingly different relationships with their father, and they cast different lights on his character. Interestingly, they have similar feelings about their paternal grandparents.

John Holland

John Holland is married with three children and lives in Bethesda, Maryland. A computer programmer, he played music professionally for many years but always with a "day job." He gave that up about twenty years ago to focus on family and work, but music remains a great interest. In his response to my initial email, John noted that his relationship with his father was "complicated and went through various phases." He elaborated on this complexity in his next email:

> As a kid I was very close to my father. When I was 15, I started being kind of anti-social and getting worse grades. This led to conflict with him which never really ended until after Jane died. We had a very nice kind of reconciliation in those last couple of years. I overhauled his website of film essays (asharperfocus.com), and he signed off on putting it in place. That was a big part of our reconciliation. I was struck by his understanding of the humanity and lives of the people in the movies when I started doing that. He seemed to understand the lives of people who were so different than him. It was like I didn't know the person who wrote the essays. I did watch all the movies on the website and read all the essays, something I mostly did after his passing. Around the same time, I found that my own relationship with my (step)son sort of resolved itself. Whether there was a connection between these two father-son relationships, I don't know. Since making peace with him, I find I have a much better feeling about him as a person, and I am able to identify with him. I see him in myself and I'm OK with that. I read *Literature and the Brain*, but it's a bit much for me to retain much from.
>
>   In skimming your book, I see a lot of familiar names and things. People like David Willbern and Murray Schwartz are people I remember from pool parties on Sundays and other social occasions. My overwhelming feeling about your book is that it is tragic that I never knew much about his work. I think when he rejected the choices I wanted to make and made, it left me rejecting him, and never really understanding what he

was about as a scholar and intellectual. This cloud over our relationship started before I was old enough to appreciate what he was about and persisted for most of my life.

In a subsequent email, I asked John if he was willing to comment on his father's relationship to his own father (John's paternal grandfather), and whether reading my manuscript heightened his knowledge of the professional side of his father's life. Here are his responses:

> I always knew that my Dad had issues with "Grandfather" (that's actually what we called him). Once I got old enough to understand, it was part of the family lore that Grandfather had wanted Dad to follow his footsteps. Dad had almost done so but then hadn't. Dad had become liberal politically and socially, and Grandfather was not. The Sunday pool parties that were a fixture of my life growing up featured a custom sign, "High Park Athletic Club," which was a sort of parody of Grandfather's membership in the New York Athletic Club. I think they must have been very close for him to pursue the patent lawyer path as effectively and as far as he did. They never resolved the different choices he made to forsake the path and become who he became. When I got out in the world myself, I started to wonder was it really so awful to end financial support after paying for a BS and a law degree? I was always sort of raised to think it was a terrible thing.
>
> I did not have a close relationship with Grandfather but it was cordial. I went to visit him a few times as he was in New York City and I wanted to be there. I remember going with him to the (in)famous New York Athletic Club. I also saw him some when I was at Columbia University. He died when I was 20 (1981).
>
> I need to read your book more closely, but it does help me know Dad's work. I sort of always knew that Shakespeare, psychoanalysis, and Freud were big parts of it, way before I had any idea of my own what those things are. What I think is tragic is that I got into this conflict with him over my own ambitions in music, and this and my high school friends turned me off the intellectual life for a long time, and also off my Dad's work. Now I appreciate his work a lot more, although I'm just more of a math and music person than an English major. I wish I could have come to that realization sooner, but at least it was before he passed. Your book might be a good thing for me to read properly, as I am probably never going to read all of his, although as I mentioned I did read *Literature and the Brain* a couple of years ago.

About his cancer, he first had lung cancer in 1991 and had an operation which I think was pretty tough. He came out of that pretty well, and was considered cancer free after 5 years. I think after he got 5 years out from the 1991 cancer, Dad was feeling like he had dodged that bullet, scary though it was. He had twenty plus good years afterwards and was very active. He then had it again in 2015 or 2016, and this was the ultimate cause of his death. As I understand these things, his later cancer is not considered to be related to the 1991 bout. He mentioned to me once that he considered a "revolver solution" to avoid the end stages of the disease, but was dissuaded from this idea by a friend saying that that would leave a horrible situation for others to deal with. I don't think it was at all a depressive or self-destructive impulse. It was just an idea to avoid unnecessary physical discomfort. If Florida had assisted suicide, I think he might have considered it.

Kelley Holland

Kelley Holland is married with three children and lives in Montclair, New Jersey. After many years as a business and financial journalist with national publications, she founded her own coaching and speaking business working with women who want to develop a healthier relationship to money.

> I had such a mix of feelings reading your book—it brought back his voice so very clearly. Also, you surfaced names that floated around our house throughout my childhood—Robert Silhol's, Claire Kahane's, and of course everyone from the SUNY Buffalo English department. I also appreciated the notes from people he had mentored academically when they were students or junior professors. We did have a pretty regular stream of students or visiting professors at the dinner table when I was growing up, and it's wonderful to hear what an impact he had on their work.
>
> I'm sure I can't add much of anything to your knowledge of Dad as an intellectual—that was only part of my relationship to him. But I can provide some color on Dad IRL, as the kids say (in real life).
>
> You are correct that for my father, breaking from the professional path his parents had planned for him was a major life event and central to his adult identity. Not only did he not become a lawyer, he became a liberal Democrat. (Dad had awful stories about his father's political comments, though I suspect Grandfather's views were not out of line for a lot of successful self-made men in those days.) Dad

also became a vehement atheist, another break from his parents. They weren't hugely devout, but they did identify as members of an Episcopal congregation.

As you pointed out, Dad did NOT like being a junior. In fact, when we were discussing his funeral and his burial in a green cemetery next to Mom, he decided not to include "Jr." on the little marker for his grave, saying something like "I think we can get rid of that."

I didn't really know my dad's parents well because he so disliked spending time with them. We would take an annual day trip to New York, sit in their apartment for an hour or two of stilted conversation, and then Dad would take me to Lord & Taylor. We would fly back to Buffalo that night.

About my grandfather's upbringing I can tell you that he "got out" because he graduated at the top of his high school class—it had all of seven students—and was accepted to Johns Hopkins. I leave it to you to decide whether he carried a variant of survivor guilt that made him laugh along with his brother at my dad. My grandmother grew up in or near Olean, NY, which is a small town in a snowy, wooded middle-of-nowhere area south of Buffalo. I wish I knew what inspired her to pursue a law degree, but clearly she had brains—and hopes of more than what Olean offered. I once saw a picture of my grandparents as a young couple in New York pre-Dad, and they both had that happy look of "Wow! Look what we did" on their faces.

For perspective: my grandmother got herself from Olean to law school, at what is now SUNY Buffalo. In fact, she met my grandfather in a prep class for the bar exam. At the time, going to law school was an exceptional thing for a woman to do, especially one who grew up in small-town western New York. The only legal work she could ever get was doing essentially what paralegals do now—the "real" jobs were for the men. She stopped working outside the home when Dad was born, if not earlier.

I find that very understandable under the circumstances, but I don't think Dad gave her much credit for her accomplishments. My theory is that Dad was angry at his mother for not pushing back against her strong-willed husband's coming down hard on Dad. But that is strictly opinion.

I will note, though, that my father and HIS father had striking similarities. Both were brilliant, both strong willed, both had systems they relied on, both were more "head" people than "heart" people, and both were quite opinionated. (Both also escaped their upbringing on the strength of their minds. I leave it to you to draw the Freudian connection to Dad's use of knowledge to dominate, after experiencing the domination of his father.)

I will also say that my dad set the bar high for his kids, as I imagine his father did for him. When I was in tenth grade, he convinced me to write a term paper on Fellini, and the two of us traipsed up to the university campus to see several of his masterworks. I loved those afternoons with Dad and having him try to teach me how to take critical notes in the dark, but the films went over my 15-year-old head. To this day I have no idea how I managed to string together a paper.

You write in various places about Dad not disclosing much about his personal history before publishing *Meeting Movies*. Agreed. But I think the statement about Dad always wanting to know and understand is more revealing than it first seems. As you point out, in *The I* Dad described a visceral need to know. I would argue that Dad's journey from New Criticism to reader response theory to neuroscience (and I'm omitting several stops along the way) is a manifestation of that drive. He was hungry for understanding, and if it took him in unexpected directions, that was fine. He went where he thought the answer might be. I loved your excerpt about Dad boring through the Alps. That was a wonderful encapsulation of his work.

Regarding Dad's interest in comedy and laughing, I can share a little bit of personal history. As an only child on the Upper West Side who went to private school in the Bronx and was not allowed to play with neighborhood kids, he spent a lot of time alone. He LOVED afternoon radio shows like "The Shadow" and also the comedians. He also liked the funny pages in the paper—his only gripe with the *New York Times* was the lack of a comics section. I also know he was a bit of a prankster at his school—perhaps because humor gives protection? But I could always get him to laugh at himself—say, at his deep reluctance to ever say "I don't know"—and it was charming.

You mention Dad's "special friend," whom he described to you. Her name is Catherine, and she is a remarkable, kind, intelligent, wonderful woman. Frankly, I was shocked at how deep their relationship became; I never thought Dad would be capable of that after losing Mom. But they made each other very, very happy, and Catherine was instrumental in enabling Dad to die at home, the way he wanted to.

Are anecdotes helpful? If so, here are a few:

1. You are correct that Dad's memory was prodigious. It was a bit of a family game to try and test it. I recall one time calling him in the early

2000s and asking whether an oyster was a mollusk or a bivalve. He knew the answer right away (it's a bivalve mollusk) and when I asked how, he answered, "Fourth grade science class."

2. Dad once told me about the moment when he understood how readers transform text. We were in Paris for the academic year 1971–1972 because Dad was teaching at the University of Paris-Vincennes, and we had an apartment in the 17th arrondissement. He was working at his desk, looking out at the Rue Prony, when this idea came to him. I've always loved both the image and the intellectual courage he showed in publicly changing his mind and taking off in a new direction.

3. An earlier one: in 1967 when Dad was working on *Dynamics*, he tried to explain his big idea to eight-year-old me. Sitting at the kitchen one night, we started talking about what it felt like when I read a book, and he got super excited by what I said. I was very proud to be quoted (on page 65). Even late in life Dad remained fascinated with the question of how and why we suspend disbelief. As I write this in the middle of the coronavirus pandemic, I find myself on Zoom call after Zoom call, and I think back to his ideas about why the small screen fails to be immersive.

A couple of factual notes. You theorize that Dad "got involved" with finances and investing in the context of being a lawyer. I don't know if that happened then, but I do know that in the early 1960s in Cambridge, having been cut off financially by his father, my parents moved several times, fixing up each house and presumably making money in the process. That could have been his reference to interest payments—maybe. Also, in the 1960s he did some investing—not much, on a professor's salary, but whatever—and of course he had a system. It actually kind of resembled a flow chart involving Y/N questions about price-earning ratios, dividend rates, etc. He sent me the thing in the early 1980s when I was trying to understand investing myself, but I can't find it now.

Also, you describe Dad reaching out to you with his question about rational suicide in 1999 and link it to his cancer diagnosis. In fact, Dad was found to have a small malignant tumor in one lung in 1991. It was completely removed via surgery, and he never needed chemo or radiation afterwards. His next experience with lung cancer didn't come until 2016. But I know that the initial experience was terrifying for him: After he died I found letters he had written to Mom, my brother and me to be opened on the occasion of his death. He also thought and talked a great deal about assisted suicide—not in a depressive way but because he was deeply intent on having the death he wanted. I was his health car proxy and executor, and he gave me the gift of complete clarity about exactly what he wanted at the end of life, and after.

Finally—It's worth noting that Dad never really stopped teaching or writing. After Mom and Dad moved to their retirement community, they found that there were regular Saturday night movie screenings in a big meeting room. Well, Dad had thoughts about the caliber of those films, so he and a friend started a Film Club where members could have serious discussions about films. Dad would propose a director to study and three of his (yes, they were almost all men) films, and the club would vote. Then Dad would re-watch the films, write an essay for each, and at the monthly screenings he would read the essay aloud and discussion would ensue. All in all, the club had more than one in four residents as members, and together they saw dozens of films. The club was so well loved that after Dad died, his friends organized a Norm Holland Film Festival for the following summer. We watched Krzysztof Kiéslowski's *Three Colors* trilogy, and Dad's colleague Andy Gordon contributed a wonderful speech. The dining room even served Dad's favorite chocolate dessert to the festivalgoers.

I hope some of this is helpful. As I said, reading your manuscript was bittersweet, but you did a remarkable job of capturing Dad's complexities—his fearsome intellect, his spikiness and his sparkle. I agree: no one beamed quite like Dad.

Writing on Holland

While writing this book, I've had the fantasy that if I could go back in time, to my exasperating encounter with Holland in 1967, I would say to him, upon storming out of his office in a huff, "Oh, by the way, Professor Holland, I intend to write a book about you in half a century." At the time, I couldn't imagine writing a book about anyone, but if I could anticipate being an author in the 1960s, Holland would have been the *last* person about whom I would write a book. Surely he would have looked at me in astonishment, wondering how an impertinent college senior could undertake such an ambitious project. "Don't relegate me to a mere footnote in literary history," he might have warned me. "Don't subordinate me to another theorist." "And," he might have cautioned, "don't confuse the two verbs, as you did today!" What would I have wanted him to say? "O my prophetic soul," Hamlet's words upon hearing his father's ghost's revelation that he was murdered by Claudius. Does my fantasy suggest a patricidal wish or a reparative desire to honor a father figure? The likely answer, of course, is both.

Why did I write a book on Holland? Though my study is not biographical, James Atlas's question—how does the biographer choose his subject?—applies to literary critics as well:

> *Does* the biographer choose his subject? Sooner ask how each of us became the person we are and how we spend our lives. Isn't it just random? A matter of genes and family background and historical circumstance? Of forturity? We come across a book, a manuscript, a letter; someone who knew the subject; the subject himself. But why this one instead of that one? It's impossible to know. (202)

In writing about Holland, I have sought to understand the central figure in American psychoanalytic literary criticism. He also happened to be the scholar who helped me the most in my own career as a psychoanalytic scholar. That alone is sufficient motivation to write a book about him. I also experienced unexpected therapeutic relief: in Loewaldian terms, Holland was transformed from a ghost into an ancestor, a welcome exorcism. But there are other motives for writing about Holland, including retracing my own long evolution as a psychoanalytic critic. Temperamentally we were different—I don't think he worried about his intellectual self-worth as a scholar, as I have, nor was he burdened by survivor guilt arising from a mentor's suicide. Nevertheless, we both shared the same passion for looking at literature and life from a psychoanalytic perspective. And we both wanted to express gratitude toward our mentors.

While woefully ignorant about literature at the time, I know *now* what I would have wanted Holland to say to me during our fateful and fitful 1967 encounter. "I greet you at the beginning of a great career, which yet must have had a long foreground somewhere, for such a start"—Emerson's 1855 letter to Walt Whitman congratulating him on the publication of *Leaves of Grass*. My fantasy is embarrassingly grandiose, to be sure, but it conveys the importance of Holland's support to me during my wounding tenure experience, and my efforts to pay him back in the only way I can, with a book that seeks to convey his crucial role in keeping alive psychoanalytic literary criticism. I often wonder how Holland would have reacted to this book. I doubt he would have felt the joy Emerson experienced reading *Leaves of Grass*, the "courage of treatment which so delights us, and which large perception can only inspire." I would like to think, however, that he would have appreciated my best efforts to honor his writings.

Works Cited

Adams, Robert M. "Interfering with Literature." *New York Review of Books*, April 10, 1969.
Adorno, T. W., Else Frenkel-Brunswik, Danie J. Levinson, and R. Nevitt Sanford. *The Authoritarian Personality*. New York: Harper & Row, 1950.
Atlas, James. *The Shadow in the Garden: A Biographer's Tale*. New York: Pantheon, 2017.
Babuts, Nicolae. "Review of *The Critical I*." *Symposium: A Quarterly Journal in Modern Literatures* 49 (1996): 310–12.
Bachelard, Gaston. *The Psychoanalysis of Fire*. Preface by Northrop Frye. Boston: Beacon Press, 1968.
Baranowski, A. M. and H. Hecht. "The Auditory Kuleshov Effect: Multisensory Integration in Movie Editing." *Perception* 45 (2017): 1–8.
Barratt, Daniel, Anna Cabak Rédei, Ase Innes-Ker, and Joost van de Weijer. "Does the Kuleshov Effect Really Exist? Revisiting a Classic Film Experiment on Facial Expressions and Emotional Contexts." *Perception* 45 (2016): 847–74.
Barrett, Marna S. and Jeffrey S. Berman. "Is Psychotherapy More Effective When Therapists Disclose Information About Themselves?" *Journal of Counseling and Clinical Psychology* 69 (2001): 597–603.
Begley, Adam. "Terminating Analysis." *Lingua Franca* 4 (1994): 24–30.
Berman, Jeffrey. *Death in the Classroom: Writing About Love and Loss*. Albany, NY: State University of New York Press, 2009.
Berman, Jeffrey. *Dying in Character: Memoirs on the End of Life*. Amherst, MA: University of Massachusetts Press, 2012.
Berman, Jeffrey. "Foreword to New York University Press's Series on Literature and Psychoanalysis." New York: New York University Press, 1991–1997.
Berman, Jeffrey. "'The Grief That Does Not Speak': Suicide, Mourning, and Psychoanalytic Teaching." In *Self-Analysis in Literary Study: Exploring Hidden Agendas*, edited by Daniel Rancour-Laferriere. New York: New York University Press, 1994, 35–54.
Berman, Jeffrey. *Joseph Conrad: Writing as Rescue*. New York: Astra, 1977.
Berman, Jeffrey. *Mad Muse: The Mental Illness Memoir in a Writer's Life and Work*. Bingley, UK: Emerald, 2019.
Berman, Jeffrey. *Narcissism and the Novel*. New York: New York University Press, 1990.
Berman, Jeffrey. *Risky Writing: Self-Disclosure and Self-Transformation in the Classroom*. Amherst, MA: University of Massachusetts Press, 2001.
Berman, Jeffrey. *Surviving Literary Suicide*. Amherst, MA: University of Massachusetts Press, 1999.

Berman, Jeffrey. *Writing the Talking Cure: Irvin D. Yalom and the Literature of Psychotherapy*. Albany, NY: State University of New York Press, 2019.
Berman, Jeffrey. *Writing Widowhood*. Albany, NY: State University of New York Press, 2015.
Berman, Jeffrey. *The Talking Cure: Literary Representations of Psychoanalysis*. New York: New York University Press, 1985.
Berman, Jeffrey and Paul W. Mosher. *Off the Tracks: Cautionary Tales About the Derailing of Mental Health Care*. 2 vols. New York: International Psychoanalytic Books, 2019.
Bernheimer, Charles and Claire Kahane, eds. *In Dora's Case: Freud—Hysteria—Feminism*. New York: Columbia University Press, 1985; 2nd ed., 1990.
Bleich, David. "A Comment on the Essays of Stephen Black and Norman Holland." *College English* 40 (1978): 223-4.
Bleich, David. "Epistemological Assumptions in the Study of Response." From *Subjective Criticism*. Baltimore, MD: Johns Hopkins University Press, 1978. Rpt. in *Reader-Response Criticism: From Formalism to Post-Structuralism*, edited by Jane P. Tompkins. Baltimore, MD: Johns Hopkins University Press, 1980, 134-63.
Bleich, David. "How I Got My Language: Forms of Self-Inclusion." In *Self-Analysis in Literary Study: Exploring Hidden Agendas*, edited by Daniel Rancour-Laferriere. New York: New York University Press, 1994, 55-83.
Bleich, David. *Know and Tell: A Writing Pedagogy of Disclosure, Genre, and Membership*. Portsmouth, NH: Boynton/Cook, 1998.
Bleich, David. *Readings and Feelings: An Introduction to Subjective Criticism*. Urbana, IL: National Council of Teachers of English, 1975.
Bleich, David. "Response to Norman Holland." *College English* 38 (1976): 299-301.
Bloom, Harold. *The Age of Anxiety: A Theory of Poetry*. New York: Oxford University Press, 1973.
Bloom, Harold. "The Critic's Critic." *New York Times*, November 5, 2009.
Bloom, Harold. *The Flight to Lucifer: A Gnostic Fantasy*. New York: Vintage, 1980.
Bloom, Harold. *Shakespeare: The Invention of the Human*. New York: Riverhead Books, 1998.
Bloom, Harold. *The Western Canon: The Books and Schools of the Ages*. New York: Harcourt, 1994.
Bollas, Christopher. *Being a Character: Psychoanalysis and Self Experience*. New York: Hill and Wang, 1992.
Bollas, Christopher. *Cracking Up: The Work of Unconscious Experience*. New York: Hill and Wang, 1995.
Bollas, Christopher. *The Shadow of the Object: Psychoanalysis of the Unthought Known*. New York: Columbia University Press, 1987.
Bonaparte, Marie. *Edgar Poe, Étude Psychanalytique*. Paris: Denöel et Steele, 1933.

Bowlby, John. "Psychoanalysis as Art and Science." In *A Secure Base: Clinical Applications of Attachment Theory*. London: Routledge, 1988.

Breuer, Josef and Sigmund Freud. *Studies on Hysteria*. In *The Standard Edition of the Complete Psychological Works of Sigmund Freud*, translated and edited by James Strachey. Vol. 2. London: The Hogarth Press, 1975.

Brody, Jane E. "The Crisis in Youth Suicide." *New York Times*, December 2, 2019.

Camus, Albert. *The Myth of Sisyphus and Other Essays*. New York: Vintage, 1955

Charney, Maurice. "Review of *Psychoanalysis and Shakespeare*." *Shakespeare Quarterly* 19 (1968): 401–3.

Chodorow, Nancy. *The Psychoanalytic Ear and the Sociological Eye: Toward an American Independent Tradition*. London: Routledge, 2020.

Chodorow, Nancy. *The Reproduction of Mothering: Psychoanalysis and the Sociology of Gender*. Berkeley, CA: University of California Press, 1978.

Chomsky, Noam. *Syntactic Structures*. The Hague/Paris: Mouton, 1957.

Crews, Frederick. "Anaesthetic Criticism." In *Psychoanalysis & Literary Process*, edited by Frederick Crews. Cambridge, MA: Winthrop, 1970, 1–24.

Crews, Frederick. *Follies of the Wise: Dissenting Essays*. New York: Shoemaker Hoard, 2006.

Crews, Frederick. *Freud: The Making of an Illusion*. New York: Metropolitan Books, 2017.

Crews, Frederick, ed., et al. *The Memory Wars: Freud's Legacy in Dispute*. New York: New York Review Book, 1995.

Crews, Frederick. *Out of My System: Psychoanalysis, Ideology, and Critical Method*. New York: Oxford University Press, 1975.

Crews, Frederick. *The Sins of the Fathers: Hawthorne's Psychological Themes*. Oxford: Oxford University Press, 1966; rpt.1970.

Crews, Frederick. *Skeptical Engagements*. New York: Oxford University Press, 1986.

Crews, Frederick, ed. *Unauthorized Freud: Doubters Confront a Legend*. New York: Viking, 1998.

Culler, Jonathan. "Prolegomena to a Theory of Reading." In *The Reader in the Text: Essays on Audience and Interpretation*, edited by Susan R. Suleiman and Inge Crosman. Princeton, NJ: Princeton University Press, 1980, 46–66.

Delany, Paul. "Review of *Poems in Persons*." *New York Times*, October 28, 1973.

Derrida, Jacques. "The Purveyor of Truth." *Yale French Studies* 52 (1975): 31–113.

Eder, Doris L. "Review of *Surfiction*: Plunging into the Surface. " *boundary* 2 (1976): 153–66.

Edmundson, Mark. *Towards Reading Freud: Self-Creation in Milton, Wordsworth, Emerson, and Sigmund Freud*. Princeton, NJ: Princeton University Press, 1990.

Eliot, T. S. *The Complete Poems and Plays, 1909–1950*. New York: Harcourt, Brace & World, 1952.

Ellenberger, Henri F. *The Discovery of the Unconscious: The History and Evolution of Dynamic Psychiatry*. New York: Basic Books, 1970.

Elovitz, Paul H. and Bob Lentz. "Nancy J. Chodorow: Psychoanalyst and Gender Theorist." *Clio's Psyche* 11 (2005): 113, 134–43.

Encyclopedia of World Literature in the 20th Century, edited by Wolfgang Bernard Fleischmann, Frederick Ungar, and Linda Mainiero. 4 vols. New York: Ungar, 1967–1975.

Erikson, Erik H. *Childhood and Society*. New York: Norton, 1963.

Erikson, Erik H. *Identity: Youth and Crisis*. New York: Norton, 1968.

Erikson, Erik H. *Identity and the Life Cycle: Selected Papers by Erik. H. Erikson*. Historical Introduction by David Rapaport. New York: International Universities Press, 1959.

Erikson, Erik H. *Young Man Luther: A Study in Psychoanalysis and History*. New York: Norton, 1958; rpt. 1962.

Falle, George. "Review Article: Comedy and Society." *University of Toronto Quarterly* 30 (1960): 95–100.

Federman, Raymond. *Critification: Postmodern Essays*. Albany, NY: State University of New York Press, 1993.

Fiedler, Leslie. *Love and Death in the American Novel*. New York: Stein and Day, rev. ed., 1966.

Fisher, Seymour and Roger P. Greenberg. *The Scientific Credibility of Freud's Theories*. New York: Basic Books, 1977.

Fisher, Seymour and Roger P. Greenberg. *Freud Scientifically Reappraised: Testing the Theories and Therapy*. New York: Wiley, 1996.

Fitzgerald, F. Scott. *The Crack-Up*. New York: New Directions, 1945.

Fitzgerald, F. Scott. *The Great Gatsby*, edited by Matthew J. Bruccoli. New York: Collier, 1992.

Fitzgerald, F. Scott. *Tender Is the Night*. 1934; rpt. New York: Scribner's, 1962.

Fitzgerald, F. Scott. *This Side of Paradise*. Garden City, NY: Scribners, 1923.

Freud, Anna. *The Ego and the Mechanisms of Defense*. 1936; rev. ed. New York: International Universities Press, 1937.

Freud, Sigmund. "Character and Anal Eroticism." 1908. In *The Standard Edition of the Complete Psychological Works of Sigmund Freud*, translated and edited by James Strachey. Vol. 9. London: The Hogarth Press, 1959.

Freud, Sigmund. *Civilization and Its Discontents*. 1930. In *The Standard Edition of the Complete Psychological Works of Sigmund Freud*, translated and edited by James Strachey. Vol. 21. London: The Hogarth Press, 1961.

Freud, Sigmund. *The Complete Letters of Sigmund Freud to Wilhelm Fliess: 1887–1904*, translated and edited by Jeffrey Moussaieff Masson. Cambridge, MA: Harvard University Press, 1985.

Freud, Sigmund. "The Dynamics of Transference." 1912. In *The Standard Edition of the Complete Psychological Works of Sigmund Freud*, translated and edited by James Strachey. Vol. 12. London: The Hogarth Press, 1958.

Freud, Sigmund. *Fragment of an Analysis of a Case of Hysteria*. 1905. In *The Standard Edition of the Complete Psychological Works of Sigmund Freud*, translated and edited by James Strachey. Vol. 7. London: The Hogarth Press, 1953.

Freud, Sigmund. *Inhibitions, Symptoms and Anxiety*. 1926. In *The Standard Edition of the Complete Psychological Works of Sigmund Freud*, translated and edited by James Strachey. Vol. 20. London: The Hogarth Press, 1959.

Freud, Sigmund. *The Interpretation of Dreams*. 1900. In *The Standard Edition of the Complete Psychological Works of Sigmund Freud*, translated and edited by James Strachey. Vols. 4–5. London: The Hogarth Press, 1953.

Freud, Sigmund. *Jokes and Their Relation to the Unconscious* 1905. In *The Standard Edition of the Complete Psychological Works of Sigmund Freud*, translated and edited by James Strachey. Vol. 8. London: The Hogarth Press, 1960.

Freud, Sigmund. *Letters of Sigmund Freud*, edited by Ernst L. Freud, translated by Tania and James Stern. New York: Basic Books, 1960.

Freud, Sigmund. *New Introductory Lectures on Psycho-Analysis*. 1933. In *The Standard Edition of the Complete Psychological Works of Sigmund Freud*, translated and edited by James Strachey. Vol. 22. London: The Hogarth Press, 1964.

Freud, Sigmund. "Obsessive Actions and Religious Practices." 1907. In *The Standard Edition of the Complete Psychological Works of Sigmund Freud*, translated and edited by James Strachey. Vol. 9. London: The Hogarth Press, 1959.

Freud, Sigmund. "Some Psychical Consequences of the Anatomical Distinctions between the Sexes." 1925. In *The Standard Edition of the Complete Psychological Works of Sigmund Freud*, translated and edited by James Strachey. Vol. 19. London: The Hogarth Press, 1961.

Freud, Sigmund. *Totem and Taboo*. 1913. In *The Standard Edition of the Complete Psychological Works of Sigmund Freud*, translated and edited by James Strachey. Vol. 13. London: The Hogarth Press, 1953.

Friedman, Susan Stanford. *Penelope's Web: Gender, Modernity, H.D.'s Fiction*. Cambridge: Cambridge University Press, 1990.

Friedman, Susan Stanford. *Psyche Reborn: The Emergence of H.D.* Bloomington, IN: Indiana University Press, 1981.

Gabbard, Glen O. *Long-Term Psychodynamic Psychotherapy: A Basic Text*. 3rd ed. New York: American Psychiatric Association, 2017.

Gilman, Sander L. *Freud, Race, and Gender*. Princeton, NJ: Princeton University Press, 1993.

Gilman, Sander L. *The Fortunes of the Humanities: Thoughts for After the Year 2000*. Stanford, CA: Stanford University Press, 2000.

Gordon, Andrew M. "Trouble in River City, or Lacan's 'The Agency of the Letter in the Unconscious.'" *PsyArt: A Hyperlink Journal for the Psychological Study of the Arts*, August 22, 1997. Accessed September 20, 2019. http://psyartjournal.com/article/show/m_gordon-trouble_in_river_city_or...

Greaney, Michael. *Contemporary Fiction and the Uses of Fiction: The Novel from Structuralism to Postmodernism*. Houndmills, UK: Palgrave Macmillan, 2006.

Greenberg, Harvey R. *The Movies on Your Mind*. New York: Saturday Review Press, 1975.

Guttman, Samuel A., Randall L. Jones, and Stephen M. Parrish, eds. *The Concordance to the Standard Edition of the Complete Psychological Works of Sigmund Freud*. 6 vols. Boston: G. K. Hall, 1980.

H.D. [Hilda Doolittle]. *Tribute to Freud: Writing on the Wall*. New York: Pantheon, 1956.

Henretty, Jennifer R., Jeffrey S. Berman, Joseph M. Currier, and Heidi M. Levitt. "The Impact of Counselor Self-Disclosure on Clients: A Meta-Analytic Review of Experimental and Quasi-Experimental Research." *Journal of Counseling Psychology* 61 (2014): 191–207.

Hogan, Patrick Colm. "Review of *Literature and the Brain*." *Style* 43 (2009): 445–50.

Holland, Norman N. "A Brainy Afterword." In *Compromise Formations: Current Directions in Psychoanalytic Criticism*, edited by Vera Camden. Kent, OH: Kent State University Press, 1989, 235–43.

Holland, Norman N. *The Brain of Robert Frost: A Cognitive Approach to Literature*. New York: Routledge, 1989.

Holland, Norman N. *The Critical I*. New York: Columbia University Press, 1992.

Holland, Norman N. "A Cyberreader Defends." In *Self-Analysis in Literary Study: Exploring Hidden Agendas*, edited by Daniel Rancour-Laferriere. New York: New York University Press, 1994, 84–110.

Holland, Norman N. *Death in a Delphi Seminar: A Postmodern Mystery*. Albany, NY: State University of New York, 1995.

Holland, Norman N. *The Dynamics of Literary Response*. New York: Oxford University Press, 1968; rpt. New York: Norton, 1975. rpt. New York: Morningside-Columbia University Press, 1989.

Holland, Norman N. *The First Modern Comedies: The Significance of Etherege, Wycherley, and Congreve*. Cambridge, MA: Harvard University Press, 1959; rpt. Bloomington, IN: Midland-Indiana University Press, 1967.

Holland, Norman N. *5 Readers Reading*. New Haven, CT: Yale University Press, 1975.

Holland, Norman N. "Freud and the Poet's Eye." In *Hidden Patterns: Studies in Psychoanalytic Literary Criticism*, edited by Leonard Manheim and Eleanor Manheim. New York: Macmillan, 1966, 151–70.

Holland, Norman N. "Hermia's Dream." In *Representing Shakespeare: New Psychoanalytic Essays*, edited by Murray M. Schwartz and Coppélia Kahn. Baltimore, MD: Johns Hopkins University Press, 1980, 1–20.

Holland, Norman N. *Holland's Guide to Psychoanalytic Psychology and Literature-and-Psychology*. New York: Oxford University Press, 1990.

Holland, Norman N. "How Can Dr. Johnson's Remarks on Cordelia's Death Add to My Own Response?" In *Psychoanalysis and the Question of the Text*, edited with a Preface by Geoffrey H. Hartman. Baltimore, MD: Johns Hopkins University Press, 1978, 18–44.

Holland, Norman N. *The I*. New Haven, CT: Yale University Press, 1985; rpt. with a new introduction as *The I and Being Human*. New Brunswick, NJ: Transaction Publishers, 2011.

Holland, Norman N. "Jude the Obscure: Hardy's Symbolic Indictment of Christianity." *Nineteenth-Century Fiction* 9 (1954): 50–60.

Holland, Norman N. *Laughing: A Psychology of Humor*. Ithaca, NY: Cornell University Press, 1982.

Holland, Norman N. "Literary Suicide: A Question of Style." *Psychocultural Review* 1 (1977): 285–303.

Holland, Norman N. *Literature and the Brain*. Gainesville, FL: PsyArt Foundation, 2009.

Holland, Norman N. *Meeting Movies*. Madison, NJ: Fairleigh Dickinson University Press, 2006.

Holland, Norman N. "The Next New Criticism." *The Nation*, April 22, 1961.

Holland, Norman N. "Obituary: Heinz Lichtenstein." *International Journal of Psycho-Analysis* 71 (1990): 527–9.

Holland, Norman N. *Poems in Persons: An Introduction to the Psychoanalysis of Literature*. New York: Norton, 1973; rpt. New York: Norton, 1975. Rpt. New York: Morningside-Columbia University Press, 1989; revised edition: *Poems in Persons: Psychology of the Literary Process*. Cybereditions, 2000.

Holland, Norman N. *Psychoanalysis and Shakespeare*. New York: McGraw-Hill, 1966; rpt. New York: Octagon Books, 1976.

Holland, Norman N. "Re-Covering 'The Purloined Letter': Reading as a Personal Transaction." In *The Reader in the Text: Essays on Audience and Interpretation*, edited by Susan R. Suleiman and Inge Crosman. Princeton, NJ: Princeton University Press, 1980, 350–70.

Holland, Norman N. "Report: Focus Group on Revisionism." *New Literary History* 29 (1998): 173–96.

Holland, Norman N. "Response to Crews." *The Scientific Review of Alternative Medicine* 10 (2006): 29–30.

Holland, Norman N. *The Shakespearean Imagination*. New York: Macmillan, 1964; rpt. Bloomington, IN: Midland-Indiana University Press, 1968.

Holland, Norman N. *A Sharper Focus*. http://www.asharperfocus.com/criticism.html. Accessed November 5, 2019.

Holland, Norman N. "Shrinking Literature: Reply to Robert M. Adams." *The New York Review of Books*, September 11, 1969.

Holland, Norman N. "Sons and Substitutions: Shakespeare's Phallic Fantasy." In *Shakespeare's Personality*, edited by Norman N. Holland, Sidney Homan, and Bernard J. Paris. Berkeley, CA: University of California Press, 1989, 66–85.

Holland, Norman N. "The Sparrow." *The Hudson Review* 8 (1955): 407.

Holland, Norman N. "The Story of a Psychoanalytic Critic." *American Imago* 56 (1999): 245–59.

Holland, Norman N. "Unity Identity Text Self." *PMLA* 90 (1975): 813–22. Rpt. in *Reader-Response Criticism: From Formalism to Post-Structuralism*, edited by Jane P. Tompkins. Baltimore, MD: Johns Hopkins University Press, 1980, 118–33.

Holland, Norman N. "You, U. K. Le Guin." In *Future Females: A Critical Anthology*, edited by Marleen S. Barr. Bowling Green, OH: Bowling Green State University Popular Press, 1981, 125–37.

Holland, Norman N. and Murray M. Schwartz. "The Delphi Seminar." *College English* 36 (1975): 789–800. Expanded into *Know Thyself: Delphi Seminars*. Gainesville, FL: PsyArt Foundation, 2009.

Horney, Karen. "The Flight from Womanhood: The Masculinity Complex in Women as Viewed by Men and Women." *International Journal of Psycho-Analysis*, 1926. In *Feminine Psychology*, edited by H. Kelman. New York: Norton, 1967, 54–70.

Horney, Karen. *Our Inner Conflicts*. New York: Norton, 1945.

Howe, Irving. *Thomas Hardy*. New York: Macmillan, 1967.

Hutter, A. D. "Review of *The I*." *International Review of Psycho-Analysis* 16 (1989): 121–4.

Hyman, Stanley Edgar. *The Armed Vision: A Study in the Methods of Modern Literary Criticism*. New York: Knopf, 1948; rpt. 1952.

Jacobs, Theodore J. "On Self-Disclosure." In *Privacy: Developmental, Cultural, and Clinical Realms*, edited by Salman Akhtar and Aisha Abbasi. London: Routledge, 2019, 147–61.

Jamison, Kay Redfield. *Robert Lowell: Setting the River on Fire*. New York: Vintage, 2017.

Jamison, Kay Redfield. *Touched with Fire: Manic-Depressive Illness and the Artistic Temperament*. New York: Simon & Schuster, 1993; rpt. Free Press, 1994.

Jones, Ernest. *The Life and Work of Sigmund Freud*. 3 vols. New York: Basic Books, 1953–1957.

Kahane, Claire. *Passions of the Voice: Hysteria, Narrative, and the Figure of the Speaking Woman, 1850–1915*. Baltimore, MD: Johns Hopkins University Press, 1985.

Kandel, Eric R. "A New Intellectual Framework for Psychiatry." *American Journal of Psychiatry* 155 (1998): 457–69.

Kandel, Eric R. *In Search of Memory: The Emergence of a New Science of Mind*. New York: Norton, 2006.

Keats, John. *Selected Poems and Letters*. Cambridge, MA: Riverside Press, 1959.

Kerrigan, William. "Terminating Lacan." *South Atlantic Quarterly* 88 (1989): 993–1008.

Kiell, Norman, ed. *Psychoanalysis, Psychology, and Literature: A Bibliography*. Madison, WI: University of Wisconsin Press, 1963.

Kohut, Heinz. "Reflections." In *Advances in Self Psychology*, edited by Arnold Goldberg. New York: International Universities Press, 1980.

Kris, Ernst. *Psychoanalytic Explorations in Art*. New York: International Universities Press, 1952.

Lacan, Jacques. "Seminar on 'The Purloined Letter.'" Translated by Jeffrey Mehlman. *French Freud: Structural Studies in Psychoanalysis. Yale French Studies* 48 (1972): 38–72.

Lakoff, George and Mark Johnson. *Metaphors We Live By*. Chicago, IL: University of Chicago Press, 1980.

Lawrence, D. H. *Studies in Classic American Literature*. New York: Viking, 1969.

Lear, Jonathan. *Wisdom Won from Illness: Essays on Philosophy and Psychoanalysis*. Cambridge, MA: Harvard University Press, 2017.

Lehrer, Ronald. *Nietzsche's Presence in Freud's Life and Thought: On the Origins of a Psychology of Dynamic Unconscious Mental Functioning*. Albany, NY: State University of New York Press, 1994.

Lehrman, Philip R. "Freud's Contributions to Science." *Harofe Haivri* [*Hebrew Physician*] 1 (1940): 161–76.

Lesser, Simon O. *Fiction and the Unconscious*. New York: Vintage, 1957.

Levin, Aaron. "Courageous Actions Led to Removal of Homosexuality as a Diagnosis in DSM." *Psychiatry* Online, October 15, 2019. https://psychnews.psychiatryonline.org/doi/10/appi.pn.2019.10b11. Accessed October 27, 2019.

Lichtenstein, Heinz. *The Dilemma of Human Identity*. New York: Jason Aronson, 1977.

Lichtenstein, Heinz. "Identity and Sexuality." *Journal of the American Psychoanalytic Association* 9 (1961): 179–260.

Loewald, Hans W. "On the Therapeutic Action of Psychoanalysis." In *Papers on Psychoanalysis*. New Haven, CT: Yale University Press, 1980.

Manheim, Leonard and Eleanor. "Introduction." In *Hidden Patterns: Studies in Psychoanalytic Literary Criticism*, edited by Leonard and Eleanor Manheim. New York: Macmillan, 1966, 1–16.

McLaughlin, James T. *The Healer's Bent: Solitude and Dialogue in the Clinical Encounter*, edited and introduced by William F. Cornell. Hillsdale, NJ: Analytic Press, 2005.

Meusel, Magdalene. *Thomas Hardy und die Bibel*. Kiel, 1937.

Millot, Catherine. *Life with Lacan*, translated by Andrew Brown. Cambridge, UK: Polity, 2018.

Mollinger, Robert. "Review of *Poems in Persons*." *The Psychoanalytic Review* 62 (1975): 183–5.

Mosher, Paul W. "Frequency of Word Use as an Indicator of Evolution of Psychoanalytic Thought." *Journal of the American Psychoanalytic Association* 46 (1998): 577–81.

Nelson, Cary. "The Psychology of Criticism, or What Can Be Said." In *Psychoanalysis and the Question of the Text*, edited with a Preface by Geoffrey H. Hartman. Baltimore, MD: Johns Hopkins University Press, 1978, 45–61.

Nietzsche, Friedrich. *Beyond Good and Evil*, translated by Helen Zimmern. In *The Philosophy of Nietzsche*. New York: Modern Library, 1954.

Nuttall, A. D. "Review of *The Dynamics of Literary Response*." *The Review of English Studies* 21 (1970): 242–4.

Pagan, Nicholas O. "The Evolution of Feeling-Dominated Response in Norman N. Holland's Theory of Literature." *PsyArt* 21 (2017): 115–28.

Pagan, Nicholas O. "In Memoriam: Norman N. Holland, 1927–2017." *PMLA* 135 (2018): 1268–70.

Panksepp, Jaak. *Affective Neuroscience: The Foundations of Human and Animal Emotions*. New York: Oxford University Press, 1998.

Papini, Giovanni. "A Visit to Freud." In *Freud as We Knew Him*, ed. Hendrik Ruitenbeek. Detroit, MI: Wayne State University Press, 1973, 98–102.

Paris, Bernard J. *Bargains with Fate: Psychological Crises and Conflicts in Shakespeare and His Plays*. New York: Insight Books, 1991.

Paris, Bernard J. *Conrad's Charlie Marlow: A New Approach to "Heart of Darkness" and Lord Jim*. New York: Palgrave Macmillan. 2005.

Paris, Bernard J. *Dostoevsky's Greatest Characters: A New Approach to "Notes from the Underground," Crime and Punishment, and The Brothers Karamazov*. New York: Palgrave Macmillan, 2008.

Paris, Bernard J. *Experiments in Life: George Eliot's Quest for Values*. Detroit, MI: Wayne State University Press, 1965.

Paris, Bernard J. *Imagined Human Being: A Psychological Approach to Character and Conflict in Literature*. New York: New York University Press, 1997.

Paris, Bernard J. *Karen Horney: A Psychoanalyst's Search for Self-Understanding*. New Haven, CT: Yale University Press, 1994.

Paris, Bernard J. "Pulkheria Alexandrovna and Raskolnikov, My Mother and Me." In *Self-Analysis in Literary Study: Exploring Hidden Agendas*, edited by Daniel Rancour-Laferriere. New York: New York University Press, 1994, 111–29.

Paris, Bernard J. *Rereading George Eliot: Changing Responses to Her Experiments in Life*. Albany, NY: State University of New York Press, 2003.

Phillips, Adam. *Promises, Promises: Essays on Literature and Psychoanalysis*. New York: Basic Books, 2000.

Phillips, Adam. *Terrors and Experts*. Cambridge, MA: Harvard University Press, 1996.

Pickering, George. *Creative Malady: Illness in the Lives and Minds of Charles Darwin, Florence Nightingale, Mary Baker Eddy, Sigmund Freud, Marcel Proust, and Elizabeth Barrett Browning*. New York: Delta, 1976.

Prochnik, George. "The Curious Conundrum of Freud's Persistent Influence." *New York Times*, August 14, 2017.

Purves, Alan C. "Poems in Persons: A Review and a Reply." *Research in the Teaching of English* 8 (1974): 9–14.

Purves, Alan C. "Review of *The Dynamics of Literary Response*." *Journal of English and German Philology* 68 (1969): 560–4.

Rashkin, Esther. *Family Secrets and the Psychoanalysis of Narrative*. Princeton, NJ: Princeton University Press, 1992.

Reik, Theodor. *Listening with the Third Ear: The Inner Experience of a Psychoanalyst*. New York: Farrar, Straus, 1948.

Rich, Adrienne. *Of Woman Born*. New York: Norton, 1976.
Rodell, Marie J. *Mystery Fiction: Theory and Technique*. New York: Hermitage House, 1952.
Rosenblatt, Louise. *The Reader, the Text, the Poem: The Transactional Theory of the Literary Work*. Carbondale IL: Southern Illinois University Press, 1978.
Rosenzweig, Saul. "Some Implicit Common Factors in Diverse Methods of Psychotherapy: 'At Last the Dodo Bird Said, Everybody Has Won and All Must Have Prizes.'" *American Journal of Orthopsychiatry* 6 (1976): 412–15.
Roudinesco, Élisabeth. *Jacques Lacan*, translated by Barbara Bray. New York: Columbia University Press, 1997.
Rudnytsky, Peter L. *Psychoanalytic Conversations: Interviews with Clinicians, Commentators, and Critics*. Hillsdale, NJ: The Analytic Press, 2000.
Rudnytsky, Peter L. "Wrecking Crews." *American Imago* 56 (1999): 285–98.
Rudnytsky, Peter L. and Andrew M. Gordon, eds. *Psychoanalyses/Feminisms*. Albany, NY: State University of New York Press, 2000.
Ruti, Mari. *Penis Envy and Other Bad Feelings: The Emotional Costs of Everyday Life*. New York: Columbia University Press, 2018.
Rymer, Russ. "Annals of Science: A Silent Childhood-I." *The New Yorker*, April 13, 1992.
Said, Edward. *On Late Style: Music and Literature Against the Grain*. Foreword by Mariam C. Said. Introduction by Michael Wood. New York: Pantheon, 2006.
Schneiderman, Stuart. *Jacques Lacan: The Death of an Intellectual Hero*. Cambridge, MA: Harvard University Press, 1983.
Schwartz, Murray M. "Critic, Define Thyself." In *Psychoanalysis and the Question of the Text*, ed. with a Preface, by Geoffrey H. Hartman. Baltimore, MD: Johns Hopkins University Press, 1978, 1–17.
Schwartz, Murray M. "Psychoanalysis in My Life: An Intellectual Memoir." *American Imago* 75 (2018): 125–52.
Schwartz, Murray M. "Review of *Out of My System*: Psychoanalysis, Ideology, and Critical Method." *The Psychohistory Review* 7 (1979): 43–5.
Schwartz, Murray M. "Where Is Literature?" *College English* 36 (1975): 756–65.
Schwartz, Murray M. and Coppélia Kahn, eds. *Representing Shakespeare: New Psychoanalytic Essays*. Baltimore, MD: Johns Hopkins University Press, 1980.
Schwartz, Murray M. and David Willbern. "Literature and Psychology." In *Interrelations of Literature*, edited by Jean-Pierre Barricelli and Joseph Gibaldi. New York: Modern Language Association, 1982, 205–23.
Schapiro, Barbara Ann. "Attunement and Interpretation: Reading Virginia Woolf." In *Self-Analysis in Literary Study: Exploring Hidden Agendas*, edited by Daniel Rancour-Laferriere. New York: New York University Press, 1994, 178–89.
Segal, Erich. "Review of *The Dynamics of Literary Response*." *Comparative Literature* 22 (1970): 376–8.
Silvio, Joseph R. "Review of *Literature and the Brain*." *Journal of the American Academy of Psychoanalysis* 39 (2011): 375–6.

Simon, Bennett. "Review of *A Case for Irony*, by Jonathan Lear." *Journal of the American Psychoanalytic Association* 61 (2013): 147–55.

Slatoff, Walter. *With Respect to Readers*. Ithaca, NY: Cornell University Press, 1970.

Smith, John Harrington. "Review: The First Modern Comedies." *Modern Philology* 57 (1960): 274–7.

Solomon, Andrew. *The Noonday Demon: An Atlas of Depression*. New York: Touchstone, 2002.

Sontag, Susan. *Against Interpretation*. New York: Delta, 1979.

Sprengnether, Madelon. *Mourning Freud*. New York: Bloomsbury Academic, 2018.

Sprengnether, Madelon. *The Spectral Mother: Freud, Feminism and Psychoanalysis*. Ithaca, NY: Cornell University Press, 1990.

Stein, Jean. "Interview with William Faulkner." *The Paris Review* 12 (1956). https://www.theparisreview.org/interviews/4954/william-faulkner-the-art-of-fiction. Accessed May 3, 2019.

Stern, Daniel N. *The Interpersonal World of the Infant: A View from Psychoanalysis and Development Psychology*. New York: Basic Books, 1985.

Stolorow, Robert D. and George E. Atwood. *Faces in a Cloud: Subjectivity in Personality Theory*. New York: Jason Aronson, 1979.

Strange, Deborah. "UF Scholar, Literary Critic Norman Holland Dies at 90." *The Gainesville Sun*, October 6, 2017. https://www.gainesville.com/news/20171006/uf-scholar-literary-critic-norm.... Accessed May 18, 2019.

Strupp, Hans and Suzanne Hadley. "Specific vs. Nonspecific Factors in Psychotherapy: A Controlled Study of Outcome." *Archives of General Psychiatry* 36 (1979): 1125–36.

Styron, Alexandria. *Reading My Father*. New York: Scribner, 2011.

Sulloway, Frank J. *Freud, Biologist of the Mind: Beyond the Psychoanalytic Legend*. New York: Basic Books, 1979.

Tene, Wylie. "American Psychoanalytic Association Issues Overdue Apology to the LGBTQ Community," June 21, 2019. http://www.apsa.org/content/news-apsaa-issues-overdue-apology-lgbtq-community. Accessed July 1, 2019.

Tompkins, Jane P. "An Introduction to Reader-Response Criticism." In *Reader-Response Criticism: From Formalist to Post-Structuralism*, ed. Jane P. Tompkins. Baltimore, MD: Johns Hopkins University Press, 1980.

Tompkins, Jane P. "Me and My Shadow." In *The Intimate Critique: Autobiographical Literary Criticism*, edited by Diane P. Freedman, Olivia Frey, and Frances Murphy Zauhar. Durham, NC: Duke University Press, 1993, 23–40.

Trilling, Lionel. *The Liberal Imagination*. Garden City: Anchor Books, 1953.

Turner, Mark. *The Literary Mind*. New York: Oxford University Press, 1996.

Turner, Mark. *Reading Minds: The Study of English in the Age of Cognitive Science*. Princeton, NJ: Princeton University Press, 1991.

Waelder, Robert. "The Principle of Multiple Function: Observations on Over-Determination." *Psychoanalytic Quarterly* 5 (1936): 45–62.

Wampold, Bruce E. and Zac E. Imel. *The Great Psychotherapy Debate: The Evidence for What Makes Psychotherapy Work*. 2nd ed. New York and London: Routledge, 2015.
Warren, Robert Penn. *All the King's Men*. New York: Bantam, 1973.
Webster, Richard. *Why Freud Was Wrong: Sin, Science, and Psychoanalysis*. New York: Basic Books, 1995.
Wedding, Danny. "Review of *Meeting Movies*." *Psychology of Aesthetics, Creativity, and the Arts* 1 (2007): 48–9.
Whitebook, Joel. *Freud: An Intellectual Biography*. Cambridge: Cambridge University Press, 2017.
Winnicott, D. W. *The Maturational Processes and the Facilitating Environment: Studies in the Theory of Emotional Development*. London: Hogarth Press, 1965.
Wright, Elizabeth. *Psychoanalytic Criticism: Theory in Practice*. London: Methuen, 1984.
Wurmser, Léon. "Shame: The Veiled Companion of Narcissism." In *The Many Faces of Shame*, edited by Donald L. Nathanson. New York: Guilford Press, 1987, 64–92.
Yalom, Irvin D. *Existential Psychotherapy*. New York: Basic Books, 1980.
Yalom, Irvin D. *Love's Executioner and Other Tales of Psychotherapy*. New York: Basic Books, 1989; rpt. Perennial, 1990.
Yalom, Irvin D. *The Schopenhauer Cure*. New York: HarperCollins, 2005.
Yalom, Irvin D. *The Theory and Practice of Group Psychotherapy*. 4th ed. New York: Basic Books, 1995.
Yalom, Irvin D. *When Nietzsche Wept*. New York: Harper Perennial, 1993.
Yalom, Irvin D. and Ginny Elkin. *Every Day Gets a Little Closer: A Twice-Told Therapy Tale*. New York: Basic Books, 1974.
Young, Philip. *Ernest Hemingway: A Reconsideration*. New York: Harcourt, Brace and World, 1966.
Zetzel, Elizabeth R. *The Capacity for Emotional Growth*. New York: International Universities Press, 1970.
Zetzel, Elizabeth R. "Represión de la Experiencia Traumática y Proceso de Aprendizaje" ("Repression of Traumatic Experience and Learning Process"). *Revista de Psicoanálisis* 25 (1968): 919–29.
Zetzel, Elizabeth R. and W. W. Meissner. *Basic Concepts of Psychoanalytic Psychiatry*. New York: Basic Books, 1973.
Ziolkowski, Theodore. "Philosophy into Fiction." *American Scholar* 66 (1997): 547–61.

Index

Abraham, Nicolas   204
Adams, Henry   239, 250
Adams, Robert M.   68–9
Adler, Alfred   30
Adorno, Theodor   201, 212
ambivalence   5, 27, 32, 35, 40, 58, 67, 98, 108, 119, 134–6, 143, 168, 169
American Psychoanalytic Association   62
"anal character"   97–9
analyzability   49–50
Andreasen, Nancy   222
Aporia   177
Armstrong, Edwin   34
Arnold, Matthew   59–60, 250
Atlas, James   202, 258
Atwood, George E.   169–70

Babuts, Nicolae   161
Bachelard, Gaston   65
Bahr, Kathy   249–50
Baranowski, A. M.   153
Barber, C. L.   244
Barrett, Marna   168
Barth, John   164
Barthes, Roland   156, 175, 209, 215
Bate, Walter Jackson   221
Bayard, Pierre   238
Begley, Adam   109–10
Benvenuto, Bice   159
Bergman, Ingmar   196–7, 208
Bergstein, Eleanor   235
Bernheimer, Charles   96
bi-active model of reading   9, 98, 115, 137, 139, 153, 164, 166–7
binding problem   216–17
Bleich, David   10, 11, 105–7, 151, 168

Bleuler, Eugen   58
Bloom, Harold   8, 31–3, 37, 214, 221
Bodkin, Maud   78
Bollas, Christopher   11, 172, 221
Bonaparte, Marie   61–2, 114
Bowlby, John   73, 146
Brantley, Richard   236
Brivic, Sheldon R.   68
Brody, Jane E.   192
Brown, Norman O.   107
Buber, Martin   122
Burbage, Richard   23

Camden, Vera   202
Camus, Albert   156, 231
Canons and codes   76, 140–3, 153, 158, 216
Carné, Marcel   196
Carroll, Lewis   147
Casablanca   196, 205, 209
Charcot, Jean-Martin   175
Charney, Maurice   44
Chaucer, Geoffrey   33, 57–8
Chekhov, Anton   222
Chodorow, Nancy   39, 50, 79, 83, 130–1, 160, 204, 207–8
Chomsky, Noam   137, 156, 158–9
Coleridge, Samuel Taylor   22–3, 57, 163, 211
Conrad, Joseph   2, 92–3, 136, 149
Contagion   14, 95, 193, 208, 223
Corvus, Andrew   95–6
Crane, Hart   94
Creative malady   222–3
Creed, Wendy   245–6
Crews, Frederick   11, 31, 66–8, 107–10, 151, 214–15, 240
Culler, Jonathan   11, 115–16, 139, 156, 159, 192–3
Curtiz, Michael   196

Da Vinci, Leonardo 62
Davis, Robert Con 128
Dayal, Samir 238
"death instinct" 7
De Beauvoir, Simone 156
deconstruction 21, 63, 115, 130, 156, 174, 179, 193
DEFT 103–4, 118, 132–3, 136, 243
Delany, Paul 111
Delboeuf, Joseph 64
Delphi seminar 10, 163, 170–81, 189, 194, 223, 240–5
De Man, Paul 156
depression 50, 95, 101, 222
Derrida, Jacques 113–16, 137, 154, 156–8, 161, 171, 174–5, 177, 215
De Saussure, Ferdinand 9, 127, 137, 156–9, 164
Desclos, Anne 152
Deutsch, Helene 47, 83
Diagnostic and Statistical Manual of Mental Disorders (DSM) 62, 141
Dickens, Charles 204, 219
Dodo bird effect 147
Dostoevsky, Feodor 39, 149
Drive theory 81, 130
Dryden, John 222

Eco, Umberto 157
Edel, Leon 54
Eder, Doris L. 179
Edmundson, Mark 40
ego psychology 17–18, 30, 50, 90, 116, 121, 130–1, 146, 150, 156, 160
Elias, Camelia 238
Eliot, George 149–50, 195
Eliot, T. S. 4, 160–1, 206–7
Ellenberger, Henri F. 128–9, 223
Elovitz, Paul H. 39
Emerson, Ralph Waldo 258
empathy 7, 100–1, 141, 189–91, 195

Erikson, Erik H. 41–2, 53, 72–3, 93, 108, 121, 172, 218, 227, 237
Esalen 183
eureka experience 71, 124, 150

Falle, George 19
Fatal Attraction 179
Faulkner, William 90, 92, 96–7, 101, 204
Federman, Raymond 178–9
feedback systems 43–4, 119–20, 125–6, 132, 134, 138–43, 151, 153, 160, 161, 198, 216
Fellini, Federico 64, 69, 196, 255
Felman, Shoshana 128, 147
Fiedler, Leslie 11, 54, 108, 176, 221
Fineman, Joel 172
Fish, Stanley 125, 139, 158–9
Fisher, Seymour 75–6, 84–5, 99, 117
Fitzgerald, F. Scott 9, 86, 90, 92–4, 121, 133–5, 151
Fitzgerald, Zelda 134
five-factor model 99
Fliess, Wilhelm 12, 23, 223
Forrester, John 110
Foucault, Michel 33, 156–7, 175, 215
Fox-Kales, Emily 249
Fraiberg, Louis and Selma 54
free association 9–10, 74, 88, 114–16, 139, 146, 154–5, 164, 172, 191, 194, 196–7
Freud, Anna 50, 56, 83, 90, 201
Freud, Sigmund 3, 5–17, 23–4, 27–32, 35, 38–42, 47–8, 50–3, 57–8, 60–2, 64–8, 72–5, 77–85, 88, 90–1, 94–101, 107–11, 118–23, 126–7, 131, 146–8, 155, 160, 166, 169–70, 174–5, 177, 190, 192, 197–8, 201, 207, 214–15, 217–18, 222–4

Beyond the Pleasure Principle 72
"Character and Anal Eroticism" 97–9
Civilization and Its Discontents 166
"The Dynamics of Transference" 58
Fragment of an Analysis of a Case of Hysteria 95–6, 100
Inhibitions, Symptoms and Anxiety 90
The Interpretation of Dreams 64
Jokes and Their Relation to the Unconscious 57
New Introductory Lectures on Psycho-Analysis 29
Notes upon a Case of Obsessional Neurosis 98
"Obsessive Actions and Religious Practices" 97
The Question of Lay Analysis 3
"Some Psychical Consequences of the Anatomical Distinctions between the Sexes" 61
Totem and Taboo 119
Freudolatry 30, 79
"Freud wars" 214–15
Friedman, Susan Stanford 83, 120
Fromm, Erich 78
Frost, Robert 111, 138–40
Frye, Northrop 33, 65
Fryer, John 63

Gaarder, Jostein 193
Gabbard, Glen O. 17, 56
Gallop, Jane 128, 147
Gardner, Howard 1
Gibbon, Edward 64
Gilman, Sander L. 84, 125, 142, 250
Gliserman, Martin 238
Godard, Jean-Luc 164, 219

Goethe, Johann Wolfgang von 22–3, 207, 224
Gogol, Nikolai 124
Gordon, Andrew 127–8, 146, 161, 238, 243, 257
Greaney, Michael 193
"great chain of being" 20
Greenberg, Harvey R. 197
Greenberg, Roger P. 75–6, 84–5, 99, 117

Hadley, Suzanne 148
Hardy, Thomas 13–15
Hartmann, Heinz 41, 50, 176
Hawthorne, Nathaniel 67, 108–9
H.D. (Hilda Doolittle) xii, 9, 74, 79–83, 86–8, 120, 241
Heidegger, Martin 71
Heider, Fritz 66
Hemingway, Ernest 90, 92–4, 102, 124–5, 158, 222
Henretty, Jennifer R. 168
Herblock 118
Hitchcock, Alfred 196–7
Hogan, Patrick Colm 225
Holland, Jane 233, 243
Holland, John 11, 250–3
Holland, Kelley 11, 250, 253–7
Holland, Norman N.
    and the "anal personality" 99, 117, 123–4
    and attitude toward the relationship between creativity and madness 222–3
    and becoming a patent lawyer 21, 186, 195, 198–200, 252
    and being a rebel 13, 33, 44, 98
    and being "something of a Puritan" 65, 188, 224
    and being torn between critical relativism and monism 6, 57–8, 98, 125

Index 275

and belief literary criticism is one of the social sciences 18
and cancer diagnosis 11, 229, 253, 256
and career as a New Critic 4, 8, 13, 21, 30, 51, 53, 76, 196, 220, 255
and character typology 99, 124
and conflicted relationship with his father 198–200, 252–5
and conflicts over lying on the couch 183–4
and countertransference difficulties 88, 100
and creating a psychoanalytic community 237
and equating active with masculine and passive with feminine 203
and experience being in psychoanalysis 182–5
and faith in science 18
and fear of closeness 207–8
and feeling "closed off" after his analysis 185, 189
and generativity xiii, 227
and gratitude 227
and his children 250–7
and his free associations 10, 114–15, 196–7
and his "observing ego" 183
and his own identity theme 9, 89, 96, 132, 135, 138, 181
and impact on colleagues and students 239–50
and intense intellectuality 9, 11, 56, 180, 183, 201
and involvement with being a therapist 184–5
and intellectualization 9, 54–7, 98, 186
and Jane Holland 4–5, 63, 180, 205, 227, 233–4

and life in retirement 234, 257
and mistrust of psychobiography 34–5
and the narcissism of minor differences 166
and need for boundaries 143, 179, 189–90, 195, 197, 207
and need for organic unity 21, 37, 76, 180, 198
and no longer being an orthodox or schematic Freudian 119
and no loose ends 136, 180, 194
as a paradoxical figure xiii, 6–7, 143
and parsimony 9, 96, 98, 123–4, 243
and personal knowledge 4, 146
and the pleasure principle 10, 15–16, 33, 64–5, 74, 90, 181, 188, 211, 218, 220, 223, 224
as a polarizing figure 1, 33, 60, 127, 173
and rational suicide 229–33
and rejecting "cookbook psychiatry" 197
and sentimentalism 25, 194–6
and a severed lifeline 10, 164–7
and shameful family secrets 203–4
and skepticism of relational, interpersonal, and intersubjective psychoanalysis 80
and tension between knowing and feeling 135, 186
and training as an engineer 6, 34, 90, 125, 198, 242
and traumatic childhood 182, 187–8, 203
and treating fictional characters as real people 22, 38, 43, 65–6

and treating literary works like a jig-saw puzzle   220
and use of charts, diagrams, and maps   125, 241–2, 256
and wariness of empathy   7, 101, 189–90, 195
as a would-be poet   124
"About Me"   10, 12, 181–9, 204, 214
The Brain of Robert Frost: A Cognitive Approach to Literature   9, 137–9, 141–3, 152, 175, 189, 208, 215
"A Brainy Afterword"   202
The Critical I   xiii, 10, 20, 41, 104, 116, 129, 152–61, 175, 193, 209, 215, 238
"A Cyberreader Defends"   10, 152, 163–7, 169, 192
Death in a Delphi Seminar: A Postmodern Mystery   7, 10, 33, 94, 152, 155, 170–81, 191, 193–4, 203, 227, 238, 245
"The Delphi Seminar" (with Murray M. Schwartz)   171–2
The Dynamics of Literary Response   xii, 8–9, 47–71, 81, 98, 107, 111, 115, 186–8, 224, 240, 242, 244
The First Modern Comedies: The Significance of Etherege, Wycherley, and Congreve   8, 15–19, 78, 196
5 Readers Reading   9, 71, 74–111, 118, 124, 139–40, 181, 189, 245
"Freud and the Poet's Eye"   27–8
"Hermia's Dream"   44
Holland's Guide to Psychoanalytic Psychology and Literature-and-Psychology   4, 10, 28, 145–51, 173, 192, 216
"How Can Dr. Johnson's Remarks on Cordelia's Death Add to My Own Response?"   101
The I   xii, 9, 20, 28, 104, 120–8, 130–3, 136–7, 141, 146, 152, 156, 175, 188, 255
"*Jude the Obscure*: Hardy's Symbolic Indictment of Christianity"   13–15
Laughing: A Psychology of Humor   9, 99, 104, 117–20, 134, 177, 194, 208
"Literary Suicide: A Question of Style"   93–5, 222
Literature and the Brain   xii, 1, 10–11, 211–27, 239, 251–2
Meeting Movies   xiii, 5, 6, 10, 15, 21, 37–8, 44, 59, 125, 187, 188, 190, 195–210, 223, 248, 249, 255
"The Next New Criticism"   53–4
"Obituary: Heinz Lichtenstein"   73–4
Poems in Persons: An Introduction to the Psychoanalysis of Literature   xiii, 9, 71–111, 118, 120, 124, 139, 140, 147, 181, 221, 241
Psychoanalysis and Shakespeare   xii, 8, 23, 27–44, 49, 51, 61, 65, 78, 220, 244
"Re-Covering 'The Purloined Letter': Reading as a Personal Transaction"   9, 113–16, 186
"Report: Focus Group on Revisionism"   197–8
"Response to Crews"   215
The Shakespearean Imagination   xii, 8, 19–22
A Sharper Focus   225–6, 229

Index

"Shrinking Literature: Reply to Robert M. Adams" 68
"Sons and Substitutions: Shakespeare's Phallic Fantasy" 44
"The Sparrow" 205–6
"The Story of a Psychoanalytic Critic" 13, 18, 37, 44, 50–4, 63, 69, 73, 91, 128, 136, 233
"Unity Identity Text Self" 197
"You, U. K. Le Guin" 89
Holmes, Oliver Wendell 86
Homan, Sidney 44
homophobia 102, 124–5
homosexuality 62–3, 102
Hopkins, Gerard Manley 213
Horney, Karen 50, 78, 83, 149–50, 204
Howe, Irving 14
Humphrey, Derek 232
Hunter, Dianne 172, 249
Huston, John 196
Hutter, Albert D. 68, 136
Hyman, Stanley Edgar 77–8

id psychology 197
identification with the aggressor 56, 201
identity theme xiii, 3, 6–10, 27, 33, 41, 71–3, 76–81, 85–111, 116–18, 121–6, 130–42, 147–9, 155, 173–5, 178, 181, 183, 185, 188–9, 194, 196, 203, 205, 207, 216, 237, 241–3
Imel, Zac E. 147
intellectualization 9, 54–6, 98, 186
intentional fallacy 31
interpretive community 139, 158
Irigaray, Luce 146
Iser, Wolfgang 137, 139, 164, 215
I-thou relationship 66, 122

Jacobs, Theodore J. 168
Jacobson, Donald F. 43
Jaeckin, Just 152
Jaffe, Lee 63
Jakobson, Roman 127
James, Henry 54, 226
Jamison, Kay Redfield 222
Jay, Martin 110
Johnson, Mark 156
Johnson, Samuel 33, 101, 201
Jones, Ernest 30–1, 38, 42, 47, 77, 220
Jonson, Ben 30, 124
Jung, Carl G. 10, 27, 30, 78, 151, 221, 238

Kahane, Claire 27, 96, 238, 240–1, 253
Kahn, Coppélia 44
Kandel, Eric 214
Kaplan, Morton 43
Katz, Henry G. 52, 208, 227
Keats, John 208, 221
Keen, Suzanne 218
Kennedy, Roger 159
Kernberg, Otto 41, 190
Kerrigan, William 127–8
Kevorkian, Jack 232
Kiell, Norman 54
Kierkegaard, Soren 232
Klein, Melanie 17, 42–8, 83
Kliban, B. 117
Kohut, Heinz 41, 73, 141–2, 190–1
Kris, Ernst 39, 41, 57, 176, 208
Kugler, Paul 151
Kuleshov effect 152–3
Kupper, Nelly G. 250

Lacan, Jacques 4, 9–10, 41, 63, 72, 77, 83, 113–15, 121, 125–30, 137, 145–6, 154, 156–61, 164–5, 167–72, 176, 179, 192–4, 215, 238, 247
Laing, R. D. 77

Lakoff, George   41, 142, 156
Lane, Anthony   219
"Late style"   212
Lawrence, D. H.   157
Lear, Jonathan   11, 148
Le Guin, Ursula K.   89
Lehrer, Ronald   148
Lehrman, Philip R.   6
Le nom du père   126
Lesser, Simon   54, 57, 91, 135, 195, 218
Leverenz, David   68
Levertov, Denise   194
Levin, Aaron   62
Lichtenstein, Heinz   xii, 9, 41, 71–4, 80, 121, 124, 132, 190, 241
life cycle   93, 227
"Listening with the third ear"   80
Loewald, Hans   294, 258
Longfellow, Henry Wadsworth   48–9
Looney, J. Thomas   35
Lowell, Robert   222
Lukes, Steven   193

Madden, John   196
Malamud, Bernard   121
Manheim, Leonard and Eleanor   27, 54
Mann, Thomas   27, 197
Marcuse, Herbert   77
Martins, Cecilia Beecher   247–8
Masling, Joseph   27, 177
Maslow, Abraham   149–50
Matrophobia and patrophobia   201
Mauron, Charles   121
McLaughlin, James T.   52
Mead, Margaret   146
Meissner, W. H.   49–50
Melnick, Burton   244–5
Melville, Herman   87
Michelangelo   66
Mill, John Stuart   64
Miller, Arthur   54

Miller, J. Hillis   149, 156–8, 215
Millot, Catherine   129
Milton, John   33, 127, 166–7
mirror neurons   218
mirror stage   126, 159
mirroring selfobject   141
Mishima, Yukio   94, 231
Mizener, Arthur   92–3
Mollinger, Robert   111
Mosher, Paul   81, 179, 186
Muller, John P.   159
Murrow, Edward R   229 n.1

narcissism   34, 61, 141, 145, 166, 190
Negative Capability   208
Nelson, Cary   111
New Criticism   xii, 8, 13, 51, 53–4, 74–6, 116, 255
"New Cryptics"   xiii, 33, 156, 176, 193, 195, 201, 215–16
Nietzsche, Friedrich   4, 33, 80, 141, 148, 169, 175, 214
Nightingale, Florence   96
Nixon, Richard   118–19
Noland, Richard   240
Nuttall, A. D.   68

Oates, Joyce Carol   235
object relations theory   49, 62, 130, 182
oedipus complex   23, 40, 42, 77
Oz, Amos   220

Pagan, Nicholas   225, 236
Panksepp, Jaak   217–18
Papini, Giovanni   207
Paris, Bernard J.   xiii, 10, 11, 44, 83, 149–50, 168, 210, 219
parsimony   9, 96, 98, 123–4, 180, 243
"penis envy"   9, 61, 81–4, 101, 119, 131–2
Perls, Fritz   77

Perry, Laura Keyes 199–200, 246–7
Phillips, Adam 39, 48
Pickering, George 222–3
plagiarism 175, 178
Plath, Sylvia 94, 175, 222
Plato 62, 202
Poe, Edgar Allan 94, 113, 115, 180
Polanski, Roman 86
pre-Oedipal stage of
  development 40, 42, 51, 83
primal scene 59, 83, 167, 186–9
projective identification 17, 56
PsyArt xiii, 3, 128, 229, 233–5, 237–50
psychobabble 18, 166
psychobiography 34
Pudovkin, V. I. 152–3
Purves, Alan C. 69, 111

Ragland-Sullivan, Ellie 128, 146–7, 154–5, 159
Rancour-Laferriere, Daniel 10, 163, 167–8, 238
Rank, Otto 30, 40
Rashkin, Esther 204
Reader-active model 9, 153, 156, 166, 216
Reich, Wilhelm 34, 77, 107
Reik, Theodor 3, 80
repetition-compulsion principle 7, 72–3, 169, 197
restoration comedy 15–19
"return of the repressed" 24
Rich, Adrienne 201
Richards, Arlene Kramer 82
Richardson, William 159
Riddel, Joseph 83
Robinson, Edward
  Arlington 139–42
Rodell, Marie J. 171
Rogers, Carl 73, 149
Rogers, Robert 27
Rose, Gilbert J. 93

Rosenblatt, Louise 104
Rosenzweig, Saul 147
Roudinesco, Élisabeth 128–9
Rudnytsky, Peter J. 39, 50, 73, 81, 109, 145–6, 238, 250
Rushdie, Salman 223
Ruti, Mari 131–2
Rymer, Russ 158

Sacks, Oliver 226
Said, Edward 212
Sartre, Jean-Paul 156
Schachter, Joseph 81
Schapiro, Barbara Ann 168–9
Schneiderman, Stuart 129–30
Schreiner, Olive 97
Schwartz, Murray M. xii–xiii, 3, 10, 11, 27, 41, 44, 47, 68, 71–2, 108–11, 120–1, 126, 140–2, 145, 171–4, 177–8, 191, 194, 221, 227, 235–41, 244, 248, 251
SEEKING 217–18, 234
Segal, Erich 69
self-actualization 150
sentimentalism 25, 195
Shakespeare, William 7, 8, 19–25, 27–45, 61, 65, 77–8, 101, 173, 196–8, 202, 233, 243–4, 252
Sharpe, Ella Freeman 34
Shaw, George Bernard 120–1, 136, 246
Silhol, Robert 128, 247, 253
Silvio, Joseph R. 225
Simon, Bennett 11
Slatoff, Walter 91–3
Smith, Gordon 54
Smith, John Harrington 16
Snow, C. P. 213
Socrates 75, 94
Solomon, Andrew 148
Sontag, Susan 203
Spencer, Theodore 153–4

Spock, Benjamin 23
Sprengnether, Madelon 40, 96
Sprich, Robert 125 n.1, 239–40
Spurgeon, Caroline 34
Stein, Richard L. 68
Stern, Daniel N. 160
Stolorow, Robert D. 169–70
Strachey, James 90, 97, 100
Strange, Deborah 236
Strupp, Hans 148
Styron, William 103
sublimation 56, 90
suicide 2, 7, 11, 13–15, 35, 91–5, 138, 169, 175, 192, 194, 208, 222, 229–33, 253, 256, 258
Suleiman, Susan 113, 115
Sullivan, Harry Stack 50, 78
Sullivan, Henry 154–5
Sulloway, Frank J. 31
Swan, Jim 27
switch words 215

text-active model of reading 9, 98, 104, 115, 137, 139, 143, 153, 156–7, 167, 204, 223
theming xiii
therapeutic alliance 50, 100
therapist self-disclosure 168
Thoret, Yves 238, 247
Tolstoy, Leo 121, 197, 229–30
Tompkins, Jane P. 106–7, 167–8
transactive mode of reading 104, 115, 139, 142–3, 167, 241
transference and countertransference 50, 58, 88, 96, 100, 136, 141, 168, 184
trauma 135, 182–3, 186–8, 197, 203–4

Trilling, Lionel 5–6, 54, 134–5, 220
Truffaut, François 247
Turner, Mark 157, 216–17
Twain, Mark 75, 221
twinning 177–8
"two cultures" 213

Updike, John 206

"*Vulgärfreudismus*" 29, 30, 52

Waelder, Robert 176–7
Wampold, Bruce E. 147
Warren, Robert Penn 135
Webster, Richard 31
Wedding, Danny 209–10
Wells, Caragh 238
Wheeler, Richard 172, 244
Whitebook, Joel 48, 223
Whitman, Walt 258
Wilde, Oscar 52
Wilden, Anthony 158
Willbern, David 27, 145, 181, 241–3, 251
Williams, Meg Harris 238, 249
Williams, Tennessee 54
Willing suspension of disbelief 57
Wilson, Edmund 2
Winnicott, D. W. 41, 47, 73, 241
Woolf, Virginia 96, 168–9
Wright, Elizabeth 88
Wurmser, Léon 204

Yalom, Irvin D. 4–5, 84, 91, 234–5
Young, Philip 94, 102

Zetzel, Elizabeth 8, 28, 47–51, 60, 62, 80, 95, 121, 166, 170, 186–9, 205, 214, 217, 227
Ziolkowski, Theodore 193–4